The Wellness
Lowfat Cookbook

UNIVERSITY OF CALIFORNIA AT BERKELEY

THE
Wellness
Lowfat
Cookbook

HUNDREDS OF DELICIOUS RECIPES

& A REVOLUTIONARY NEW

EATING PLAN THAT CAN HELP

PREVENT HEART DISEASE

By the Editors of The Wellness Cooking School
and The University of California at Berkeley
WELLNESS LETTER

PUBLISHED BY REBUS, INC., NEW YORK

Distributed by Random House

THE UNIVERSITY OF CALFORNIA AT BERKELEY WELLNESS LETTER
The Wellness Lowfat Cookbook comes from the editors of the Wellness Cooking School
and the editors of America's top-rated health newsletter, the
University of California at Berkeley Wellness Letter.

The Wellness Letter is a monthly eight-page newsletter that delivers brisk, useful
coverage on health, nutrition and exercise topics in language that is clear, engaging and nontechnical. It's
a unique resource that covers fundamental ways to prevent illness.
For information on how to order this award-winning newsletter from the world-famous School of Public
Health at the University of California at Berkeley, write to:
Health Letter Associates, Department 1108, 632 Broadway, New York, New York 10012.

Library of Congress Cataloging-in-Publication Data

The Wellness lowfat cookbook: hundreds of delicious recipes & a revolutionary new eating plan
that can help prevent heart disease/by the editors of the Wellness Cooking School
and the University of California at Berkeley wellness letter.
p.   cm.
At head of title: University of California at Berkeley
Includes index.
ISBN 0-929661-11-7
1. Low-fat diet—Recipes. 2. Coronary heart disease—Prevention.
I. Wellness Cooking School II. University of California, Berkeley, wellness letter.
RM237.7.W45 1993   93-7466
641.5′6311—dc20   CIP

Printed in the United States of America
10 9 8 7 6 5 4 3
Distributed by Random House, Inc.

This book is not intended as a substitute for medical advice.
Readers who suspect they may have specific medical problems should consult
a physician about any suggestions made in this book.

Cover: Chicken Scaloppini with Peppers, pages 95-96

C O N T E N T S

INTRODUCTION

Many people are at a loss when it comes to achieving a heart-healthy diet. Most know that they should be eating a diet low in fat, saturated fat and cholesterol, but surveys by the American Dietetic Association and the Food Marketing Institute reveal that about a third of adults find what they hear about diet confusing, and nearly half want to cut back on the fat in their diets, but aren't sure how.

The Wellness Lowfat Cookbook addresses this confusion. Not only does it provide a thorough understanding of the connection between diet and heart disease; it also shows how to apply this knowledge to the foods you eat every day through a simple lowfat diet plan. And, to make it easy for you to maintain the plan, the book features some 300 delicious lowfat, nutrient-packed recipes that prove once and for all that heart-healthy eating doesn't have to mean boring, tasteless food.

The book begins with "Your Diet and Your Heart," a comprehensive nontechnical discussion of the role diet plays in preventing heart disease. You'll learn what causes heart attacks; where cholesterol comes from; whether the antioxidants—vitamins C and E and beta carotene—can really help in preventing a heart attack; and how dietary fiber, calcium, potassium, iron, sodium and alcohol affect your heart.

Once you have gained a basic understanding of diet and heart disease, you can better appreciate the importance of *The Healthy Heart Solution*, the unique lowfat eating plan developed especially for this book by doctors and nutritionists at the University of California at Berkeley School of Public Health in conjunction with The Wellness Cooking School. Meal by meal, over a six-week period, you'll gradually learn to cut fat from your diet, ensuring that lowfat eating becomes a permanent part of your life.

What makes this eating plan work is its simplicity: It does not involve calculating the percentage of calories from fat for every food or every meal you eat, as so many other lowfat eating plans do. Instead, you simply establish a "daily fat target" and strive to achieve it by adding up the grams of fat you eat each day. As long as you do not exceed your daily fat target, no foods are forbidden. To help you understand where the fat in your diet comes from, an extensive glossary, "A Guide to Heart-Healthy Foods," features nutritional information on many commonly eaten foods. Each entry details the health benefits or drawbacks of the food in addition to providing ways to reduce its fat content if necessary.

The Recipes and Nutritional Analyses

After spending a few weeks on *The Healthy Heart Solution* eating plan, you'll find that one of the best ways to keep fat intake down is to cook lowfat meals at home. Beginning on page 46, you will find hundreds of delicious lowfat recipes for appetizers, snacks, soups, meat, poultry and fish dishes, meatless main courses, pastas, main-course salads, sandwiches, desserts, breads and breakfasts. Who would have thought you could have Banana Pancakes with Strawberry Sauce (3 grams of fat/serving) for breakfast; Black Bean and Orange Soup (0.6 grams) and Chinese Chicken Salad (8 grams) for lunch; a few Rye-Cheese Crackers (0.6 grams/cracker) as a snack; Spinach Lasagna (6 grams) for dinner and Hazelnut Cheesecake (10 grams) for dessert—and still be on a lowfat diet?

Indeed, as you begin to prepare the recipes in this book you will be amazed to find foods often forbidden on other heart-healthy diets: eggs, butter, cheese and even bacon, for example. As *The Healthy Heart Solution* will prove to you, it isn't necessary to eliminate high-fat foods from your diet in order to maintain a lowfat diet. What is required, however, is moderation: When high-fat foods are used in a recipe, they are used in small quantities and only to enhance the flavor of a dish.

To help you decide what lowfat dishes to make, use the nutritional analyses provided with the recipes. The nutritional analyses not only give information on the grams of fat per serving, but also values for calories, saturated fat, cholesterol, sodium, dietary fiber, calcium, iron, potassium and the antioxidants (beta carotene, vitamin C and vitamin E). For simplicity, all nutritional values have been rounded to the nearest whole number, with the exception of fat, saturated fat, and beta carotene, which are rounded to the nearest tenth. (Consult the box on page 48 for the recommended daily intake for all of these nutrients.) Bear in mind, however, that the values are averages. The nutritional content of any dish depends on the quality of the ingredients you use. Finally, remember that learning to cook and eat the lowfat way should be an enjoyable—and mouth-watering—process. If you stick with the *The Healthy Heart Solution*, and utilize the recipes in this book, you will ultimately be assured of a healthier heart and satisfying, nutritious meals for the rest of your life.

YOUR DIET AND YOUR HEART

Heart disease kills more men and women each year than cancer, accidents, AIDS or any other cause of death; in fact, nearly one in two deaths in the United States is the result of heart disease. Many people believe that genetics—or fate—is the sole determinant of who gets heart disease, and that how they lead their lives has little impact. But it is becoming increasingly clear that many risk factors for heart disease are within an individual's control—and that changing one's diet is one of the most effective ways to reduce that risk. Indeed, recent studies show that four of the leading risk factors for heart disease—high blood cholesterol, hypertension (high blood pressure), obesity and diabetes—can be reduced, or in some cases eliminated, through diet. As former surgeon general C. Everett Koop stated in his landmark report on nutrition and health, "For the two out of three adult Americans who do not smoke and do not drink excessively, one personal choice seems to influence long-term health prospects more than any other: what we eat."

Still, questions remain in many people's minds about exactly what kind of diet will help prevent heart disease. Do you have to become a vegetarian, or at least give up red meat? What's the limit on fat? What's so bad about saturated fat? Can you boost your level of "good" cholesterol? Will eating oat bran help your heart? Can foods high in vitamin C, vitamin E and beta carotene prevent heart disease? This chapter answers these and many other commonly asked questions about the role diet plays in heart disease.

What causes heart attacks?

The buildup of fats, cholesterol and other substances, collectively called plaque, in the coronary arteries—the arteries in the heart—is the leading cause of heart attacks. The medical term for this condition is atherosclerosis. As the amount of plaque in the arteries increases, the openings in the arteries are narrowed and the blood flow is hindered. Eventually, the plaque may grow so dense that it closes off an artery. Usually, a blood clot forms on the plaque in an artery, thus blocking off the flow of blood. When the flow of blood is blocked in an artery leading to the heart, a part of the heart muscle is deprived of oxygen and other nutrients, and the result is a heart attack. (If the artery that is blocked is one that leads to the brain, the result is a stroke.) It doesn't take very much plaque to narrow an artery since even the largest coronary arteries are only about the thickness of a ball-point pen.

Who gets heart disease?

In general, a person who eats a high-fat diet is more prone to developing atherosclerosis than one who eats a diet low in fat. One of the earliest studies to illustrate the relationship between a high-fat diet and atherosclerosis compared the dietary habits of men from seven countries to their rate of heart disease. The study showed that the higher the intake of fat, the higher the number of deaths from heart disease. For example, the Americans, whose diet derived an average of 38 percent of its calories from fat, experienced 770 heart attacks per 10,000 men; the Italians, whose diet derived 27 percent of its calories from fat, experienced 515 heart attacks per 10,000 men; and the Japanese, whose diet derived only about 9 percent of its calories from fat, experienced just 127 heart attacks per 10,000 men.

While it has been found that men are more likely than women to develop atherosclerosis, this holds true only for premenopausal women. Researchers believe that estrogen somehow protects women from heart disease before menopause, but after menopause, when estrogen levels drop significantly, women begin to develop atherosclerosis at an increasing rate. By the time women reach the age of 60, they develop cardiovascular disease at the same rate as men at the age of 50.

Risk factors for developing heart disease include: age, male sex, a high blood cholesterol level, smoking, a sedentary lifestyle, obesity, hypertension and diabetes. Risk factors have a compounding effect. This means, for example, that someone who has a moderately high cholesterol level and moderately high blood pressure may be at greater risk of heart disease than someone whose only risk factor is a very high cholesterol level. Fortunately, one strategy—a lowfat diet—can help control a multitude of risk factors, including a high cholesterol level, high blood pressure, obesity and diabetes.

How does atherosclerosis start?

No one knows exactly how atherosclerosis begins, but most scientists agree that it starts with an injury to the lining of the arterial walls, called the endothelium. An artery can be injured by a number of things: high blood pressure, a high blood cholesterol level or cigarette smoking, for example. When this happens, platelets—cells involved in blood clotting—begin to congregate at the injury site, releasing a substance that causes the smooth muscle cells normally present in the artery walls to multiply rapidly and form a foundation for the development of plaque. The platelets create a sticky surface that traps monocytes—a type of white blood cell—on the artery wall. The monocytes burrow into the endothelium, where they are then called macrophages. The macrophages gorge themselves on oxidized cholesterol circulating in the bloodstream. (Oxidation is a process by which energy is produced in the body. During the process, oxygen is activated and reacts with many substances, including cholesterol. Oxygen effects cholesterol in the bloodstream in much the same way oxygen in the air can break down vegetable oils and turn them rancid.) The cholesterol then becomes part of the plaque; in fact, about 70 percent of plaque by weight is cholesterol. At this point the cholesterol triggers further proliferation of smooth muscle cells, thereby causing the plaque to grow.

This process takes place over many years. The beginning stages of atherosclerosis often appear in childhood and accelerate rapidly in a person's thirties or forties. Yet the symptoms of atherosclerosis—angina (chest pain that originates in the heart), heart attack or stroke—do not become evident until an artery is 50 to 70 percent blocked by plaque. This is why it is important to take steps to prevent heart disease before any symptoms occur. In fact, parents should pay attention to their children's diets (see "Children and a Lowfat Diet" on page 18 for guidelines) and children should, of course, be encouraged to be physically active and to avoid smoking.

What kind of diet helps keep arteries clear?

A diet that is low in fat, especially saturated fat, is key to preventing atherosclerosis. In addition, eating foods that provide complex carbohydrates, fiber, potassium (and certain other minerals) and vitamins (especially vitamin C, beta carotene and vitamin E) and avoiding too much sodium will help control blood cholesterol, obesity, high blood pressure and diabetes. This means eating plenty of whole grains, cereals, breads, pasta, dried beans and peas, and fresh vegetables and fruits.

Is it necessary to become a vegetarian?

No. While grains, legumes, vegetables and fruits are the foundation of a heart-healthy diet, it's possible to eat red meat, poultry, fish, eggs and dairy products and not hurt your heart. In fact, these foods make important nutritional contributions, such as supplying high-quality protein, vitamins B_{12} and B_6, iron, zinc and, in the case of dairy products, calcium. It's not the animal foods themselves that increase your risk of heart disease, it's the fat they contain. If you choose lean cuts of red meat, light-meat poultry without the skin and low- or nonfat dairy products, you can safely include these foods in your diet.

Where does the cholesterol in the body come from? Do you get it from foods you eat, such as eggs?

Cholesterol is a white, waxy, fatlike substance produced by the liver and intestines from the carbohydrates, proteins and fats you eat. It is absolutely essential to life, since it makes up 50 percent of the membranes that surround all the body's cells, is part of the fatty insulation sheaths around nerve fibers and serves as a building block for many hormones. But since the body can produce all the cholesterol it needs to carry out these functions, you do not need to eat any cholesterol to stay healthy.

Still, the animal products you eat—meats, fish, poultry, dairy products and eggs—do contain cholesterol because, like humans, animals produce cholesterol. The cholesterol you consume in your diet is called "dietary cholesterol" to distinguish it from the cholesterol produced in your body, which is called "blood cholesterol." While you may eat foods that contain cholesterol, most of the cholesterol in your bloodstream is manufactured by your body. (Plants do not produce cholesterol, and so plant foods—grains, vegetables, vegetable oils, fruits, legumes and nuts—do not contain any cholesterol.)

Isn't there "good" and "bad" cholesterol?

The body makes different types of blood cholesterol packages called lipoproteins. Since cholesterol is a fat, it is not soluble in water and, therefore, not soluble in blood (which is mostly water). For cholesterol to get to the cells, the liver puts together lipoproteins, made of cholesterol and fatty substances such as triglycerides and phospholipids wrapped in protein molecules. The protein enables the cholesterol to be carried through the blood.

The largest of the lipoproteins is called very-low-density lipoprotein, or VLDL. As VLDL circulates through the bloodstream, it drops off triglycerides to the cells, which will be used for energy or stored for later use. After VLDL drops off its triglycerides, it breaks up into smaller, low-density lipoprotein, or LDL. LDL, containing 60 to 70 percent of the cholesterol found in the body, carries cholesterol through the bloodstream, dropping it off where it can be used for cell metabolism. When high levels of LDL circulate in the bloodstream, the LDL can become attached to the artery walls. The cholesterol found in LDL is subject to oxidation, which some researchers believe is what causes cholesterol to contribute to clogged arteries. Thus, LDL is often called "bad" cholesterol (even though some LDL cholesterol is needed for proper metabolism).

The liver also makes another type of molecular package known as high-density lipoprotein, or HDL. Like the other lipoproteins, HDL is composed of proteins, fatty substances and cholesterol, but HDL carries less cholesterol than LDL. As it circulates through the bloodstream, HDL seems to have the beneficial capacity to collect cholesterol from the bloodstream, tissues and arteries, and bring it back to the liver for reprocessing or excretion. Consequently HDL has been termed "good" cholesterol.

What should your blood cholesterol levels be?

Blood cholesterol is measured by withdrawing a small amount of blood—usually from the arm—to be analyzed in a lab. The result is the number of milligrams of cholesterol per deciliter of blood (about $\frac{1}{10}$ of a quart or a little less than half a cup), expressed as mg/dl. Doctors and scientists have come to realize that the higher your cholesterol, the greater the chance you will develop heart disease. As a result, doctors now recommend that your total cholesterol level be 200 mg/dl or less. Yet 58 percent of Americans have a cholesterol level of 200 mg/dl or higher (and 28 percent have a cholesterol level of 240 mg/dl or higher). While there is no "magic number" where your cholesterol level passes from safe to dangerous, the risk of heart disease rises continually with increasing blood cholesterol, though it doesn't rise markedly until that level exceeds 200 mg/dl. The rate of heart disease begins to accelerate even more rapidly above the 220 level.

Your LDL and HDL levels are as important as your total cholesterol level. Regardless of your total cholesterol level, if you have an LDL level of 130

EVALUATING CHOLESTEROL LEVELS	Total cholesterol (mg/dl)	LDL cholesterol (mg/dl)
Desirable	under 200	under 130
Borderline high	200 to 239	130 to 159
High	240 or over	160 or over

HDL CHOLESTEROL AND RISK OF HEART DISEASE	WOMEN	MEN
Very low risk	over 75*	over 65
Low risk	65	55
Average risk	55	45
Moderate risk	40	25
High risk	less than 40	less than 25

*HDL cholesterol in milligrams per deciliter

mg/dl or higher you are at greater risk of developing heart disease. At least four studies have found that people with a "safe" total cholesterol level—below 200 mg/dl—may still be at risk for heart disease if their HDL level is low; and conversely, that some people with elevated total cholesterol (usually women) may not be at high risk if their HDL level is high. However, no study has found that people with a low HDL level can decrease their risk of heart disease solely by raising their HDL.

Can your cholesterol level be too low?

According to some studies, people with low total cholesterol (below 160 mg/dl), especially those who have lowered it through drugs and/or diet, do reduce their heart attack risk, but are more prone to die from lung cancer and other respiratory diseases, as well as cerebral hemorrhage (one kind of stroke), alcoholism, accidental death and suicide. But there is not enough evidence to say that a very low cholesterol level is as dangerous as a high one. Heart disease is still the major killer in this country, and men with a blood cholesterol level of 240 or higher are three times more likely to suffer a heart attack than those whose level is under 160. If a low cholesterol level does have a down side, the evidence is complicated.

In 1990, the *British Medical Journal* published a statistical analysis combining six studies of a total of 25,000 men, half of whom had lowered their cholesterol level, primarily with drugs. The cholesterol-lowering group had 28 fewer heart attacks than the other men, but the benefit was canceled by 29 violent deaths. That same year the National Heart, Lung, and Blood Institute (NHBLI) called a conference to review all data on cholesterol and mortality rates. The NHBLI analysis of 19 large studies revealed that while elevated cholesterol (above 200) was certainly associated with heart disease, at least in men, a level below 160 in both men and women went along with a 40 percent higher rate of death by noncardiac causes, such as violent death, lung disease and some cancers. Another re-review of a large-scale study involving some 351,000 men showed that a cholesterol level below 160 was associated with increased risk for hemorrhagic stroke, as well as liver and pancreatic cancer, digestive disease, suicide, cirrhosis of the liver and alcoholism.

The increases in risk, however, were extremely small. For example, those with a blood cholesterol level of 160 to 239 had a hemorrhagic-stroke risk of about 1 in 20,000. Below 160, the risk doubled—but it was still only 1 in 10,000. In those with a level of 160 to 199, the risk of noncancerous lung disease was 2 per 10,000; in those below 160, the risk rose to 2.4. Yet the overall death rate for people with a level under 160 was still less than that for people with a level above 200. The cholesterol range with the lowest overall mortality rate was between 160 and 200.

One theory that attempts to explain the increased mortality rate from noncardiac causes in people whose blood cholesterol level is below 160 suggests that low blood cholesterol in people with cancer and other illnesses may be the result, not the cause, of some of the diseases. Another theory states that certain cholesterol-lowering drugs themselves may somehow cause the increase in noncardiac deaths. There's much here requiring further study—but it's far too soon to conclude that lowering your cholesterol may harm you.

Many experts have assumed that the lower your cholesterol level, the better—and that's still fair to say. Often, the first warning sign of heart disease is a heart attack. Reducing blood cholesterol is one way to head off a heart attack. Though a blood cholesterol level below 160 may pose other risks, relatively few middle-aged or older Americans are so affected. It is unlikely that a lowfat diet will reduce cholesterol to levels that will increase noncardiac risk, if any risk from low cholesterol does exist.

How can you boost your HDL level?

You cannot increase your level of HDL through diet. However, cutting back on fat and replacing saturated fats with unsaturated ones will reduce LDL and improve the ratio of HDL to LDL, thus decreasing the risk of heart disease. Using olive oil in cooking instead of butter and substituting fish for some of the red meat you eat are two ways to accomplish this. Exercising, losing weight and quitting smoking have also been shown to produce increases in HDL.

Is the key, then, to avoid foods high in cholesterol?

Surprisingly, for most people there does not seem to be a simple direct relationship between the dietary cholesterol you get from foods and the amount of cholesterol in your bloodstream. Researchers have found a much stronger link between the intake of fat—specifically saturated fat—and blood cholesterol. Since your body carefully regulates the production of cholesterol, when you eat foods that contain cholesterol, your body simply produces less of it. However, eating too much saturated fat upsets the body's regulating mechanism. As a result, limiting your intake of fat and saturated fat will help reduce your risk of heart disease more than decreasing your intake of dietary cholesterol alone.

However, you still need to watch the amount of cholesterol you eat. Researchers estimate that about 20 percent of Americans are hypersensitive to dietary cholesterol, meaning that the mechanism that regulates the cholesterol in their blood is faulty. Since it is difficult to determine who is cholesterol-sensitive, most experts recommend that everyone keep their dietary cholesterol intake at 300 milligrams a day or less (slightly more than the amount found in one large egg). Fortunately, with few exceptions, saturated fat and cholesterol go hand in hand; when you cut back on saturated fat you automatically reduce the amount of cholesterol you are eating.

What's so bad about saturated fat?

Eating a lot of saturated fat—more accurately called saturated fatty acids—stimulates your body's production of LDL or "bad" cholesterol. In addition, saturated fat seems to decrease the number of LDL receptors in the cells. Every cell in the body—but especially those in the liver—contains these LDL receptors, which function like tiny vacuum cleaners, sucking cholesterol from the bloodstream to be used by the cell. If the number of these receptors is decreased, the cells cannot pick up the cholesterol already in the bloodstream, and as a result, the body mistakenly makes more cholesterol to compensate. This can leave too much LDL cholesterol circulating in the bloodstream where it can accu-mulate in arterial walls. Some animal studies suggest that a diet high in saturated fat may inhibit the proper functioning of LDL receptors by as much as 90 percent.

Which foods contain saturated fat?

Saturated fat is found primarily in animal products, specifically beef, pork, poultry skin, whole milk, cheese and butter. In beef, pork and lamb, much of the saturated fat is found in the fat that surrounds the cut of meat and in the fatty streaks, known as marbling, that run through the lean tissue. If you choose cuts with little marbling and trim all the external fat, you will cut down on the saturated fat content of these meats. Removing the skin from poultry signficantly reduces the saturated fat content. For example, 4 ounces of roasted chicken breast with skin contains 3 grams of saturated fat, whereas the same amount of skinless chicken breast contains 1 gram.

Saturated fat is also found in certain vegetable oils, the so-called tropical oils—coconut, palm and palm kernel. Hydrogenated and partially hydrogenated vegetable oils found in stick margarines and in packaged foods (such as some baked goods, snack foods and cereals) are sources of saturated fat as well. Read ingredients lists on packaged foods carefully, and reduce your consumption of foods that contain tropical or hydrogenated oils.

What is hydrogenation?

Manufacturers hydrogenate—that is, add hydrogen atoms to—soybean, corn and other liquid oils when using them in products such as baked goods and cereals to make the oils more solid and stable. But hydrogenation *transforms* many of an oil's unsaturated fatty acids, making them more saturated and changing their structure in other subtle ways—they are thus called trans fatty acids. (Partially hydrogenated oils also contain trans fatty acids.) Scientists have been concerned that trans fats may increase the risk of heart disease. While a diet high in regular unsaturated fat lowers total blood cholesterol, a diet high in trans fats lowers it much less—or may even raise it—by increasing LDL. In addition, trans fats lower HDL. Like all vegetable oils, however, hydrogenated oils contain no cholesterol.

VEGETABLE OILS: A FAT BREAKDOWN

The chart below gives the breakdown of unsaturated and saturated fats in a tablespoon of various vegetable oils, listed from least to most saturated. A tablespoon of each contains 14 grams of total fat; however, the values given here may not add up to 14 because of rounding.

	Poly-unsaturated (g)	Mono-unsaturated (g)	Saturated (g)
Canola	4	8	1
Safflower	10	2	1
Sunflower	9	3	1
Corn	8	3	2
Soybean	8	3	2
Olive	1	10	2
Peanut	4	6	2
Sesame	6	6	2
Cottonseed	7	2	4
Palm kernel	0.2	2	11
Coconut	0.2	0.8	12

Aren't there some types of saturated fats that don't raise your cholesterol?

A few years ago a study reported that stearic acid, one of the main components of the saturated fat in meats and cocoa butter (which is used to make chocolate), actually lowered cholesterol. The study received a lot of press, and from the headlines and the news briefs, you might have concluded that hamburgers and chocolate bars are good for you. As it happens, the study's results can't be applied to everyday life because the composition of fats in the subjects' diets was artificial—that is, the diets were designed so that the individuals' only source of fat was stearic acid—and consequently unlike the composition of fat found in any food. Indeed, the saturated fat in food is never of purely one type. For example, although beef contains stearic acid, it also contains twice as much palmitic acid, a saturated fat that is known to raise cholesterol levels.

How do polyunsaturated and monounsaturated fats affect the risk of heart disease? In what foods are they found?

Polyunsaturated and monounsaturated fats (collectively known as unsaturated fats) do not increase the risk of heart disease because they don't raise cholesterol levels. In fact, they may lower them. Polyunsaturated fats—which predominate in safflower oil, sunflower oil and corn oil, as well as in walnuts, sunflower seeds and pumpkin seeds—tend to lower the amount of LDL cholesterol in the blood. However, some animal studies using large quantities of polyunsaturated fats have suggested that in addition to lowering LDL cholesterol, polyunsaturated fats can also lower beneficial HDL cholesterol. This may not increase the risk of heart disease, though, if the levels of both types of cholesterol drop proportionately.

Some studies have shown that monounsaturated fats—which are found in such foods as avocados, olives and olive oil, canola oil and almonds—may reduce total cholesterol by decreasing the amount of LDL cholesterol without decreasing the amount of HDL cholesterol.

Can you eat as much unsaturated fat as you want?

No. While poly- and monounsaturated fats do tend to lower cholesterol, they only do so when substituted for saturated fats in the diet. The goal is to reduce the total amount of fat in your diet while increasing the proportion of unsaturated to saturated fats; it is not beneficial simply to add unsaturated fats to your diet. One way to do this is to substitute unsaturated fats for saturated ones whenever possible. For example, use olive oil or canola oil instead of butter to sauté vegetables.

There are several reasons not to overload on unsaturated fats. A diet that is high in fat—no matter what type of fat—increases the chances of obesity, which in itself is an independent risk factor for heart disease, and may also be a risk factor for certain types of cancer. Moreover, fat in all foods is a mixture of unsaturated and saturated fats; no fat found in any food is 100 percent unsaturated (or 100 percent saturated). Even highly unsaturated vegetable oils contain some saturated fat.

What about the fat in fish? Isn't it good for your heart?

Fish contain a unique type of polyunsaturated fatty acids called omega-3s, which they get by eating certain plants, especially those that grow in cold water. Omega-3s help prevent heart disease because they make the blood platelets less likely to stick together, which reduces the chances of a blood clot forming. Moreover, fish oils seem to increase "good" HDL slightly, whereas polyunsaturated fats from vegetable sources do not. The general consensus among experts is that, as part of an overall lowfat diet, eating two servings of fish per week—particularly fatty fish such as salmon, mackerel or swordfish—can help reduce your risk of developing heart disease.

What's the limit on fat?

You need to consume some fat every day to remain healthy. Fat has several important functions in the body including maintaining healthy skin and hair, carrying fat-soluble vitamins (A, D, E and K) through the bloodstream, storing energy and making several hormonelike substances that are necessary for such functions as controlling blood pressure. The body can make much of the fat it needs from the foods you eat, but you need to eat some unsaturated fat in order to supply linoleic acid and other so-called essential fatty acids that the body cannot make on its own. However, the amount of unsaturated fat you need to eat each day is so small that is is easily supplied through diet. Even if you tried to cut all the fat from your diet, you'd get enough essential fatty acids from the small amounts of fat found in vegetables, fruits, grains and legumes.

To help keep blood cholesterol low and consequently help prevent heart disease, the American Heart Association (AHA) and a number of other health organizations recommend that fat make up no more than 30 percent of your daily calories, with just 10 percent of that coming from saturated fat. Americans currently get about 36 percent of their calories from fat, and about 12 percent of that from saturated fat.

Other health experts believe that deriving 30 percent of your total daily calories from fat is still too much, and that fat consumption should drop to 20 or even 10 percent. Cutting fat consumption by that much, however, may be difficult for some people, especially when they are just beginning to reduce the amount of fat in their diets. Even so, if you can get your fat consumption down to 20 or 25 percent of your daily calories, you are improving your odds of avoiding heart disease. A diet that derives 10 percent of its calories from fat would require eliminating virtually all animal products (except nonfat dairy products, egg whites and some very lean fish). Yet studies have shown that such a diet might be beneficial for people who already have heart disease, as evidenced by angina, previous heart attack or a bypass operation. Dr. Dean Ornish and his colleagues at the University of San Francisco found that a diet deriving less than 10 percent of its calories from fat, in combination with vigorous exercise, stress management and quitting smoking, reversed atherosclerosis in patients who had had heart attacks or bypass surgery.

What results can you expect to see in your cholesterol level if you cut back on the saturated fat in your diet?

On average, a diet that derives 30 percent of its calories from fat and a third of that from saturated fat will lower blood cholesterol 5 to 10 percent; if you cut back on fat even more, you can expect greater results. However, since other factors aside from diet affect blood cholesterol (including heredity, cigarette smoking and exercise habits), it's impossible to determine exactly how much a lowfat diet can lower cholesterol in an individual. Some people will experience great reductions in cholesterol and other people will show very little change. In general, the higher your cholesterol level is to begin with, the greater a reduction you can expect to achieve.

But if reducing the amount of fat and saturated fat in your diet doesn't produce dramatic reductions in your total cholesterol, don't despair; even small reductions can significantly lower your risk of developing heart disease. According to the results of the ongoing Framingham study, which has followed thousands of men and women in Framingham, Massachusetts, since 1949, for every

The recommendations in this book are geared to adults, but evidence shows that children over age two can benefit from a lowfat diet. Not only will a lowfat diet help control blood cholesterol, it will set the foundation for a lifetime of healthy eating. Children under age two, however, need fat for proper growth and development, and their fat intake should not be limited.

While major symptoms of atherosclerosis seldom manifest themselves before adulthood, the fatty streaks and fibrous plaque that are probable precursors of atherosclerosis can begin to appear in early childhood. Autopsies of many young soldiers killed in battle during World War II and in the Korean and Vietnam conflicts have revealed a significant accumulation of coronary plaque. It is estimated that 36 percent of youths age 19 and younger in the United States have a blood cholesterol level of 170 mg/dl or higher (a 170 mg/dl level in children is the equivalent of a 200 mg/dl level in adults).

Although you may be concerned about your children's fat intake, be careful not to cut so much from their diet that it is no longer nutritionally sound. It is not appropriate or necessary to keep track of the fat in a child's diet in the same way you would keep track of the fat in your own—by counting the number of grams of fat eaten each day. Instead, take these common sense steps: encourage consumption of fresh fruit and vegetables, grains and legumes; watch the amount of high-fat snacks a child eats; serve reasonable portions of lean meats, poultry and fish; and substitute low- or nonfat dairy products for whole-milk products. Such measures are all it takes to provide your child with a base on which to build a life-long healthy eating style.

1-percent reduction in the total cholesterol level, there is a 2-percent reduction in heart disease risk.

Is there an easy way to keep track of fat?

Calculating the percentage of your calories that comes from fat can be time-consuming and confusing. First you need to determine how many calories you eat each day, then you need to figure out what 30 percent of that number is. Many people trying to follow this recommendation believe that every food they eat must get 30 percent or less of its calories from fat. This line of thinking places many foods that would be perfectly acceptable on a lowfat diet off limits. For example, a garden salad containing 2 cups of lettuce and mixed vegetables topped with 1 tablespoon of Italian dressing would get 68 percent of its calories from fat, simply because the calorie content of the lettuce and vegetables is so low. But this doesn't mean you shouldn't eat the salad. It's not the amount of fat in any single food that matters as much as the amount of fat you consume over the course of a day.

It's much easier and more realistic simply to count grams of fat instead. *The Healthy Heart Solution,* the lowfat eating plan developed for this book, follows this prescription. Regardless of the number of calories you eat per day, you limit your fat intake to a fat gram-target based on your gender, activity level and risk of heart disease. For most people, the fat target will be closer to 20 or 25 percent of calories from fat than to 30 percent. When you've reached your fat target for the day, you're finished with fat, but not necessarily with food. You can and should still eat foods that are virtually fat free, such as vegetables, fruits, grains and nonfat dairy products. And since the amount of food you can eat is not limited, satiety shouldn't be a problem. To figure out how much fat is in certain foods, you can refer to the chart on pages 238-243 or check foods labels. (For example, the salad mentioned previously would contain 7 grams of fat, all from the tablespoon of Italian dressing.)

Is there any reason to eat oat bran to help lower cholesterol?

Oats and oat bran have received a lot of attention as cholesterol-lowering agents thanks to research funding (and ad campaigns) from cereal companies. But there is nothing magical about oats and oat bran. It's the soluble fiber they contain that lowers blood cholesterol. Oats and oat bran aren't the only foods that contain soluble fiber; it is found in many other foods, including barley, carrots, pears, dried beans, peas and lentils, apples and grapefruit, to name just a few. Soluble fiber is so named because it is easily dissolved in water. It works chemically to prevent or reduce the absorption of certain substances into the bloodstream, and this is how researchers believe soluble fiber lowers cholesterol. Some studies suggest that soluble fiber produces a reduction in LDL cholesterol without decreasing HDL cholesterol.

Not surprisingly, the cholesterol-lowering record of oats and oat bran has been a controversial one. In the mid-1980s, oat bran was touted as a surefire way to lower cholesterol. Then, in 1990, its reputation seemed in dispute when a small study found oat bran no more effective at lowering blood cholesterol than white bread. In 1991, a larger study found that people who ate just 2 ounces of instant oats per day reduced their cholesterol by an average of 12 mg/dl in eight weeks. The latest word on oats and oat bran comes from researchers at the University of Minnesota, who reviewed all published studies on oat bran and cholesterol and concluded that consuming 3 grams of soluble fiber a day (the amount in 1⅓ cups of oat bran cereal or three packets of instant oatmeal) reduces blood cholesterol by an average of 2 to 3 percent. People with elevated cholesterol tended to have larger drops of 6 to 7 percent. The more soluble fiber consumed, the greater the reduction in blood cholesterol levels.

What about wheat bran? Will it help lower your cholesterol?

No. A different type of dietary fiber, called insoluble fiber because it does not dissolve in water, predominates in wheat bran. Insoluble fiber does not help lower your cholesterol, but it does have many other important functions, such as preventing constipation and perhaps protecting against colon cancer. Health experts recommend that you get 25 to 30 grams of fiber a day from both sources—soluble and insoluble—to get all the benefits fiber provides.

If you regularly eat soluble fiber, does that mean you can eat more fat?

No. Soluble fiber will only help lower cholesterol significantly when it is eaten as part of a lowfat diet. This is why it's a waste of time—and money—to eat oat bran cereals or oat bran muffins that contain hydrogenated oils, coconut or other sources of saturated fat. Any cholesterol-lowering benefit from the oats would be canceled out by the saturated fat.

Will cutting back on salt help prevent heart disease?

Studies have found that populations that consume a lot of sodium have a higher incidence of hypertension than those that consume little sodium. (Hypertension is an independent risk factor for heart disease, since it increases the chances of heart attack or stroke.) In northern Japan, for example, sodium consumption is enormous—about 20 to 25 grams a day, three to four times higher than average consumption in the United States—and the prevalence of hypertension is also very high. In contrast, members of the Luo tribe in Kenya, who eat a diet low in sodium, tend to have a low incidence of hypertension. It has been shown, however, that when members of this tribe move to urban areas, where the diet is higher in sodium, their blood pressure goes up.

Does everyone need to watch sodium intake?

A number of experts question the sensibility of advising everyone to cut back on sodium. It appears that a high intake of sodium raises blood pressure only in people who are sensitive to it, that is to say, those who cannot effectively remove the excess from their bodies. It is estimated that 5 to 10 percent of Americans are sodium-sensitive, and this group makes up about half of the cases of hypertension in the United States.

Still, there are good reasons for everyone to cut back on salt and other sources of sodium. Americans eat far more sodium than their bodies need, and it is impossible to determine who is sodium-sensitive and who isn't before hypertension develops. If you were sodium-sensitive and you restricted your sodium intake before high blood pressure occurred, it's possible that you would

SODIUM CONTENT OF FOODS

The maximum amount of sodium a healthy person should consume in a day is 2400 milligrams. However, people with high blood pressure may be advised to consume less. The list below gives the amount of sodium in a standard serving size of some commonly eaten foods; the foods are listed from lowest to highest sodium content.

Shredded wheat, *1 cup* 3 mg	Ketchup, *1 tbsp* 156 mg
Tomato, *1 large* 11 mg	Cheddar cheese, *1 oz* 174 mg
Broccoli, *1 cup, chopped* 24 mg	Parmesan, *grated, 2 tbsp* 186 mg
Tomato sauce, *canned, no-salt-added, 1 cup* 37 mg	Mustard, *1 tbsp* 189 mg
Turkey breast, *skinless, roasted, 4 oz* 59 mg	Shrimp, *boiled, 4 oz* 255 mg
Egg, *1 large* 63 mg	Oat circles, *1 cup (1 oz)* 303 mg
Beef, *lean, broiled, 4 oz* 75 mg	Green beans, *canned, drained, 1 cup* 341 mg
Chicken breast, *skinless, roasted, 4 oz* 84 mg	Blue cheese, *1 oz* 391 mg
Celery, *3 stalks* 104 mg	Bran cereal, *1 cup* 457 mg
Yogurt, *plain, lowfat, 1 cup* 105 mg	Cottage cheese, *1%, 1 cup* 918 mg
Flatfish, *broiled, 4 oz* 120 mg	Chicken vegetable soup, *canned, 1 cup* 1068 mg
Milk, *1%, 1 cup* 123 mg	Tomato sauce, *canned, with salt, 1 cup* 1476 mg
Potato chips, *1 oz* 132 mg	Pickles, *dill, 2 medium* 1667 mg

never develop it. Moreover, sodium sensitivity tends to increase with age.

What's a healthy amount of sodium?

Some sodium is necessary for survival. All cells in the body are bathed in a fluid that maintains cell function; this fluid contains particles that are 90 to 95 percent sodium. Though your body requires very little sodium each day—approximately 115 milligrams, or roughly the amount in $\frac{1}{20}$ of a teaspoon of salt—the National Academy of Sciences recommends 500 milligrams of sodium daily to promote good health (though if you are sweating profusely, you may need more). Amazingly, the average American consumes 5000 to 7000 milligrams a day. The Food and Drug Administration (FDA) and various professional groups have been carefully reviewing the evidence for and against sodium and have decided that a sodium intake of 2400 milligrams per day is the maximum amount for a healthy individual. A person under a doctor's care for hypertension may be advised to consume less.

What are the main sources of sodium?

Table salt is the most obvious source of sodium in the diet, but it is probably not the leading source for most people. Many packaged and processed foods—such as bottled spaghetti sauce, canned vegetables, packaged rice mixes, snack foods, cold cuts, canned soups and fast foods—tend to be high in sodium. And sodium is found naturally in many foods, such as milk and celery. Look for packaged and processed foods that are low in sodium.

Even seemingly healthy packaged foods can contain a lot of sodium. For example, an ounce of most ready-to-eat breakfast cereals contains 200 to 500 milligrams of sodium, whereas an ounce of potato chips contains 132 milligrams. Read ingredient lists, too, for other sources of sodium besides salt; there are at least seventy such compounds. Anything with sodium in its name (calcium disodium, monosodium glutamate, sodium phosphate) is a source as is any type of special salt such as garlic salt, onion salt or sea salt. Baking powder and baking soda also contain sodium.

Besides eating less sodium, are there other dietary measures that might lower blood pressure?

Yes. You can eat plenty of fruits and vegetables high in potassium. Potassium helps to counter the effects of sodium and has been shown to lower blood pressure in people with hypertension. In a year-long study, fifty-four individuals between the ages of 30 and 65, all of whom were taking medication for essential hypertension (that is, hypertension without any clear cause), were split into two groups. One group maintained their normal diet, the other ate a high-potassium diet rich in fruits and vegetables. Over the course of the year, members of the group on the potassium-rich diet lowered their blood pressure enough so that 81 percent were able to reduce the amount of medication they took by half, and 38 percent were able to discontinue their medication entirely.

Calcium and magnesium are two other minerals that have been shown in some studies to have a positive effect on lowering blood pressure. However, evidence of a connection between a high calcium or magnesium intake and lowered blood pressure is not as clear as the connection between low sodium/high potassium intake and lowered blood pressure. Good sources of calcium include low- and nonfat dairy products, leafy green vegetables such as kale, and almonds. Magnesium is found in whole grains, legumes, nuts and seeds and green vegetables.

Which foods are good sources of potassium?

Potassium is abundant in many foods. Fruits, vegetables, grains and legumes are particularly rich in this mineral and have the added benefit of being low in fat. Meats, dairy products and fish also contain good amounts of potassium. There is no Recommended Dietary Allowance for potassium, but most health experts do suggest that you get 3000 to 3500 milligrams a day.

What are antioxidants?

Antioxidants are chemical compounds—either produced by the body or obtained from foods—that fight free radicals (unstable molecules that can damage cells). Free radicals are produced by the body in response to the cells' natural process of using oxygen for metabolism, and their development is also promoted by outside factors such as heat, cigarette smoke, alcohol, pollutants such as nitrogen dioxide and ozone, and ultraviolet light and other forms of radiation, including x-rays. If the damage remains unrepaired, the affected cells are unable to do their molecular work effectively. Antioxidants counter this damage. Beta carotene, vitamin C and vitamin E have all been identified as antioxidants.

Can antioxidants fight heart disease?

Though the evidence is not yet conclusive, there are strong suggestions that adequate levels of antioxidants in the body can slow down the development of heart disease or even prevent it from occurring in the first place because they block the action of free radicals. One theory on how free radicals can contribute to heart disease is that they may react with artery walls, eventually irritating or wounding them, whereupon fatty deposits build up around the scars. A related idea is that free radicals might combine with or oxidize LDL cholesterol, making it more likely to accumulate in arterial walls.

Several studies have pointed to the protective effect of antioxidants against heart disease. In The Physicians' Health Study—the study known for reporting that taking an aspirin every other day reduces the incidence of heart attack—333 of the participants (all men) who had angina or other evidence of heart disease were followed to determine the effect of beta carotene on the risk of heart attack, stroke or the need for surgery to bypass or open clogged arteries. About half of the individuals were given a 50-milligram beta carotene supplement, the other half were given a placebo. The beta carotene group suffered about half as many cardiac events as the placebo group. Another study of women—The Nurses' Health Study, which has followed 120,000 registered nurses for fifteen years—found that the women whose diets contained foods rich in beta carotene were significantly less likely to suffer heart attacks or strokes than the women whose diets were low in these foods.

Beta carotene is not the only antioxidant that seems to have a protective effect. According to an

LEADING SOURCES OF BETA CAROTENE AND VITAMIN C

While it is not yet clear how much beta carotene you need to consume for this antioxidant to have a protective effect against heart disease, experts generally recommend that you consume 5 to 6 milligrams a day. For vitamin C, the Recommended Dietary Allowance is 60 milligrams for adults, but studies suggest that you need to consume more of this vitamin each day—possibly 150 to 250 milligrams—to get the antioxidant benefits. The leading sources of beta carotene and vitamin C are listed below, from highest to lowest. All values are for 3½-ounces, uncooked.

BETA CAROTENE

Carrots, *1⅓ carrots* 17 mg

Sweet potato, *¾ potato* 12 mg

Dandelion greens, *2-3 cups* 8 mg

Peppers, hot, red, *2 peppers* 6 mg

Turnip greens, *2-3 cups* 5 mg

Kale, *2-3 cups* 5 mg

Butternut squash, *1 cup* 5 mg

Beet greens, *2-3 cups* 4 mg

Spinach, *2 cups* 4 mg

Arugula, *2 cups* 4 mg

Lamb's lettuce, *2 cups* 4 mg

Mustard greens, *2-3 cups* 3 mg

Watercress, *2 cups* 3 mg

Hubbard squash, *1 cup* 3 mg

Peppers, red bell, *1 cup* 3 mg

Apricots, *3 fresh* 2 mg

Cantaloupe, *⅔ cup* 2 mg

Swiss chard, *2-3 cups* 2 mg

Collard greens, *2-3 cups* 2 mg

Romaine lettuce, *2 cups* 2 mg

Chicory, *2 cups* 2 mg

Mango, *½ fruit* 2 mg

Broccoli, *1 cup* 1 mg

Brussels sprouts, *1 cup* 1 mg

VITAMIN C

Peppers, hot, red, *2 peppers* 243 mg

Persimmon, Fuyu, *⅔ fruit* 218 mg

Peppers, red bell, *1 cup* 190 mg

Kale, *2-3 cups* 120 mg

Kiwi fruit, *1 large* 98 mg

Fennel, *1 cup* 93 mg

Broccoli, *1 cup* 93 mg

Arugula, *2 cups* 91 mg

Brussels sprouts, *1 cup* 85 mg

Cauliflower, *1 cup* 72 mg

Mustard greens, *2-3 cups* 70 mg

Papaya, *⅓ fruit* 62 mg

Turnip greens, *2-3 cups* 60 mg

Strawberries, *⅔ cup* 57 mg

Cabbage, red, *1½ cups, shredded* 57 mg

Orange, *¾ fruit* 53 mg

Cabbage, green, *1½ cups, shredded* 47 mg

Cabbage, bok choy, *1½ cups, shredded* 45 mg

Watercress, *2 cups* 43 mg

Cantaloupe, *⅔ cup* 42 mg

Peas, *⅔ cup* 42 mg

Grapefruit, *⅔ cup* 37 mg

Asparagus, *8 stalks* 33 mg

Tangerine, *½ cup sections* 31 mg

Cabbage, savoy, *1½ cups, shredded* 31 mg

Honeydew melon, *⅔ cup* 25 mg

international study by the World Health Organization, a low level of vitamin E in the blood was the most important predictor of death from heart disease. Another study comparing men with angina to healthy men found that those individuals with high levels of vitamin E and other antioxidants in their blood were less likely to suffer angina.

How much of these antioxidants do you need? What are the sources?

No one is yet sure how much beta carotene, vitamin E or vitamin C you need to fight heart disease. What is known, however, is that these nutrients seem to have no significant side effects even in large amounts. The best sources of beta carotene are dark orange and yellow fruits and vegetables and leafy green vegetables. Vitamin C is found in citrus fruits and kiwi fruit, broccoli and other members of the cabbage family, hot and sweet peppers, berries and tomatoes. (See the chart on page 22 for the beta carotene and vitamin C content of selected foods.) Vitamin E is present in whole grains, wheat germ and nuts. It is also abundant in vegetable oils, but you should not increase your intake of these because of their high fat content.

Should you take antioxidant supplements?

It is still not proven whether antioxidants work alone or with other substances in foods, and for that reason, it's probably best to get your antioxidants from foods, not supplements. A lowfat diet that contains plenty of fruits and vegetables will easily supply you with good amounts of beta carotene and vitamin C. Vitamin E, however, can be more difficult to get on a lowfat diet; it takes a cup of peanuts or three-quarters of a stick of margarine just to meet the RDA for vitamin E (8 to 10 milligrams of alpha-tocopherol, the most potent form of vitamin E, which translates to 12 to 15 International Units, or IUs). And studies that have shown vitamin E to be protective against heart disease have used doses of 100 to 800 IUs, far above the RDA. Therefore, many people take supplements. Reasonable supplementation—100 IUs daily—certainly won't harm you. Keep in mind, though, that the long-term effects of such doses of vitamin E supplements have not been studied in humans.

What role does iron play in heart disease?

The idea that iron could be a cause of heart disease has been around for about a decade. However, the idea wasn't taken seriously in the scientific community until 1992, when a Finnish study found that men who had a high level (more than 200 micrograms per liter of blood) of ferritin, one of the body's chief storage forms of iron, were twice as likely to have a heart attack as men with a low level of ferritin. The study, which followed more than 1900 men aged 42 to 60 for more than five years, also found that the men who had a high LDL ("bad") cholesterol level as well as a high ferritin level had four times as great a risk of heart attack.

The Finnish researchers hypothesized that iron increases the risk of heart attack by increasing the formation of free radicals, which in turn oxidize the LDL cholesterol (that is, add oxygen atoms to the LDL, which in effect makes it rancid) so that it promotes atherosclerosis and ultimately the coronary blockage that results in a heart attack. A high level of stored iron may also weaken the heart muscle itself and worsen the effects of a heart attack should one occur.

According to Dr. Jerome Sullivan of the Veterans Administration Medical Center in Charleston, South Carolina, the researcher who first proposed the theory that a low level of iron in the body can protect against heart disease, many factors that alter the risk for heart attack may be explained by their effect on the body's iron level. For instance, young women may be at lower cardiac risk because their menstrual blood loss keeps their iron store low. Aspirin may protect the heart by causing gastrointestinal bleeding, thereby reducing iron. And the ability of regular exercise to cut the risk of heart disease may also be explained by the low iron level found in some athletes.

Should you cut back on iron?

The Finnish study was just one study and further research is needed to confirm or disprove the iron/heart disease theory. Many questions remain: Could the small amount of aspirin currently recommended for the prevention of heart attack actually produce enough stomach bleeding to lower the level of ferritin? Could the moderate amount of aerobic exercise recommended to protect the heart re-ally reduce ferritin? Isn't it a high estrogen level, not low iron, that protects premenopausal women? Will the iron theory hold for more varied groups (American women, for instance, instead of Finnish men)? Does a high level of stored iron cause heart disease, or is it just a marker for another factor that is the real culprit? (For example, a person may eat a lot of red meat, which is high in iron, but the real problem is the saturated fat in the meat.)

Iron remains an extremely important mineral, essential for the formation of hemoglobin (which stores oxygen in red blood cells) and many other physiological functions. It is especially crucial for children and infants, who need the mineral to sus-tain growth and development, and for pregnant women. Menstruating women, in particular, should not worry about consuming too much iron—just the opposite. Iron deficiency remains a real prob-lem in this country. The bottom line is that there is not nearly enough solid evidence supporting the link between iron and heart disease, so you should continue to eat the foods that supply you with the RDA for iron (10 milligrams for men, 15 milligrams for women).

Will a glass of wine help your heart?

There is a growing body of research suggesting that drinking moderate amounts of alcohol may actual-ly be healthy for the heart. One of the most con-vincing studies comes from researchers at Har-vard's School of Public Health. As part of a contin-uing study over the course of two years, they looked at 44,000 men between the ages of 40 to 75 (mostly dentists and veterinarians) and found that those who drank light to moderate amounts of al-cohol had a 25- to 40-percent lower chance of de-veloping heart disease. Moderate drinking was defined as one or two drinks a day, a standard drink being 12 ounces of beer, 4 ounces of wine or 1½ ounces of 80-proof spirits.

The researchers attributed alcohol's beneficial effect to its ability to raise HDL cholesterol, the "good" type that protects against coronary artery disease. While some scientists have questioned whether alcohol raises the type of HDL that is car-dio-protective (some types apparently aren't), the

Harvard researchers concluded that it does. But ad-ditional factors may also be involved: Some re-searchers have suggested that alcohol may also lower LDL ("bad") cholesterol, for instance, or help prevent the excessive blood clotting that can cause a heart attack. One thing is certain, however: Only light to moderate drinking may benefit the heart. Drinking a lot of alcohol is a good way to cause heart disease.

Other studies, however, have found that only certain types of alcoholic beverages protect against heart disease. For instance, a small French study found that only red wine was cardio-protective, and recently scientists from Cornell University claimed to identify the special chemical in red-wine grapes responsible for this benefit. Another study of more than 81,000 drinkers found that those who drank wine—red or white—had the lowest risk of coronary disease. But the research pointed out that they could not rule out the possibility that wine drinkers may have other traits (such as a more healthful diet) that protect them.

If you don't drink, does this evidence suggest you should start?

No one is recommending that people who don't al-ready drink alcohol take up the habit. Alcohol has many other effects on the body, all proven to be adverse. Most of these toxic effects are due to chronic heavy drinking (more than two drinks a day, depending on body weight) and include ele-vated risk of stroke, cirrhosis, heart failure and ar-rhythmias, fetal damage in pregnant women and certain cancers. Alcoholism also has devastating emotional costs, such as damage to family life.

Moderate drinking may be beneficial, but don't assume that wine, beer or a martini will counteract the effects of a high-fat diet, smoking or being over-weight. And if your doctor has prescribed a choles-terol-lowering medication, a daily cocktail is no substitute. Though moderate drinking is safe for many, some people find it difficult to be moderate once they start drinking. And even consuming two drinks in a short period of time can be risky if you are driving, operating heavy equipment or taking certain medications. Pregnant women and recover-ing alcoholics should not drink alcohol at all.

THE HEALTHY HEART SOLUTION

While most strategies for reducing the risk of heart disease through lifestyle changes are straightforward—if you smoke, quit smoking, or if you are sedentary, adopt an exercise program—starting a diet that is good for the heart can be confusing. *The Healthy Heart Solution*, an eating plan created especially for this book, clears up that confusion. This plan focuses on dietary elements that have been shown to play an important role in the development or prevention of heart disease—fat, saturated fat, cholesterol, sodium, complex carbohydrates, fiber, potassium, beta carotene, vitamin C and vitamin E—and with one simple strategy helps you design a diet that increases the good elements and decreases the bad.

The Healthy Heart Solution is not a "diet" in the sense that you follow it until you've lost a certain number of pounds. Nor is it a "gimmicky" eating program that focuses on one food (such as grapefruit or oat bran) or on some bizarre rotation of foods (such as eating nothing but fruit in the morning). Instead, the plan aims to make lowfat eating a lifetime habit by putting forth a single simple and straightforward goal: to limit fat intake to a certain number of grams per day, depending on your gender, activity level and risk of heart disease (see the chart, "Your Daily Fat Target," on page 28). By cutting back on your total daily fat intake, you will automatically cut down on saturated fat and cholesterol as well. Moreover, as long as you do not exceed your daily fat target, you can eat practically any foods you like, and at the same time lower your blood cholesterol level, your blood pressure and most likely even your weight (see the box, "A Note About Weight Control," on page 26).

Why the plan works

The Healthy Heart Solution works because it reduces the amount of fat in your diet while taking your personal tastes into account—a factor that cannot be overemphasized. For many people the words "healthy diet" are synonymous with "giving up all the foods I like." Nothing could be more untrue—or more unrealistic. It's not necessary to completely eliminate certain foods to achieve a healthy diet, and, indeed, that approach is likely to backfire. While most diets and eating plans present overwhelming lists of forbidden and permitted foods and expect them to satisfy a multitude of tastes and individual preferences, on *The Healthy Heart Solution* program no foods are forbidden as long as you stay at or below your daily fat target. Moreover, when you try to change your diet too much too fast, you wind up feeling frustrated and deprived, which often leads to a return to old eating habits. With this plan, you ease into lowfat eating gradually, so the changes you make are more likely to become permanent.

The Healthy Heart Solution does require that you take a critical look at the foods you are eating now and then consciously decide which high-fat foods are important to you and which ones you could easily limit, find substitutes for or eliminate. For example, let's say you know you can't do without mayonnaise on your turkey sandwich at lunch, but you might not miss the butter on your morning toast if you used jam instead. Or, perhaps you love Cheddar cheese, but aren't a big fan of red meat; by cutting back on the red meat you eat, you can still permit yourself some cheese. Is ice cream your regular bedtime snack? Try substituting lowfat or nonfat frozen yogurt, or if that does not appeal to you, cut back on the portion size of your ice cream (serve yourself half a cup instead of a cup, for example), and have it three times a week instead of every day.

Counting the fat, not the calories

The Healthy Heart Solution provides an easy way to control the amount of fat you're eating without having to do a lot of math or calorie counting. You simply count grams of fat. To help you do this, the chart on pages 238-243 gives the grams of fat in over 350 commonly eaten foods. For packaged foods, you should refer to the nutritional information on the food labels. (See "The New Food Labels,"

A NOTE ABOUT WEIGHT CONTROL

If you are familiar with the various weight–loss diets that have been popular over the years, you may wonder how an eating plan that doesn't count calories can help you lose weight. The fact is that many people are overweight because they eat too much fat, not too much food. Because dietary fat is a concentrated energy source, every gram of fat contains 9 calories, compared to just 4 calories in a gram of carbohydrate or protein. Thus, high–fat foods are high–calorie foods. And though fat provides satiety—that is, it helps you feel full and satisfied—calorie for calorie, high–fat foods may leave you hungry. For example, let's say you had an ounce of Cheddar cheese and 4 whole–wheat crackers for an afternoon snack. For the 200 calories in that snack, you could have had 7 cups of air–popped popcorn, 12 apricots, 60 grapes, 40 celery stalks, 7 carrots, or 3 cups of raspberries. While the cheese and crackers might have barely satisfied your hunger, most likely you would not have eaten the equivalent calorie amounts of the other snacks before you were full, thus saving calories. And the cheese and crackers would have added 13 grams of fat to your daily intake, whereas the alternative snacks would be virtually fat–free.

In addition, research suggests that fat is more fattening because it is converted to body fat more easily than carbohydrates. The evidence shows that the body burns carbohydrates from foods more efficiently than fat since the carbohydrates take more metabolic energy to convert to body fat. Experiments at the University of Massachusetts Medical School indicate that if you consume 100 extra calories in the form of carbohydrate, 23 of those will be used simply to process that carbohydrate and 77 of them will end up being stored as body fat. But if you consumed 100 extra calories in the form of fat, only 2 calories would be burned to process that fat and 98 calories would be stored as body fat.

One could deduce from the University of Massachusetts study that simply watching the fat in your diet would probably cause you to lose weight. However, just as not everyone's cholesterol responds in the same way to a lowfat diet, not everyone's weight responds the same way. Other factors—such as heredity and the amount of exercise you get—also effect weight. If you do not lose weight once you achieve your daily fat target on the six–week program, you can try eating even less fat. But a better option is to begin an exercise program, since the combination of exercise· and diet is the best strategy for permanent weight loss. Moreover, exercise has its own heart–strengthening benefits.

on page 247, for how to read the nutritional information on a food label.) To determine your daily fat target, consult the chart on page 28.

The key to the plan is not just to reduce the high-fat foods in your diet, but to replace them with lowfat or fat-free foods, such as fruits, vegetables, grains, legumes and low- and nonfat dairy products. In this way, you aren't simply cutting back on fat, saturated fat and dietary cholesterol, you're also increasing the amount of complex carbohydrates, dietary fiber, vitamin C, vitamin E, beta carotene, calcium, potassium and other important nutrients in your diet. While the amount of fat you can eat each day on this plan is limited, the amount of food you can eat is not. Once you've reached your daily fat target, you must stop eating fat for the day, but not necessarily food.

How's your current diet?

The Healthy Heart Solution is designed to help you cut fat from your diet meal by meal over a six-week period. Before you begin the six-week program, however, you need to pinpoint the areas in your diet that need attention. This is essential if you want to make lasting changes. The best way to do this is to keep a record of everything you eat for four consecutive days. Pick four days (three weekdays and one weekend day) when you'll be eating as you normally do; in other words, don't pick a time period that includes a holiday, wedding or some other special event that centers around food. Moreover, if you don't usually eat in restaurants, don't pick a period when you know you're going to be doing so. If eating out for business or pleasure is part of your regular routine, however, be sure to include those days in your recording period.

To accurately record what you are eating, you have to be aware of the amount of food you are consuming. When eating at home, use measuring spoons, measuring cups and a small kitchen scale to measure and weigh your foods. You should also pay attention to the serving sizes listed on packaged foods. For example, the label on an indvidual can of soup may say that a serving contains 3 grams of fat. Only upon careful inspection will you discover that the can contains two servings. If you ate the whole can for lunch, you would have to record 6 grams of fat. When eating out, use your eye to estimate portion sizes. For example, 3 to 4 ounces of cooked meat, poultry or fish is about the size of a deck of cards. When you don't know the exact amount of food you're eating, or the ingredients used in preparing it, make your best guess.

The best way to keep a record of what you're eating over the four-day period is to get a small notebook or pad and keep it with you. Assign a page for each of the four days, then divide the pages into two columns. On the left-hand side write down the foods you've eaten and the serving sizes. On the right-hand side, record the number of grams of fat in each portion.

Record the grams of fat right away if this information is easily obtainable, such as from a food label. Wait until the end of the four-day period to record the number of fat grams in nonpackaged foods, such as meats, dairy products, vegetables, fruits and nuts, by using the chart on pages 238-243; this way you won't be constantly looking things up. For a homemade dish that contains a variety of ingredients, like a stew or casserole, you'll have to "guesstimate" the amount of fat in a serving by considering the ingredients that go into it—unless, of course, the recipe features a nutritional analysis like the ones in this book. Do the same thing with restaurant meals. Don't worry about

being precise; the goal is simply to get an idea of how much fat is in your typical diet.

Though you don't have to be exact in your record-keeping, there are two caveats you must keep in mind. Be sure to record *everything* you eat and drink. This includes any spreads (mayonnaise, butter, cream cheeese, margarine), toppings (salad dressing, whipped cream, nuts, gravy, hollandaise sauce) and "tastes" you might unwittingly consume during the course of a day (such as the spoonful of peanut butter eaten while making the kids' sandwiches or the handful of chips absent-mindedly munched while watching the ball game). Though foods like these may seem inconsequential, they can add a significant amount of fat to your diet; for example, just an ounce of potato chips contains 10 grams of fat.

Evaluating your food diary

At the end of the four days, add up the number of grams of fat you have eaten per day and spend some time reviewing your food diary. It can provide you with valuable information about the areas of your diet that need changing. For example, you can pinpoint the foods you regularly eat that are high in fat and think about ways to reduce the portion sizes for those foods. You can also consider how to replace those foods with foods lower in fat (see the "Fat Tradeoffs" chart on page 30). In addition, the diary will help you spot patterns, like a tendency to eat lowfat foods during most of the day but to load up on fatty foods at dinner or to snack on them after dinner.

The diary may also show you that while you regularly eat vegetables high in beta carotene and vitamin C, such as carrots or broccoli, you tend to eat those foods with butter, cheese or hollandaise sauce, which are high in fat. Making some adjustments in how you serve these foods may be all you need to do to reduce their fat content. On the other hand, you may find that some of the foods you eat can't easily be altered to lower their fat content. For example, there's no way to make a fast-food lunch consisting of a hamburger, french fries and a milk shake lower in fat—except to change what you eat for lunch. (Or, if you do eat these foods, you'll have to compensate for them at another meal.)

Implementing The Healthy Heart Solution

The Healthy Heart Solution is an effective way to permanently change your eating style for the better because it allows you to make changes gradually. The first step is to determine your daily fat target by consulting the chart below. Then, over the course of a six-week period, you'll learn to make changes in what you eat meal by meal. You'll spend the first two weeks focusing on breakfast, then two weeks on lunch and snacks and finally two weeks on dinner. By the end of the six-week period you will have altered your daily diet so that it contains no more fat than your target allows.

Because you won't be cutting back to your daily fat target all at once, fat-allotment goals have been set for each meal. During the first week of each two-week period—the Training Week—you won't be limited to a specific amount of fat; instead you will simply begin to learn how much fat is in the foods you eat and what to substitute for the high-fat items. Think of the Training Week as a practice period for that meal. During the second week—the Goal Week—you will be limited to a specific number of fat grams for that meal, though you will still be able to decide what foods will provide the fat. As you master breakfast and move on to lunch and snacks and then to dinner, you must, of course, continue to meet the goals from previous meals. You will find this increasingly easy to do as the days go by.

As this plan will prove, it's well worth starting to cut fat slowly. Focusing on one meal at a time gives you the opportunity to adjust to a new way of eating, making it more likely that you will be able to sustain the changes you've made. Indeed, you can compare making changes in your eating style

to starting an exercise program. If you attempt to run six miles on your first day, you will surely become tired and feel that it's too much for you. You probably won't try to run again since it seems like a lot of work. But if you start by walking a mile or two, then running a mile or two, and so on, gradually building your stamina and endurance, you'll soon be running six miles with ease. It's the same when you make changes in your diet. If you cut the fat out gradually and give yourself time to get used to a lower-fat way of eating, it will easily become part of your routine.

During this six-week period, it is useful to continue to record the foods you eat—and how many grams of fat they have—in your notebook. Writing things down helps you become familiar with the amount of fat in different foods and reinforces low-fat eating habits. In addition, keeping a food diary lets you see in black and white the fat choices you're making. After the six weeks have passed, you should have a very good idea of the fat content of most of the foods you eat regularly, and can stop keeping the diary if you are so inclined.

Setting your daily fat target

How much fat you should eat each day depends on a number of factors: your sex (men use more energy than women, even at rest, so they can eat more fat), your level of physical activity and your personal or family history of heart disease. To determine your daily fat target, refer to the chart below. You fall into the Active category for your sex if you exercise aerobically at least 2½ hours a week for at least half an hour every time you exercise. Aerobic exercise includes activities such as

YOUR DAILY FAT TARGET						
	WOMEN				**MEN**	
	Sedentary	*Active*			*Sedentary*	*Active*
Normal Risk	40 grams/day	50 grams/day		**Normal Risk**	50 grams/day	60 grams/day
High Risk	30 grams/day	40 grams/day		**High Risk**	40 grams/day	50 grams/day

brisk walking (at least 4 miles per hour), jogging, swimming, cycling, aerobic dancing, rowing, circuit training and cross-country skiing. Some household chores—raking leaves, chopping wood, mowing the lawn, gardening and housecleaning—also qualify as aerobic activities if they are done vigorously for 20 minutes or more without stopping. You can also count leisure-time activities, such as singles tennis, racquetball, squash, golf (if you walk the course instead of using a golf cart) and full-court basketball. You also fall into the Active category if you have a physically active job, such as construction worker, landscaper or mail carrier. If this activity schedule does not apply to you, and you do not have a physically active job, you fall into the Sedentary category, which requires that you eat less fat than an active person.

For both men and women at both levels of activity, you will find two levels of fat intake included in the chart—Normal Risk and High Risk, referring to your risk of heart disease. You fit into the High Risk category if you have a personal history of heart disease, a cholesterol level of 220 mg/dl or higher (for more on cholesterol see pages 12-16) or a family history of heart disease. You have a family history of heart disease if a relative (parent, grandparent or sibling) developed heart disease before the age of 55.

Strategies for cutting fat

How do you begin to make changes in your diet so that it includes less fat? There are three strategies you can employ to reduce the amount of fat you eat overall. Each tactic by itself can result in a significant reduction in fat consumption, but adopting a combination of the three strategies gives you more fat-cutting options and results in even greater fat reduction.

1. Substitute lowfat foods for high-fat ones. Many high-fat foods have lowfat alternatives, as the "Fat Tradeoffs" chart on page 30 shows. For example, instead of using a whole egg in recipes, consider using two egg whites, and save 5 grams of fat. Rather than slathering butter on your baked potato, use no-fat salsa instead. In some muffin and cookie recipes, all of the oil or other shortening can be replaced by applesauce, which has no fat. If you

replace the half-cup of whole milk you use on your morning cereal with skim milk, you save 4 grams of fat. Or, if you choose 4 ounces of a Select grade cut of top round steak instead of fattier Prime grade sirloin, you save 8 grams of fat. Simply using 4 ounces of water-packed tuna instead of oil-packed tuna saves you 8 grams of fat, and if you skip adding the typical tablespoon of mayo and dress the tuna with mustard instead, you save an additional 11 grams of fat.

2. Limit portion sizes of higher-fat foods and "stretch" them with lower-fat foods. You can still eat foods that are high in fat if you control the portions you eat. For example, instead of having an 8-ounce steak, ½ cup of rice and ½ cup of broccoli for dinner, stir-fry 3 or 4 ounces of beef with broccoli, peppers, mushrooms and snow peas, and serve it over a generous portion of brown rice; this halves the amount of fat in your meal, but should more than satisfy your hunger. In a recipe for lasagna, blend part-skim milk ricotta cheese with lowfat cottage cheese or nonfat ricotta cheese; you'll be cutting fat and probably won't even notice any difference in taste.

3. Evaluate carefully which high-fat foods to include in your diet. High-fat foods do not have to be banned from your diet, but you do need to plan for them. If some of your favorite foods are high in fat, make room for them in your diet by eating smaller portions, eating them less often and passing up other high-fat foods that day. For example, if you're craving french fries at lunch, go ahead and have a small order. But compensate for the fries by making sure that everything else in the meal is relatively low in fat., or by having an extra-lowfat dinner.

Use these strategies during the Training Week and Goal Week for each meal to help you reduce the amount of fat you eat. In addition, begin to experiment with the recipes in this book to discover some delicious meals and snacks that will easily fit into your new way of eating. (A nutritional analysis has been provided for every recipe to help you see at a glance how much fat is in a serving of that particular dish.) In addition, refer to "A Guide to Heart-Healthy Foods, pages 35 to 45, for information on the nutritional content of various foods, along with suggestions for recipes made with them.

FAT TRADEOFFS

This chart will give you an idea of how a few simple tradeoffs in the foods you eat can significantly reduce the fat in your diet. Some of the changes are direct substitutions—skim milk for whole milk, for example, which saves you 8 grams of fat per cup. Others are a little more creative—such as angelfood cake for carrot cake. While this tradeoff may not seem so appealing at first glance, consider that it saves you 16 grams of fat—a good part of what you should be eating for an entire lunch or dinner. On the following pages, you'll find additional fat substitution and replacement strategies for breakfast, lunch, snacks and dinner.

FOOD	FOOD SUBSTITUTE
Sirloin steak, *Prime grade, untrimmed, 4 oz* 12 g	Top round steak, *Select grade, trimmed, 4 oz* 4 g
Regular ground beef, *broiled, 4 oz* 24 g	Extra-lean ground beef, *broiled, 4 oz* 19 g
Chicken breast, *roasted with skin, 4 oz* 9 g	Chicken breast, *roasted skinless, 4 oz* 5 g
Oil-packed light tuna, *4 oz* 9 g	Water-packed light tuna, *4 oz* 1 g
Pizza with cheese and pepperoni, *1 slice* 7 g	Pizza with cheese and mushrooms, *1 slice* 3 g
Baked potato, *with 1 tbsp butter* 11 g	Baked potato, *with salsa* 0 g
Croissant, 12 g	Bagel, 2 g
Potato chips, *1 oz* 10 g	Pretzels, *1 oz* 1 g
Peanuts, *dry-roasted, 1 oz* 14 g	Chestnuts, *roasted, 1 oz* 1 g
Buttered oil-popped popcorn, *1 cup* 11 g	Air-popped unbuttered popcorn, *1 cup* 0 g
Carrot cake, *with cream cheese frosting, 1 slice* 16 g	Angelfood cake, *with puréed fruit, 1 slice* 0 g
Chocolate chip cookies, *2 small* 6 g	Fig bars, *2* 2 g
Premium ice cream, *vanilla, ½ cup* 12 g	Premium frozen yogurt, *vanilla, ½ cup* 4 g
Unsweetened chocolate, *1 oz* 15 g	Cocoa powder, *1 oz* 4 g
Whole-milk ricotta cheese, *½ cup* 16 g	Fat-free ricotta cheese, *½ cup* 0 g
Cheddar cheese, *shredded, ¼ cup* 9 g	Part-skim mozzarella cheese, *shredded, ¼ cup* 5 g
Whole milk, *1 cup* 8 g	Skim milk, *1 cup* 0 g
Heavy cream, *½ cup* 44 g	Evaporated skimmed milk, *½ cup* 0 g
Sour cream, *½ cup* 24 g	Plain nonfat yogurt *½ cup* 0 g
Eggnog, *1 cup* 19 g	Apple cider, *mulled, 1 cup* 0 g
Whole egg, *in recipes* 5 g	Two egg whites 0 g
Oil, *¼ cup (in quick bread or muffin recipes)* 54 g	Applesauce, *¼ cup* 0 g
Mayonnaise, *1 tbsp* 11 g	Mustard, *1 tbsp* 0 g

WEEKS 1 AND 2: BREAKFAST

Some of the foods in the American diet that are highest in fat—bacon, sausage, eggs, cream cheese and hash browns among them—are traditionally eaten at breakfast. Despite a decrease in the average American's consumption of eggs—from 236 eggs per person per year in 1980 to 184 today—egg breakfasts with all the trimmings remain a popular choice, especially on the weekend. During the week, breakfast tends to be eaten on the run and often includes high-fat fast-food breakfast sandwiches, doughnuts and pastries. Even some of the seemingly healthy muffins are high in fat and provide few nutrients for the calories they contain. All in all, a high-fat breakfast can easily pack in more than half the fat and all the cholesterol you should be eating in a day.

On the other hand, breakfast is probably the easiest meal to make low in fat and, if you choose your foods wisely, it can be virtually fat-free. Moreover, it's an excellent meal in which to include foods high in complex carbohydrates, fiber and vitamins and minerals (such as vitamin C and calcium), because so many traditional breakfast foods—cold cereal, bread, oatmeal, milk, orange juice, fruit—are naturally high in these nutrients and low in fat. However, there's no rule that says your breakfast has to be cereal and toast with a glass of orange juice: What people eat for breakfast is largely a cultural matter. In Japan, for example, breakfast often includes fish, salad and soup. But if you'd rather leave out the whole grains and fruits at breakfast, do include them in other meals during the day.

Moreover, breakfast doesn't have to "stick to the ribs." A piece of fruit, a container of yogurt or an English muffin, like the Cornmeal-Cheese English Muffins on page 206, all provide a light breakfast that's nutrient-dense. And if you're one of those people who just isn't hungry until you've been awake for an hour or two, you can take something light and nourishing with you to the office—such as a slice of Oatmeal Bread, page 199, or Pumpkin-Spice Bread, page 204, or some Brown Rice Crackers, page 57—and eat it mid-morning as a snack.

Week 1/Breakfast Training Week

Use the substitution and replacement strategies suggested on pages 29 and 30 to make your breakfast lower in fat. Also try these suggestions:

• Use 1-percent or skim milk instead of whole milk on your cereal or try fruit juice instead of the milk.

• Use 1-percent or skim milk instead of cream or half-and-half in your coffee.

• Experiment with omelets made with two egg whites and one whole egg. Fill the omelets with chopped vegetables, such as peppers, tomatoes, onions or scallions, instead of cheese. If you must have a cheese omelet, use part-skim mozzarella or a small amount of your favorite cheese grated. To fry the omelet, use a nonstick pan sprayed with vegetable cooking spray instead of butter or oil.

• Use jam, jelly or fruit butters in place of butter, margarine or cream cheese on your morning toast, English muffin or bagel.

• Try some of the healthy pancake and waffle recipes in this book, such as Blueberry Cornmeal Pancakes on page 225 or French Toast Waffles on page 229.

• If you crave bacon, use Canadian bacon instead of regular bacon.

Week 2/Breakfast Goal Week

Using what you have learned in Week 1/ Breakfast Training Week, limit your fat intake at breakfast as follows:

YOUR BREAKFAST FAT TARGET		
WOMEN		
	Sedentary	*Active*
Normal Risk	8 grams	10 grams
High Risk	6 grams	8 grams
MEN		
	Sedentary	*Active*
Normal Risk	10 grams	12 grams
High Risk	8 grams	10 grams

WEEKS 3 AND 4: LUNCH AND SNACKS

For most working people, lunch is the most difficult meal to make lowfat. In the middle of a busy workday, it's easiest to grab a bite at the local deli, sandwich shop or fast-food restaurant and, in the quest for convenience, unwittingly choose foods high in fat and sodium. For example, a roast beef and cheese sandwich can contain 33 grams of fat, and ham and cheese on a croissant can supply 50 grams of fat. Even a plain regular-sized fast-food hamburger and a small order of french fries can contribute 23 grams of fat. Lunch accompaniments such as potato salad, coleslaw and potato chips are all high-fat foods. And those who do not eat lunch at all tend to snack more during the day, mostly on vending machine snacks, such as candy bars, cheese and crackers and cookies, which are high in fat and offer very little nutritional value.

The best way to control the fat content of your lunch is to make it yourself. You can choose from a wide variety of foods—vegetables, fruits, lowfat dairy products, legumes, breads, pasta and even meat and poultry—that will fill you up without adding a lot of fat to your diet. Lunch can consist of such portable items as fruit, yogurt, cottage cheese or a healthful sandwich. If you like, you can invest in an insulated lunch box, a thermos and a few plastic containers. That way such dinner leftovers as soup, chili, salads, pasta and stews can become part of the next-day's lunch routine. If your office has a refrigerator and a microwave oven, you have even more options open to you.

Even people who eat a good breakfast and lunch may feel the urge to snack either at mid-morning or mid-afternoon. Snacking is certainly allowed on this eating plan; indeed, diets that forbid you to grab something to tide you over between meals often leave you feeling hungry and unsatisfied, which may cause you to overeat at meals. Many popular snacks, however, contribute lots of fat and few nutrients, so it's important to choose your snacks wisely. Good lowfat snack choices include fruit, air-popped popcorn, or unsalted pretzels. For example, a ripe pear lightly spread with Camembert or Brie cheese can make a satisfying snack. You can also try the Three-Grain Breadsticks on page 62 or the Rye-Cheese Crackers on page 57.

Week 3/Lunch and Snacks Training Week

Stick to your breakfast fat target. Use the substitution and replacement strategies suggested on pages 29 and 30 to lower the fat content of your lunch and snacks. Also try these suggestions:

• Choose a fresh roast turkey sandwich over pastrami or bologna, and use mustard instead of mayonnaise on the bread.

• Order a fast-food roast beef sandwich rather than a regular hamburger; the roast beef is often lower in fat. And skip the sauce.

• Choose any kind of fruit for a lowfat snack.

• At the salad bar, watch out for high-fat items, such as avocados, cheese, pasta and bean salads, olives and meats, and skip or at least go easy on the salad dressing.

• Make a batch of healthy muffins or cookies to take with you to work for a mid-morning or afternoon snack. Good recipes to try include the Peach Muffins on page 209; the Biscotti on page 182; and the Molasses Cookies on page 180.

Week 4/ Lunch and Snack Goal Week:

Stick to your breakfast fat target. Use what you have learned in Week 3/ Lunch and Snacks Training Week and divide the grams of fat allotted for your category below between lunch and snacks.

YOUR LUNCH AND SNACK FAT TARGET		
	WOMEN	
	Sedentary	*Active*
Normal Risk	16 grams	20 grams
High Risk	12 grams	16 grams
	MEN	
	Sedentary	*Active*
Normal Risk	20 grams	24 grams
High Risk	16 grams	20 grams

WEEKS 5 AND 6: DINNER

For many Americans, dinner is often the largest meal of the day. According to a survey of food consumption trends, Americans eat about half their daily calories at dinner. Moreover, dinner can be a complicated meal for many families, since everyone's tastes and schedules must be accommodated. Not surprisingly, many people try to simplify dinner as much as possible, relying on convenience or packaged foods such as frozen dinners, canned vegetables, canned soups, bottled spaghetti sauces and packaged rice or stuffing mixes, all of which can be high in fat or sodium or both.

Dinner is also the meal most likely to feature meat as a centerpiece, usually in large portions. Meat can supply a hefty dose of fat and cholesterol; for example, an 8-ounce sirloin steak has 16 grams of fat. Match that with a baked potato with 2 tablespoons of sour cream, a salad with 2 tablespoons of Italian dressing and a roll with a pat of butter, and you'll have a dinner with 40 grams of fat. But there are many ways to lower the fat content of dinners and still eat meat. For example, you can prepare stir-fry dishes with a small amount of meat and a generous quantity of vegetables and rice or another grain. Or you could have spaghetti with a meatball or two (if you want a few more meatballs, make them from ground skinless light-meat turkey rather than ground beef). Remember, too, that meatless dishes can make satisfying dinners (see pages 111 to 130 for some ideas).

Week 5/Dinner Training Week
Stick to the fat targets for breakfast and lunch and snacks. Use the substitution and replacement strategies on pages 29 and 30 to lower the fat content of your dinners. Also try these suggestions:
• Substitute poultry or fish for some of the red meat you eat.
• Choose light-meat poultry over dark meat and always remove the skin.
• Trim all visible fat from meats before cooking.
• In recipes that traditionally contain a lot of meat, reduce the amount of meat called for and round out the recipe with extra vegetables or grains instead. Two good examples of this can be found in the Lamb and Mushroom Stew with Rosemary recipe on page 86 and the Stir-fried Chicken and Vegetables recipe on page 96.
• Prepare meatless dinners a few times a week. You will probably find them just as satisfying as those with meat. Try the following recipes: Vegetable Gumbo, page 118; Pasta with Creamy Coriander Pesto, page 135; or Shepherd's Pie, page 111.
• When sautéing or stir-frying vegetables, use a nonstick pan and try cooking the vegetables in wine, water or even fruit juice instead of butter or oil. If you need to use oil to prevent sticking, use a small amount of highly unsaturated oil, such as olive, safflower or canola, or a light mist of vegetable cooking spray.
• Bake or broil foods instead of deep-frying them.
• Choose lowfat desserts. Fruit is always a good choice. Try Cranberry Poached Pears with Yogurt on page 193 or Papaya and Apples with Berry Sauce on page 191. Often, traditional dessert recipes can be reworked to contain less fat; for example, the Hazelnut Cheesecake on page 173 uses part-skim ricotta cheese and lowfat lemon yogurt instead of the usual cream cheese.

Week 6/Dinner Goal Week
Stick to the fat goals for breakfast and lunch and snacks. Use what you learned in Week 5/Dinner Training Week and eat no more fat for dinner than allotted below for your category.

YOUR DINNER FAT TARGET		
	WOMEN	
	Sedentary	Active
Normal Risk	16 grams	20 grams
High Risk	12 grams	16 grams
	MEN	
	Sedentary	Active
Normal Risk	20 grams	24 grams
High Risk	16 grams	20 grams

Sticking with The Healthy Heart Solution

At the end of the six-week period you should be eating no more than your daily fat target. Now you can begin dividing the grams of fat any way you choose over the course of the day, while still paying attention to your daily fat target. For example, if your daily fat target is 50 grams, you could have a fat-free breakfast and fat-free snacks and then have 25 grams of fat at lunch and 25 grams of fat at dinner. Indeed, the proportion of fat per meal can change from day to day. Let's say you're going out to dinner and you know the restaurant has terrific cheesecake. If you control your fat intake earlier in the day, you can have the cheesecake for dessert. Once you become familiar with the fat content of different foods, planning the amount of fat you eat per meal will become second nature. Remember, however, that it is best to spend a few minutes each morning thinking about what you will be eating during the day. This will help prevent overloading on fat at one meal and having very little fat to work with the rest of the day.

Keep in mind that you should change your daily fat target if your physical activity level changes. For example, if you fall into the Sedentary category for your sex and you begin a regular exercise program, you could increase your fat intake by moving to the Active level. Conversely, if you fall into the Active level and you stop exercising, you will need to reduce your fat consumption.

If you find yourself sliding back toward your old eating habits, start keeping a food diary again so you can see where the extra fat is coming from. Whatever you do, don't use an occasional slip as an excuse to completely abandon your new eating style. Instead, just start over again, even if it means repeating the six-week program. The box below offers some tips on dealing with backsliding.

A NOTE ABOUT BACKSLIDING

Even if you conscientiously limit your fat intake to no more than your fat target, there will be days when your fat intake exceeds that amount. If that happens, it is important not to punish yourself: A setback doesn't mean failure, and it certainly shouldn't be used as an excuse to return to old eating patterns. Simply view the event as a fork in the road: One path leads to total relapse, the other to continued change for the better. You could say to yourself: "I ate a pint of ice cream last night. It's no use. I obviously can't limit the fat I eat, so there's no reason to even try." Or you could give yourself a break and adopt this attitude: "Well, I ate a pint of ice cream last night and went over my fat limit. That's not so good, but that was last night. Today I'll stick to my eating plan and forget about last night." In other words, you give yourself permission not to be perfect.

According to studies by G. Alan Marlatt and his colleagues at the University of Washington, three primary high-risk situations account for 75 percent of all relapses.

1. Negative emotional states. You're more likely to slip if you're bored, angry or frustrated.

2. Interpersonal conflicts. If you've had an argument at home or at work, you may return to high-fat eating habits in compensation or revenge.

3. Social pressure. Family, friends and co-workers may pressure you into eating high-fat foods. Or you might not be able to resist high-fat foods offered to you at a party or restaurant.

If you do go over your fat target, ignore any feelings of guilt or inadequacy and concentrate on the reasons why you decided to eat a lowfat diet in the first place. You want to lower your cholesterol, prevent heart disease and perhaps lose weight. Then review the situation that led to the slip-up. Was it a simple miscalculation? Were you bored? Were you upset? Did someone pressure you to eat high-fat foods? Evaluating these events can be helpful in preventing backsliding in the future.

A GUIDE TO
HEART-HEALTHY FOODS

The following glossary of foods will help you stick with *The Healthy Heart Solution* by showing you how to make wise fat choices. Included are the health benefits of various foods—as well as their nutritional drawbacks—information on substitutions and shopping tips. Consult this glossary for fat-cutting ideas during the six-week program, then continue to refer to it as needed afterwards.

Bacon and sausage Anyone concerned about heart disease should be particularly wary of bacon and sausage, both of which are especially high in fat and sodium. However, an occasional small serving of bacon or sausage can still be part of a lowfat, low-sodium diet if fat and sodium intake are controlled at other meals.

A good alternative to regular bacon is Canadian bacon; 2 ounces of Canadian bacon (about 2 slices) contains 8 grams of fat, while 2 ounces of regular bacon (about 8 slices) contains 24 grams of fat. An alternative to regular sausages are "lean" or "light" sausages—usually made by adding turkey, rice or other filler to the pork or beef. These are slightly lower in fat than their standard counterparts, containing about 5 grams of fat per ounce versus about 8 grams in regular sausage. Don't assume that these lower-fat options are necessarily lower in sodium, however. All types of bacon and sausage are high in sodium. Be sure to look at the package labels and remember that sodium in these products comes in many forms besides salt, including monosodium glutamate (MSG), sodium nitrite and sodium phosphate.

Breads *(see also Crackers and Muffins and quickbreads)* Most breads—including bagels and rolls—are low in fat and can be eaten freely. Biscuits and croissants are an exception, however. A typical biscuit recipe calls for 2 to 3 tablespoons of a hard fat (such as butter, stick margarine, shortening or lard) for each cup of flour. As a result, a small bis-

cuit (about 2 inches in diameter) can contain 3 to 5 grams of fat. An average-sized croissant has about 12 grams of fat, mostly from the large amount of butter used in the dough. Add chocolate or cheese and the fat content of a croissant increases even more.

In most cases, however, it's not the bread that's fattening, but the toppings you put on it. Butter, margarine and cream cheese are almost pure fat, most of it saturated. In place of butter or margarine on toast, use jam or jelly, fruit spread or fruit butter. Or, instead of regular cream cheese, try one of the reduced-fat or fat-free cream cheeses now available. Other good substitutes for cream cheese are pot cheese, farmer's cheese, lowfat cottage cheese or part-skim or fat-free ricotta cheese. To make cottage cheese or ricotta thicker and more spreadable, spoon them into a strainer lined with cheesecloth or a paper coffee filter, place the strainer over a bowl and refrigerate for 2 to 3 hours. This will remove some of the liquid whey from the cheese and make it less watery. To add flavor without fat, you can season these cheeses with your favorite herbs and spices. Homemade yogurt cheese can also be prepared this way; see page 52.

When shopping for bread, always check the label for fiber content, since not all breads are equal in terms of fiber. Look for loaves that have 2 or 3 grams per slice. Most breads are made of what is called wheat flour, which isn't whole wheat, but simply white flour that has had most of the fiber-rich bran and the nutritious germ mechanically removed. If you want 100-percent whole-wheat bread, look for breads labeled "whole wheat."

Some white breads (especially diet breads) contain added fiber from oat bran, wheat bran or soy flour, making them higher in fiber than many "6-grain" or "12-grain" loaves. Watch out for breads that claim they are made from triticale, wheat bran or rye flour; they may prove to have very little whole grain when you check the list of ingredients.

Butter and margarine Many people concerned about diet believe that using margarine instead of butter is better for their health. The bottom line is that if your diet is low in fat to begin with, you needn't worry about eating a small amount of either butter or margarine since butter and stick margarines contain exactly the same amount of fat—11 grams per tablespoon.

Because most margarines are made with vegetable oils, they do not contain any cholesterol, whereas butter contains 31 milligrams per tablespoon. Many margarines, however, are made with hydrogenated oils—oils that have been chemically changed to make them more saturated and thus extend their shelf life. These artificially saturated fats are no better for you than the saturated fat contained in butter.

There are some forms of margarine that do have clear advantages over butter, however. Softer spreads, such as tub and squeeze margarines, are often made with no hydrogenated oils, or contain less hydrogenated oil than stick margarines. They are therefore lower in saturated fat. Their total fat content, however, is the same as stick margarines and butter. Diet margarines are even better, since they are very soft and contain more water and only half the fat of regular margarines. However, the high water content makes them unsuitable for cooking purposes.

Canned fish As a sandwich filling or served on a bed of greens, canned fish is a good lowfat food if you choose carefully. Water-packed tuna has 0.5 to 2 grams of fat per 4-ounce serving, but tuna packed in oil has 9 grams of fat per 4 ounces even after the oil is drained. Moreover, draining oil-packed tuna removes 15 to 25 percent of the cardio-protective polyunsaturated fatty acids called omega-3s (see page 17 for more on omega-3s), whereas draining water-packed tuna removes only 3 percent.

Other canned fish options include salmon and sardines. The advantage these fish have over tuna is their high calcium content; if eaten with the bones (which are soft and chewable), 3½ ounces of salmon or sardines provide 175 to 350 milligrams of calcium. The disadvantage of salmon and sardines is that they are considerably higher in fat than canned tuna, even when packed in water. A 4-ounce portion of canned sockeye (red) salmon has about 10 grams of fat; pink salmon has 7 grams of fat. Four ounces of sardines canned in water or tomato sauce contain 13 grams of fat. Canned fish can also be extremely high in sodium; look for brands with a low sodium content or no salt added.

Even if you choose water-packed canned fish, you still should be careful about the way you prepare it. Mayonnaise, typically used to dress tuna or salmon salads, adds a lot of fat. A half-cup of tuna salad made with regular mayonnaise has 11 grams of fat—virtually all from the mayonnaise. Use fat-free mayonnaise or a mixture of lowfat yogurt and mustard instead. Other ways to add moistness and flavor to seafood salads without adding fat are to include celery, bell peppers, tomatoes, corn kernels, scallions, chives, shallots, onions, carrots or fresh herbs. Grated apple also complements tuna salad nicely.

Cereals Ready-to-eat cereals are by far the most popular American breakfast choice. They're convenient for quick meals and many are high in fiber, low in fat and provide good amounts of vitamins and minerals. Still, you must shop with care when choosing a cold cereal since some are loaded with fat or sodium or both. Granola is a good example. While it seems healthful—oats are the main ingredient and granola often contains seeds, nuts and dried fruit—most commercial brands are exceedingly high in fat. Oil is used in toasting the oats; the nuts and seeds are already high in fat; and coconut (which is high in saturated fat) is often added. Rather than buying commercial granola, consider making your own lowfat granola (see the recipe on page 221). Alternatively, look for one of the fat-free brands that are on the market.

When buying a ready-to-eat cereal, choose one that will boost your fiber intake. While some bran cereals contain as much as 14 grams of fiber in a 1-ounce serving, others, like crisped rice, have less than a gram of fiber per serving. (As a general rule, high-fiber cereals contain 7 or more grams of fiber per ounce.) In addition, different cereals contain different types of fiber. Wheat-bran cereals, for example, are good sources of insoluble fiber—the kind that helps prevent constipation and may protect against colon cancer—while cereals made with oats or barley provide soluble fiber, which may lower cholesterol.

Whatever lowfat, high-fiber cereal you decide on, serve it with skim milk, for a virtually fat-free breakfast or snack. For variety, flavor the milk with vanilla, almond or another flavoring extract. Or, instead of milk, add low- or nonfat plain or flavored yogurt to the cereal (stir it briskly to thin it before spooning it into the cereal). You could also use fruit juice instead of milk. Consider mixing different types of cereal in the same bowl, then adding fresh or dried fruit, such as apples, berries, bananas, nectarines, peaches, kiwi, raisins, dates, figs, prunes or apricots for additional fiber and nutrients.

As far as hot cereals are concerned, oatmeal is probably the most familiar, though any whole grain (such as bulgur, barley, millet, amaranth, brown rice or buckwheat) can be mixed with water or another liquid, such as fruit juice or skim milk, and then cooked into a porridge (see pages 217-221 for some hot cereal recipes using a variety of whole grains). As long as you don't add butter or cream, oatmeal and other whole-grain cereals are very low in fat. And because whole-grain cereals are excellent sources of fiber, they make an especially filling breakfast. You can boost the fiber content of these cereals even further by eating them with dried or fresh fruit. Try oatmeal with raisins, dates or dried figs; rice with dried apricots; millet with sliced or grated apples, or barley with bananas.

Cheese Cheese is one food that must be limited on a lowfat diet. Just 1 ounce of most hard cheeses—such as Cheddar, Swiss, or provolone—contains 8 to 9 grams of fat. In fact, the only cheeses that can truly be called lowfat are part-skim ricotta and 1- and 2-percent fat cottage cheese. While part-skim mozzarella is lower in fat than many cheeses, it still contains about 5 grams of fat per ounce. However, even high-fat cheeses can be included in your diet if you use them sparingly: For example, try a thin slice of Swiss or Cheddar on a chicken or turkey sandwich, a sprinkling of grated Parmesan as a topping for vegetables or pastas, or a little blue cheese crumbled over a salad.

There is now a wide variety of commercially manufactured lowfat, reduced-fat and fat-free cheeses available on the market. You'll find lowfat substitutes for Cheddar, Swiss, Monterey Jack, and American, and some fat-free brands of mozzarella and ricotta as well. Lowfat cheeses are made by substituting skim milk, lowfat milk, or even water for whole milk or cream, and, in some cases, using vegetable oil instead of butterfat. Unfortunately, the taste and texture of most of these lowfat cheeses doesn't come close to that of true cheese; indeed, most tend to be bland and rubbery. Moreover, lowfat cheeses don't melt well. Still, in some instances, the loss of flavor might not be noticeable. For example, a slice of lowfat Swiss might be fine for a meat sandwich, and fat-free ricotta is virtually indistinguishable from part-skim ricotta in a baked pasta casserole.

If lowfat cheese really doesn't appeal to you, then consider eating less of the cheeses you do like: To enjoy the full flavor of a cheese, eat a small amount by itself, or perhaps with an apple or a pear or some lowfat crackers. When cooking with cheese, choose strong-flavored varieties—such as blue cheese, asiago, Parmesan, Romano, sharp Cheddar or Limburger—since a small amount goes a long way in adding flavor to foods. Grating or shredding a cheese helps it go further while still adding flavor. The Vegetable Quesadillas on page 112, for example, are enhanced by the addition of grated Montery Jack cheese.

Chips, pretzels, puffs and popcorn These crunchy, salty foods are favorite snack choices, but anyone serious about a lowfat diet should be aware of the fat differences among them. Popcorn, if prepared by the air-popping method, can be virtually fat-free. Of course, if you add butter, the fat content goes up considerably. Pre-popped packaged popcorn varies in fat content; be sure to check the nutritional information carefully for grams of fat per serving. Many brands of microwave popcorn also contain an inordinate amount of fat—about 8 grams per 3-cup serving.

Look for the lower-fat brands (about 4 grams per 3-cup serving) that are available. Packaged popcorn can also be high in sodium—250 to 300 milligrams per 3-cup serving. Making your own popcorn lets you control sodium as well as fat. For an interesting topping for popcorn, see the recipe for Popcorn with Herbed Goat Cheese on page 61.

Pretzels can also be a good snack choice: An ounce of pretzels—about 5 medium pretzels or 2 large ones—contains just a gram of fat. Pretzels are usually heavily salted, however, and can contain 400 to 650 milligrams of sodium per ounce; so choose unsalted types.

Almost all kinds of chips and puffs are high in fat and sodium. An ounce of potato chips, for example, has 10 grams of fat and 190 grams of sodium, and an ounce of corn chips has 9 grams of fat and 190 grams of sodium. Flavored chips—such as barbecue, bacon or nacho—usually have the highest sodium content. Cheese puffs are no better—1 ounce has 8 grams of fat and 360 milligrams of sodium. In most instances, the fat in these products comes from the oil used in manufacturing them; often it is vegetable oil or partially hydrogenated vegetable oil, which is high in saturated fat. Some snack food manufacturers are now producing "light" versions of their products, containing about a third less fat. While these products are better than their high-fat counterparts, they are still, by no means, lowfat foods.

Cold cuts Cold cuts such as bologna, salami and pastrami are typically high in saturated fat and cholesterol and also contain hefty amounts of sodium (some products have 450 milligrams of sodium or more per ounce). Today, many of these traditional processed meats are being made with turkey or chicken. Unfortunately, even these cold-cuts are frequently not as lean as they could be, since they may be made with dark meat (and some brands contain high-cholesterol organ meats). In fact, turkey bologna and turkey salami are not much lower in fat than the meats they're intended to replace. Turkey ham and turkey pastrami, on the other hand, are good lowfat choices; look for brands that contain a gram of fat or less

per ounce, and try to choose low-salt or no-salt-added varieties.

Instead of ordering processed luncheon meats at the deli, select extra-lean ham, lean roast beef, or fresh roasted turkey breast. Stay away from turkey roll: While low in fat, it is often not composed solely of turkey; the meat has frequently been processed and filled with additives. Moreover, the fat content of turkey roll depends on whether it is made primarily from dark or light meat.

The best cold cuts are those sliced from meats you prepare yourself. Leftover chicken, turkey breast, lean beef (such as sirloin, round or loin cuts) or lean pork (loin or tenderloin) are the most healthful meats for sandwiches. You can control the fat content by choosing lean cuts, trimming all the visible fat and, in the case of poultry, removing the skin. When you cook the meat yourself, you can also avoid any added sodium.

Condiments Mayonnaise, which is made from vegetable oil, egg yolks and vinegar, is the only condiment that is high in fat, containing 11 grams of fat per tablespoon (yet, despite its egg content, a tablespoon of real mayonnaise has just 5 milligrams of cholesterol). In buying mayonnaise, look for products labeled "salad dressing" or "light," "diet" or "imitation" mayonnaise. These mock-mayonnaise products may contain less than half the fat of real mayonnaise because water and starch or another thickener has replaced some of the oil. Some brands are even fat-free. When shopping for fat-free mayonnaise, be sure the label says "fat-free" in addition to "no cholesterol" since some mayonnaises may contain no cholesterol and still be high in fat.

When considering condiments, keep in mind that ketchup, mustard, salsa, soy sauce and Worcestershire sauce are all virtually fat-free. The problem with some of these, however, is their sodium content. A tablespoon of soy sauce can contain more than 1000 milligrams of sodium, while Dijon mustard may have 465 milligrams of sodium per tablespoon and ketchup, 156 milligrams per tablespoon. Look for low-sodium versions, or consider using horseradish and chutney, two fat-free condiments that contain very little sodium.

Cookies You don't have to give up cookies on a heart-healthy diet. In fact, there is a wide variety of healthful cookies available today. You must choose carefully, though. Some brands are truly healthful—made with little fat and whole grains—but others are simply sweetened with fruit juice instead of sugar and contain all the fat of standard cookies. Your only clue to fat content may be the list of ingredients. Check for palm oil, palm kernel oil, coconut oil and hydrogenated and partially hydrogenated oils, and try to avoid cookies that contain them. Your best bet is to find a cookie made with a plain unhydrogenated vegetable oil, such as soybean or corn; while unhydrogenated vegetable oils are not lower in fat, they are lower in saturated fat than tropical or hydrogenated oils. Shortbread and butter cookies, along with cookies made with chocolate, peanut butter or nuts, tend to be the highest in fat. Fig bars (and other fruit-filled bars), ginger snaps and graham crackers are relatively low in fat. Making your own cookies allows you to control the amount of fat they contain. Try the recipes for lowfat Molasses Cookies on page 180, Apple-Pumpkin Chewies on page 181 and Butternut Squash Hermits on page 181.

Crackers Ounce for ounce, some popular crackers contain as much fat and sodium as the cheese you put on them. Others have virtually no fat or sodium and pack healthy amounts of fiber. Crackers made with "100 percent vegetable oil," for example, are no better for you than those made with butter or lard if the oil is coconut, palm or palm kernel—all highly saturated oils. Watch out, too, for hydrogenated or partially hydrogenated oils, which are also saturated. One way to test how much fat is in a cracker is to rub the cracker with a paper napkin. If it leaves a grease mark, there's lots of fat.

Choose crackers that are virtually fat-free, such as rice cakes, crispbread, matzo or melba toast, or those that are relatively low in fat, such as certain thin wheat crackers (containing only about 2 grams of fat per ounce), or saltines or graham crackers (with 2 to 3 grams of fat per ounce). Watch out for water crackers and round snack-type crackers, which can contain 5 to 9 grams of fat per ounce.

And choose cheese-flavored crackers infrequently, since they are much higher in fat.

Most crackers contain a fair amount of salt, some providing as much as 400 milligrams of sodium per ounce. However, there are many low- or no-salt varieties available, and many crackers actually taste better with less salt.

As far as fiber is concerned, cracker labels are like bread labels in that words like "wheat," "stone ground wheat" or "blend of hearty wheats" don't necessarily mean that the product is made with whole wheat. In fact, most wheat crackers are made with 50 to 90 percent white flour. If you're looking for a fiber boost from crackers, you'll have to look for those labeled "whole wheat."

Eggs Eggs aren't particularly high in fat—one large egg contains about 5 grams, with only 2 grams of that saturated—but they are exceptionally high in cholesterol, with one egg supplying about two-thirds of the total cholesterol you should eat in a day. This means that you shouldn't eat more than four whole eggs a week (and that people with high cholesterol need to limit themselves to one whole egg per week). This includes whole eggs used as part of other dishes, such as the eggs used in baking. Egg whites can be used freely, however, since all the cholesterol (and all of the fat) in an egg is in the yolk. You can also use egg substitutes, which contain no cholesterol and little fat.

Learn to be creative with your use of eggs. For example, you can extend scrambled eggs by using one whole egg and one egg white. Omelets—often made with 2 or 3 eggs as well as cheese, ham and other high-fat ingredients—can be made healthier by using one whole egg and two egg whites. And instead of adding ham and cheese, fill the omelet with vegetables, such as onions, tomatoes, peppers, spinach, asparagus or mushrooms, and lowfat cottage or part-skim ricotta cheese. You can also add a cheesy flavor without adding a lot of fat by sprinkling a little grated Parmesan or part-skim mozzarella cheese into the omelet mixture. Cook the omelet in a nonstick pan or in a pan lightly brushed with vegetable oil or sprayed lightly with vegetable cooking spray.

Fish and shellfish Fish and shellfish are good for your heart. Not only are most types low in fat, but fish contains the special polyunsaturated fatty acids called omega-3s. Omega-3s seem to be able to protect against heart disease by reducing the potential for the blood to clot, which lessens the chance of heart attack (see page 17). In fact, it has been shown that eating even small amounts of fish once or twice a week seems to have a beneficial effect. Fatty fish—such as salmon, herring, mackerel, sardines, swordfish, rainbow trout, pompano, bluefish, ocean perch, striped or freshwater bass, shad, catfish, butterfish, carp, smelt and mullet—contain the most omega-3s. Lean fish, such as cod, flounder and sole, have less fat, but a greater percentage of the fat they do have is in the form of omega-3 fatty acids.

Contrary to popular belief, most fish—even most types of shellfish—are very low in cholesterol. Shrimp is the exception with 221 milligrams of cholesterol per 4-ounce serving. But all types of fish and shellfish are very low in saturated fat. Shrimp, for example, has less than a gram of saturated fat per 4-ounce serving. Seafood ceases to be low in fat, however, when it is cooked with butter or topped with a high-fat cream sauce. Add flavor without fat by using lemon or lime juice, wine, or herbs and spices, or by making a creamy sauce with lowfat sour cream or lowfat or nonfat yogurt. Baking, poaching, steaming, broiling and microwaving are all excellent methods for cooking fish and shellfish to keep them moist without the addition of fat. Try the Tex-Mex Steamed Snapper on page 103, for example, or the baked Stuffed Trout on page 104.

Frozen desserts Anyone concerned with counting fat grams can delight in the fact that ice cream is no longer the only frozen dessert option. All sorts of new frozen desserts are now on the market, including frozen yogurt, fat-free frozen dairy desserts and nondairy frozen desserts.

While most standard ice cream contains about 7 grams of fat per half cup, premium ice cream can contain up to 12 grams of fat per half cup, much of it saturated. Frozen yogurt is usually a better bet, but check to see whether it is made from whole milk and cream (both high in fat) or skim milk. In general, frozen yogurt contains 3 to 4 grams of fat per half cup; and some frozen yogurts are fat-free. Frozen dairy desserts (a new name for ice milk) are made from skim milk and contain 3 grams of fat per half cup. Nondairy frozen desserts, which contain 0 to 3 grams of fat per half cup, use an array of ingredients to match the texture of ice cream. These include Simplesse (a fat substitute), polydextrose and maltodextrin (food starch derivatives) and a variety of natural gums (such as guar and cellulose). Tofu is also used in nondairy frozen desserts, but some of these can be high in fat, though the fat is largely unsaturated. Still other frozen desserts are fruit-based. Sherbets usually contain some milk as well as fruit and have about 4 grams of fat per cup; fruit ices, sorbets and fruit bars contain little or no fat.

While even the richest ice cream can safely be eaten as an occasional treat, in general frozen desserts should be limited to those that contain 4 grams of fat or less per half cup. Remember, too, that crushed cookies, candy, nuts and other "mix-ins" can significantly boost the fat content, as can a topping of whipped cream. To be sure you're getting a lowfat frozen dessert, consider making your own. Try the recipes for Ruby Sorbet and Lemon-Lime Sherbet, both found on page 195.

Fruit Because fruit is high in fiber (which helps to fill you up), it makes an especially satisfying snack or dessert. Indeed, most of the fiber in fruits is in the form of pectin, a soluble fiber that has been shown to help lower cholesterol. Apples and citrus fruits have the most pectin. Another advantage of eating fruit for snacks and desserts is that it provides vitamin C, beta carotene and potassium. And, of course, most fruits are fat-free.

When choosing fruit, don't overlook dried fruits. Because they are concentrated by drying, ounce for ounce dried fruits contain greater amounts of vitamins, minerals and fiber than fresh fruits—and, though higher in calories, they are also fat-free. For example, 2 ounces of dried apricots (about 16 halves) contains 2 milligrams of beta carotene, while 2 ounces of fresh apricots (about 2 fruits) has just 1 milligram. Similarly, prunes have at least three times more iron than the fresh plums they're made from. Vitamin C, however, is one nutrient that is destroyed by the drying process, so dried fruits are not a good source of vitamin C.

Grains The United States Department of Agriculture (USDA) has revised the concept of the four food groups and the basics of a healthy diet; in doing so, they determined that grains and grain products (including breads and pastas) should be the foundation of a lowfat eating plan. Grains are virtually fat-free and supply complex carbohydrates, protein, fiber and a host of vitamins and minerals. Whole grains and whole-grain products are the best sources of fiber since their nutritious layers (the bran and germ) have not been removed, and they are also excellent sources of essential nutrients, such as vitamin E, copper, magnesium and zinc.

While most people aren't used to thinking of grains as main-course fare, a host of grains easily lend themselves to casseroles, main-dish salads, fillings for vegetables and bases for stews. Rice, wheat berries, bulgur (a quick-cooking form of wheat), kasha (buckwheat groats), whole oat groats, barley, millet and triticale are the most common types of grains found in supermarkets and health food stores. Amaranth and quinoa, which are not botanically classified as grains, can also be used like grains. Both are becoming increasingly popular for their interesting flavors and high protein content.

You can keep grain dishes low in fat by simply not adding high-fat ingredients. For example, the directions on packaged rice, rice mixes and other grain products often call for the addition of oil or butter; this can usually be eliminated without substantially affecting the flavor of the dish.

Legumes Dried beans, peas and lentils are collectively known as legumes. Because legumes are a rich source of protein, soluble fiber and vitamins and minerals—and because most types are virtually fat-free—nutritionists are now suggesting that anyone interested in adopting a lowfat diet eat more of these foods.

Legumes are extremely versatile: They come in a wide variety of shapes, sizes, colors and flavors.

Some popular legumes include adzuki beans, kidney beans, navy beans, black beans, pinto beans, flageolets, lentils and green and yellow split peas, although there are many more to choose from. Most legumes can be readily substituted for each other in recipes and, fortunately, legumes don't need a lot of fat to give them flavor. Try them in soups or stews, combined with rice or pasta, in salads or in such classic dishes as baked beans and chili. See page 83 for Three-Bean Chili, which uses pinto beans, black beans and red kidney beans.

Legumes cease to be a lowfat food, however, when they are combined with large amounts of fat. Take hummus, for example: This Middle Eastern dip traditionally features chickpeas as its main ingredient, but it also includes large amounts of olive oil and tahini (a paste made from sesame seeds), which makes it high in fat.

Meat In this country, beef is by far the most popular meat choice, far outranking veal, pork and lamb. And while beef consumption has declined 28 percent since the mid-1970s, a Gallup poll found that in most American's minds beef is still considered the "perfect" entrée.

Today beef and other meats can be included in a heart-healthy diet because they aren't nearly as fatty as they used to be. Beef is about 27 percent leaner, and pork 31 percent leaner, than 15 years ago, thanks to breeding and feeding techniques that produce leaner animals—and to the growing number of retailers who are trimming the external fat down to about $\frac{1}{10}$ of an inch. You can reduce the fat content of meat even further by choosing lean cuts and trimming all the external fat remaining *before cooking*. One study of beef cuts conducted by researchers at Texas A & M University found that trimming the fat before cooking had no effect on the flavor, juiciness or tenderness of the beef.

The type of cut is an important clue to its fat content. Cuts of meat from parts of the animal that do a lot of work—the shoulder, for example (called the chuck in beef)—are higher in fat than cuts from the areas that do little work, such as the loin. This is because muscles that are exercised build connective tissue, and fat in the animal's body is deposited around connective tissue first.

In beef, grading can also provide a clue to the fat content. The cuts with the most marbling and, therefore, the most fat, are given the grade of Prime, followed by Choice and Select. On average, a cut of beef graded Select has 5 to 20 percent less fat than Choice beef of the same cut, and 40 percent less fat than Prime. About 44 percent of the beef you find in supermarkets is ungraded, however. Often sold under the store's brand, this meat is usually of Choice or Select quality. Don't assume, however, that Select beef is always preferable to Choice. It only applies when comparing grades from the same cut. For example, a 4-ounce Choice cut of eye of round has 6 grams of fat, while the same size Select cut of eye of round has 4 grams of fat. However, 4 ounces of Select trimmed blade roast (chuck) has 16 grams of fat, as compared to 8 grams of fat in Choice trimmed top round.

The three keys to making meat part of a lowfat diet are eating small portions (3½ to 5 ounces when cooked), trimming all visible fat and choosing lean cuts—those with 10 grams or less of fat per 3½ ounces.

When serving meat, round out small portions with generous quantities of vegetables, legumes or grains. For example, when making beef or lamb stew, cut back on the amount of meat called for in the recipe and include plenty of vegetables—carrots, onions, sweet potatoes, potatoes, canned whole tomatoes (include the juice, which will help tenderize the meat), parsnips, celery, summer or winter squash, mushrooms and turnips—and serve the stew over bulgur, rice, couscous or barley. When making stir-fries, combine a small amount of beef, pork or lamb with Oriental vegetables, such as nappa cabbage, water chestnuts, snowpeas, baby corn, scallions and bamboo shoots. Add broccoli, cauliflower, carrots and red or green peppers, if you like, and serve the mixture over brown or white rice. When making dishes that call for ground beef, choose a lean cut of beef and have the butcher trim and grind it for you. Alternatively, choose extra-lean ground beef and mix it with an equal amount of ground light-meat turkey. If using ground meat in spaghetti sauce or chili, or as a filling, brown it in a nonstick skillet first, then pour off the fat before combining the meat with other ingredients.

Milk and cream   All types of milk are high in calcium and potassium, but they vary widely in fat content. The best milk choice on a heart-healthy diet is skim or nonfat milk. A cup of skim milk has less than half a gram of fat. If you don't like the taste of skim milk, choose lowfat (1%) milk, which has 3 grams of fat per cup. Alternatively, you can make skim milk seem richer by blending in a tablespoon or two of nonfat dry milk; this also boosts the calcium content, since a tablespoon of nonfat dry milk contains 94 milligrams of calcium.

Using 2-percent milk is a good way to wean yourself off whole milk, but it is still relatively high in fat, containing nearly 5 grams per cup. Stay away from whole milk, which contains 8 to 9 grams of fat per cup, nearly half of which is saturated.

Because half-and-half, light cream and heavy cream are high in fat, they should be used sparingly, if at all. Just a tablespoon of half-and-half contains 2 grams of fat; a tablespoon of light cream, 5 grams; and a tablespoon of heavy cream, 6 grams. Three tablespoons of whipped heavy cream contains 9 grams of fat.

Muffins and quickbreads   Muffins and quickbreads that you make yourself—or selectively choose at the store—can be good lowfat sources of complex carbohydrates and fiber. If they contain dried fruit, such as apricots, raisins or prunes, they provide even more fiber along with vitamins and minerals, such as beta carotene and iron.

But beware of the muffins or quickbreads available at delis or bakeries or from the coffee cart—they may contain more fat than you think. Commercially made muffins and quickbreads often contain hydrogenated oils, whole eggs and nuts, which boost the fat content. And those made with honey or fruit juice are no healthier than those made with sugar, since they aren't necessarily low in fat. Even bran muffins are often made with the same high-fat ingredients as other muffins and quickbreads, and may contain very little bran. If a muffin or a slice of quickbread is heavy in your hand or feels sticky, it's apt to be high in fat.

Some commercial muffins and quickbreads, however, do have a lower fat content. Look at the ingredient list. Flour (preferably whole-grain) should be the first ingredient. Oil should be far down on the list and it should not be hydrogenated. Look for products made with soy, safflower or canola oil, all of which are low in saturated fat.

Nuts Extremely nutritious, nuts are rich in protein, fiber, potassium, calcium, iron, vitamin E, the B vitamins, copper, magnesium and zinc. Unfortunately, they are also high in fat and, therefore, must be eaten in limited quantities by anyone on a heart-healthy diet. Just an ounce of nuts can supply anywhere from 13 to 22 grams of fat. The one exception is chestnuts, which have 1 gram of fat per ounce. Because the fat in nuts is mostly unsaturated (except for coconut, which is high in saturated fat), nuts will not raise blood cholesterol.

Organ meats Organ meats, such as liver, spleen, sweetbreads and heart, are not high in fat, but are very high in cholesterol. For example, 4 ounces of braised beef liver has just 6 grams of fat, but packs 440 milligrams of cholesterol. Because of the extraordinarily high cholesterol content of organ meats, you should not eat them more than once a week and then only eat them in small portions.

Pancakes and waffles When you want a lowfat, high-fiber breakfast that's also tasty and festive, pancakes and waffles are an excellent choice. Making your own pancakes and waffles from scratch is a sure way to decrease the amount of fat and boost the fiber (see the recipes for homemade pancakes and waffles on pages 223 to 229).

You can also prepare pancakes and waffles made from store-bought mixes with less fat per serving if you make them with skim milk, egg whites and only a small amount of oil. The problem with most mixes is not fat and cholesterol but sodium—almost 900 milligrams per serving in some cases—which comes from added salt and such leavening agents as baking powder and baking soda. Watch out especially for the so-called "complete" mixes to which you add only water; these may contain partially hydrogenated oils, as well as whole milk, and are considerably higher in fat than those mixes to which you add your own ingredients. Waffle lovers may want to try the frozen ready-to-heat varieties, some of which now include oat bran and other whole grains. Most are relatively low in fat and sodium (generally, one waffle has 4 to 5 grams of fat and roughly 220 milligrams of sodium).

In terms of fiber, pancakes and waffles can range from less than 1 gram per serving in products made from refined flour to 12 grams for those made from whole grains. To boost the fiber content of any pancake or waffle recipe, add any of the following to the batter: wheat bran or germ, oat bran, instant oatmeal, diced apples, blueberries or grated carrots.

Of course, pancakes and waffles are no longer lowfat foods when topped with lots of butter or whipped cream. Use cooked or fresh fruit as toppings to avoid the fat while adding vitamins, minerals and fiber. Try sliced strawberries alone or mixed with other berries; apples stewed in apple juice with cinnamon; mixed pear and apple slices; or sliced bananas, peaches, nectarines or kiwis.

Pasta Once thought of as fattening, pasta has earned a new reputation as a health food. High in complex carbohydrates and protein and low in fat, pasta is only fattening when it is served with high-fat cream-, meat- or oil-based sauces, or stuffed with fatty cheeses or meats.

There are many different types of pasta to choose from. Traditional pasta is made from semolina, a type of refined wheat flour, and is sold plain or flavored with spinach, tomato, saffron, basil, garlic, herbs and other seasonings. Pastas made from corn, rice or vegetable starch are also available, as is whole-wheat pasta, which is very high in dietary fiber. Asian noodles, which include bean thread (cellophane) noodles, buckwheat noodles (called *soba*), wheat noodles (called *udon* or *somen*) and rice noodles, are among the more exotic pastas now becoming widely available.

The healthiest toppings for pasta include tomato sauce, broth-based sauces, vegetable purées or sliced vegetables. Small amounts of sharp-flavored cheeses can also add lots of flavor with little fat.

(For example, a tablespoon of grated Parmesan cheese contains just 2 grams of fat). Part-skim or fat-free ricotta cheeses are also good complements to pasta. Try Linguine with Tuna Sauce, page 132, or Spinach Lasagna, page 135; both contain less than 10 grams of fat per serving.

Poultry If you want a meal where meat is the focus, skinless light-meat chicken and turkey are both good choices since they are low in fat and very low in saturated fat. Four ounces of skinless chicken breast contains just 5 grams of fat (including 1 gram of saturated fat), and turkey breast is even leaner, supplying just 1 gram of fat per serving, with a negligible amount of saturated fat. If you eat your poultry with the skin on, however, the fat and saturated fat content doubles, since poultry skin is mostly fat.

It is also important to note that dark-meat poultry is much higher in fat than light meat. Dark-meat chicken has two times the fat of chicken breast. Dark-meat turkey has four times as much fat as turkey breast. Because duck and goose meat is all dark, both are extremely high in fat even when eaten without the skin, and neither is a good choice for a lowfat diet. Eat duck and goose only on occasion, and always take off the skin.

While you should remove the skin before eating any type of poultry, there's no reason to remove it before baking, broiling or roasting the bird. Researchers at the University of Minnesota found that no signficiant amount of fat is transferred from the skin to the meat during cooking by these methods. In fact, removing the skin from poultry before cooking by these methods only leads to drier—not leaner—meat.

Recently, more and more supermarkets have begun to offer ground poultry. Make sure, however, that the ground poultry comes from white meat only. Some packaged ground turkey, for example, contains dark meat or turkey skin. You can be sure you're getting lean ground poultry if you buy chicken breasts or turkey breast cutlets or tenderloins and then have them ground for you. Ground poultry often needs added moisture and more seasoning than ground beef. Tomato juice and egg white will add moisture, and herbs will add flavor.

In dishes that call for ground meat, use ground turkey or chicken alone or combined with lean ground beef.

Salad dressings Salad dressings are extremely high in fat, containing 6 to 8 grams per tablespoon. In fact, according to the USDA, salad dressing is the leading source of fat in the diets of American women between the ages of 19 and 50.

On a heart-healthy diet, it's best to skip the salad dressing and use lemon juice, salsa or mild plain vinegar instead. Another option is a sprinkling of Parmesan cheese; a tablespoon is enough to provide intense flavor but contains only 2 grams of fat. Try using specialty vinegars, such as raspberry vinegar, balsamic vinegar, or garlic- or tarragon-flavored vinegar. If you prefer a traditional salad dressing, use a small measured amount. Or make your own lowfat vinaigrette by mixing one part vinegar (two parts if the vinegar is a mild one, such as balsamic or rice vinegar), one part chicken stock, and two parts flavorful oil, such as olive. You can add some yogurt or mustard for extra body. Alternatively, use one of the bottled low- or nonfat dressings now on the market.

Vegetable oils Vegetable oils are widely used to prepare and flavor foods and are one of the biggest sources of fat in the American diet. Though Americans have cut their consumption of animal fats (such as lard and butter) by 36 percent since 1968, they have increased their consumption of vegetable oils by 46 percent. Today Americans consume, on average, 51 pounds of vegetable oils per person per year. Since just 1 tablespoon of vegetable oil contains 14 grams of fat, limiting its use can signifcantly reduce fat intake. For a fat breakdown of various vegetable oils, see the chart on page 16.

There are several ways to cut back on the amount of vegetable oil you eat. In cooking, use nonstick cookware, or just lightly coat the pan with a nonstick vegetable cooking spray or a small amount of vegetable oil. Alternatively, sauté foods in broth or wine instead of oil. And when preparing rice or other grains, eliminate any oil called for in the recipe directions.

Vegetables If there is one food group that best meets the requirements of a heart-healthy diet, it has to be vegetables, which, with a few exceptions, are low in fat and sodium, high in fiber and complex carbohydrates and packed with vitamins and minerals, especially beta carotene, vitamin C and potassium. And with the wide assortment of tastes and textures vegetables provide, it's easy to get the five or more daily servings recommended for good health.

Indeed, studies have shown that a diet high in vegetables and other plant foods can help fight heart disease. In one recent study conducted by researchers in India, 406 men who had had heart attacks were divided into two groups. Both groups were advised to cut back on fat, saturated fat and dietary cholesterol. But one of the groups was also instructed to increase their consumption of vegetables, fruits, grains, nuts, legumes and fish; individuals in that group kept their fruit and vegetable intake at or above 14 ounces a day. After one year, the vegetable/fruit group had 39 percent fewer cardiac events and 45 percent fewer deaths than the group that had simply been advised to eat a lowfat diet. The researchers speculated that a diet high in soluble fiber, antioxidants and protective minerals like potassium is cardio-protective.

Not all vegetables are equally nutritious, however. Some of the most popular "diet" vegetables—iceberg lettuce, celery and cucumbers—are low in fat, but contain very few nutrients. While other vegetables—broccoli, kale, potatoes, carrots and peppers, for example—are nutritional powerhouses, supplying hefty amounts of vitamin C, beta carotene and potassium among other vitamins and minerals. To gain the most nutrients from vegetables, buy them fresh and eat them soon after purchase. Serve them raw when possible—as part of a crudité platter, perhaps.

If the fresh vegetables in your local grocery store appear to be past their prime, buy frozen vegetables (without added salt or sauces). Most frozen vegetables retain much of their nutrient content because they are flash-frozen soon after picking. But the taste and texture of frozen vegetables is not equal to fresh, and they may suffer nutrient loss if improperly stored or cooked. Canned vegetables, which undergo a heating process that destroys much of the vitamin C and B vitamins, should be used only in a pinch. The nutrients that survive the canning process may leach into the canning liquid and will be lost if the liquid isn't used in the recipe. Moreover, canned vegetables often contain copious amounts of sodium, although there are reduced- and no-salt brands available.

Don't spoil the freshness and lowfat content of vegetables by topping them with heavy sauces, such as cheese or hollandaise, or by using sour cream or butter. Instead, try flavoring your vegetables with herbs and spices, a tablespoon or two of chopped toasted nuts or a little Parmesan cheese.

Yogurt and cottage cheese Whether eaten alone or mixed with fruits, vegetables or cereals, these dairy products make a satisfying breakfast, lunch or snack. Fortunately, there are many low- and nonfat forms of these products available. Lowfat yogurt typically contains 2 to 5 grams of fat per cup, while whole-milk yogurt contains 6 to 8 grams. Creamed cottage cheese has 10 grams of fat per cup, 2-percent cottage cheese, 4 grams, and 1-percent cottage cheese, 2 grams. Dry-curd cottage cheese is virtually fat-free.

Plain low- or nonfat yogurt and cottage cheese are the most versatile types. You can eat them as is, straight from the carton, or you can dress them up with honey, flavoring extracts, jam, applesauce, fresh or dried fruits or fresh vegetables. You can add some crunch—plus fiber and vitamin E—to yogurt or cottage cheese by topping it with wheat germ or bran cereal.

Low- or nonfat yogurt is also an excellent source of calcium, supplying between 314 and 452 milligrams per 8-ounce serving. Cottage cheese, on the other hand, is one dairy product that is not a superior choice for calcium: An 8-ounce serving contains just 64 to 138 milligrams of calcium.

Yogurt and cottage cheese also make excellent substitutions for high-fat condiments and recipe ingredients. Use either instead of mayonnaise or sour cream in most recipes. Or blend either with herbs or chopped vegetables and use as a sandwich spread, a binder for tuna or chicken salad, a dip for sliced vegetables or a topping for baked potatoes.

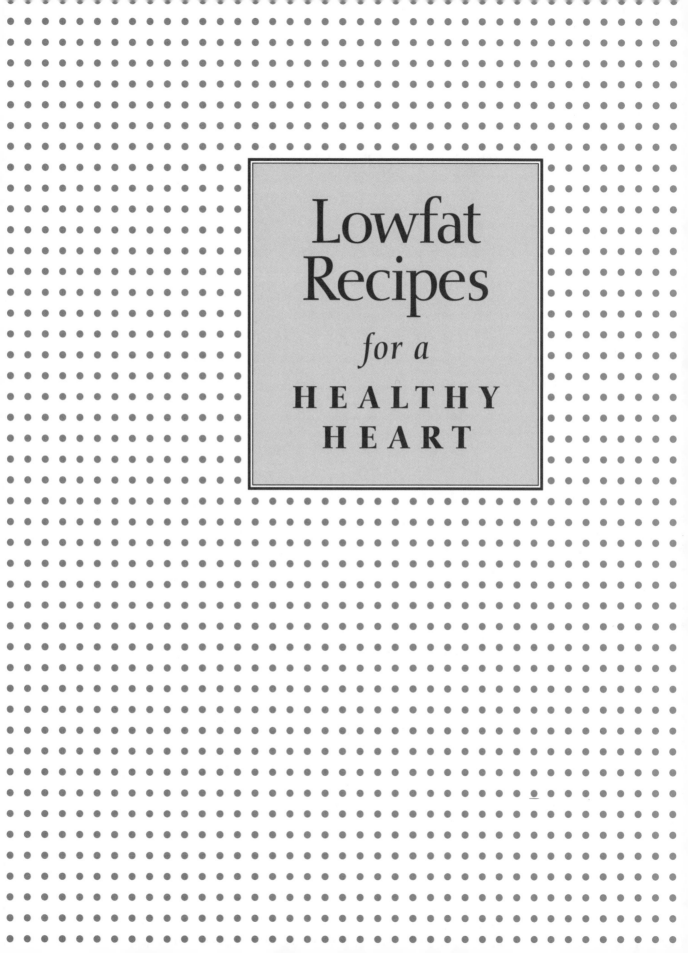

Lowfat Recipes

for a

HEALTHY HEART

RECOMMENDED DAILY INTAKES

To put the nutritional analyses that accompany the recipes on the following pages into perspective, the list below gives the recommended daily intakes for the nutrients featured in the analyses. These values are based on the Recommended Dietary Allowances (RDA) and guidelines established by various health organizations and experts. The recommendations are for adults and, unless otherwise noted, apply to both men and women.

Total Fat: Consult page 28 to determine your daily fat target

Saturated Fat: Approximately ⅓ of your daily fat target

Cholesterol: No more than 300 milligrams

Sodium: No more than 2400 milligrams

Dietary Fiber: 25 to 30 grams

Calcium: 1200 milligrams

Iron: 10 milligrams for men; 15 milligrams for women

Potassium: 3000 to 3500 milligrams

Beta carotene: 5 to 6 milligrams

Vitamin C: At least 60 milligrams*

Vitamin E: 10 milligrams for men; 8 milligrams for women**

* See page 23 for more information on vitamin C.
** See page 23 for more information on vitamin E.

EGGPLANT CAVIAR

Real caviar is a double indulgence: Perhaps the costliest of all foods, it's also one of the highest in cholesterol. Try this vegetable version instead.

2¼ pounds eggplant
1 red bell pepper
1 medium-size onion
1 garlic clove
1 tablespoon toasted sesame seeds
1 tablespoon chopped fresh parsley
1 teaspoon olive oil
1 teaspoon lemon juice
¼ teaspoon salt
Black pepper
4 slices whole-wheat bread

1. Preheat the oven to 375°.

2. Prick the eggplant and bell pepper with a fork, place them on a baking sheet with the onion and bake 45 minutes, or until the eggplant is completely soft and the onion is fork-tender; set aside to cool.

3. Halve the eggplant and scoop the flesh into a food processor or blender. Halve, stem and seed the pepper, and peel the onion and garlic. Add them to the eggplant. Process the mixture, pulsing the machine on and off, just until very coarsely chopped.

4. Transfer the mixture to a bowl and stir in the sesame seeds, parsley, oil, lemon juice, salt, and pepper to taste. Cover and refrigerate at least 1 hour.

5. To serve, toast the bread, cut it into quarters and spread the caviar on it. *Makes 4 servings*

NUTRITION INFORMATION
values are per serving
• • •

CALORIES	159	CALCIUM	125 MG
TOTAL FAT	3 G	IRON	3 MG
SATURATED FAT	0.3 G	POTASSIUM	589 MG
CHOLESTEROL	0 MG	BETA CAROTENE	TRACE
SODIUM	318 MG	VITAMIN C	44 MG
DIETARY FIBER	7 G	VITAMIN E	TRACE

♦♀

CHINESE BAKED EGGPLANT

A little chicken stock (instead of a lot of oil) keeps the eggplant halves moist during cooking. The small amount of fragrant dark sesame oil in this recipe is used mainly for flavor.

1½ pounds eggplant (preferably 2 or more Japanese or
    other small eggplants)
1 tablespoon Oriental sesame oil
1 tablespoon minced fresh ginger
2 garlic cloves, chopped
Pinch of salt
Black pepper
½ cup low-sodium chicken stock
2 dried Mission figs, chopped (2 ounces)
½ cup chopped scallions

1. Preheat the oven to 375°.

2. Line a baking sheet with foil. Trim the eggplant and halve lengthwise. Cut each half lengthwise into ½-inch-thick slices, lay them on the baking sheet and sprinkle them with the oil, ginger, garlic, salt and pepper to taste.

3. Drizzle the chicken stock over the eggplant, scatter the figs on top and bake 30 minutes, or until the figs are golden brown.

4. Top the eggplant with scallions and serve.

Makes 4 servings

NUTRITION INFORMATION
values are per serving
• • •

CALORIES	242	CALCIUM	187 MG
TOTAL FAT	8 G	IRON	3 MG
SATURATED FAT	1 G	POTASSIUM	1037 MG
CHOLESTEROL	1 MG	BETA CAROTENE	0.5 MG
SODIUM	237 MG	VITAMIN C	21 MG
DIETARY FIBER	8 G	VITAMIN E	2 MG

SCANDINAVIAN-STYLE CANAPES

There is one type of fat that's good for you: The oils in fatty fish—such as the sablefish used in this recipe—contain omega-3 fatty acids, which can help prevent heart disease.

¼ cup plain lowfat yogurt
2 teaspoons Dijon mustard
1 tablespoon chopped fresh dill, plus 16 dill sprigs
16 slices cocktail pumpernickel bread
Sixteen ¼-inch-thick cucumber slices
1 red bell pepper, cut into sixteen 1-inch squares
2 ounces smoked sablefish, cut into 16 pieces

1. In a small bowl stir together the yogurt, mustard and chopped dill.

2. Spread the bread with the yogurt mixture. Place a cucumber slice and a bell pepper square on each piece of bread and top with a piece of fish and a dill sprig.

3. Arrange the canapés on a platter and serve. If not serving immediately, cover the platter tightly with plastic wrap and refrigerate.

Makes 4 servings

NUTRITION INFORMATION
values are per serving

• • •

CALORIES	134	CALCIUM	54 MG
TOTAL FAT	4 G	IRON	1 MG
SATURATED FAT	0.8 G	POTASSIUM	320 MG
CHOLESTEROL	10 MG	BETA CAROTENE	0 MG
SODIUM	338 MG	VITAMIN C	37 MG
DIETARY FIBER	2 G	VITAMIN E	TRACE

Scandinavian-Style Canapés

BUCKWHEAT-MUSHROOM PATE

Pâté de fois gras, made from goose liver and fat, is a gourmet's delight and a "no-no" on a heart-healthy diet. Instead, try his delicious pâté made with kasha (buckwheat groats) and vegetables. It is cholesterol-free and also a good source of beta carotene.

1 cup kasha (medium grain)
1 tablespoon plus 1 teaspoon peanut oil
2 medium-size whole carrots plus 1 cup shredded carrots
2 cups thinly sliced mushrooms
1 cup finely chopped onion
4 cups packed whole spinach leaves, washed but not dried
¼ cup wheat germ
¼ cup Dijon mustard
4 large egg whites
1 teaspoon salt
½ teaspoon dried rosemary, crushed
½ teaspoon dried thyme, crumbled
¼ teaspoon black pepper

1. Bring 2 cups of water to a boil in a small saucepan. Stir in the kasha, reduce the heat to low, cover and simmer 8 to 10 minutes, or until the kasha is fluffy and the water is absorbed; set aside, covered.

2. Brush a 9 x 4-inch glass loaf pan with 1 teaspoon of oil; set aside.

3. Fill a large saucepan half full of water. Add the whole carrots, bring to a simmer and cook the carrots 20 minutes, or until tender when pierced with a fork; drain and cool under cold water.

4. Heat the remaining oil in a large nonstick skillet over medium heat. Stir in the mushrooms, onion and shredded carrots, cover and cook about 5 minutes, or until the mushrooms release their liquid. Uncover the skillet, reduce the heat to low and cook, stirring, about 10 minutes, or until the vegetables are soft and all the liquid has evaporated; transfer to a large bowl and set aside.

5. Wipe out the skillet with paper towels. Place the spinach in the skillet, cover and steam over low heat about 3 minutes, or just until wilted; set aside.

6. Preheat the oven to 350°.

7. Using a fork, break up the kasha and stir it into the vegetable mixture. Add the wheat germ, 1 tablespoon of the mustard, the egg whites, salt, rosemary, thyme and pepper and stir until well blended.

8. Line the loaf pan with spinach leaves, overlapping them and leaving a 2-inch overhang around the top. Pack half of the kasha mixture into the pan, then lay the whole carrots lengthwise on top, 1 inch apart. Pack in the remaining kasha mixture and fold the overlapping spinach leaves over the top. Cover the pâté with foil, prick the foil in several places with a fork and place the loaf pan in a large roasting pan. Add ½ inch of hot water to the roasting pan and bake the pâté 1½ hours.

9. When the pâté is done, cool it on a rack 30 minutes, then refrigerate it overnight. Turn the pâté out onto a platter and use a sharp knife to cut it into sixteen ½-inch-thick slices. Serve the remaining mustard with the pâté. *Makes 16 servings*

NUTRITION INFORMATION
values are per serving

• • •

CALORIES	78	CALCIUM	26 MG
TOTAL FAT	2 G	IRON	1 MG
SATURATED FAT	0.3 G	POTASSIUM	263 MG
CHOLESTEROL	0 MG	BETA CAROTENE	3 MG
SODIUM	255 MG	VITAMIN C	6 MG
DIETARY FIBER	2 G	VITAMIN E	TRACE

STUFFED EGGS

A generous spoonful of spicy potato filling takes the place of the yolks in this version of deviled eggs.

1 pound new potatoes
8 large eggs
1 small apple, peeled and cored
1 large celery stalk
3 tablespoons chutney
2 tablespoons lowfat sour cream
2 tablespoons dry bread crumbs
1 tablespoon chopped fresh chives
1½ teaspoons curry powder
¼ teaspoon salt
Hot pepper sauce
¼ teaspoon paprika

1. Place the potatoes and eggs in a medium-size saucepan and add cold water to cover. Bring to a boil over medium heat and cook 12 minutes. With a slotted spoon, remove the eggs and cool them under cold running water.

2. Cook the potatoes another 15 minutes, drain and let cool 15 minutes. Meanwhile, shell the eggs, cut them in half lengthwise and remove and discard the yolks; set aside the whites.

3. Peel and quarter the potatoes, place them in a medium-size bowl and mash them until smooth.

4. Finely chop the apple and celery in a food processor or by hand, then add them to the mashed potatoes. Add the chutney, sour cream, bread crumbs, 2 teaspoons of chives, the curry powder, salt and hot pepper sauce to taste, and stir until well blended. Spoon the mixture onto the egg whites and place them on a plate; cover with plastic wrap and refrigerate at least 2 hours.

5. Just before serving, garnish the eggs with the remaining chives and sprinkle them with paprika.

Makes 8 servings

NUTRITION INFORMATION
values are per serving

• • •

CALORIES	102	CALCIUM	14 MG
TOTAL FAT	1 G	IRON	TRACE
SATURATED FAT	0.3 G	POTASSIUM	296 MG
CHOLESTEROL	1 MG	BETA CAROTENE	0 MG
SODIUM	170 MG	VITAMIN C	8 MG
DIETARY FIBER	1 G	VITAMIN E	TRACE

YOGURT CHEESE WITH PEPPER AND HERBS

Yogurt cheese—made by draining the liquid from yogurt—is a healthful substitute for high-fat dairy products such as cream cheese, sour cream and heavy cream. A cheesecloth-lined strainer works well for the process; you can also use a coffee filter or one of the special yogurt cheese funnels sold at kitchen specialty shops.

2 cups plain lowfat yogurt
¾ teaspoon coarsely ground black pepper
¼ teaspoon salt
3 tablespoons chopped fresh chives
48 Buckwheat Crackers (see page 56)

1. Place a cheesecloth-lined strainer over a bowl. Spoon the yogurt into the strainer, cover with plastic wrap and refrigerate 24 hours, or until the yogurt is the consistency of thick sour cream. (Discard the whey, or reserve it to use in soups or in baking recipes requiring buttermilk or sour milk.)

2. Transfer the yogurt cheese to a small bowl and stir in ¼ teaspoon of pepper, the salt and 1½ tablespoons of the chives.

3. Mound the cheese on a platter and, using a spatula, shape it into a 5-inch disk. Sprinkle the cheese with the remaining chives and pepper.

4. Serve the yogurt cheese with the crackers.

Makes 4 servings

NUTRITION INFORMATION
values are per serving

• • •

CALORIES	232	CALCIUM	255 MG
TOTAL FAT	7 G	IRON	2 MG
SATURATED FAT	2 G	POTASSIUM	424 MG
CHOLESTEROL	8 MG	BETA CAROTENE	0 MG
SODIUM	363 MG	VITAMIN C	3 MG
DIETARY FIBER	3 G	VITAMIN E	4 MG

WHITE BEAN-CHEVRE SPREAD

Sour cream or cheese dips can turn low-calorie crudités into high-fat snacks. Instead, try this bean purée flavored with herbs and just a little cheese.

1 cup cooked, drained white beans (½ cup dried)
2 ounces chèvre (mild goat cheese)
½ cup chopped fresh parsley
2 tablespoons chopped fresh basil
2 tablespoons chopped fresh chives
1 tablespoon lemon juice
⅛ teaspoon salt
⅛ teaspoon black pepper
12 asparagus stalks, trimmed and blanched
2 cups Brussels sprouts, blanched
4 small new potatoes, boiled and cut into large chunks
5 carrots, cut into sticks
2 green and 2 red bell peppers, cut into
*   1-inch-wide strips*

1. Place the beans, chèvre, herbs and lemon juice in a food processor or blender and process until puréed.

2. Transfer the spread to a small serving bowl and stir in the salt and pepper.

3. Arrange the vegetables in bowls and on platters and serve with the spread. *Makes 6 servings*

NUTRITION INFORMATION
values are per serving

• • •

CALORIES	160	CALCIUM	98 MG
TOTAL FAT	3 G	IRON	3 MG
SATURATED FAT	2 G	POTASSIUM	822 MG
CHOLESTEROL	4 MG	BETA CAROTENE	11 MG
SODIUM	117 MG	VITAMIN C	123 MG
DIETARY FIBER	7 G	VITAMIN E	1 MG

SALMON MOUSSE

The small, edible bones found in canned salmon are a good source of calcium. Bone-in canned sardines offer a similar nutritional dividend.

One 1-pound can red salmon, with its liquid
1 envelope unflavored gelatin
Vegetable cooking spray
2 large scallions
1 cup frozen lima beans, thawed
2 teaspoons tomato paste
2 teaspoons prepared horseradish
1 teaspoon green peppercorns
½ cup lowfat sour cream
½ cup plain lowfat yogurt
¼ cup lemon juice
1 cup shredded Romaine lettuce
1 cup shredded spinach leaves
½ pound asparagus, blanched

1. Place ¼ cup of the salmon liquid in a small bowl, sprinkle in the gelatin and set aside 5 minutes. Meanwhile, drain the salmon and remove and discard any skin and large pieces of bone. Bring ½ cup of water to a boil, add it to the gelatin mixture and stir until the gelatin dissolves completely; set aside.

2. Spray a 1-quart mold with cooking spray; set aside. In a food processor or blender, process the scallions until minced. Add the salmon (including any small bones), the beans, tomato paste, horseradish and peppercorns, and process about 1 minute, or until smooth. Add the gelatin mixture, sour cream, yogurt and lemon juice and process just until combined, scraping down the container with a rubber spatula as necessary. Pour the mixture into the prepared mold and refrigerate about 4 hours, or until the mousse is set.

3. To unmold the mousse, invert the mold on a platter and briefly cover it with a kitchen towel wrung out in hot water. Surround the mousse with the Romaine, spinach and asparagus and serve.

Makes 6 servings

NUTRITION INFORMATION
values are per serving

• • •

CALORIES	218	CALCIUM	230 MG
TOTAL FAT	9 G	IRON	2 MG
SATURATED FAT	3 G	POTASSIUM	688 MG
CHOLESTEROL	50 MG	BETA CAROTENE	1 MG
SODIUM	625 MG	VITAMIN C	28 MG
DIETARY FIBER	3 G	VITAMIN E	5 MG

CREAMY SALSA WITH DIPPERS

Lowfat yogurt is a healthy base for dips and dressings, and contains roughly one-tenth the fat (and one-twelfth the saturated fat) of sour cream. Yogurt is also an excellent source of protein and calcium. Though many people think that all dairy products supply good amounts of calcium, some, such as cottage cheese and cream cheese, are actually poor sources of this vital mineral.

1 pound plum tomatoes
1 medium-size onion
1 jalapeño pepper
¼ cup plain lowfat yogurt
¼ cup chopped fresh cilantro
½ teaspoon salt
¼ teaspoon ground black pepper
1½ pounds new potatoes
2 cups cauliflower florets

1⅓ cups broccoli florets
¼ pound green beans
1 red bell pepper
4 large flour tortillas

1. For the salsa, core and dice the tomatoes. Peel and coarsely chop the onion. Seed and chop the jalapeño.

2. In a food processor or blender, working in batches if necessary, combine the tomatoes, onion, jalapeño, yogurt, cilantro, salt and pepper. Process the mixture, pulsing the machine on and off, until the vegetables are coarsely chopped. Transfer the salsa to a bowl and set aside.

3. Preheat the oven to 500°. Bring two medium-size saucepans of water to a boil.

4. Cook the potatoes in one pan of boiling water 20 minutes, or until tender.

5. Meanwhile, blanch the cauliflower in the other pan 3 minutes, or until crisp-tender. Reserving the boiling water, transfer the cauliflower to a colander, cool it under cold running water and set aside to drain. Blanch, cool and drain the broccoli and beans in the same fashion until crisp-tender.

6. Stem and core the bell pepper and cut it into 1-inch-wide strips; set aside.

7. Dip each tortilla in a bowl of water, then cut into 8 triangles. Place the triangles on a baking sheet and bake 3 to 4 minutes, or until crisp. If the tortillas begin to curl, lay another baking sheet on top of them. Reduce the oven temperature to 300° and bake the triangles another 2 to 3 minutes, or until just beginning to brown. Remove from the oven and set aside.

8. Drain the potatoes and cut them into ½-inch-thick slices.

9. To serve, place the bowl of salsa in the center of a platter and surround it with the vegetables and tortilla chips. *Makes 4 servings*

NUTRITION INFORMATION
values are per serving

• • •

CALORIES	311	CALCIUM	148 MG
TOTAL FAT	3 G	IRON	5 MG
SATURATED FAT	0.3 G	POTASSIUM	1349 MG
CHOLESTEROL	TRACE	BETA CAROTENE	1 MG
SODIUM	369 MG	VITAMIN C	148 MG
DIETARY FIBER	8 G	VITAMIN E	1 MG

SPICY SALSA

This homemade salsa is tastier than storebought—and it's an excellent source of vitamin C.

¾ pound ripe plum or cherry tomatoes, coarsely chopped
1 tablespoon finely chopped canned jalapeño peppers
½ cup chopped Spanish onion
2 tablespoons fresh lime juice
4 tablespoons fresh coriander

Combine all the ingredients in a bowl. Let the salsa stand at room temperature 30 to 45 minutes to allow the flavors to blend. *Makes 2 cups*

NUTRITION INFORMATION
values are per ½-cup serving

• • •

CALORIES	27	CALCIUM	17 MG
TOTAL FAT	0.3 G	IRON	1 MG
SATURATED FAT	0 G	POTASSIUM	239 MG
CHOLESTEROL	0 MG	BETA CAROTENE	0.7 MG
SODIUM	40 MG	VITAMIN C	23 MG
DIETARY FIBER	1 G	VITAMIN E	TRACE

NACHOS

Corn tortillas, made with whole-grain cornmeal and no shortening, are a better choice than flour tortillas, which are made with white flour and fat.

Eight 6-inch corn tortillas
1¼ cups cooked kidney beans, drained, liquid reserved
¼ teaspoon chili powder
2 cups Salsa (above), drained
1 cup shredded Monterey Jack cheese

1. Preheat the oven to 500°.

2. Immerse the tortillas one at a time in water; drain and lay them on baking sheets. Bake the tortillas 6 or 7 minutes, or just until crisp, turning them after 4 to 5 minutes. If the tortillas begin to curl, lay another baking sheet on top of them. Remove the tortillas from the baking sheet, using a metal spatula to loosen them if necessary, and set aside to cool. Reduce the oven temperature to 350°.

Rice Cakes with Vegetable-Cheese Spread

3. Combine the beans and chili powder in a small skillet and heat over medium heat, mashing the beans with a fork, until the mixture is hot. Stir in the reserved bean liquid a little at a time until the mixture is smooth and spreadable.

4. Cut each tortilla into 6 wedges, then reassemble the wedges into rounds on the baking sheet.

5. Spread the bean mixture equally over the tortillas and top each with ¼ cup of Salsa and 2 tablespoons of cheese. Layer on the remaining Salsa and cheese. Bake 4 to 5 minutes, or until the cheese is melted. Serve hot. *Makes 8 servings*

NUTRITION INFORMATION
values are per serving

• • •

CALORIES	170	CALCIUM	168 MG
TOTAL FAT	6 G	IRON	2 MG
SATURATED FAT	3 G	POTASSIUM	290 MG
CHOLESTEROL	13 MG	BETA CAROTENE	TRACE
SODIUM	280 MG	VITAMIN C	13 MG
DIETARY FIBER	4 G	VITAMIN E	TRACE

RICE CAKES WITH VEGETABLE-CHEESE SPREAD

The carrots and peppers in this colorful spread supply the recommended daily intake for beta carotene.

½ cup part-skim ricotta cheese
2 cups grated carrots
¾ cup finely chopped red bell pepper
¼ cup finely chopped celery
3 tablespoons chopped scallion
2 tablespoons chopped fresh parsley
½ teaspoon chopped fresh thyme, or ¼ teaspoon
  dried thyme
1 tablespoon lemon juice
¼ teaspoon grated lemon zest
6 rice cakes

1. Place the ricotta in a food processor or blender and purée until smooth. Add the vegetables, herbs, lemon juice and lemon zest, and stir until combined.

2. Spread ½ cup of the mixture on each rice cake and serve.   *Makes 6 servings*

NUTRITION INFORMATION
values are per serving

• • •

CALORIES	86	CALCIUM	75 MG
TOTAL FAT	2 G	IRON	TRACE
SATURATED FAT	1 G	POTASSIUM	233 MG
CHOLESTEROL	6 MG	BETA CAROTENE	6 MG
SODIUM	55 MG	VITAMIN C	32 MG
DIETARY FIBER	2 G	VITAMIN E	TRACE

BLUE CHEESE SPREAD WITH TORTILLA TRIANGLES

Though it boasts a rich blue-cheese flavor, this creamy spread is made mainly from potatoes, with just an ounce of the tangy cheese added.

1 pound new potatoes
Four 8-inch corn tortillas
½ cup skim milk
1 ounce blue cheese, crumbled
1 tablespoon chopped fresh chives
¼ teaspoon coarsely ground black pepper

1. Scrub the potatoes, place them in a medium-size saucepan with cold water to cover and bring to a boil over medium heat. Cover the pan, reduce the heat to low and simmer 20 minutes, or until the potatoes are tender when pierced with a knife. Drain the potatoes and set aside to cool. Meanwhile, preheat the oven to 500°.

2. Dip each tortilla in a bowl of water, then cut it into 8 triangles. Place the triangles on a baking sheet and bake 3 to 4 minutes, or until crisp. If the tortillas begin to curl, lay another baking sheet on top of them. Reduce the oven temperature to 300°, Return the tortilla triangles to the oven and bake another 2 to 3 minutes, or until golden brown; set aside.

3. When the potatoes are cool enough to handle, peel and quarter them. Place them in a medium-size

bowl and mash them, then gradually stir in the milk, cheese, chives and pepper. The mixture should be well blended but not completely smooth.

4. Transfer the spread to a serving bowl and serve with the warm tortilla triangles.   *Makes 4 servings*

NUTRITION INFORMATION
values are per serving

• • •

CALORIES	195	CALCIUM	128 MG
TOTAL FAT	3 G	IRON	2 MG
SATURATED FAT	1 G	POTASSIUM	531 MG
CHOLESTEROL	6 MG	BETA CAROTENE	0 MG
SODIUM	174 MG	VITAMIN C	14 MG
DIETARY FIBER	3 G	VITAMIN E	TRACE

BUCKWHEAT CRACKERS

Making crackers is almost as easy as baking cookies, and your efforts are rewarded with a delicious whole-grain snack that's low in fat and sodium.

1 cup buckwheat flour, approximately
1 cup unbleached all-purpose flour
1 tablespoon sugar
¼ teaspoon baking soda
¼ teaspoon salt
3 tablespoons margarine
⅔ cup plain lowfat yogurt

1. Preheat the oven to 325°.

2. Combine 1 cup of buckwheat flour, the all-purpose flour, sugar, baking soda and salt in a food processor. Add the margarine while pulsing the machine on and off for 15 seconds, or until the mixture resembles coarse cornmeal. Add the yogurt and process another 5 to 10 seconds, or until the mixture begins to form a ball of dough. (To mix the dough by hand, combine the dry ingredients in a large bowl and cut in the margarine, using a pastry blender or 2 knives. Add the yogurt and stir with a wooden spoon until the dough forms a ball and leaves the sides of the bowl.) Divide the dough into 2 equal pieces.

3. Dust a work surface and a rolling pin with buckwheat flour and roll out 1 piece of dough to a 10 x 10-inch rectangle. Prick the dough all over with a fork. Using a ruler and a sharp knife, cut the dough into 25 two-inch squares, then cut them diagonally into triangles. Or, use a small cookie cutter to cut 50 crackers.

4. Transfer the crackers to a baking sheet and bake 20 minutes, or until crisp and slightly browned. Transfer the crackers to racks to cool and repeat with the remaining dough. *Makes 100 crackers*

NUTRITION INFORMATION
values are per cracker

• • •

CALORIES 13 CALCIUM MG
TOTAL FAT 0.4 G IRON TRACE
SATURATED FAT 0 POTASSIUM 12 MG
CHOLESTEROL TRACE BETA CAROTENE 0 MG
SODIUM 13 MG VITAMIN C TRACE
DIETARY FIBER TRACE VITAMIN E TRACE

BROWN RICE CRACKERS

Commercial crackers—even the ones you buy at health-food stores—are often made with saturated fats. In contrast, these nutty-tasting whole-wheat crackers contain no saturated fat at all.

2 tablespoons skim milk
1 tablespoon walnut oil
1 cup whole-wheat flour, approximately
1 cup cooked brown rice
1 teaspoon salt
½ teaspoon coarsely ground black pepper

1. In a small bowl stir together the milk, oil and 2 tablespoons of water; set aside.

2. Place 1 cup of flour, the rice, salt and pepper in a food processor and process 2 to 3 seconds, or just until mixed. With the machine running, add the milk mixture and process just until the dough forms a cohesive mass. If necessary, add up to 1 tablespoon of water. The dough will be sticky but should hold its shape when a small piece is pinched off. Form the dough into a ball, wrap it loosely in plastic wrap and set aside 15 minutes.

3. Lightly flour a work surface and a rolling pin. Pat the dough into a disk, then roll it to a ½-inch thickness. Let it rest 10 to 15 minutes, then roll it out

again. Repeat the process twice, rolling the dough somewhat thinner each time and dusting with flour if necessary. Let the dough rest between rollings.

4. Preheat the oven to 350°.

5. Roll the dough out to a 10 x 9-inch rectangle about ⅛ inch thick. Using a ruler and a sharp knife, cut the dough into thirty 1 x 3-inch rectangles. Place the crackers ½ inch apart on a baking sheet and bake 20 minutes, or until crisp and golden.

6. Transfer the crackers to racks to cool and repeat with the remaining dough. *Makes 60 crackers*

NUTRITION INFORMATION
values are per cracker

• • •

CALORIES 13 CALCIUM 2 MG
TOTAL FAT 0.3 G IRON TRACE
SATURATED FAT 0 G POTASSIUM 12 MG
CHOLESTEROL TRACE BETA CAROTENE 0 MG
SODIUM 36 MG VITAMIN C TRACE
DIETARY FIBER TRACE VITAMIN E TRACE

RYE-CHEESE CRACKERS

Among the fattiest of all storebought crackers are the cheese-flavored and -filled varieties. These rye-cheese crisps are sprinkled with just a small amount of Parmesan for robust flavor but little added fat.

1 cup unbleached all-purpose flour, approximately
½ cup light rye flour
½ teaspoon salt
1 tablespoon unsalted butter or margarine, well chilled
1½ teaspoons caraway seeds
2 tablespoons grated Parmesan cheese

1. In a medium-size bowl stir together 1 cup of the all-purpose flour, the rye flour and salt.

2. Cut the butter into pieces, then with your fingers work it into the dry ingredients until the mixture resembles coarse cornmeal. Add the caraway seeds and ½ cup of cold water and stir until the dough begins to gather into a mass, then form it into a ball with your hands. Flatten the dough into a disk, wrap it in plastic wrap and let it rest at room temperature 30 minutes.

3. Preheat the oven to 300°.

4. Lightly flour a work surface and a rolling pin. Cut the dough in half and roll out half to a 1/16-inch-thick rectangle. Using 2-inch cookie cutters, cut out about 30 crackers, cutting them as close together as possible. (Do not reroll any excess dough; it will be tough when baked.)

5. Transfer the crackers to a baking sheet and repeat with the remaining dough.

6. Sprinkle the crackers with Parmesan and bake 12 minutes, or until crisp and lightly browned. Transfer the crackers to racks to cool, then store in an airtight container up to one week. *Makes 30 crackers*

NUTRITION INFORMATION
values are per cracker

• • •

CALORIES	29	CALCIUM	7 MG
TOTAL FAT	0.6 G	IRON	TRACE
SATURATED FAT	0.3 G	POTASSIUM	11 MG
CHOLESTEROL	1 MG	BETA CAROTENE	0 MG
SODIUM	42 MG	VITAMIN C	0 MG
DIETARY FIBER	TRACE	VITAMIN E	TRACE

Guacamole with Chips and Crudités

GUACAMOLE WITH CHIPS AND CRUDITES

The avocado is a rarity among fruits: It is exceptionally high in fat and should be eaten in moderation. But the fat in avocados is monounsaturated, the type that may lower blood cholesterol. This light guacamole gives you the flavor (and health benefits) of the avocado, but cuts the richness by blending the velvety green fruit with lowfat cottage cheese.

1 medium-size ripe avocado
1 cup lowfat cottage cheese (1%)
1 tablespoon lime juice
1 teaspoon chopped chives
1/4 to 1/2 teaspoon red pepper flakes
7-ounce package corn tortillas
2 teaspoons corn oil
Small head leaf lettuce
Assorted raw vegetables for dipping

1. Halve and peel the avocado and cut into chunks. Place in a blender with the cottage cheese, lime juice, chives and red pepper flakes; blend to the desired consistency. Refrigerate the guacamole 2 hours.

2. Just before serving, preheat the oven to 400°.

3. Brush the tortillas lightly with oil. Cut each tortilla into 8 triangles and place on a baking sheet. Bake the tortilla triangles 5 to 6 minutes, or until browned and crisp. If the tortillas begin to curl, lay another baking sheet on top of them.

4. Line a serving bowl with lettuce leaves and mound the guacamole on top. Serve with the tortilla chips and raw vegetables. *Makes 8 servings*

NUTRITION INFORMATION
values are per serving

• • •

CALORIES	169	CALCIUM	88 MG
TOTAL FAT	7 G	IRON	2 MG
SATURATED FAT	1 G	POTASSIUM	627 MG
CHOLESTEROL	1 MG	BETA CAROTENE	8 MG
SODIUM	184 MG	VITAMIN C	66 MG
DIETARY FIBER	4 G	VITAMIN E	2 MG

TOFU HUMMUS WITH PITA CRISPS

Hummus, a Near-Eastern dip, is usually made with chickpeas. Here, calcium-rich tofu (bean curd) is added, enhancing this already nutritious dip.

3 squares firm tofu (¾ pound), quartered
1 cup cooked, drained chickpeas
3 tablespoons lemon juice
1 tablespoon tahini (sesame paste)
1 garlic clove, peeled and crushed
2 tablespoons chopped fresh dill
Six 1-ounce pita breads
1 medium-size sweet potato, boiled, cooled and peeled
¼ teaspoon salt
Black pepper
1½ teaspoons sesame seeds
1½ cups broccoli florets, blanched and cooled

1. Place the tofu in a food processor or blender with the chickpeas, lemon juice, tahini and garlic, and process until smooth. Transfer the mixture to a serving bowl, stir in the dill, cover and refrigerate.

2. Preheat the oven to 350°.

3. Split the pita breads and cut each piece into quarters. Spread the pieces on a baking sheet and toast them 10 minutes, or until lightly browned around the edges.

4. Meanwhile, cut the sweet potato into finger-length sticks.

5. To serve, season the hummus with salt, and pepper to taste. Divide it among 6 plates and sprinkle each portion with sesame seeds. Arrange the broccoli florets, sweet potato sticks and pita triangles around the hummus and serve.   *Makes 6 servings*

NUTRITION INFORMATION
values are per serving

• • •

CALORIES	257	CALCIUM	200 MG
TOTAL FAT	8 G	IRON	8 MG
SATURATED FAT	1 G	POTASSIUM	428 MG
CHOLESTEROL	0 MG	BETA CAROTENE	2 MG
SODIUM	275 MG	VITAMIN C	36 MG
DIETARY FIBER	4 G	VITAMIN E	1 MG

BABAGANOUSH

Eggplant, like most vegetables, starts out virtually free of fat, but its spongy flesh will absorb seemingly infinite quantities of oil if you sauté or fry it. Therefore, broiling, grilling and baking are the best cooking methods for this vegetable. In this recipe, eggplant is broiled until its skin chars, giving the flesh a rich, smoky flavor. It's easy to scoop the softened flesh out of the skin after cooking.

1¾ pounds eggplant
1 garlic clove
1 tablespoon plus 1 teaspoon olive oil
3 tablespoons unbleached all-purpose flour
¾ cup skim milk
¼ cup lowfat cottage cheese (1%)
2 tablespoons chopped fresh parsley
1 tablespoon lemon juice
½ teaspoon salt

1. Preheat the broiler.

2. Stem and halve the eggplant and place the halves cut side down on a foil-lined baking sheet. Broil the eggplant 6 inches from the heat 15 minutes, or until the skin is well charred. Reduce the oven temperature to 375°. (Transfer the eggplant from the broiler to the oven if using a separate broiler.) Place the unpeeled garlic on the baking sheet. Bake the eggplant and garlic 15 minutes; remove them from the oven and set aside to cool.

3. Heat the oil in a small saucepan over medium heat.

4. Meanwhile, peel and mash the garlic, add it to the pan and cook 2 minutes. Whisk in the flour and continue whisking until combined, then gradually add the milk, whisking constantly until the mixture forms a smooth, thick sauce. Remove the pan from the heat and set aside.

5. Place the cottage cheese in a food processor or blender and process it 5 to 10 seconds, or until smooth. Add the garlic sauce and process the mixture 5 seconds more. Scoop the eggplant flesh from its skin into the processor, add the parsley, lemon juice and salt, and process another 5 seconds, or just until combined.

6. Transfer the babaganoush to a bowl and serve immediately, or cover and refrigerate it until well chilled.   *Makes 6 servings*

NUTRITION INFORMATION
values are per serving

• • •

CALORIES	85	CALCIUM	88 MG
TOTAL FAT	3 G	IRON	1 MG
SATURATED FAT	0.6 G	POTASSIUM	312 MG
CHOLESTEROL	TRACE	BETA CAROTENE	TRACE
SODIUM	264 MG	VITAMIN C	5 MG
DIETARY FIBER	2 G	VITAMIN E	2 MG

RED LENTIL DIP

Served with an assortment of raw vegetables, such as carrots, celery and green beans, this dip makes a filling, high-fiber snack. If you can't get red lentils, use brown or green ones instead.

½ cup red lentils
¼ cup plain lowfat yogurt
2 tablespoons medium-hot bottled salsa
1 tablespoon chopped fresh chives
Dash of hot pepper sauce
Pinch of salt

1. Place the lentils and 1 cup of water in a small saucepan and bring to a boil over medium heat. Cover the pan, reduce the heat to low and simmer the lentils about 20 minutes, or until they are tender.
2. Transfer the lentils and any remaining liquid to a food processor or blender and process until smooth. Add the remaining ingredients and process until smooth, scraping down the sides of the container with a rubber spatula as necessary.
3. Transfer the dip to a small bowl and serve.

Makes about 1¼ cups

NUTRITION INFORMATION
values are per tablespoon

• • •

CALORIES	19	CALCIUM	8 MG
TOTAL FAT	0.1 G	IRON	TRACE
SATURATED FAT	0 G	POTASSIUM	63 MG
CHOLESTEROL	TRACE	BETA CAROTENE	0 MG
SODIUM	14 MG	VITAMIN C	TRACE
DIETARY FIBER	TRACE	VITAMIN E	TRACE

CURRIED CHICKPEA DIP WITH VEGETABLES

Thanks to the broccoli, asparagus and other vegetables that accompany the zesty dip, this appetizer is a good source of antioxidants, supplying more than 50 percent of your daily vitamin C requirement. The sweet potato (eaten raw, it is delectably crisp and juicy) is an excellent source of beta carotene.

1 garlic clove
1 tablespoon chopped scallion
¾ cup canned chickpeas, rinsed and drained
½ cup part-skim ricotta cheese
2 teaspoons curry powder
½ teaspoon brown sugar
¼ teaspoon Worcestershire sauce
2 dashes of hot pepper sauce
½ cup lowfat sour cream
½ cup coarsely chopped cooked spinach, squeezed dry
¼ pound mushrooms, trimmed
3 ounces snow peas, blanched
8 asparagus spears, blanched
1 cup broccoli florets, blanched
¼ pound yellow squash, cut into 3-inch sticks
1 raw sweet potato, thinly sliced

1. Bring a small saucepan of water to a boil. Add the garlic clove and cook for 5 minutes. Rinse the garlic under cold water and discard the peel.
2. Process the garlic and scallion in a food processor or blender until minced. Add the chickpeas, ricotta, curry powder, sugar, Worcestershire sauce and hot pepper sauce, and process about 30 seconds, or until smooth. Add the sour cream and spinach and process just until combined.
3. Transfer to a bowl and serve with the vegetables as dippers.

Makes 6 servings

NUTRITION INFORMATION
values are per serving

• • •

CALORIES	163	CALCIUM	124 MG
TOTAL FAT	7 G	IRON	3 MG
SATURATED FAT	2 G	POTASSIUM	516 MG
CHOLESTEROL	13 MG	BETA CAROTENE	4 MG
SODIUM	198 MG	VITAMIN C	43 MG
DIETARY FIBER	3 G	VITAMIN E	2 MG

BERRY-CHEESE DIP WITH PITA SCOOPS

A half cup of cream cheese contains about 125 milligrams of cholesterol and 25 grams of saturated fat; the same quantity of lowfat cottage cheese has a mere 5 milligrams of cholesterol and less than half a gram of saturated fat.

1½ cups fresh or unsweetened frozen raspberries or
*   strawberries, thawed*
1 tablespoon light brown sugar
1 banana
½ cup lowfat cottage cheese (1%)
Four 1-ounce pita breads
1 tablespoon toasted sesame seeds

1. Combine the berries and sugar in a food processor or blender and process until puréed.

2. Strain the purée into a small bowl, then return ¼ cup of it to the food processor. Cover and refrigerate the remaining purée.

3. Peel and quarter the banana.

4. For the dip, add the banana and cottage cheese to the food processor, and process until smooth. Transfer the dip to a small serving bowl, cover and refrigerate until ready to serve.

5. Preheat the broiler.

6. Split each pita bread to form 2 rounds, then cut each round into quarters and spread them on a baking sheet. Toast the pita triangles under the broiler 3 minutes on each side, or just until lightly browned.

7. Meanwhile, pour the reserved raspberry purée on top of the dip and swirl it in with a knife, then sprinkle the dip with sesame seeds.

8. Place the bowl of dip in the middle of a platter, surround it with the pita scoops and serve

Makes 4 servings

NUTRITION INFORMATION
values are per serving

• • •

CALORIES	173	CALCIUM	77 MG
TOTAL FAT	2 G	IRON	2 MG
SATURATED FAT	0.4 G	POTASSIUM	263 MG
CHOLESTEROL	1 MG	BETA CAROTENE	0 MG
SODIUM	277 MG	VITAMIN C	14 MG
DIETARY FIBER	3 G	VITAMIN E	TRACE

POPCORN WITH HERBED GOAT CHEESE

Drenching popcorn in melted butter adds lots of saturated fat and cholesterol to what started out as a high-fiber, low-calorie snack. By substituting a modest amount of a relatively lowfat cheese, you add plenty of flavor but very little fat (and you won't need to shake on lots of salt, either). If garlic-herb goat cheese is not available, you can substitute plain goat cheese (a young, soft cheese such as Montrachet) blended with a little minced fresh garlic and a pinch of your favorite dried herbs. If you can't find any kind of goat cheese in your market—or if you don't care for it—use an ounce of lowfat cottage cheese mixed with garlic and herbs.

3 tablespoons popcorn, approximately (about 3 cups popped)
1 ounce garlic-herb goat cheese
1 tablespoon chopped fresh parsley
¼ teaspoon black pepper

1. Pop the corn in a hot-air popper.

2. Meanwhile, heat the cheese in a large nonstick skillet over low heat, stirring constantly, until melted.

3. Add the popcorn, parsley and pepper to the skillet and toss quickly to combine. Serve warm.

Makes 4 servings

NUTRITION INFORMATION
values are per serving

• • •

CALORIES	40	CALCIUM	17 MG
TOTAL FAT	2 G	IRON	TRACE
SATURATED FAT	1 G	POTASSIUM	15 MG
CHOLESTEROL	3 MG	BETA CAROTENE	0 MG
SODIUM	27 MG	VITAMIN C	1 MG
DIETARY FIBER	TRACE	VITAMIN E	TRACE

THREE-GRAIN BREADSTICKS

Storebought breadsticks might seem like a healthful, lowfat snack, but many brands are made with a lot of oil. In particular, beware of breadsticks heavily coated with sesame seeds, which may have up to 7 grams of fat per ounce. The peppery homemade breadsticks here, made with whole-grain flours and zesty seasonings, are satisfying snacks whether eaten alone or with a yogurt dip or a lowfat cheese.

1 package active dry yeast
1 cup whole-wheat flour, approximately
1 cup unbleached all-purpose flour
½ cup rye flour
1 teaspoon coarsely ground black pepper
½ teaspoon salt
Pinch of ground red pepper
2 tablespoons cornmeal

1. Place the yeast in a large bowl, add 1 cup of warm water (105-115°) and cover the bowl with plastic wrap; set aside for 10 minutes.

2. In another large bowl combine 1 cup of whole-wheat flour, the all-purpose and rye flours, black pepper, salt and ground red pepper. Gradually stir the dry ingredients into the yeast mixture until a stiff dough forms. Turn the dough out onto a lightly floured work surface and knead it, adding more flour if necessary, 8 to 10 minutes, or until the dough is smooth and elastic. Spray the bowl with nonstick cooking spray, place the dough in the bowl, cover with a kitchen towel and let rise in a warm place 1 to 1½ hours, or until the dough is doubled in bulk.

3. Preheat the oven to 350°. Sprinkle two nonstick baking sheets lightly with the cornmeal.

4. Punch down the dough and knead it 2 to 3 minutes, then let it rest 10 minutes. Divide the dough into 4 equal pieces, then divide each piece into 10 equal parts. With floured hands, quickly roll each piece of dough into a stick about 12 inches long and ¼ inch thick. Place the breadsticks on the baking sheets and bake 15 to 20 minutes, or until lightly browned, switching the position of the baking sheets halfway through the baking time.

5. Transfer the breadsticks to wire racks to cool, then leave at room temperature, uncovered, for 12 to 24 hours to crisp. Store the breadsticks loosely wrapped to keep them crisp. *Makes 40 servings*

NUTRITION INFORMATION
values are per breadstick

• • •

CALORIES	29	CALCIUM	2 MG
TOTAL FAT	0.1 G	IRON	TRACE
SATURATED FAT	0 G	POTASSIUM	23 MG
CHOLESTEROL	0 MG	BETA CAROTENE	0 MG
SODIUM	27 MG	VITAMIN C	TRACE
DIETARY FIBER	TRACE	VITAMIN E	TRACE

OVEN-BAKED POTATO CHIPS

Although commercial potato chips retain some of the nutrients of the fresh potatoes they were made from—including fiber, potassium and niacin—they also come laden with about 10 grams of fat per ounce. Try these no-fat-added chips instead.

1 large Idaho potato (about ¾ pound)
Paprika

1. Preheat the oven to 400°.

2. Scrub the potato well and cut it crosswise into ⅛-inch-thick slices.

3. Lightly coat a large baking sheet with nonstick cooking spray. Arrange the potato slices in one layer (overlapping them slightly if necessary) then spray the slices lightly with cooking spray. Sprinkle lightly with paprika.

4. Bake the chips 30 minutes, turning once, then reduce the heat to 300°. Bake another 15 to 20 minutes, or until the chips are crisp and browned.
Makes 1 serving

NUTRITION INFORMATION
values are per serving

• • •

CALORIES	310	CALCIUM	30 MG
TOTAL FAT	1 G	IRON	4 MG
SATURATED FAT	0.2 G	POTASSIUM	1175 MG
CHOLESTEROL	0 MG	BETA CAROTENE	0 MG
SODIUM	22 MG	VITAMIN C	36 MG
DIETARY FIBER	7 G	VITAMIN E	TRACE

Corn Thins

CORN THINS

Make these crackers with whole cornmeal, rather than the bolted (degermed) type, from which the nutritious bran and germ have been removed.

1 cup white cornmeal, approximately
½ cup unbleached all-purpose flour
1 tablespoon sugar
½ teaspoon salt
¼ teaspoon baking soda
¼ teaspoon black pepper, or more to taste
½ cup plain lowfat yogurt
1 tablespoon margarine, melted

1. Preheat the oven to 350°.

2. In a medium-size bowl combine 1 cup of the cornmeal, the flour, sugar, salt, baking soda and pepper. Add the yogurt and margarine and stir until combined.

3. Divide the dough into two portions. Spray a nonstick baking sheet with nonstick cooking spray; lightly dust a rolling pin with cornmeal. Place one portion of dough on the baking sheet and roll it out to a ¼-inch thickness. Place a sheet of plastic wrap over the dough and roll it out to a 10 x 10-inch square. Remove the plastic wrap. Using a ruler and a sharp knife, cut the dough into 2-inch squares, then into triangles; do not separate them.

4. Bake the crackers 20 minutes, or until crisp and golden. Check after 8 minutes; if the crackers are browning unevenly, turn the baking sheet. Transfer the crackers to a rack to cool (they will separate as you remove them from the pan).

5. Rinse and respray the baking sheet, then make a second batch of crackers in the same fashion.

Makes 100 crackers

NUTRITION INFORMATION
values are per cracker

• • •

CALORIES	10	CALCIUM	2 MG
TOTAL FAT	0.2 G	IRON	TRACE
SATURATED FAT	0 G	POTASSIUM	6 MG
CHOLESTEROL	TRACE	BETA CAROTENE	0 MG
SODIUM	15 MG	VITAMIN C	TRACE
DIETARY FIBER	0 G	VITAMIN E	TRACE

ANTIPASTO SNACK

This mixture of pickled fruits and vegetables, a variation on an Italian condiment, makes a delicious and unusual snack or appetizer. Although it is not preserved like commercial pickles, it will keep for about a week in the refrigerator. The okra and dried fruits supply calcium, potassium and fiber; the apricots are rich in beta carotene.

1½ pounds fresh okra
¾ pound pitted prunes (about 40)
1 pound yellow onions, peeled and thinly sliced
¼ pound dried apricots (about 16)
1 sprig fresh thyme
1 medium-size fresh or dried hot red pepper
4 garlic cloves, peeled
4 cups white wine vinegar
2 tablespoons coriander seeds
2 tablespoons sugar
¼ teaspoon coarse salt
4 bay leaves
½ pound provolone cheese
16 breadsticks

1. Wash and trim the okra and pack the pods vertically into a 3-quart canning jar.

2. Toss the prunes with the onion slices and place the mixture on top of the okra. Place the apricots on top of the prunes and onions and tuck the thyme sprig, red pepper and garlic cloves down into the jar.

3. In a nonreactive saucepan combine 3 cups of water with the vinegar, coriander seeds, sugar, salt and bay leaves, and bring to a rolling boil.

4. Pour the boiling liquid into the jar, filling it to the top. Let cool, then close the jar tightly and refrigerate for 2 to 3 days to allow the flavors to develop.

5. Accompany each serving with 1 ounce of provolone and 2 breadsticks. *Makes 8 servings*

NUTRITION INFORMATION
values are per serving

• • •

CALORIES	383	CALCIUM	342 MG
TOTAL FAT	9 G	IRON	3 MG
SATURATED FAT	5 G	POTASSIUM	1020 MG
CHOLESTEROL	20 MG	BETA CAROTENE	2 MG
SODIUM	639 MG	VITAMIN C	33 MG
DIETARY FIBER	7 G	VITAMIN E	TRACE

☙ *Soups* ☙

CHICKEN NOODLE SOUP WITH VEGETABLES

Using canned low-sodium chicken stock and fresh vegetables and herbs, you can turn out a delicious soup with a moderate sodium content and plenty of fiber and vitamin C in about half an hour—rather than simmering a "from scratch" soup for hours.

2 tablespoons olive oil
2½ cups diced carrots
1½ cups chopped scallions
1 green bell pepper, seeded and diced
3 cups low-sodium chicken stock
6 ounces linguine
⅓ cup chopped fresh parsley
2 tablespoons chopped fresh dill, or 2 teaspoons dried
½ teaspoon salt
½ teaspoon black pepper

1. Heat the oil in a medium-size skillet over medium heat. Add the carrots, scallions and bell pepper, and sauté 4 minutes, or until the carrots are softened. Add the stock and 1 cup of water, and bring the mixture to a simmer.

2. Break the linguine into 2-inch lengths and stir it into the soup.

3. When the soup returns to a simmer, stir in the parsley, dill, salt and black pepper, and cook another 10 minutes, or until the linguine is al dente. Ladle the soup into 6 bowls and serve. *Makes 6 servings*

NUTRITION INFORMATION
values are per serving
• • •

CALORIES	191	CALCIUM	50 MG
TOTAL FAT	5 G	IRON	3 MG
SATURATED FAT	0.7 G	POTASSIUM	485 MG
CHOLESTEROL	0 MG	BETA CAROTENE	11 MG
SODIUM	284 MG	VITAMIN C	31 MG
DIETARY FIBER	3 G	VITAMIN E	1 MG

QUICK CHICKEN NOODLE SOUP WITH PEAS

Before using canned stock or broth, stand the unopened can upright in the freezer for a few minutes. When you remove the top of the can, you'll find that any fat in the stock will have congealed on the surface; simply scrape it off with a spoon and discard.

4 cups low-sodium chicken stock
1 cup julienned carrots
¼ pound superfine egg noodles
1 cup fresh or frozen peas
2 tablespoons chopped fresh parsley
½ teaspoon black pepper

1. Bring the stock to a boil in a medium-size saucepan over medium-high heat. Add the carrots and cook 2 to 3 minutes, or until barely tender.

2. Add the noodles, reduce the heat to medium and cook 3 minutes.

3. Add the peas, parsley and pepper. Bring the soup to a boil, cook 1 minute longer and serve.
Makes 4 servings

NUTRITION INFORMATION
values are per serving
• • •

CALORIES	170	CALCIUM	30 MG
TOTAL FAT	2 G	IRON	3 MG
SATURATED FAT	0.3 G	POTASSIUM	532 MG
CHOLESTEROL	27 MG	BETA CAROTENE	6 MG
SODIUM	180 MG	VITAMIN C	19 MG
DIETARY FIBER	1 G	VITAMIN E	TRACE

Miso Chicken Soup with Rice Noodles

MISO CHICKEN SOUP WITH RICE NOODLES

Flavorful miso is a soy-and-grain-based seasoning paste that is often used as a soup base in Japanese cooking. When shopping for miso, ask for the mildest kind; it will have the lowest sodium content.

> 4 dried shiitake mushrooms, soaked 30 minutes in 1 cup
>   warm water
> 4 cups low-sodium chicken stock
> 1 ounce dried rice noodles (mei fun) or spaghettini
> ¼ cup miso
> 6 ounces skinless, boneless chicken breast, cut into thin
>   strips
> ½ cup lightly packed spinach or bok choy leaves, torn into
>   small pieces
> ⅛ teaspoon Oriental sesame oil

1. Strain the mushroom-soaking liquid into a medium-size saucepan. Add the stock and bring the mixture to a boil.

2. Cut off and discard the mushroom stems. Slice the caps into slivers, add them to the stock along with the rice noodles and simmer 3 to 4 minutes.

3. Remove about ¼ cup of stock and combine it with the miso in a small bowl; mix well and add to the soup. Add the chicken strips and bring the soup

just to a boil. Add the spinach, remove the pan from the heat and stir in the sesame oil.   *Makes 4 servings*

BEEF, CABBAGE AND BEER SOUP

Lean cuts of beef, such as eye of round or top loin, can toughen in cooking, but the addition of acid ingredients can help tenderize them. Tomato purée, beer, lemon juice and honey do the trick in this Belgian-inspired soup.

> 1 tablespoon plus 1 teaspoon vegetable oil
> ½ pound lean beef, cut into 1-inch cubes
> 6 cups thinly sliced cabbage
> 1 cup chopped onion
> 1 teaspoon caraway seeds
> ¼ teaspoon black pepper
> 1½ cups beer
> 1 cup canned tomato purée
> ¼ cup lemon juice
> 2 tablespoons honey
> ¾ pound potatoes, peeled and cut into 1-inch cubes
> ½ teaspoon salt

1. In a large heavy-gauge saucepan or Dutch oven, heat the oil over medium heat. Brown the beef 3 to 5 minutes, or until well browned on all sides. Using a slotted spoon, transfer the beef to a plate and set aside.

2. Add the cabbage, onion, caraway seeds and pepper to the pan. Cook over medium heat, stirring occasionally, about 10 minutes, or until the cabbage is wilted. Stir in 2 cups of water, the beer, tomato purée, lemon juice and honey. Bring the mixture to a boil and return the beef to the pan. Reduce the heat, cover the pan and simmer 30 minutes, stirring occasionally.

3. Add the potatoes, cover and simmer 1¼ to 1½ hours, or until the beef is very tender. Just before serving, add the salt, and additional pepper if desired.

Makes 6 servings

NUTRITION INFORMATION
values are per serving

• • •

CALORIES	200	CALCIUM	69 MG
TOTAL FAT	6 G	IRON	2 MG
SATURATED FAT	1 G	POTASSIUM	701 MG
CHOLESTEROL	21 MG	BETA CAROTENE	TRACE
SODIUM	226 MG	VITAMIN C	67 MG
DIETARY FIBER	3 G	VITAMIN E	4 MG

mushrooms and remaining liquid to the soup and bring it to a boil over medium-high heat.

4. Meanwhile, whisk the egg white in a small bowl. When the soup boils, stir in the cornstarch mixture and the egg white, and cook, stirring, 1 minute, or until the egg white is opaque. Serve the soup immediately.

Makes 2 servings

NUTRITION INFORMATION
values are per serving

• • •

CALORIES	144	CALCIUM	32 MG
TOTAL FAT	3 G	IRON	2 MG
SATURATED FAT	0.3 G	POTASSIUM	750 MG
CHOLESTEROL	0 MG	BETA CAROTENE	0 MG
SODIUM	360 MG	VITAMIN C	5 MG
DIETARY FIBER	1 G	VITAMIN E	TRACE

HOT AND SOUR SOUP

In traditional Chinese fashion, this soup is thickened with cornstarch, rather than the butter or cream that might go into a French soup. Ginger, rice vinegar and tamari add plenty of flavor but no fat.

1 ounce dried shiitake mushrooms
2 cups low-sodium chicken stock
¾ cup chopped scallions
⅓ cup sliced bamboo shoots
½ ounce thinly sliced fresh ginger
2 tablespoons diced tofu
2 tablespoons Japanese rice vinegar
1 teaspoon tamari
½ teaspoon Oriental sesame oil
½ teaspoon sugar
⅛ teaspoon white pepper
1 tablespoon plus 1 teaspoon cornstarch
1 egg white

1. Place the mushrooms in a small bowl, add 2 cups of boiling water and set them aside to soak 15 minutes. Reserving the liquid, cut the mushrooms into slivers; set aside.

2. In a large saucepan combine the stock, scallions, bamboo shoots, ginger, tofu, vinegar, tamari, oil, sugar and pepper.

3. Transfer ¼ cup of the mushroom soaking liquid to a cup and stir in the cornstarch. Add the

SCALLOP BISQUE

A bowl of this soup supplies more potassium than two bananas, more vitamin C than two glasses of orange juice and more calcium than 8 ounces of milk.

1 tablespoon vegetable oil
3 tablespoons unbleached all-purpose flour
¼ cup minced shallots
2 cups skim milk
½ cup low-sodium chicken stock
1 cup grated carrots
1 cup each diced red and yellow bell peppers
1 cup sliced mushrooms
¼ pound bay scallops
2 tablespoons lowfat sour cream
1½ teaspoons grated lemon zest
¼ teaspoon salt
Black pepper
2 tablespoons chopped fresh parsley

1. Heat the oil in a large saucepan over medium heat. Add the flour and shallots, and cook, stirring, 2 minutes. Do not let the flour brown. Whisk in the milk, stock and ½ cup of water, and continue whisking until smooth. Add the carrots, bell peppers and mushrooms, and bring the mixture to a boil. Reduce the heat to low and simmer the soup 15 minutes, or until the vegetables are tender.

2. Transfer the soup to a food processor or blender and process until puréed.

3. Return the soup to the saucepan, add the scallops, and cook over medium-low heat 5 minutes, or until the scallops are opaque. Stir in the sour cream, lemon zest, salt, and pepper to taste, and ladle the soup into 2 bowls. Sprinkle with parsley and serve.

Makes 2 servings

NUTRITION INFORMATION
values are per serving

• • •

CALORIES	352	CALCIUM	358 MG
TOTAL FAT	12 G	IRON	3 MG
SATURATED FAT	2 G	POTASSIUM	1237 MG
CHOLESTEROL	28 MG	BETA CAROTENE	11 MG
SODIUM	661 MG	VITAMIN C	147 MG
DIETARY FIBER	4 G	VITAMIN E	6 MG

MANHATTAN FISH CHOWDER

If you prefer not to make your own fish stock, see if your fish market carries it. Or, make this chowder with 3 cups of low-sodium chicken stock.

2 tablespoons olive oil
1 cup finely chopped onion
1 garlic clove, peeled and crushed
1½ cups peeled, diced potatoes
1½ cups fish stock plus 1½ cups low-sodium chicken stock
Small bay leaf
½ teaspoon salt
1 pound skinless, boneless halibut, cut into 1-inch chunks
1 cup canned crushed tomatoes
¼ teaspoon dried thyme
¼ teaspoon crushed fennel seed
¼ teaspoon red pepper flakes
¼ cup finely chopped parsley

1. Heat the oil in a large saucepan over medium heat. Add the onion and garlic, and cook 3 to 5 minutes, or until softened.

2. Add the potatoes, stock, bay leaf and salt, cover the pan and bring to a simmer. Cook for about 15 minutes, or until the potatoes are tender.

3. Add the remaining ingredients except the parsley, bring to a slow boil and cook, stirring gently, 1 minute, or until the fish is cooked through. Remove the pan from the heat, sprinkle the chowder with parsley and serve.

Makes 4 servings

NUTRITION INFORMATION
values are per serving

• • •

CALORIES	272	CALCIUM	97 MG
TOTAL FAT	10 G	IRON	2 MG
SATURATED FAT	1 G	POTASSIUM	1099 MG
CHOLESTEROL	36 MG	BETA CAROTENE	TRACE
SODIUM	551 MG	VITAMIN C	20 MG
DIETARY FIBER	2 G	VITAMIN E	1 MG

ORIENTAL SCALLOP SOUP

This delicately flavored soup is made with *sake*, a Japanese brewed rice wine that can be purchased at most liquor stores. If you cannot find *sake*, dry sherry makes a good substitute.

2 teaspoons vegetable oil
¼ pound bay scallops
4 cups low-sodium chicken stock
1½ cups chopped carrots
⅓ cup chopped scallions
1 teaspoon minced fresh ginger
1¾ cups sliced fresh shiitake mushrooms,
    or fresh white mushrooms
¾ cup cooked white rice
½ cup finely diced red bell pepper
3 ounces snow peas, trimmed
¼ cup sake (Japanese rice wine)

1. Heat the oil in a medium-size saucepan over medium heat. Add the scallops and sauté 2 minutes, or until the scallops are opaque and firm; transfer the scallops to a small bowl and set aside.

2. Place the stock, carrots, scallions and ginger in the saucepan, bring to a simmer over medium heat and cook 15 minutes.

3. Strain the stock into a large bowl and discard the solids. Return the stock to the pan, add the mushrooms and simmer 2 minutes, or until the mushrooms are soft. Stir in the scallops, rice, bell pepper, snow peas, sake and ½ cup of water, and cook another 3 minutes, or until the soup is heated through. Ladle the soup into 4 bowls and serve.

Makes 4 servings

NUTRITION INFORMATION
values are per serving
• • •

CALORIES 148 CALCIUM 45 MG
TOTAL FAT 3 G IRON 2 MG
SATURATED FAT 0.4 G POTASSIUM 748 MG
CHOLESTEROL 9 MG BETA CAROTENE 9 MG
SODIUM 229 MG VITAMIN C 34 MG
DIETARY FIBER 3 G VITAMIN E 3 MG

turn the purée to the pot, stir to recombine and re-heat the soup briefly over low heat. Ladle the soup into 6 bowls and serve.

Makes 6 servings

NUTRITION INFORMATION
values are per serving
• • •

CALORIES 112 CALCIUM 59 MG
TOTAL FAT 0.6 G IRON 1 MG
SATURATED FAT 0 G POTASSIUM 582 MG
CHOLESTEROL TRACE BETA CAROTENE 4 MG
SODIUM 191 MG VITAMIN C 16 MG
DIETARY FIBER 3 G VITAMIN E TRACE

CHILI VEGETABLE SOUP

Puréeing some of the vegetables in this zesty soup produces a satisfying texture and makes the addition of cream or other high-fat thickeners unnecessary. Starchy vegetables, such as potatoes, work especially well for thickening soups.

1 pound all-purpose potatoes, peeled and diced (2½ cups)
1 cup frozen corn kernels
1 cup unpeeled, sliced zucchini
¾ cup coarsely chopped celery
¾ cup sliced carrots
½ cup chopped scallions
½ cup coarsely chopped onion
2 garlic cloves, crushed and peeled
2 cups low-sodium chicken stock
½ cup skim milk
1 tablespoon mild chili powder
¼ teaspoon salt
¼ teaspoon black pepper

1. Place all of the vegetables, including the onion and garlic, in a large pot. Add 1 cup of water, the stock, milk, chili powder, salt and pepper, and bring to a boil over medium-high heat. Cover the pot, reduce the heat to low and simmer the vegetables 15 to 20 minutes, or until the potatoes are tender. Remove the pot from the heat and let the soup cool for about 20 minutes.
2. Transfer 2 cups of the cooled soup to a food processor or blender and process until puréed. Re-

VEGETABLE SOUP

Although the variety of vegetables in this soup makes it a good source of vitamin C, fiber and calcium, the recipe is not ironclad: You can substitute according to what looks best at your market.

2 teaspoons olive oil
1½ cups chopped onion
1 cup diced red bell pepper
⅔ cup diced celery
½ cup diced carrot
2 garlic cloves, minced
⅔ cup broccoli florets
⅓ cup thinly sliced zucchini
⅓ cup thinly sliced yellow squash
⅓ cup yellow cornmeal
¼ cup thinly sliced scallions
2 tablespoons grated Parmesan cheese
2 teaspoons chopped fresh coriander

1. In a large saucepan, heat the oil over medium heat. Add the onion, bell pepper, celery, carrot and garlic, reduce the heat to low and cook about 10 minutes, or until the onions are soft.
2. Increase the heat to high and add 6 cups of water. Bring the soup to a boil and add the broccoli, zucchini and yellow squash. Reduce the heat to medium-low and simmer about 7 minutes, or until the broccoli is tender.
3. Increase the heat to high and bring the soup to a rolling boil. Slowly pour in the cornmeal, whisking constantly. Continue whisking about 1 minute, or

until the soup thickens. Remove the pan from the heat and ladle the soup into 4 bowls. Sprinkle each serving with scallions, Parmesan and coriander.

Makes 4 servings

2. Stir in the corn, tomato paste and lemon juice. Return the soup to a boil, then cover the pan, reduce the heat and simmer 30 minutes.

3. Add the salt and hot pepper sauce, and pepper to taste, and serve.

Makes 8 servings

CHICKPEA AND ESCAROLE SOUP

The combination of rice and legumes in this Italian-inspired soup provides protein as complete as you would get in meat, but with much less fat.

2 tablespoons olive oil
1 cup chopped onion
1 tablespoon minced garlic
1½ teaspoons minced fresh thyme, or ½ teaspoon dried thyme, crumbled
1½ teaspoons minced fresh oregano, or ½ teaspoon dried oregano, crumbled
8 cups coarsely chopped escarole leaves
2½ cups cooked chickpeas (1¼ cups dried)
¼ cup long-grain white rice
1 cup frozen or canned corn kernels
2 tablespoons tomato paste
2 tablespoons lemon juice
1½ teaspoons salt
¼ teaspoon hot pepper sauce
Black pepper

1. In a 6- to 8-quart pot, heat the oil over medium heat. Stir in the onion, garlic, thyme and oregano, and sauté 3 to 5 minutes, or until the onion is wilted. Add the escarole, chickpeas and rice, and stir to coat lightly with oil. Add 10 cups of water, cover the pot and bring to a boil. Reduce the heat and simmer, covered, 30 minutes.

PISTOU SOUP

This French soup would traditionally be made with a cup of oil and a cup of cheese. Here, 2 tablespoons each of margarine and Parmesan are all that's needed.

2 large tomatoes (1 pound total weight), cored and quartered
5 garlic cloves, chopped
3 tablespoons chopped fresh basil
2 tablespoons grated Parmesan cheese
2 tablespoons butter or margarine
1 large all-purpose potato, peeled and coarsely diced (1¼ cups)
1 cup thickly sliced carrots
¾ cup coarsely chopped scallions
1 cup low-sodium chicken stock
1 cup cooked red kidney beans
1 cup fresh or frozen green peas
1 tablespoon chopped fresh parsley
½ teaspoon salt

1. Place the tomatoes, garlic, basil and Parmesan in a food processor or blender, and process just until blended, scraping down the sides of the container with a rubber spatula.

2. Melt the butter in a medium-size saucepan over medium-high heat. Add the potato, carrots and scallions, and sauté 3 to 4 minutes, or until the scallions are limp. Add the tomato mixture, stock, kidney beans and ½ cup of water, and bring to a boil. Cover

Chickpea and Escarole Soup

the pan, reduce the heat to low and simmer 20 to 25 minutes, or until the potato is tender.

3. Add the peas, parsley and salt, and cook another 5 minutes.   *Makes 8 servings*

NUTRITION INFORMATION
values are per serving

• • •

CALORIES	118	CALCIUM	58 MG
TOTAL FAT	4 G	IRON	2 MG
SATURATED FAT	2 G	POTASSIUM	450 MG
CHOLESTEROL	9 MG	BETA CAROTENE	4 MG
SODIUM	219 MG	VITAMIN C	25 MG
DIETARY FIBER	1 G	VITAMIN E	TRACE

RATATOUILLE SOUP

Canned tomatoes are exceptionally high in sodium due to the salt and other sodium compounds added in processing. However, many tomato products come in no-salt-added forms.

½ pound eggplant
6 ounces zucchini
¼ pound onions
¼ pound carrots
2 garlic cloves
Two 14-ounce cans no-salt-added tomatoes,
    with their liquid
2 tablespoons chopped fresh parsley
1 teaspoon dried basil
½ teaspoon dried oregano
⅛ teaspoon ground black pepper
Pinch of sugar
1 bay leaf

1. Wash, trim and dice the eggplant, zucchini and carrots. Peel and coarsely chop the onions and garlic; set aside.

2. Place the tomatoes and their liquid in a medium-size saucepan and bring to a boil over medium-high heat. Add the eggplant, zucchini, onions, carrots, garlic, parsley, basil, oregano, pepper, sugar and bay leaf. Cover the pan, reduce the heat to medium-low and simmer the vegetables 30 minutes. Remove the pan from the heat, and allow the soup to cool slightly; remove and discard the bay leaf.

3. Transfer 3 cups of the solids to a food processor or blender and process 1 minute, or until coarsely puréed. Return the purée to the pan and stir to combine. Reheat the soup and serve it hot, or chill it well and serve it cold.   *Makes 2 servings*

NUTRITION INFORMATION
values are per serving

• • •

CALORIES	166	CALCIUM	212 MG
TOTAL FAT	1 G	IRON	5 MG
SATURATED FAT	0.2 G	POTASSIUM	1590 MG
CHOLESTEROL	0 MG	BETA CAROTENE	10 MG
SODIUM	78 MG	VITAMIN C	84 MG
DIETARY FIBER	8 G	VITAMIN E	TRACE

LENTIL MINESTRONE

There's just enough ground beef in this Italian classic to add a meaty flavor. A serving of the soup provides 14 grams of protein, much of which comes from the lentils and macaroni.

1 teaspoon olive oil
2 cups coarsely diced green bell peppers
1½ cups coarsely chopped onions
1 cup diced celery
2 ounces ground chuck
2 garlic cloves, minced
⅓ cup dried lentils
¼ cup white rice
4 small tomatoes, preferably green (unripe) ones,
    cut into 1-inch cubes
2 ounces elbow macaroni
1 bay leaf
1 tablespoon lime juice
¾ teaspoon salt
½ teaspoon dried oregano
Black pepper
¼ cup grated Parmesan cheese

1. Heat the oil in a Dutch oven or large heavy-gauge saucepan over medium heat. Add the bell peppers, onions, celery, ground chuck and garlic, and cook, stirring, about 5 minutes, or until the vegetables are softened. Stir in the lentils, rice, tomatoes, macaroni, bay leaf and 2 quarts of water, cover the pan and bring to a boil. Reduce the heat to low and simmer 45 minutes.

2. Add the lime juice, salt, oregano, and black pepper to taste. Remove and discard the bay leaf. Ladle the soup into 4 bowls and sprinkle it with the Parmesan.

Makes 4 servings

NUTRITION INFORMATION
values are per serving

• • •

CALORIES	288	CALCIUM	143 MG
TOTAL FAT	7 G	IRON	4 MG
SATURATED FAT	2 G	POTASSIUM	733 MG
CHOLESTEROL	15 MG	BETA CAROTENE	0.6 MG
SODIUM	547 MG	VITAMIN C	74 MG
DIETARY FIBER	5 G	VITAMIN E	1 MG

4. Transfer the soup to a food processor or blender and process until smooth, then return it to the pan and reheat 5 to 10 minutes over medium heat. Ladle the soup into 4 bowls and serve.

Makes 4 servings

NUTRITION INFORMATION
values are per serving

• • •

CALORIES	137	CALCIUM	63 MG
TOTAL FAT	3 G	IRON	2 MG
SATURATED FAT	2 G	POTASSIUM	687 MG
CHOLESTEROL	8 MG	BETA CAROTENE	17 MG
SODIUM	154 MG	VITAMIN C	16 MG
DIETARY FIBER	4 G	VITAMIN E	TRACE

CARROT AND LEEK SOUP

Mild-flavored leeks, which resemble overgrown scallions, are—ounce for ounce—more nutritious than onions; they contain more B vitamins and iron. The tightly overlapping layers of a leek's stem may entrap soil or grit, so it's important to separate the layers and wash the vegetable thoroughly.

½ pound leeks
2 garlic cloves, peeled and crushed
1 tablespoon butter or margarine
1 pound carrots, trimmed and cut into 2-inch pieces
½ pound red potatoes, peeled and quartered
2 cups low-sodium chicken stock
¼ cup chopped fresh dill
¼ teaspoon black pepper

1. Trim the leeks, split them lengthwise and wash them carefully under cold running water to remove any grit and sand. Cut the leeks into 2-inch pieces.

2. Place the leeks, garlic and butter in a medium-size saucepan, cover and cook over low heat 5 minutes. Add the carrots, potatoes, stock, dill, pepper and 1 cup of water, increase the heat to medium-high and bring the mixture to a boil. Cover the pan, reduce the heat to low and simmer the soup 15 to 20 minutes, or until the potatoes are tender.

3. Remove the pan from the heat, uncover it and allow the soup to cool 20 minutes.

PINTO BEAN VEGETABLE SOUP

Check the labels on supermarket brands of canned bean and vegetable soups and you'll commonly find sodium contents of 800, 900 or even 1000 milligrams per serving. That makes a convincing case for cooking up a homemade soup like this one, which has only 181 milligrams of sodium per serving.

1 cup dried pinto beans
1½ cups chopped onions
2 garlic cloves, chopped
¼ cup chopped fresh dill
1 bay leaf
¼ teaspoon salt
¼ teaspoon black pepper
3½ cups peeled, diced sweet potatoes
4 cups thickly sliced green cabbage
1 cup sliced carrots
1 cup sliced yellow squash
¼ cup chopped fresh parsley

1. Place the beans in a large pot, add enough cold water to cover and refrigerate overnight.

2. Rinse and drain the beans and return them to the pot. Stir in the onions, garlic, 3 tablespoons of the dill, the bay leaf, salt and pepper. Add the potatoes and 2 quarts of water, and bring to a boil over medium-high heat. Reduce the heat to medium-low, cover the pot and simmer 35 to 45 minutes, or until the beans are tender.

3. Add the cabbage, carrots and squash, return the soup to a boil and cook another 5 to 10 minutes, or until the carrots are tender. Remove and discard the bay leaf, then stir in the parsley. Ladle the soup into 4 bowls and garnish with the remaining dill.

Makes 4 servings

NUTRITION INFORMATION
values are per serving

• • •

CALORIES	350	CALCIUM	171 MG
TOTAL FAT	1 G	IRON	6 MG
SATURATED FAT	0.2 G	POTASSIUM	1270 MG
CHOLESTEROL	0 MG	BETA CAROTENE	18 MG
SODIUM	181 MG	VITAMIN C	73 MG
DIETARY FIBER	7 G	VITAMIN E	7 MG

CARROT-BEET SOUP

This low-calorie soup is a great way to use beets, an often-overlooked vegetable. If the beets you buy have fresh-looking green leaves, reserve the greens to cook and serve with another meal.

> 1 tablespoon corn oil
> 1 cup coarsely chopped onion
> ½ cup chopped shallots
> 3 cups low-sodium chicken stock
> 2 cups peeled, sliced fresh beets
> 2 cups sliced carrots
> 4 thin lemon slices for garnish

1. Heat the oil in a medium-size saucepan over medium heat. Add the onion and shallots, and cook, stirring frequently, 10 minutes. Add the stock, beets, and carrots, increase the heat to medium-high and bring the mixture to a boil. Cover the pan, reduce the

Carrot-Beet Soup

the heat to medium-low and simmer 30 minutes, or until the vegetables are tender.

2. Remove the pan from the heat and allow the soup to cool slightly. Using a slotted spoon, transfer the solids to a food processor and process 1 minute, or until puréed.

3. Return the purée to the pan. Let the soup cool, then cover and refrigerate it until well chilled. Stir the soup to reblend it, then ladle it into 4 bowls and garnish with lemon slices.   *Makes 4 servings*

NUTRITION INFORMATION
values are per serving

• • •

CALORIES	122	CALCIUM	44 MG
TOTAL FAT	4 G	IRON	1 MG
SATURATED FAT	0.5 G	POTASSIUM	755 MG
CHOLESTEROL	0 MG	BETA CAROTENE	13 MG
SODIUM	180 MG	VITAMIN C	15 MG
DIETARY FIBER	4 G	VITAMIN E	3 MG

BLACK BEAN AND ORANGE SOUP

You save yourself lots of excess sodium by cooking dried beans rather than using canned ones. If time is tight on weeknights, cook up a pot of beans on the weekend: They'll keep for about four days in the refrigerator.

1½ cups orange juice, preferably freshly squeezed
1¼ cups cooked black beans (½ cup dried)
2 carrots, cut into 3-inch pieces
1 cup finely chopped onion
1 teaspoon ground coriander
4 orange slices, for garnish

1. Place the juice, beans, carrots, onion and coriander in a medium-size nonreactive saucepan. Bring to a boil, reduce the heat to low and simmer, covered, 20 minutes. Set the soup aside to cool briefly, then process it in a food processor or blender just until puréed.

2. Reheat the soup over low heat, then ladle it into 4 bowls and garnish with orange slices.
Makes 4 servings

NUTRITION INFORMATION
values are per serving

• • •

CALORIES	142	CALCIUM	46 MG
TOTAL FAT	0.6 G	IRON	2 MG
SATURATED FAT	0.1 G	POTASSIUM	562 MG
CHOLESTEROL	0 MG	BETA CAROTENE	6 MG
SODIUM	15 MG	VITAMIN C	54 MG
DIETARY FIBER	4 G	VITAMIN E	TRACE

BLACK-EYED PEA SOUP

Firm-textured black-eyed peas, also called cow peas, have a single black dot on their creamy skins. They are sold dried, canned and frozen, and in some areas are available fresh in season.

1 cup dried black-eyed peas
2 tablespoons plus 2 teaspoons margarine
1 cup chopped onion
2 garlic cloves, chopped
One 14-ounce can plum tomatoes, with their liquid
1 cup diced carrots
1 cup diced celery
1 cup frozen lima beans
½ cup low-sodium chicken stock
1 teaspoon ground cumin
1 teaspoon coriander seeds
¼ teaspoon black pepper

1. Place the peas in a medium-size bowl with cold water to cover by 2 inches. Let the peas soak overnight in the refrigerator.

2. Drain the peas and set aside.

3. Melt the margarine in a large saucepan over medium-high heat. Add the onion and garlic, and sauté 2 to 3 minutes, or until the onion begins to turn translucent. Add the black-eyed peas, the tomatoes with their liquid, the carrots, celery, lima beans, stock, cumin, coriander, pepper and 1 cup of water, and stir to combine. Bring the mixture to a boil, then cover the pan, reduce the heat to low and simmer 30 minutes.

4. Using a slotted spoon, transfer about two-thirds of the solids from the soup to a food processor or blender, and purée. Return the purée to the saucepan and stir to combine. Bring the soup to a boil over medium-high heat and simmer it, stirring constantly, 2 minutes, or until heated through. Ladle the soup into 4 bowls and serve.   *Makes 4 servings*

NUTRITION INFORMATION
values are per serving

• • •

CALORIES	314	CALCIUM	266 MG
TOTAL FAT	9 G	IRON	4 MG
SATURATED FAT	2 G	POTASSIUM	1326 MG
CHOLESTEROL	0 MG	BETA CAROTENE	7 MG
SODIUM	252 MG	VITAMIN C	33 MG
DIETARY FIBER	15 G	VITAMIN E	13 MG

CREAMY MUSHROOM BARLEY SOUP

To most Americans, this old-fashioned soup is the most familiar use of barley. However, mild-flavored, easy-to-cook barley, which is an excellent source of soluble fiber, deserves wider use.

½ pound onions
2 garlic cloves
2 cups low-sodium chicken stock
6 tablespoons barley
½ pound fresh mushrooms
¼ cup chopped fresh parsley
2 tablespoons chopped fresh dill

1. Peel and coarsely chop the onions and garlic; set aside.
2. Bring the stock and 2 cups of water to a boil in a medium-size saucepan over medium-high heat. Stir in the onions, garlic and barley, cover the pan, reduce the heat to low and simmer 45 minutes.
3. Meanwhile, wash, trim and coarsely chop the mushrooms; set aside.
4. Add the mushrooms to the soup, cover the pan and simmer another 15 minutes.
5. Using a slotted spoon, transfer the solids to a food processor or blender and process until puréed.
6. Return the purée to the saucepan, then stir in the parsley and dill. Bring the soup to a boil over medium-high heat, then ladle it into 4 bowls.
Makes 4 servings

NUTRITION INFORMATION
values are per serving

• • •

CALORIES	111	CALCIUM	36 MG
TOTAL FAT	0.8 G	IRON	2 MG
SATURATED FAT	0 G	POTASSIUM	511 MG
CHOLESTEROL	0 MG	BETA CAROTENE	TRACE
SODIUM	88 MG	VITAMIN C	11 MG
DIETARY FIBER	4 G	VITAMIN E	TRACE

KALE-MUSHROOM SOUP

Kale, like other dark green leafy vegetables, is a good nondairy source of calcium as well as the antioxidants beta carotene and vitamin C. Mushrooms provide substantial amounts of B vitamins.

2 garlic cloves, thinly sliced
2 teaspoons butter or margarine
¾ pound fresh kale, washed and cut into
     ¼-inch-wide strips
4 cups Vegetable Stock (see recipe opposite) or low-sodium
     chicken stock
2 cups sliced fresh mushrooms
¼ teaspoon black pepper
Pinch of salt

1. Sauté the garlic in the butter in a large saucepan over low heat 2 to 3 minutes.
2. Add the kale, stock, mushrooms, pepper and salt, and bring to a boil. Cover the pan, reduce the heat to low and simmer the mixture 10 to 15 minutes, or until the vegetables are tender.
Makes 4 servings

NUTRITION INFORMATION
values are per serving

• • •

CALORIES	82	CALCIUM	97 MG
TOTAL FAT	3 G	IRON	2 MG
SATURATED FAT	1 G	POTASSIUM	479 MG
CHOLESTEROL	6 MG	BETA CAROTENE	5 MG
SODIUM	239 MG	VITAMIN C	51 MG
DIETARY FIBER	5 G	VITAMIN E	TRACE

VEGETABLE STOCK

Homemade stock improves any soup recipe and gives you greater control over the sodium and fat content. Making poultry or meat stock can be complicated undertakings, but this virtually fat-free vegetable stock is easy to prepare—you don't have to deal with a turkey carcass or a veal bone. For convenience, freeze 1-cup portions of stock to use in your favorite recipes; it will keep for about one month. Or, refrigerate the stock for up to a week.

1 pound green cabbage
½ pound leeks
¼ pound parsnips
1 large carrot
1 celery stalk
1 unpeeled garlic clove
6 parsley sprigs
½ teaspoon salt
½ teaspoon whole black or white peppercorns

1. Core and coarsely chop the cabbage; you should have about 3 cups. Trim the leeks, split them lengthwise and wash them carefully under cold running water to remove any grit and sand. Coarsely chop the leeks. Wash, trim and halve the parsnips, carrot and celery.

2. Place the vegetables in a large pot, add the garlic, parsley, salt, peppercorns and 2 quarts of water, and bring to a boil over medium-high heat. Reduce the heat to medium-low, cover the pot and simmer the stock 1 hour. Uncover the pot and simmer the stock another 45 minutes.

3. Strain the stock through a colander set over a large bowl; discard the solids.

4. Transfer the stock to jars or food-storage containers and refrigerate or freeze it.   *Makes 7 cups*

NUTRITION INFORMATION
values are per cup
• • •

CALORIES	25	CALCIUM	27
TOTAL FAT	0.1 G	IRON	TRACE
SATURATED FAT	0 G	POTASSIUM	138 MG
CHOLESTEROL	0 MG	BETA CAROTENE	1 MG
SODIUM	165 MG	VITAMIN C	13 MG
DIETARY FIBER	1 G	VITAMIN E	TRACE

CREAMY CORN AND OAT SOUP

Oats are not just for breakfast porridge: They do a fine job of thickening this super-quick soup while adding fiber, iron and B vitamins.

2 cups fresh or frozen corn kernels
1 cup rolled oats
½ cup chopped onion
2 garlic cloves, minced
¼ teaspoon black pepper
Pinch of salt
2 tablespoons chopped fresh parsley

1. In a medium-size saucepan combine the corn, oats, onion, garlic, pepper, salt and 3½ cups of water. Bring the mixture to a boil over medium heat, reduce the heat to low and simmer 15 minutes. If a thinner soup is preferred, add up to ½ cup of water.

2. Remove the pan from the heat, stir in 1 tablespoon of the parsley and divide the soup among 4 bowls. Sprinkle the soup with the remaining parsley and serve.   *Makes 4 servings*

NUTRITION INFORMATION
values are per serving
• • •

CALORIES	152	CALCIUM	23 MG
TOTAL FAT	1 G	IRON	1 MG
SATURATED FAT	0.2 G	POTASSIUM	230 MG
CHOLESTEROL	0 MG	BETA CAROTENE	0.2 MG
SODIUM	38 MG	VITAMIN C	6 MG
DIETARY FIBER	3 G	VITAMIN E	TRACE

LEEK AND POTATO SOUP

This hot version of *vichyssoise* is made without the butter and heavy cream that go into the classic chilled soup. A warming, delicately seasoned purée, it is a superb source of potassium and calcium.

4 to 5 leeks (about 1 pound)
2 potatoes, peeled and quartered
1 cup thinly sliced celery

4 cups low-sodium chicken stock
2 cups skim milk
1 tablespoon chopped fresh parsley
White pepper

1. Cut off the root ends and green tops from the leeks. Halve the leeks lengthwise, separate the layers and wash them thoroughly. Cut the leeks into 1-inch pieces.

2. In a large saucepan, combine the leeks, potatoes, celery and stock. Bring to a boil, skimming off any scum. Reduce the heat and simmer, uncovered, about 40 minutes, or until the vegetables are tender. Cool the soup briefly, then purée in a blender or food processor or mash to a coarse purée by hand.

3. Return the soup to the saucepan, add the milk and reheat the soup just until heated through; do not boil. Ladle the soup into bowls or mugs and sprinkle with parsley and pepper.   *Makes 4 servings*

NUTRITION INFORMATION
values are per serving

• • •

CALORIES	155	CALCIUM	199 MG
TOTAL FAT	0.8 G	IRON	2 MG
SATURATED FAT	0.2 G	POTASSIUM	866 MG
CHOLESTEROL	2 MG	BETA CAROTENE	0 MG
SODIUM	263 MG	VITAMIN C	15 MG
DIETARY FIBER	2 G	VITAMIN E	TRACE

SPICY WINTER SQUASH SOUP

Novice cooks will appreciate this recipe: You don't have to worry about getting the seasoning just right because a can of spicy vegetable juice does most of the work for you. Just measure out a spoonful of basil and add a pinch of salt, and you'll have a perfectly seasoned soup.

One 2½-pound acorn squash
One 12-ounce can spicy vegetable juice
1 cup chopped green bell pepper
1 cup fresh or frozen corn kernels
1 tablespoon chopped fresh basil
Pinch of salt

1. Preheat the oven to 400°.

2. Line a medium-size baking pan with foil.

3. Halve the squash, remove the seeds and place the squash cut side down in the pan. Bake 20 to 25 minutes, or until the squash is tender when pierced with a knife. Set aside to cool about 15 minutes.

4. Scoop the squash into a large saucepan and mash it with a potato masher or fork to remove any large lumps (or purée the squash in a food processor or blender). Add 1½ cups of water, the vegetable juice, bell pepper, corn, basil and salt, and bring to a boil over medium-high heat. Reduce the heat to low and simmer 10 to 15 minutes. Serve hot, or cool the soup to room temperature and then refrigerate it and serve it chilled.   *Makes 6 servings*

NUTRITION INFORMATION
values are per serving

• • •

CALORIES	106	CALCIUM	67 MG
TOTAL FAT	0.2 G	IRON	2 MG
SATURATED FAT	0 G	POTASSIUM	735 MG
CHOLESTEROL	0 MG	BETA CAROTENE	0.5 MG
SODIUM	238 MG	VITAMIN C	40 MG
DIETARY FIBER	3 G	VITAMIN E	TRACE

INDIAN SPICED PUMPKIN SOUP

Saving pumpkin for one or two holiday meals means you miss out on an excellent source of beta carotene. If you cook fresh pumpkin for this recipe, toast the seeds—a rich source of iron—and shell them to use as a garnish for the soup.

2 teaspoons butter
¾ cup coarsely chopped onion
1 teaspoon ground coriander
½ teaspoon each ground cumin and turmeric
2 cups canned or cooked pumpkin
¼ cup chopped fresh coriander
2 tablespoons brown sugar
2 tablespoons tomato paste
1 tablespoon peanut butter
¼ teaspoon black pepper
Pinch of salt

Herbed Gazpacho

1. Melt the butter in a medium-size saucepan over medium heat. Add the onion and sauté 3 to 4 minutes, or until light golden. Add the coriander, cumin and turmeric, and cook, stirring, 1 minute.

2. Add the pumpkin, coriander, sugar, tomato paste, peanut butter, pepper, salt and 3 cups of water, and stir gently to mix well. Bring the mixture to a boil, then cover the pan, reduce the heat to low and simmer the soup about 30 minutes, or until the flavors are well blended. *Makes 4 servings*

NUTRITION INFORMATION

values are per serving

• • •

CALORIES	113	CALCIUM	46 MG
TOTAL FAT	4 G	IRON	2 MG
SATURATED FAT	2 G	POTASSIUM	492 MG
CHOLESTEROL	6 MG	BETA CAROTENE	0.9 MG
SODIUM	83 MG	VITAMIN C	15 MG
DIETARY FIBER	TRACE	VITAMIN E	TRACE

HERBED GAZPACHO

Gazpacho, often called a liquid salad, is traditionally thickened with oil and bread crumbs, but without those ingredients it's lighter and more refreshing. Served over ice, this low-calorie soup will get a hot-weather brunch off to a sparkling start.

Two 14½-ounce cans peeled tomatoes, with their liquid
½ pound unpeeled cucumber, finely chopped (1½ cups)
½ cup finely chopped scallions
⅓ cup finely diced celery
¼ cup chopped fresh basil
2 tablespoons herbed vinegar or red wine vinegar
1 small garlic clove, minced
½ teaspoon black pepper
Pinch of salt

1. Combine the tomatoes and their liquid with all the remaining ingredients in a large bowl; stir well to break up the tomatoes. Cover the bowl and refrigerate the gazpacho 4 hours, or until thoroughly chilled.

2. Stir the soup to reblend it before serving and ladle it over ice cubes, if desired. *Makes 4 servings*

NUTRITION INFORMATION
values are per serving

• • •

CALORIES 58 CALCIUM 98 MG
TOTAL FAT 0.7 G IRON 2 MG
SATURATED FAT 0.1 G POTASSIUM 648 MG
CHOLESTEROL 0 MG BETA CAROTENE 1 MG
SODIUM 378 MG VITAMIN C 41 MG
DIETARY FIBER 3 G VITAMIN E TRACE

to release their flavor. Cover the bowl and refrigerate the soup overnight to blend the flavors.

5. To serve, remove the mint, ladle the soup into 4 bowls and garnish with a fresh mint sprig.

Makes 4 servings

NUTRITION INFORMATION
values are per serving

• • •

CALORIES 262 CALCIUM 230 MG
TOTAL FAT 2 G IRON 1 MG
SATURATED FAT 0.7 G POTASSIUM 1247 MG
CHOLESTEROL 5 MG BETA CAROTENE 13 MG
SODIUM 109 MG VITAMIN C 124 MG
DIETARY FIBER 4 G VITAMIN E 5 MG

MIDSUMMER CANTALOUPE SOUP

Cantaloupe and sweet potato, two of the best sources of beta carotene, are combined in this summertime treat. When choosing a cantaloupe, look for one with golden-yellow undertones beneath the netting. The stem end should show a slight indentation and the melon's fragrance should be flowery-sweet.

2 medium-size cantaloupes
1 pound sweet potatoes
1 cup skim milk
1 cup plain lowfat yogurt
¼ cup frozen apple juice concentrate
1 tablespoon grated lemon zest
8 mint sprigs

1. Quarter and seed the cantaloupes. Scoop out the flesh with a spoon or cut off the rind and then cut the flesh into large chunks. Place the cantaloupe flesh in a food processor or blender, process until liquefied and transfer to a large bowl; set aside.

2. Trim the sweet potatoes. Place them in a medium-size saucepan with cold water to cover and bring to a boil over medium-high heat. Reduce the heat to low, partially cover the pan and simmer 45 minutes, or until the potatoes are tender; drain and set aside to cool.

3. When the potatoes are cool enough to handle, peel them, cut them into large chunks and process until puréed. Gradually add the cantaloupe juice, the milk, yogurt, apple juice concentrate and lemon zest, and process until well blended.

4. Return the soup to the bowl and add 4 mint sprigs, crushing them gently with a wooden spoon

PINEAPPLE GAZPACHO

If you want a sound, sweet pineapple, look for a tag identifying the fruit as jet-shipped from Hawaii. Pineapples from Hawaii are picked at their sweetest, and the quick transport preserves quality.

2 medium-size cucumbers
6 cups fresh pineapple, or drained juice-packed
    pineapple chunks
One 14-ounce can plum tomatoes, with their liquid
1 red bell pepper
½ cup orange juice
3 tablespoons lemon juice
¼ cup chopped fresh mint

1. Wash, halve and seed the cucumbers, and cut them into chunks.

2. Process the cucumbers and pineapple in a food processor or blender 45 seconds, or until finely chopped, pulsing the machine on and off. Add the tomatoes and their liquid, and process 15 seconds; transfer to a serving bowl.

3. Stem and seed the pepper, cut it into large chunks and process it with the orange juice, lemon juice and mint 5 seconds. Add this mixture to the serving bowl and stir to combine. Cover the bowl and refrigerate the gazpacho 4 hours, or until the soup is well chilled. Just before serving, stir the gazpacho to reblend it, then divide it among 4 bowls.

Makes 4 servings

NUTRITION INFORMATION

values are per serving

• • •

CALORIES	171	CALCIUM	66 MG
TOTAL FAT	2 G	IRON	2 MG
SATURATED FAT	0.2 G	POTASSIUM	771 MG
CHOLESTEROL	0 MG	BETA CAROTENE	0.6 MG
SODIUM	167 MG	VITAMIN C	113 MG
DIETARY FIBER	5 G	VITAMIN E	TRACE

ONION SOUP WITH SHALLOT TOASTS

Think of onion soup and you probably picture a dark broth topped with a hefty layer of melted cheese. This soup, however, is a dense leek-and-onion purée that has a light topping of crisp Parmesan-dusted toasts. Like its traditional French cousin, it is also graced with a touch of sherry.

4 cups coarsely chopped leeks
2 cups low-sodium chicken stock
1 cup coarsely chopped onion
2 garlic cloves, chopped
2 tablespoons sherry
½ teaspoon dried thyme
1 bay leaf
⅛ teaspoon white pepper
1 tablespoon margarine
1 cup coarsely chopped shallots
6 ounces Italian bread
2 tablespoons grated Parmesan cheese

1. In a medium-size saucepan combine the leeks, stock, onion, garlic, sherry, thyme, bay leaf, white pepper and 1½ cups of water, and bring to a boil over medium-high heat. Cover, reduce the heat to low and simmer 1 hour.

2. Remove and discard the bay leaf. Using a slotted spoon, transfer the solids from the soup to a food processor or blender and process until puréed. Return the purée to the pan, cover and set aside.

3. Preheat the broiler.

4. Meanwhile, melt the margarine in a small skillet over medium-high heat. Add the shallots and sauté 1 to 2 minutes, or until they begin to brown.

5. Toast the bread slices under the broiler 1 minute on each side, or until golden; set aside.

6. Reheat the soup over medium-high heat, stirring occasionally, 3 to 5 minutes, or until heated through.

7. Meanwhile, divide the shallots among the slices of toast, sprinkle them with Parmesan and broil for another minute, or until golden brown and fragrant. Divide the soup among 4 bowls, top with the toasts and serve. *Makes 4 servings*

NUTRITION INFORMATION

values are per serving

• • •

CALORIES	279	CALCIUM	137 MG
TOTAL FAT	4 G	IRON	4 MG
SATURATED FAT	1 G	POTASSIUM	563 MG
CHOLESTEROL	2 MG	BETA CAROTENE	3 MG
SODIUM	370 MG	VITAMIN C	20 MG
DIETARY FIBER	4 G	VITAMIN E	3 MG

CREAM OF TOMATO SOUP WITH CROUTONS

This soup has the same amount of protein—but one-sixth the fat and less than half the sodium—of canned tomato soup prepared with whole milk. The homemade version also has about one-third more vitamin C—as well a much more robust flavor.

One 14-ounce can plum tomatoes, with their liquid
1 cup tomato juice
½ pound small red potatoes, peeled and diced
1¼ cups diced red bell peppers
1 cup coarsely chopped onion
3 tablespoons chopped fresh coriander
1 garlic clove, peeled and crushed
¼ teaspoon black pepper
1 slice whole-wheat bread
¾ cup skim milk

1. Preheat the oven to 375°.

2. In a medium-size saucepan combine the tomatoes and their liquid, the tomato juice, potatoes, bell peppers, onion, 2 tablespoons of the coriander, the garlic and black pepper, and bring to a boil over medium heat. Cover the pan, reduce the heat to low and simmer 15 minutes.

3. Meanwhile, cut the bread into ½-inch cubes, spread them on a baking sheet and bake 5 to 10 minutes, or until golden; set aside to cool.

4. Remove the pan of soup from the heat and set aside to cool for a few minutes. Purée the soup in a food processor or blender 1 minute, or until smooth. With the machine running, gradually add the milk.

5. Return the soup to the pan and reheat it over medium-high heat; do not boil. Ladle the soup into bowls, top with croutons and garnish with the remaining coriander.   *Makes 4 servings*

NUTRITION INFORMATION
values are per serving

• • •

CALORIES	128	CALCIUM	111 MG
TOTAL FAT	0.9 G	IRON	2 MG
SATURATED FAT	0.2 G	POTASSIUM	739 MG
CHOLESTEROL	TRACE	BETA CAROTENE	0.7 MG
SODIUM	449 MG	VITAMIN C	93 MG
DIETARY FIBER	3 G	VITAMIN E	TRACE

TOMATO-RICE SOUP WITH BASIL

Keep a pot of cooked brown rice on hand to add body to soups; you'll also be boosting the fiber, iron and B vitamin content. To shorten the cooking time, soak the rice overnight in cold water.

> *2 pounds fresh, ripe tomatoes, or one 32-ounce*
> *   can tomatoes, with their liquid*
> *1½ cups cooked brown rice (½ cup raw)*

> *1 cup chopped celery*
> *½ cup chopped onion*
> *¼ cup chopped fresh basil*
> *3 tablespoons tomato paste*
> *2 garlic cloves, chopped*
> *1 tablespoon sugar*
> *Pinch of salt*
> *¼ teaspoon black pepper*
> *1 bay leaf*

1. If using fresh tomatoes, core and quarter them. Place the tomatoes in a large nonreactive pot and add ½ cup of the rice, the celery, onion, basil, tomato paste, garlic, sugar, salt, pepper, bay leaf and 1 quart of water. Bring the mixture to a boil over medium heat, then cover the pot, reduce the heat to low and simmer the soup about 30 minutes, stirring occasionally and breaking up the tomatoes with the edge of the spoon.

2. Remove the pot from the heat, uncover it and allow the soup to cool about 30 minutes; remove the bay leaf.

3. Transfer the soup to a food processor or blender, in 2 batches if necessary, and process until puréed.

4. Return the soup to the pot and stir in the remaining rice. Reheat the soup over medium heat. Divide it among 6 bowls and serve.   *Makes 6 servings*

NUTRITION INFORMATION
values are per serving

• • •

CALORIES	111	CALCIUM	48 MG
TOTAL FAT	0.8 G	IRON	2 MG
SATURATED FAT	0 G	POTASSIUM	503 MG
CHOLESTEROL	0 MG	BETA CAROTENE	1 MG
SODIUM	56 MG	VITAMIN C	32 MG
DIETARY FIBER	3 G	VITAMIN E	TRACE

CHINESE BEEF SAUTE

The Chinese serve lots of rice and vegetables with a small amount of meat, which keeps their meals high in carbohydrates and low in fat.

1 cup white rice
2 cups thinly sliced carrots
1 tablespoon vegetable oil
¼ pound lean beef flank steak, well-trimmed, cut into thin strips
1 red and 1 green bell pepper, cut into thin strips
1½ cups chopped scallions
3 garlic cloves, minced
2 cups shredded Chinese cabbage
½ pound fresh mushrooms, thinly sliced
16 water chestnuts, thinly sliced
3 tablespoons reduced-sodium soy sauce
2 tablespoons Japanese rice vinegar
1 teaspoon sugar
¼ teaspoon red pepper flakes

1. Bring 2 cups of water to a boil in a medium-size saucepan over medium-high heat and stir in the rice. Cover the pan, reduce the heat to medium-low and simmer 15 minutes, or until the rice is tender and the water is absorbed.

2. Meanwhile, bring a large saucepan of water to a boil. Blanch the carrots in the boiling water 3 minutes, or until crisp-tender; drain, cool under cold running water and set aside to drain thoroughly.

3. When the rice is cooked, remove the pan from the heat and set aside.

4. Heat the oil in a large nonstick skillet or wok over medium-high heat until hot but not smoking. Add the beef and sauté 3 to 4 minutes, or until browned. Using a slotted spoon, transfer the beef to a small bowl and set aside.

5. Add the bell peppers, scallions and garlic to the skillet and cook, stirring occasionally, 5 minutes. Add the carrots, cabbage, mushrooms and water chestnuts, increase the heat to high, and cook, stirring frequently, 5 minutes.

6. Meanwhile, in a small bowl, stir together the soy sauce, vinegar, sugar and red pepper flakes. Add

this mixture, the rice and the beef to the skillet, and cook, stirring constantly, 4 to 5 minutes, or until all the ingredients are heated through. Divide the mixture among 4 plates and serve.   *Makes 4 servings*

NUTRITION INFORMATION
values are per serving

• • •

CALORIES	349	CALCIUM	122 MG
TOTAL FAT	7 G	IRON	5 MG
SATURATED FAT	2 G	POTASSIUM	969 MG
CHOLESTEROL	12 MG	BETA CAROTENE	14 MG
SODIUM	521 MG	VITAMIN C	94 MG
DIETARY FIBER	6 G	VITAMIN E	4 MG

THREE-BEAN CHILI

Beefing up a bean dish with just a small amount of meat—in this case, two ounces of lean ground beef per serving—completes the protein in the beans.

⅔ cup each canned pinto (pink) beans, black beans and red kidney beans
½ pound lean ground beef
1 cup coarsely chopped onion
1 garlic clove, chopped
1½ cups coarsely chopped green bell pepper
1 cup sliced celery
2 teaspoons chili powder
1 teaspoon ground cumin
½ teaspoon ground oregano
2 cups coarsely chopped tomatoes
¼ cup tomato paste
1 cup reduced-sodium beef stock
2 cups hot cooked rice
2 cups Spicy Salsa (see page 54), or bottled salsa
½ cup coarsely chopped Spanish onion
½ cup shredded Cheddar cheese

1. Drain the beans thoroughly in a colander, rinse them well under cold running water and set them aside to drain again.

2. Heat a large nonstick saucepan over medium heat. Add the beef, onion and garlic to the pan and sauté until the beef is browned and the onion is translucent. Add 1 cup of the bell pepper and the celery, and continue cooking 5 to 7 minutes, or until the vegetables begin to soften. Add the chili powder, cumin and oregano, and sauté another minute. Add the tomatoes and tomato paste, the stock and the drained beans, reduce the heat to medium-low and simmer, partially covered, 30 minutes.

3. Divide the chili among 4 bowls and top each serving with ½ cup of rice and ½ cup of salsa. Sprinkle each serving with the remaining ½ cup of bell pepper, the Spanish onion and the Cheddar cheese.

Makes 4 servings

NUTRITION INFORMATION
values are per serving

• • •

CALORIES	495	CALCIUM	227 MG
TOTAL FAT	14 G	IRON	7 MG
SATURATED FAT	6 G	POTASSIUM	1500 MG
CHOLESTEROL	53 MG	BETA CAROTENE	2 MG
SODIUM	381 MG	VITAMIN C	94 MG
DIETARY FIBER	6 G	VITAMIN E	TRACE

BEEF ENCHILADAS

In Mexican restaurants, the food is often buried under a heavy layer of cheese. These hearty enchiladas, made with steak strips, vegetables and rice, are abundantly flavorful without any cheese at all.

1 tablespoon olive oil
2 cups finely chopped onion
1⅓ cups finely chopped green bell pepper
2 cups long-grain white rice
¼ teaspoon salt
2 teaspoons chili powder
½ teaspoon ground cumin
¼ teaspoon ground coriander
1 cup canned whole tomatoes, with their liquid
Eight 6-inch corn tortillas
¼ teaspoon turmeric
1 pound lean beef strip steak, well trimmed
2 cups shredded lettuce
2 medium-size fresh tomatoes, diced

½ cup frozen or canned corn kernels
1 medium-size avocado, peeled and thinly sliced
½ cup Spicy Salsa (see page 54), or bottled salsa

1. Heat the oil in a large saucepan over medium-low heat. Add 1 cup of the onions and ⅔ cup of the peppers and sauté 4 minutes, or until the vegetables are soft. Add the rice, salt and half of the chili powder, cumin and coriander, and cook, stirring constantly, 1 minute. Add 4 cups of water and the canned tomatoes with their liquid, and bring to a boil. Reduce the heat to low and simmer, covered, 20 minutes.

2. Meanwhile, preheat the broiler.

3. Wrap the tortillas tightly in foil and place them on the lower rack of the oven to heat.

4. In a small bowl, combine the turmeric with the remaining chili powder, cumin and coriander.

5. Cut the steak in half lengthwise and sprinkle it on all sides with the chili-powder mixture. Place the steak on a broiler pan and broil it 5 inches from the heat for 3 minutes, then turn the steak and broil it another 2 minutes, or until the juices run pink when the meat is pierced. Turn off the broiler, leaving the tortillas in the oven. Slice the steak into 24 thin strips.

6. When the rice is cooked, in a large bowl toss together the remaining onions and peppers, the lettuce, fresh tomatoes and corn. Unwrap the tortillas and lay each one on a plate. Spread ¼ cup of rice on each tortilla and top with 3 strips of steak. Divide the vegetable mixture among the tortillas, garnish with avocado slices and drizzle 1 tablespoon of salsa over each enchilada. Serve the remaining rice on the side.

Makes 8 servings

NUTRITION INFORMATION
values are per serving

• • •

CALORIES	428	CALCIUM	95 MG
TOTAL FAT	12 G	IRON	5 MG
SATURATED FAT	3 G	POTASSIUM	738 MG
CHOLESTEROL	39 MG	BETA CAROTENE	0.9 MG
SODIUM	252 MG	VITAMIN C	37 MG
DIETARY FIBER	5 G	VITAMIN E	TRACE

Beef Enchiladas

VEAL SCALOPPINI WITH GREMOLATA

Veal scaloppini—slices of lean veal leg that have been pounded thin—cook in minutes and are a fine choice for a heart-healthy diet. Gremolata is a Milanese specialty, a bright-tasting sauce of chopped parsley, citrus zest and garlic that is usually served with *osso buco* (braised veal shanks).

¼ cup fine unseasoned bread crumbs
¾ teaspoon oregano
¼ teaspoon black pepper
1 egg white
8 veal scaloppini (about 1 pound total)
1 tablespoon olive or other vegetable oil
½ cup chicken stock
1 teaspoon grated lemon zest
2 teaspoons grated orange zest
2 tablespoons lemon juice
1 teaspoon cornstarch
1 garlic clove, minced or crushed through a press
2 tablespoons chopped parsley

1. In a shallow bowl, combine the bread crumbs, oregano and pepper. In another shallow bowl, beat the egg white. Dip the veal in the beaten egg white, then lightly dredge the veal in the seasoned bread-crumbs.

2. In a large skillet, warm the oil over medium-high heat until hot but not smoking. Add the veal and sauté until golden on both sides, about 3 minutes total. Remove the veal to a plate and cover loosely to keep warm.

3. In a small bowl, stir together the chicken stock, lemon zest, orange zest, lemon juice, cornstarch, garlic and parsley. Add this mixture to the skillet and stir to combine. Bring the mixture to a boil, return the veal (and any juices that have accumulated on the plate) to the skillet and cook until heated through, about 1 minute.

4. Top the veal with the pan juices and serve.

Makes 4 servings

NUTRITION INFORMATION
values are per serving

• • •

CALORIES	215	CALCIUM	38 MG
TOTAL FAT	10 G	IRON	1 MG
SATURATED FAT	3 G	POTASSIUM	368 MG
CHOLESTEROL	88 MG	BETA CAROTENE	0 MG
SODIUM	161 MG	VITAMIN C	8 MG
DIETARY FIBER	TRACE	VITAMIN E	TRACE

VEAL PATTIES IN BASIL CREAM SAUCE

Evaporated skimmed milk is something of a miracle ingredient for healthy cooking. It is as thick as heavy cream, but contains not a speck of fat. Thickened further with a little flour, it makes a rich sauce.

4 medium scallions
¼ cup (packed) basil leaves
1 egg white
½ pound ground veal
⅓ cup fine unseasoned bread crumbs
¾ cup evaporated skimmed milk
½ teaspoon nutmeg
¼ teaspoon allspice
¼ teaspoon black pepper
1 tablespoon olive oil
1 tablespoon flour
1 cup low-sodium chicken stock

1. Finely chop the scallions. Mince the basil.
2. In a medium-size bowl, beat the egg white until frothy. Stir in the scallions, half the basil, the

veal, bread crumbs, ¼ cup of the evaporated skimmed milk, the nutmeg, allspice and pepper. Form the mixture into 4 patties a scant ½ inch thick.

3. In a large nonstick skillet, warm the oil over medium-high heat until hot but not smoking. Add the patties and cook until browned, 3 to 4 minutes per side. Remove the patties to a plate and cover loosely to keep warm.

4. In a small bowl, combine the remaining ½ cup evaporated skimmed milk and the flour, and blend well.

5. Add the chicken stock to the skillet and bring to a boil over medium-high heat, scraping up any browned bits from the bottom of the pan. Stir in the flour-milk mixture and cook, stirring, until the sauce has thickened slightly, about 2 minutes.

6. Stir the remaining basil into the skillet. Return the veal patties (and any juices that have accumulated on the plate) to the skillet and cook until the patties are heated through and well coated with the sauce, 1 to 2 minutes.

Makes 4 servings

NUTRITION INFORMATION
values are per serving

• • •

CALORIES	182	CALCIUM	205 MG
TOTAL FAT	7 G	IRON	2 MG
SATURATED FAT	2 G	POTASSIUM	452 MG
CHOLESTEROL	36 MG	BETA CAROTENE	TRACE
SODIUM	199 MG	VITAMIN C	4 MG
DIETARY FIBER	TRACE	VITAMIN E	TRACE

LAMB AND MUSHROOM STEW WITH ROSEMARY

Fat "carries" flavor in food, so lowfat meals often require slightly more assertive seasoning than richer dishes do. This tomato-based stew, made with just a tablespoon of oil, is flavored with pungent rosemary and garlic; parsley and bay leaf add subtler notes.

2 tablespoons unbleached all-purpose flour
¼ teaspoon each salt and black pepper
½ pound lean stewing lamb, well-trimmed,
    cut into 1-inch cubes
1 tablespoon olive oil

One 14-ounce can plum tomatoes, with their liquid
¼ pound small fresh mushrooms
1 garlic clove, crushed and peeled
1 bay leaf
¾ teaspoon fresh rosemary, or ¼ teaspoon dried rosemary, crumbled
2 tablespoons chopped fresh parsley
1 cup long-grain white rice
½ cup frozen peas, thawed

1. Mix the flour, salt and pepper on a sheet of waxed paper and dredge the lamb cubes in the mixture. Reserve the excess flour.

2. Heat the oil in a large nonstick skillet over medium heat, add the lamb and sauté 5 to 10 minutes, or until the meat is well browned all over. Add the remaining flour mixture and cook, stirring, 1 minute. Add the tomatoes and their liquid, the mushrooms, garlic, bay leaf, rosemary and 1 tablespoon of the parsley and bring to a boil. Reduce the heat to medium-low, cover the pan and simmer the stew 30 minutes.

3. Meanwhile, bring 3 cups of water to a boil in a medium-size saucepan. Stir in the rice, cover the pan, reduce the heat to medium-low and simmer 20 minutes, or until the rice is tender and the water is completely absorbed.

4. Remove the bay leaf from the stew and stir in the peas. Cover the pan and let stand 5 minutes, then divide the rice among 4 plates, spoon the stew over it and sprinkle with the remaining parsley.

Makes 4 servings

NUTRITION INFORMATION
values are per serving

• • •

CALORIES	336	CALCIUM	61 MG
TOTAL FAT	8 G	IRON	5 MG
SATURATED FAT	2 G	POTASSIUM	532 MG
CHOLESTEROL	34 MG	BETA CAROTENE	0.5 MG
SODIUM	342 MG	VITAMIN C	20 MG
DIETARY FIBER	3 G	VITAMIN E	TRACE

LAMB MEDALLIONS WITH TOMATO-MINT SALSA

Fresh tomato salsa is more commonly made with fresh coriander, but for this dish, mint—a classic partner for lamb—is used instead. Mint is also added to the basting sauce for the lamb.

⅓ cup packed fresh mint leaves, or 1 tablespoon dried
2 tablespoons olive or other vegetable oil
4 garlic cloves, minced or crushed through a press
¾ teaspoon salt
½ teaspoon black pepper
8 small boneless loin lamb medallions
    (1½ to 1¾ pounds total), well trimmed
1½ cups quartered cherry tomatoes
2 tablespoons cider vinegar
2 teaspoons sugar
Pinch of ground red pepper

1. Preheat the broiler; line a broiler pan with foil.

2. In a food processor, finely chop the fresh mint; remove and set aside. (Do not clean the work bowl.)

3. In a small bowl, combine the oil, garlic, half of the mint, ½ teaspoon of the salt and the pepper.

4. Place the lamb medallions on the broiler pan. Brush the lamb with half of the mint oil. Broil the lamb 4 inches from the heat 8 minutes.

5. Turn the lamb over, brush with the remaining mint oil and broil 4 inches from the heat about 8 minutes for medium-rare; about 10 minutes for medium; about 12 minutes for well-done.

6. Meanwhile, in a medium-size bowl, combine the tomatoes, remaining mint, vinegar, sugar, ground red pepper and remaining ¼ teaspoon salt.

7. Serve the lamb with the tomato-mint salsa on the side. *Makes 4 servings*

NUTRITION INFORMATION
values are per serving

• • •

CALORIES	356	CALCIUM	39 MG
TOTAL FAT	19 G	IRON	3 MG
SATURATED FAT	5 G	POTASSIUM	629 MG
CHOLESTEROL	119 MG	BETA CAROTENE	0.5 MG
SODIUM	511 MG	VITAMIN C	13 MG
DIETARY FIBER	TRACE	VITAMIN E	TRACE

Lamb Kebabs with Cucumber-Yogurt Sauce

LAMB KEBABS WITH CUCUMBER-YOGURT SAUCE

Broiling is one of the best cooking techniques for meat because it allows the fat to drain away: A broiler pan with a rack will facilitate the process. For easy cleanup, line the lower pan with foil.

¾ cup lemon juice

2 teaspoons olive oil

2 garlic cloves, minced

¼ teaspoon salt

½ teaspoon ground cumin

¼ teaspoon ground red pepper

½ pound boneless lean leg of lamb, well-trimmed,
cut into 1-inch cubes

1 medium-size cucumber

½ cup plain lowfat yogurt

½ cup chopped fresh mint leaves

1 cup couscous

1 pint cherry tomatoes

1 large onion, cut into wedges

1 green and 1 red bell pepper, cut into 1-inch squares

10 pitted prunes, cut into ¼-inch dice

1. In a small bowl stir together ½ cup of the lemon juice, the oil, garlic, salt, cumin and ground red pepper. Add the lamb cubes and set aside to marinate 1 hour at room temperature.

2. Meanwhile, for the sauce, peel, seed, grate and squeeze dry the cucumber; you should have about ½ cup. In a small bowl, combine the cucumber, yogurt, mint and remaining lemon juice. Stir well, cover and refrigerate until ready to serve.

3. Fifteen minutes before serving, preheat the broiler.

4. Bring 1½ cups of water to a boil in a small saucepan. Place the couscous in a medium-size heatproof bowl, pour the boiling water over it and cover the bowl tightly; set the couscous aside to steam 10 minutes.

5. Meanwhile, thread the lamb cubes, tomatoes, onion wedges and bell pepper squares alternately on 6 skewers. Broil the kebabs 4 inches from the heat 4 minutes, then turn and broil another 4 minutes.

6. Uncover the couscous and fluff it with a fork. Add the prunes and mix well. Turn the couscous

onto a platter, arrange the kebabs on top, and serve the cucumber-yogurt sauce on the side.

Makes 6 servings

NUTRITION INFORMATION
values are per serving

· · ·

CALORIES	256	CALCIUM	72 MG
TOTAL FAT	4 G	IRON	2 MG
SATURATED FAT	1 G	POTASSIUM	500 MG
CHOLESTEROL	24 MG	BETA CAROTENE	0.6 MG
SODIUM	128 MG	VITAMIN C	59 MG
DIETARY FIBER	7 G	VITAMIN E	TRACE

LAMB IN PITA BREAD

Pitas, Near-Eastern pocket breads, are usually made without fat, although sometimes they do include a small amount of oil. These versatile hollow breads come in several sizes and a variety of flavors, including white, whole-wheat, onion and sesame.

½ pound lean loin lamb, well trimmed, cut into
1-inch cubes

Eight 6-inch pitas

¼ cup chopped onion

½ cup chopped green bell pepper

2 garlic cloves, crushed

8-ounce can whole tomatoes, with their liquid

1 cup cooked chickpeas

¼ cup chopped black olives

1½ teaspoons chopped fresh rosemary, or ½ teaspoon
dried rosemary, crumbled

¼ teaspoon cinnamon

1 cup plain lowfat yogurt

¼ cup chopped fresh mint

¼ teaspoon freshly ground black pepper

¼ cup crumbled feta cheese

1. Place the lamb in a food processor and process just until ground. Set aside.

2. Preheat the oven to 300°.

3. Stack the pitas, wrap in foil and set aside.

4. In a medium-size nonstick skillet, brown the lamb, onion, bell pepper and garlic over medium-high heat, stirring constantly until the lamb is no longer pink; spoon the lamb mixture into a strainer to drain the fat and return to the skillet. Add the tomatoes and their liquid, the chickpeas, olives, rosemary and cinnamon, stirring and mashing the chickpeas and tomatoes with a spoon, and cook until heated through.

5. Meanwhile, heat the pitas in the oven.

6. Combine the yogurt, mint and pepper in a small bowl; set aside.

7. Add the cheese to the skillet and heat until the cheese melts.

8. Cut a small slice from the top of each pita. Spoon the lamb mixture into the pitas and top with the yogurt mixture.   *Makes 8 servings*

NUTRITION INFORMATION
values are per serving

• • •

CALORIES	248	CALCIUM	150 MG
TOTAL FAT	8 G	IRON	2 MG
SATURATED FAT	3 G	POTASSIUM	328 MG
CHOLESTEROL	27 MG	BETA CAROTENE	TRACE
SODIUM	405 MG	VITAMIN C	12 MG
DIETARY FIBER	2 G	VITAMIN E	0 MG

LAMB CURRY

Many Indian lamb dishes are cooked with yogurt sauces because their creamy smoothness provides a perfect foil for pungent spices. Yogurt can break, or curdle, if cooked at high temperatures, but here it is stirred into the sauce after the pan has been taken off the heat, so there's no chance of spoiling the dish. Cauliflower and green beans, favorite Indian vegetables, round out the dish nutritionally and make for generous portions.

1 tablespoon plus 1 teaspoon peanut oil
1 cup coarsely chopped onion
1 teaspoon minced garlic
½ teaspoon red pepper flakes
1 bay leaf
1 teaspoon curry powder
1 teaspoon turmeric
½ pound lean lamb, well-trimmed, cut into
   2 x ¼-inch strips
1 cup tomato purée

¾ cup golden raisins
1 tablespoon red wine vinegar
½ teaspoon salt
2 cups cauliflower florets, cut into ½-inch pieces
2 cups green beans, cut into 2-inch pieces
1 cup long-grain white rice
½ cup plain lowfat yogurt

1. In a heavy saucepan or Dutch oven, heat the oil over medium heat. Sauté the onion and garlic with the red pepper flakes, bay leaf and half of the curry powder and turmeric, stirring occasionally, about 5 minutes, or until the onion is wilted and fragrant. Stir in the lamb strips and cook 2 to 3 minutes, or until browned on all sides. Stir in 2 cups of water, the tomato purée, raisins, vinegar, salt and remaining curry powder and turmeric. Bring to a boil, cover and simmer 45 minutes, or until the lamb is tender.

2. While the lamb is cooking, bring 1 inch of water to a boil in a medium-size saucepan. Place the cauliflower and green beans in a vegetable steamer and steam 7 to 10 minutes, or just until tender; remove from the pan and set aside.

3. In the same saucepan, bring 2½ cups of water to a boil. Stir in the rice, cover, reduce the heat to low and cook 20 minutes, or until the water is absorbed.

4. When the lamb is tender, add the cauliflower and beans, cover and simmer another 5 minutes, or until heated through. Remove the pan from the heat; remove and discard the bay leaf. Stir the yogurt into the curry and serve immediately over the rice.

Makes 4 servings

NUTRITION INFORMATION
values are per serving

• • •

CALORIES	482	CALCIUM	160 MG
TOTAL FAT	10 G	IRON	6 MG
SATURATED FAT	3 G	POTASSIUM	988 MG
CHOLESTEROL	39 MG	BETA CAROTENE	0.8 MG
SODIUM	341 MG	VITAMIN C	67 MG
DIETARY FIBER	5 G	VITAMIN E	2 MG

Garlic-Studded Pork Loin with Potatoes and Carrots

Pork is much leaner than it used to be: Thanks to modern breeding and feeding methods, pork is more than 30 percent lower in fat than it was a decade ago.

⅓ cup frozen pineapple juice concentrate, thawed
3 tablespoons Dijon mustard
1 teaspoon reduced-sodium soy sauce
¼ teaspoon salt
¼ teaspoon black pepper
6 garlic cloves
1 small boneless pork loin (about 1¾ pounds), trimmed and tied
1 cup chicken stock
1 pound small red potatoes, unpeeled
3 medium-size carrots
2 teaspoons cornstarch

1. Preheat the oven to 425°.

2. In a small bowl, combine the pineapple juice concentrate, mustard, soy sauce, salt and pepper.

3. Peel the garlic and cut each clove lengthwise into thirds. With a sharp knife, make 18 slits randomly in the pork loin. Tuck a piece of garlic into each slit.

4. Place the pork loin in a small roasting pan and brush the pork with half of the pineapple-mustard mixture. Pour ½ cup of the chicken stock into the bottom of the pan. Roast the pork loin 30 minutes.

5. Meanwhile, quarter the potatoes. Cut the carrots into ½-inch-thick slices. Spray a shallow pan with nonstick cooking spray, place the vegetables in the pan and roast them until the pork is done.

6. Reduce the oven temperature to 350°. Brush the pork with the remaining pineapple-mustard mixture and continue roasting until it is cooked through and the internal temperature registers 160° on a meat thermometer, about 45 minutes longer.

7. Remove the pork from the roasting pan and let it rest for 5 minutes before slicing. Meanwhile, skim and discard the fat from the pan juices. Stir together the cornstarch and the remaining ½ cup stock.

8. Add the stock mixture to the roasting pan and set over medium-low heat. Stir to incorporate any browned bits clinging to the pan and cook 2 to 3 minutes, or until the sauce is slightly thickened.

9. Slice the pork and serve it with the roasted vegetables and sauce.   *Makes 8 servings*

Nutrition Information
values are per serving

• • •

CALORIES	207	CALCIUM	25 MG
TOTAL FAT	6 G	IRON	1 MG
SATURATED FAT	2 G	POTASSIUM	563 MG
CHOLESTEROL	42 MG	BETA CAROTENE	5 MG
SODIUM	395 MG	VITAMIN C	15 MG
DIETARY FIBER	2 G	VITAMIN E	TRACE

Pear-Braised Pork Chops with Cabbage

The loin is one of the leanest cuts of pork (and of beef, veal and lamb as well). To further reduce the fat content, trim any visible fat from the edges of the chops before cooking them.

1 small Bosc or Anjou pear
1 small onion
¼ pound green cabbage
2 tablespoons cornstarch
½ teaspoon salt
½ teaspoon black pepper
Four ¼-inch-thick lean center-cut loin pork chops (about ¾ pound total), well trimmed
1 tablespoon vegetable oil
½ cup frozen apple juice concentrate, thawed
1 tablespoon lemon juice
½ teaspoon caraway seeds, lightly crushed

1. Core and peel the pear and chop it roughly. In a food processor with shredding blade, shred the pear, onion and cabbage.

2. In a shallow bowl, combine the cornstarch with ¼ teaspoon of the salt and ¼ teaspoon of the pepper. Dredge the pork lightly in the seasoned cornstarch, reserving the excess.

3. In a large nonstick skillet, warm the oil over medium-high heat until hot but not smoking. Add the pork chops and cook 5 minutes per side.

4. Slowly add the apple juice concentrate and bring the liquid back to a boil. Reduce the heat to medium-low, cover and simmer 5 minutes. Remove the pork chops to a plate and cover loosely.

5. Add the shredded pear, onion and cabbage to the skillet. Increase the heat to medium-high and bring the mixture to a boil.

6. Meanwhile, in a small bowl, stir together the reserved cornstarch mixture and the lemon juice.

7. Add the caraway seeds, the remaining ¼ teaspoon salt and ¼ teaspoon pepper, and the cornstarch mixture, and stir until slightly thickened. Reduce the heat to medium-low, cover and simmer, stirring occasionally, 5 minutes, or until the cabbage is just tender.

8. Return the pork chops to the pan and cook them 1 to 2 minutes, or until heated through. Serve the pork chops topped with some of the cabbage and pear. *Makes 4 servings*

NUTRITION INFORMATION
values are per serving

• • •

CALORIES	270	CALCIUM	35 MG
TOTAL FAT	12 G	IRON	1 MG
SATURATED FAT	3 G	POTASSIUM	513 MG
CHOLESTEROL	51 MG	BETA CAROTENE	0 MG
SODIUM	322 MG	VITAMIN C	18 MG
DIETARY FIBER	1 G	VITAMIN E	4 MG

MEDALLIONS OF PORK WITH SWEET-AND-SOUR CABBAGE

A little pork goes a long way in this German-style dish; sautéed apples and cabbage complement its flavor and add complex carbohydrates.

Four ¼-inch-thick center-cut lean loin pork medallions
  (¾ pound total weight), well-trimmed
2 tablespoons Dijon mustard
1 pound small new potatoes
1 medium-size apple
2 tablespoons olive oil
2 tablespoons brown sugar
4 cups shredded red cabbage
2 tablespoons cider vinegar

½ cup unsweetened apple juice
¼ cup chopped fresh parsley
2 teaspoons margarine
2 tablespoons unbleached all-purpose flour
2 tablespoons sherry

1. Spread the pork with mustard, wrap it loosely in plastic wrap and set refrigerate until needed.

2. Scrub the potatoes, place them in a medium-size saucepan with cold water to cover and bring to a boil over medium-high heat. Cover the pan, reduce the heat to medium-low and simmer the potatoes 20 minutes, or until tender.

3. Meanwhile, wash but do not peel the apple. Core and quarter it and cut it into ¼-inch-thick slices. Heat 1 tablespoon of the olive oil in a medium-size skillet over medium-high heat until hot but not smoking. Add the apple and sauté 3 minutes. Sprinkle the apple with the sugar and cook 1 minute, or until the sugar dissolves. Add the cabbage, vinegar and apple juice, bring to a boil and cover the skillet. Reduce the heat to medium and cook 5 minutes, then uncover the skillet and increase the heat to medium-high. Cook, stirring constantly, 5 minutes, or until the liquid is almost completely evaporated. Remove the skillet from the heat, stir in 3 tablespoons of the parsley, cover and set aside.

4. Drain and halve the potatoes, return them to the warm pan and toss them with the margarine and the remaining parsley; cover and set aside.

5. Heat the remaining 1 tablespoon of oil in a medium-size nonstick skillet over medium-high heat until hot but not smoking. Dredge the pork medallions in the flour and cook them 1 to 2 minutes on each side, or until they are golden-brown all over. Add the sherry and 1 tablespoon of water, and cook 1 minute more, or until the pan juices thicken. Divide the pork medallions, the potatoes and the cabbage mixture among 4 plates and serve. *Makes 4 servings*

NUTRITION INFORMATION
values are per serving

• • •

CALORIES	414	CALCIUM	66 MG
TOTAL FAT	17 G	IRON	3 MG
SATURATED FAT	4 G	POTASSIUM	915 MG
CHOLESTEROL	53 MG	BETA CAROTENE	TRACE
SODIUM	238 MG	VITAMIN C	59 MG
DIETARY FIBER	4 G	VITAMIN E	3 MG

Lettuce-Wrapped Spring Rolls

LETTUCE-WRAPPED SPRING ROLLS

Standard Chinese spring rolls are deep-fried. These lettuce-wrapped rolls, filled mostly with vegetables, have much less fat and more fiber than fried ones.

6 ounces ⅛-inch-wide rice noodles
1 tablespoon plus 1 teaspoon grated fresh ginger
2 tablespoons reduced-sodium soy sauce
2 tablespoons Japanese rice vinegar
1½ tablespoons honey
1 cup shredded carrots
½ cup thinly sliced scallions
1 tablespoon cornstarch
¼ teaspoon salt
2 teaspoons vegetable oil
½ pound well-trimmed lean pork loin, finely chopped

2 teaspoons Chinese chili oil
2 garlic cloves
2 cups julienned nappa cabbage
1 cup bean sprouts
12 large Boston or red leaf lettuce leaves
1 tablespoon chopped unsalted dry-roasted peanuts

1. Bring 2 quarts of water to a boil. Place the noodles in a large heatproof bowl, pour the water over them and set aside 7 minutes. Drain the noodles and cool under cold water. Return 3 cups of noodles to the bowl and add 1 teaspoon of the ginger, 1½ tablespoons of the soy sauce, 1 tablespoon plus 1 teaspoon of the vinegar, 1 teaspoon of the honey, ¼ cup of the carrot and ¼ cup of the scallions; toss to combine and set aside.

2. Coarsely chop the remaining noodles; set aside.

3. In a small bowl mix the cornstarch, salt, the remaining soy sauce, vinegar, honey and 2 tablespoons of water; set aside.

4. Heat the vegetable oil in a wok or large skillet over medium-high heat. Stir-fry the pork and remaining scallions 2 minutes, or until the pork is opaque and cooked through; transfer to a large bowl.

5. Add the chili oil to the wok and stir-fry the garlic and remaining ginger 1 minute. Add the cabbage, bean sprouts and remaining carrot, and stir-fry 1 minute. Add the cornstarch mixture and cook another minute, then add the vegetable mixture to the bowl with the pork. Stir in the chopped noodles.

6. Spoon equal amounts of the pork mixture onto each of 8 lettuce leaves and roll the leaves up; divide among 4 plates. Place the remaining lettuce leaves on the plates to serve as cups and fill them with the noodle-vegetable mixture. Sprinkle the noodles with chopped peanuts and serve.

Makes 4 servings

NUTRITION INFORMATION
values are per serving

• • •

CALORIES	368	CALCIUM	75 MG
TOTAL FAT	11 G	IRON	2 MG
SATURATED FAT	3 G	POTASSIUM	506 MG
CHOLESTEROL	35 MG	BETA CAROTENE	5 MG
SODIUM	482 MG	VITAMIN C	24 MG
DIETARY FIBER	2 G	VITAMIN E	4 MG

CHICKEN WITH GRAPES

Dried mushrooms, which lend an intensely savory, almost "meaty" taste—but no fat—to soups and sauces, are one of the flavor secrets of health-minded cooks. Italian *porcini* are especially flavorful, but can be pricey. Less expensive are Polish dried mushrooms, which can be found in the gourmet sections of most supermarkets.

1¼ cups brown rice
1 ounce dried mushrooms, such as porcini
2 shallots, thinly sliced
2 tablespoons olive oil
4 skinless chicken breast halves, with bone in (about 1½ pounds total weight)
1 cup coarsely chopped celery
½ teaspoon dried thyme
1 bay leaf
Pinch of salt
Pinch of black pepper
¼ cup low-sodium chicken stock
2 cups seedless green grapes
1 teaspoon cornstarch

1. Bring 3 cups of water to a boil in a medium-size saucepan over medium-high heat. Stir in the rice, cover, reduce the heat to low and simmer 45 minutes, or until the rice is tender and the water is completely absorbed.

2. While the rice is cooking, place the mushrooms in a small bowl, pour 1 cup of hot water over them and set aside to soak about 20 minutes.

3. In a medium-size nonstick skillet over medium heat, sauté the shallots in 1 tablespoon of the olive oil 2 minutes. Add the remaining 1 tablespoon of olive oil to the skillet, then add the chicken breasts and cook about 2 minutes on each side, or until lightly browned.

4. Strain the mushroom-soaking liquid and add it to the chicken, then add the mushrooms, celery, thyme, bay leaf, salt, pepper and stock. Reduce the heat to low, cover and simmer the chicken 15 to 20 minutes, or until tender. Add 1½ cups of grapes and simmer another 5 minutes.

5. In a small bowl combine the cornstarch with ½ cup cold water and stir well. Stir the cornstarch mixture into the chicken sauce and cook about 2 minutes, or until the sauce is slightly thickened. Divide the rice among 4 plates and place one chicken-breast half on each plate. Spoon the sauce and grapes over the chicken and garnish with the remaining grapes.

Makes 4 servings

NUTRITION INFORMATION
values are per serving

• • •

CALORIES	530	CALCIUM	55 MG
TOTAL FAT	13 G	IRON	3 MG
SATURATED FAT	3 G	POTASSIUM	741 MG
CHOLESTEROL	80 MG	BETA CAROTENE	TRACE
SODIUM	144 MG	VITAMIN C	11 MG
DIETARY FIBER	4 G	VITAMIN E	2 MG

INDIAN CHICKEN WITH VEGETABLES

Tandoori chicken, a renowned dish from northwestern India, is traditionally cooked in urn-shaped clay ovens that reach very high temperatures. Here, skinless chicken breasts are marinated, tandoori-style, in yogurt and spices, then baked in a hot oven along with chunks of satisfying root vegetables.

2 skinless, boneless chicken breast halves
½ cup plain lowfat yogurt
1 tablespoon lemon juice
1 teaspoon curry powder
½ teaspoon ground cumin
⅛ teaspoon ground red pepper
½ teaspoon salt
½ teaspoon black pepper
2 large baking potatoes (about 1 pound total weight)
1 large sweet potato
½ pound carrots
½ pound onions
5 garlic cloves
1½ tablespoons olive oil
1½ tablespoons chopped fresh coriander

1. Cut each chicken breast into two pieces.
2. In a glass bowl stir together the yogurt, lemon juice, curry powder, cumin, ground red pepper, ¼ teaspoon of the salt and ¼ teaspoon of the black pepper. Add the chicken, turning it to coat it evenly with the marinade. Cover the bowl with plastic wrap and let stand at room temperature 1 hour (or marinate the chicken in the refrigerator up to 24 hours).
3. Meanwhile, wash and peel all the potatoes. Wash and trim the carrots; peel the onions and garlic cloves. Cut the potatoes, carrots and onions into 1-inch pieces; mince the garlic cloves; set aside.
4. Preheat the oven to 400°.
5. Combine the vegetables in a large baking dish, sprinkle them with the oil and the remaining salt and pepper, and toss to coat the vegetables with oil. Bake 30 minutes, or until the potatoes are softened. Add the chicken and marinade to the baking dish and stir to combine. Cover the dish with foil, reduce the oven temperature to 350° and bake another 30 minutes, or until the chicken is tender. Transfer the chicken and vegetables to a serving dish, sprinkle with coriander and serve. *Makes 4 servings*

NUTRITION INFORMATION
values are per serving

• • •

CALORIES	441	CALCIUM	126 MG
TOTAL FAT	14 G	IRON	3 MG
SATURATED FAT	3 G	POTASSIUM	1121 MG
CHOLESTEROL	85 MG	BETA CAROTENE	15 MG
SODIUM	386 MG	VITAMIN C	37 MG
DIETARY FIBER	6 G	VITAMIN E	4 MG

CHICKEN SCALOPPINI WITH PEPPERS

A traditional scaloppini recipe might call for 4 tablespoons of butter rather than the 4 teaspoons of olive oil used in this lighter version.

1 lemon
4 skinless, boneless chicken breast halves (about 1 pound)
2 tablespoons flour
¼ teaspoon salt
⅛ teaspoon freshly ground black pepper
4 teaspoons olive oil
1 garlic clove, crushed
1 green, 1 red and 1 yellow bell pepper, cut into ¼-inch-wide strips
⅓ cup dry white wine
½ cup low-sodium chicken stock
2 teaspoons cornstarch
1 tablespoon finely chopped parsley

1. Halve the lemon and slice one half; squeeze 1 tablespoon of juice from the other half.
2. Cut the chicken breasts in half crosswise and pound gently to flatten them. Sprinkle the chicken with flour, salt and pepper, and pat in the coating.
3. Heat the oil and garlic in a large nonstick skillet over medium-high heat until the oil is hot but not smoking. Discard the garlic. Add a single layer of chicken pieces to the skillet, increase the heat to high and sauté about 1 minute on each side, or until golden brown. Transfer the cooked chicken to a platter and cover loosely to keep warm. Sauté the remaining chicken and transfer it to the platter.
4. Add the peppers, wine and lemon juice to the skillet, and cook, covered, over medium-low heat 5

minutes, or until the peppers are slightly softened. Uncover and cook over high heat 5 minutes to reduce the sauce to about 2 tablespoons.

5. Stir together the stock and cornstarch, then stir this mixture into the sauce. Bring to a boil and cook 1 minute. Stir in the parsley. Pour the sauce and peppers over the chicken and garnish with the reserved lemon slices. *Makes 4 servings*

NUTRITION INFORMATION
values are per serving

• • •

CALORIES	228	CALCIUM	25 MG
TOTAL FAT	8 G	IRON	2 MG
SATURATED FAT	2 G	POTASSIUM	392 MG
CHOLESTEROL	70 MG	BETA CAROTENE	TRACE
SODIUM	217 MG	VITAMIN C	75 MG
DIETARY FIBER	1 G	VITAMIN E	1 MG

MOROCCAN STEW

Chicken combined with vegetables, fruit, legumes and nuts makes an abundantly nutritious meal.

½ pound acorn squash, peeled and cut into ¾-inch dice
1 medium red bell pepper, cut into ½-inch-wide strips
2 carrots, cut into ¼-inch diagonal slices
1 cup low-sodium chicken stock
4 teaspoons olive oil
1 medium-size onion, cut into ¼-inch dice
1 pound skinless, boneless chicken breast
3 garlic cloves, minced
One 14-ounce can plum tomatoes, with their liquid
1 medium-size zucchini, cut into ¼-inch-thick slices
¼ cup golden raisins
¼ teaspoon salt
¼ teaspoon black pepper
⅛ teaspoon ground cinnamon
Dash of hot pepper sauce
½ cup cooked chickpeas, drained and rinsed
2 tablespoons sliced toasted almonds
2 teaspoons chopped fresh mint

1. Place the acorn squash, bell pepper, carrots and stock in a medium-size saucepan, cover and cook over medium heat 10 minutes, or until the vegetables are crisp-tender; set aside.

2. Heat 2 teaspoons of the oil in a large nonstick skillet over medium-high heat. Add the onion, and cook, stirring occasionally, 3 to 5 minutes, or until the onion is golden. Transfer the onion to a plate and set aside.

3. Cut the chicken into ½-inch cubes.

4. Heat the remaining oil in the skillet, then add the chicken and garlic, and cook 5 minutes, or just until the chicken is browned. Transfer the chicken and garlic to the plate with the onion.

5. In the same skillet, combine the tomatoes and their liquid, the zucchini, raisins, salt, black pepper, cinnamon and hot pepper sauce. Bring the mixture to a boil, breaking up the tomatoes with a spoon, and simmer about 5 minutes, or until the vegetables are tender.

6. Add the squash mixture and cook about 4 minutes more to combine the flavors. Return the onion, chicken and garlic to the skillet, then add the chickpeas, and cook 2 minutes, or until the ingredients are heated through.

7. Spoon the stew into 4 bowls and top with almonds and mint. *Makes 4 servings*

NUTRITION INFORMATION
values are per serving

• • •

CALORIES	335	CALCIUM	112 MG
TOTAL FAT	10 G	IRON	4 MG
SATURATED FAT	2 G	POTASSIUM	1116 MG
CHOLESTEROL	60 MG	BETA CAROTENE	7 MG
SODIUM	405 MG	VITAMIN C	66 MG
DIETARY FIBER	5 G	VITAMIN E	1 MG

STIR-FRIED CHICKEN AND VEGETABLES

If the fresh shiitake mushrooms called for here are not available, substitute fresh white mushrooms.

1⅓ cups brown rice
1 tablespoon plus 1 teaspoon Oriental sesame oil
3 cups broccoli florets
6 ounces parsnips, cut into 2¼-inch strips
1 medium-size onion, sliced
½ red bell pepper, cut into ¼-inch-wide strips

1½ teaspoons grated fresh ginger
1½ teaspoons minced garlic
1 teaspoon red pepper flakes
10 ounces skinless, boneless chicken breast,
     cut into 2 x ¼-inch strips
4 cups packed spinach leaves
5 ounces fresh shiitake mushrooms, trimmed and sliced
     (2 cups)
¼ cup roasted cashews
2 tablespoons Japanese rice vinegar
1½ teaspoons reduced-sodium soy sauce
¼ teaspoon salt

1. Bring 3¼ cups of water to a boil in a medium-size saucepan. Stir in the rice, cover, reduce the heat to low and cook 40 minutes, or until the rice is tender and all of the water is absorbed; remove from the heat and set aside.

2. In a large nonstick skillet or wok, heat 1 tablespoon of the oil over high heat until hot but not smoking. Add the broccoli, parsnips, onion and bell pepper, and stir-fry 2 minutes, then add the ginger, garlic and red pepper flakes, and stir-fry another 2 minutes. Using a slotted spoon, transfer the vegetables to a large bowl; set aside.

3. Add the remaining oil to the wok or skillet. Add the chicken and stir-fry 1½ minutes, separating the pieces. Return the cooked vegetables to the skillet and add the spinach, mushrooms and cashews. Add the vinegar, soy sauce and salt, and stir-fry 2 minutes, or until the mushrooms are just cooked and the spinach is wilted. Divide the rice among 4 plates and spoon the chicken and vegetables on top.

Makes 4 servings

NUTRITION INFORMATION
values are per serving

• • •

CALORIES	501	CALCIUM	155 MG
TOTAL FAT	13 G	IRON	5 MG
SATURATED FAT	3 G	POTASSIUM	1282 MG
CHOLESTEROL	44 MG	BETA CAROTENE	3 MG
SODIUM	325 MG	VITAMIN C	106 MG
DIETARY FIBER	7 G	VITAMIN E	5 MG

Stir-fried Chicken and Vegetables

Oven-Baked Chicken Nuggets

Fast food-style chicken nuggets are easy to make at home. The ingredients are pantry staples and, with a food processor, you can prepare the breading in minutes. Made from skinless chicken breast (not ground-up chicken), these oven-baked (not fried) morsels contain less fat, saturated fat, cholesterol and sodium than take-out nuggets. For fast-food convenience, prepare the chicken nuggets a few hours in advance, then pop them in the oven at mealtime.

2 garlic cloves
¼ cup parsley sprigs
4 slices whole wheat or white bread, preferably stale
¼ cup grated Parmesan cheese (about 1 ounce)
½ teaspoon onion powder
½ teaspoon black pepper
¼ teaspoon salt
2 tablespoons chilled margarine
1 pound skinless, boneless chicken breasts
1 egg white

1. Preheat the oven to 425°.
2. Line a baking sheet with foil and spray with nonstick cooking spray.
3. To make the breading, peel the garlic cloves and place them in a food processor or blender. Process until finely chopped. Add the parsley and process until finely chopped.
4. Tear the bread into small pieces and add it to the parsley mixture in the processor, then add the Parmesan, onion powder, pepper and salt, and process, pulsing the machine on and off, until the bread is coarsely crumbed.
5. Cut the margarine into small pieces and add it to the processor. Process until the margarine is completely incorporated. Transfer the breading to a paper or plastic bag.
6. Cut the chicken into 1-inch cubes. In a medium-size bowl, beat the egg white. Add the chicken and stir to moisten well.
7. Drain the chicken cubes in a colander, then place them in the bag of breading and shake until well coated.
8. Place the chicken nuggets on the prepared baking sheet, leaving space between them, and bake them 12 to 15 minutes, or until crisp.

Makes 4 servings

NUTRITION INFORMATION
values are per serving
• • •

CALORIES	283	CALCIUM	140 MG
TOTAL FAT	12 G	IRON	2 MG
SATURATED FAT	3 G	POTASSIUM	298 MG
CHOLESTEROL	72 MG	BETA CAROTENE	TRACE
SODIUM	497 MG	VITAMIN C	4 MG
DIETARY FIBER	3 G	VITAMIN E	5 MG

Chicken Pot Pie

Decorative pastry cutouts take the place of a full crust atop this hearty chicken pie and keep the fat content low. Plenty of vegetables—broccoli, potatoes, corn and onions—in the filling make this a more satisfying meal while adding a good deal of fiber.

½ cup unbleached all-purpose flour, approximately
Pinch of salt
2 tablespoons chopped fresh dill
2 tablespoons margarine, well chilled
1 tablespoon ice water
1 cup low-sodium chicken stock
3 cups unpeeled, diced new potatoes
1 cup chopped onions
3 cups broccoli florets
1 cup corn kernels
1 tablespoon cornstarch
½ pound skinless cooked chicken breast, cut into large chunks

1. In a small bowl stir together the flour, salt and 1 tablespoon of the dill. Cut in the margarine with a pastry blender or two knives until the mixture resembles coarse cornmeal. Add the ice water and stir until the dough forms a ball. Cover the bowl with a kitchen towel and set aside.
2. Bring the stock to a boil in a medium-size saucepan over medium heat. Add the potatoes and onions and return the mixture to a boil. Reduce the heat to medium-low, cover the pan and simmer the vegetables 10 to 15 minutes, or until the potatoes are tender when pierced with a knife.
3. Preheat the oven to 400°.
4. Uncover the pan, add the broccoli and corn and return the mixture to a boil.

5. In a small bowl stir together the cornstarch and ¼ cup of cold water until smooth. Add the chicken to the saucepan, then stir in the cornstarch mixture and simmer 1 to 2 minutes, or until the sauce thickens. Stir in the remaining dill. Turn the chicken mixture into a shallow 10-inch baking dish and set aside.

6. Lightly flour a work surface and rolling pin. With your hands, flatten the dough into a disk, then roll it out ¼-inch thick. Using a sharp knife, cut out a decorative chicken shape. (You may find it easier to make a cardboard pattern first.) Or cut small shapes from the dough with cookie cutters. Place the cut-out dough on top of the chicken mixture and bake 15 to 20 minutes, or until the pastry is golden.

Makes 4 servings

NUTRITION INFORMATION
values are per serving

• • •

CALORIES	384	CALCIUM	75 MG
TOTAL FAT	9 G	IRON	4 MG
SATURATED FAT	2 G	POTASSIUM	1060 MG
CHOLESTEROL	48 MG	BETA CAROTENE	0.7 MG
SODIUM	273 MG	VITAMIN C	83 MG
DIETARY FIBER	5 G	VITAMIN E	5 MG

HERBED TURKEY BURGERS

To be sure of getting the leanest possible ground turkey, have the butcher grind a piece of skinless turkey breast for you. Or, chop the turkey at home in a food processor. Preground turkey may contain dark meat, which is fattier than white.

3 medium scallions
2 cloves garlic
¼ cup packed parsley sprigs
1 pound ground skinless turkey breast
½ cup fine, unseasoned bread crumbs
2 tablespoons Dijon mustard
2 teaspoons Worcestershire sauce
1 egg white
1 teaspoon thyme
¼ teaspoon black pepper
1 tablespoon olive oil

1. In a food processor, mince the scallions, garlic and parsley.

2. In a medium-size bowl, combine the minced vegetables with the turkey, bread crumbs, mustard, Worcestershire sauce, egg white, thyme and pepper, and mix to blend well.

3. Divide the mixture into 4 equal portions and form them into patties ½ inch thick.

4. In a large nonstick skillet, warm the oil over medium-high heat until hot but not smoking. Add the turkey patties and cook until well browned on both sides, 3 to 5 minutes for the first side and 2 to 4 minutes for the second side. *Makes 4 servings*

NUTRITION INFORMATION
values are per serving

• • •

CALORIES	261	CALCIUM	51 MG
TOTAL FAT	13 G	IRON	3 MG
SATURATED FAT	3 G	POTASSIUM	376 MG
CHOLESTEROL	83 MG	BETA CAROTENE	TRACE
SODIUM	419 MG	VITAMIN C	11 MG
DIETARY FIBER	TRACE	VITAMIN E	TRACE

TURKEY SCALOPPINI WITH VEGETABLES

Turkey breast comes in many forms: Roast a whole breast for a special occasion; try steaks or cutlets for quick everyday meals. Scaloppini are cutlets that have been pounded to a quarter-inch thickness.

2 tablespoons flour
1 teaspoon basil
½ teaspoon salt
½ teaspoon black pepper
4 turkey cutlets (about 1 pound total), pounded thin
1 tablespoon olive oil or other vegetable oil
¼ pound mushrooms
1 medium yellow squash
1 cup cherry tomatoes, halved
½ cup chicken stock
3 tablespoons chopped parsley (optional)

1. In a plastic or paper bag, combine the flour, ½ teaspoon of the basil and the salt and pepper. Add the turkey cutlets and lightly dredge them in the seasoned flour.

2. In a large skillet, preferably nonstick, warm the oil over medium-high heat until hot but not smoking. Add the turkey and cook until light golden on both sides, 3 to 4 minutes per side.

3. Meanwhile, slice the mushrooms ¼ inch thick. Cut the squash into ¼-inch-thick slices.

4. Remove the turkey from the skillet and cover loosely to keep warm. Add the mushrooms, squash, cherry tomatoes, chicken stock and remaining ½ teaspoon of basil to the skillet. Reduce the heat to medium, cover and simmer 3 minutes.

5. Return the turkey to the pan. Increase the heat to medium-high, cover and cook until the turkey is heated through, about 2 minutes.

6. Serve the turkey with the vegetables and some of the pan juices. Sprinkle with parsley if desired.

Makes 4 servings

NUTRITION INFORMATION
values are per serving

• • •

CALORIES 216   CALCIUM 45 MG
TOTAL FAT 7 G   IRON 3 MG
SATURATED FAT 1 G   POTASSIUM 643 MG
CHOLESTEROL 62 MG   BETA CAROTENE TRACE
SODIUM 349 MG   VITAMIN C 19 MG
DIETARY FIBER 2 G   VITAMIN E TRACE

LIME-MARINATED TURKEY WITH FETTUCCINE

Marinades infuse meat and poultry with flavor but add no fat. Here, contrary to the usual procedure, the turkey is marinated after it is poached, rather than before cooking. The sliced turkey breast is served atop fettuccine and vegetables.

1 pound skinless, boneless turkey breast
Grated zest of 1 lime
3 tablespoons lime juice
¼ cup low-sodium chicken stock
1 tablespoon rinsed, drained capers

1 cup golden raisins
¼ teaspoon salt
¼ teaspoon black pepper
½ pound fettuccine
1 tablespoon vegetable oil
2 cups julienned cucumber
2 cups green beans, blanched
1 cup julienned carrots, blanched
1 cup sliced fresh mushrooms
¼ cup chopped fresh parsley

1. Bring 1 cup of water to a boil in a medium-size skillet over medium heat. Add the turkey, reduce the heat to low and simmer, uncovered, 15 minutes, or until cooked through. Remove the skillet from the heat and let the turkey cool in the cooking liquid.

2. In a large bowl combine the lime zest, juice, stock, capers, raisins, salt and pepper. Drain the turkey, place it in the marinade, cover and refrigerate at least 4 hours, or overnight.

3. Bring a large pot of water to a boil. Cook the fettuccine according to the package directions until al dente; drain, transfer to a large bowl and toss with the oil. Add the vegetables and toss well.

4. Drain the turkey, reserving the marinade, and cut the turkey on the diagonal into thin slices. Divide the fettuccine mixture among 5 plates and arrange the turkey slices on top. Drizzle with the marinade and sprinkle with parsley.

Makes 5 servings

NUTRITION INFORMATION
values are per serving

• • •

CALORIES 425   CALCIUM 80 MG
TOTAL FAT 4 G   IRON 5 MG
SATURATED FAT 0.8 G   POTASSIUM 684 MG
CHOLESTEROL 59 MG   BETA CAROTENE 5 MG
SODIUM 184 MG   VITAMIN C 16 MG
DIETARY FIBER 3 G   VITAMIN E 3 MG

Rice-Stuffed Roasted Hens with Kale

RICE–STUFFED ROASTED HENS WITH KALE

Leave the skin on the hens while roasting to keep the meat juicy, but remove the skin before eating.

2 teaspoons olive oil
½ cup chopped scallions
3 garlic cloves, chopped
1½ cups cooked brown rice
1 cup cooked couscous
1 cup frozen corn kernels, thawed
1 tablespoon chopped fresh rosemary
2 small Cornish game hens (about ¾ pound each)
2 medium-size onions, peeled and sliced ¼ inch thick
½ pound kale, trimmed

1. Preheat the oven to 425°.
2. Heat the oil in a small nonstick skillet over medium heat. Add the scallions and garlic and sauté 3 minutes, then transfer to a medium-size bowl, add the rice, couscous, corn and rosemary, and mix well.
3. Fill the hens with the rice mixture. Place any extra stuffing in a baking dish and cover with foil.
4. Line a roasting pan with foil and spread the onion slices in the pan. Place the hens in the pan and roast 15 minutes, basting with the pan juices.
5. Add ¾ cup of water to the roasting pan, reduce the heat to 350° and place the dish of stuffing in the oven. Cook the stuffing and the hens 30 minutes, or until the juices run clear when the thigh is pierced with a sharp knife.
6. Remove the dish of stuffing from the oven. Transfer the hens to a serving platter and cover loosely with foil. Scrape the onions and pan juices into a medium-size saucepan and bring to a boil over medium-high heat. Add the kale and cover the pan. Reduce the heat to medium low and simmer the kale, stirring occasionally, 10 minutes, or until tender.
7. Divide the stuffing and kale among 4 plates. Split the hens and place one half on each plate. Remove the skin before eating.   *Makes 4 servings*

NUTRITION INFORMATION
values are per serving

• • •

CALORIES	425	CALCIUM	104 MG
TOTAL FAT	11 G	IRON	3 MG
SATURATED FAT	2 G	POTASSIUM	627 MG
CHOLESTEROL	91 MG	BETA CAROTENE	3 MG
SODIUM	108 MG	VITAMIN C	36 MG
DIETARY FIBER	6 G	VITAMIN E	TRACE

TUNA STEAKS WITH PINEAPPLE SAUCE

Fresh tuna steaks have a dense, beef-like texture. But Choice-grade sirloin steak contains eight times more fat and one-third more cholesterol than yellowfin tuna, one of the most popular varieties.

1 small red onion
One 8-ounce can juice-packed crushed pineapple
3 garlic cloves, minced
3 tablespoons ketchup
2 tablespoons chopped scallion greens
2 teaspoons cornstarch
1 teaspoon brown sugar
½ teaspoon salt
¼ teaspoon hot pepper flakes
Pinch of ground red pepper
2 large tuna steaks (1 inch thick, about 1½ pounds total)

1. Coarsely chop the onion.
2. In a medium-size saucepan, combine the chopped onion, the pineapple and its juice, the garlic, ketchup, scallion greens, cornstarch, sugar, salt, hot pepper flakes and ground red pepper. Bring to a boil over medium heat, stirring frequently. Cook, uncovered, 10 minutes, stirring occasionally.
3. Reduce the heat to low and simmer, uncovered, until thickened, about 10 minutes.
4. Meanwhile, preheat the broiler. Line a broiler pan with foil and lightly spray with nonstick cooking spray.
5. Cut the tuna steaks in half to make 4 portions. Place the tuna steaks on the broiler pan. Top each steak with one-fourth of the pineapple sauce and broil 4 inches from the heat 12 minutes, or until the fish just flakes when tested with the tip of a knife.

Makes 4 servings

NUTRITION INFORMATION
values are per serving

• • •

CALORIES 307   CALCIUM 22 MG
TOTAL FAT 8 G   IRON 2 MG
SATURATED FAT 2 G   POTASSIUM 580 MG
CHOLESTEROL 64 MG   BETA CAROTENE TRACE
SODIUM 452 MG   VITAMIN C 11 MG
DIETARY FIBER TRACE   VITAMIN E TRACE

CRISPY BAKED SCROD WITH SWEET-AND-SOUR SAUCE

Instead of frying, bake delicate scrod fillets with a Parmesan-crumb coating. Scrod is young codfish.

½ cup plain lowfat yogurt
1 tablespoon peach jam
2 teaspoons Dijon mustard
1 teaspoon cider vinegar
1 tablespoon chopped parsley (optional)
1 egg white
2 tablespoons lowfat milk (1%)
¾ cup fine, unseasoned bread crumbs
¼ cup grated Parmesan cheese
½ teaspoon salt
¼ teaspoon black pepper
1½ pounds scrod fillets (about ½ inch thick)

1. In a medium-size bowl, combine the yogurt, peach jam, mustard, vinegar and parsley (if using), and stir to blend.
2. Preheat the oven to 400°.
3. Line a baking sheet with foil and lightly spray with nonstick cooking spray.
4. In a shallow bowl, beat the egg white and milk together. In another shallow bowl, combine the bread crumbs, Parmesan, salt and pepper.
5. Dip the fish first into the egg mixture and then into the bread crumbs, coating well on both sides.
6. Place the fish on the prepared baking sheet in a single layer. Bake, uncovered, for 10 to 12 minutes, or until the fish is opaque and flakes easily when tested with the tip of a knife.
7. Serve the fish hot with the sweet-and-sour sauce on the side.

Makes 4 servings

NUTRITION INFORMATION
values are per serving

• • •

CALORIES 288   CALCIUM 212 MG
TOTAL FAT 5 G   IRON 2 MG
SATURATED FAT 2 G   POTASSIUM 841 MG
CHOLESTEROL 82 MG   BETA CAROTENE 0 MG
SODIUM 726 MG   VITAMIN C 2 MG
DIETARY FIBER TRACE   VITAMIN E TRACE

Tex-Mex Steamed Snapper

Steaming is one of the most healthful of all cooking techniques, and steamed dishes need not be bland. For this one-pot meal, fish fillets are cooked along with vegetables; vibrant seasonings—including lime juice, chili powder, cumin and hot red pepper—provide a burst of flavor. In keeping with the Tex-Mex theme, warm tortillas round out the meal.

2 medium red snapper fillets (about 1¼ pounds total)
1 large yellow or red bell pepper
1 medium red onion
2 cups spinach leaves
2 limes
1 tablespoon vegetable oil
1 teaspoon chili powder
¾ teaspoon cumin
¼ teaspoon red pepper flakes
¼ teaspoon salt
¼ teaspoon black pepper
8 corn tortillas (5½-inch diameter)

1. Cut the snapper fillets in half to make 4 equal serving portions. Cut the bell pepper and onion into thin rings.

2. Line a flat vegetable steamer or steamer insert with the spinach, bell pepper and onion. Bring the water in the steamer to a boil and steam the vegetables for about 1 minute.

3. Meanwhile, grate the zest from one of the limes. Cut both limes into quarters.

4. In a small bowl, combine the vegetable oil, lime zest, chili powder, cumin, red pepper flakes, salt and black pepper.

5. Remove the steamer from the heat. Place the fish skin side down on top of the steamed vegetables. Brush the fish with the seasoned oil. Recover and steam until the fish just flakes when tested with a fork, about 4 minutes.

6. Meanwhile, wrap the tortillas in foil and warm them in the oven or a toaster oven. Or, wrap them in a damp paper towel and warm in a microwave.

7. Dividing evenly, serve the fish with the steamed vegetables. Using one-quarter lime per portion, squeeze the lime juice over the fish. Serve with one lime wedge and two tortillas per person.

Makes 4 servings

NUTRITION INFORMATION
values are per serving

· · ·

CALORIES	337	CALCIUM	179 MG
TOTAL FAT	8 G	IRON	3 MG
SATURATED FAT	0.9 G	POTASSIUM	981 MG
CHOLESTEROL	53 MG	BETA CAROTENE	1 MG
SODIUM	361 MG	VITAMIN C	68 MG
DIETARY FIBER	5 G	VITAMIN E	4 MG

Salmon with Cucumber-Chive Sauce

Hollandaise or béarnaise sauce can considerably elevate the fat and cholesterol content of a heart-healthy fish dinner. Here, a creamy lemon-herb sauce is made with lowfat yogurt, nonfat sour cream and chopped vegetables—no egg yolks, no butter.

2-inch-long piece of cucumber
¼ cup minced red bell pepper
1 tablespoon margarine
¼ cup snipped fresh chives
½ teaspoon salt
½ teaspoon black pepper
4 small salmon fillets or other firm-fleshed fish
    (about 1½ pounds total)
½ cup nonfat sour cream
½ cup plain lowfat yogurt
3 tablespoons lemon juice
2 teaspoons grated lemon zest (optional)
½ teaspoon dry mustard

1. Preheat the broiler. Line a broiler pan with foil and spray the foil with nonstick cooking spray.

2. Peel and finely chop the cucumber. Mince the bell pepper. Melt the margarine in a small saucepan.

3. In a small bowl, combine the melted margarine with 1 tablespoon of the fresh chives, ¼ teaspoon of the salt and ¼ teaspoon of the black pepper.

4. Place the fish on the broiler pan. Spread the chive mixture over the fish and broil 4 inches from the heat until the fish is opaque and just flakes when tested with the tip of a knife, about 7 minutes.

5. Meanwhile, in a medium-size bowl, combine the sour cream, yogurt, lemon juice, lemon zest (if using), mustard, the remaining 3 tablespoons fresh chives, ¼ teaspoon salt and ¼ teaspoon black pepper. Stir in the cucumber and bell pepper.

6. Serve the fish with the cucumber-chive sauce on the side.

Makes 4 servings

NUTRITION INFORMATION
values are per serving

• • •

CALORIES	283	CALCIUM	88 MG
TOTAL FAT	10 G	IRON	1 MG
SATURATED FAT	2 G	POTASSIUM	932 MG
CHOLESTEROL	128 MG	BETA CAROTENE	TRACE
SODIUM	408 MG	VITAMIN C	23 MG
DIETARY FIBER	TRACE	VITAMIN E	2 MG

STUFFED TROUT

Trout is a good source of omega-3 fatty acids, which may help reduce the risk of heart attack. Eating as little as one or two servings of fish each week is considered a protective measure.

½ cup low-sodium chicken stock
2 tablespoons margarine
2 cups diced red bell peppers
1½ cups sliced mushrooms
1 cup corn kernels
1 cup sliced yellow squash
1 cup chopped scallions
2 garlic cloves, chopped
5 cups whole-wheat bread cubes
One 1½-pound brook trout, cleaned
1 lemon

Stuffed Trout

1. Preheat the oven to 400°.

2. For the stuffing, bring the stock to a boil in a large skillet over medium-high heat. Add the margarine, bell peppers, mushrooms, corn, squash, scallions and garlic, and cook, stirring constantly, until the mixture returns to a boil. Remove the skillet from the heat and stir in the bread until thoroughly combined; set aside.

3. Rinse the trout and pat it dry with paper towels. Transfer three-fourths of the stuffing to a large, shallow baking pan and pat it into an even layer. Place the trout on top and fill the cavity of the fish with the remaining stuffing. Cover the pan with foil and bake 20 to 25 minutes, or until the fish flakes when tested with a fork.

4. Halve the lemon and squeeze the juice of one half over the trout; slice the other half and use it to garnish the fish.   *Makes 4 servings*

NUTRITION INFORMATION
values are per serving

• • •

CALORIES   368   CALCIUM   103 MG
TOTAL FAT   14 G   IRON   5 MG
SATURATED FAT   2 G   POTASSIUM   817 MG
CHOLESTEROL   48 MG   BETA CAROTENE   1 MG
SODIUM   388 MG   VITAMIN C   117 MG
DIETARY FIBER   8 G   VITAMIN E   5 MG

FLOUNDER ROLLS STUFFED WITH CHEESE AND SPINACH

In a fancy restaurant, fish fillets baked on a bed of spinach might be topped with a rich mousseline sauce—Hollandaise sauce enriched with whipped heavy cream. No less impressive for being homemade and heart-healthy are these stuffed and rolled fillets. The fish is wrapped around a savory mixture of spinach, ricotta and Swiss cheese.

3 garlic cloves
3 medium scallions, cut into 2-inch pieces
Half of a 10-ounce package frozen chopped spinach, thawed
½ cup part-skim ricotta cheese
½ cup grated Swiss cheese
1 egg white
2 teaspoons grated lemon zest (optional)
3 tablespoons flour
1 teaspoon oregano
¼ teaspoon black pepper
4 flounder or sole fillets (about 1 pound total)
¼ cup lemon juice
4 teaspoons margarine

1. Preheat the oven to 350°.

2. Butter an 11 x 7-inch baking dish.

3. In a food processor, mince the garlic. Add the scallions and chop finely.

4. Place the spinach between several sheets of paper towels and squeeze it as dry as possible.

5. In a medium-size bowl, combine the garlic-scallion mixture, the spinach, ricotta, Swiss cheese, egg white, lemon zest (if using), flour, oregano and pepper.

6. Place the fillets on a work surface. Dividing evenly, spread each fillet with the filling. Loosely roll up the fillets and place them seam side down in the prepared baking dish.

7. Pour the lemon juice over the fish and dot each roll with 1 teaspoon of the margarine. Bake the fish 20 minutes, or until the fish just flakes when tested with a fork. About halfway through the baking, spoon some of the pan juices over the fish.
                        Makes 4 servings

NUTRITION INFORMATION
values are per serving

• • •

CALORIES   249   CALCIUM   339 MG
TOTAL FAT   11 G   IRON   2 MG
SATURATED FAT   5 G   POTASSIUM   604 MG
CHOLESTEROL   23 MG   BETA CAROTENE   1 MG
SODIUM   174 MG   VITAMIN C   12 MG
DIETARY FIBER   TRACE   VITAMIN E   4 MG

STEAMED SCALLOPS WITH CABBAGE SLAW

Scallops are a sophisticated, lowfat "fast food." They are sold shucked, trimmed and ready for the pan, and take only minutes to cook.

¾ pound sea scallops
3 cups shredded red cabbage
1 cup julienned green bell pepper
1 cup shredded carrots
1 medium-size cucumber, peeled and thinly sliced
1⅓ cups sliced celery
1½ teaspoons salt
1 teaspoon celery seed
¼ teaspoon white pepper
2 teaspoons olive oil
¼ cup red wine vinegar
¼ cup dry vermouth

1. Cut any large scallops in half or in quarters so the scallops are of uniform size.
2. Place the cabbage, bell pepper, carrots, cucumber and celery in a large bowl. Add the salt, toss to mix and set aside 30 minutes, or until the cabbage is wilted. Add the celery seed, pepper, oil and vinegar, mix well and set aside.
3. Just before serving, heat the vermouth in a medium-size saucepan. Add the scallops and cook 1 to 2 minutes, or just until cooked through. Spoon the scallops and liquid over the slaw and serve.

Makes 4 servings

NUTRITION INFORMATION
values are per serving

• • •

CALORIES	162	CALCIUM	89 MG
TOTAL FAT	3 G	IRON	2 MG
SATURATED FAT	0.4 G	POTASSIUM	704 MG
CHOLESTEROL	28 MG	BETA CAROTENE	5 MG
SODIUM	459 MG	VITAMIN C	73 MG
DIETARY FIBER	3 G	VITAMIN E	TRACE

MARINATED SCALLOPS AND VEGETABLES

This "pickled" seafood dish is a cooked variation of South American *cebiche*, which is traditionally made with uncooked fish or shellfish. Despite the continuing popularity of "raw bars" and sushi bars, uncooked seafood is no longer considered safe to eat.

½ pound sea scallops
¼ pound cherry tomatoes, halved
½ cup freshly squeezed orange juice
3 tablespoons freshly squeezed lemon juice
1 tablespoon olive oil
2 tablespoons chopped fresh coriander
1 tablespoon grated orange zest
1 large yellow or red bell pepper
1 cup broccoli florets, blanched

1. Cut any large scallops in half or quarters so that the scallops are of uniform size.
2. Bring 2 cups of water to a boil in a small saucepan. Add the scallops, reduce the heat to low and simmer 1 to 2 minutes, or until the scallops are opaque and just firm; drain the scallops and place them in a medium-size nonreactive bowl. Add the tomatoes, orange juice, lemon juice, oil, coriander, and orange zest, and stir to combine.
3. Stem and seed the bell pepper, cut it into l-inch squares and add it to the marinade. Add the broccoli, cover the bowl and place it in the refrigerator to marinate 2 hours.
4. Gently toss the salad before serving.

Makes 4 servings

NUTRITION INFORMATION
values are per serving

• • •

CALORIES	121	CALCIUM	42 MG
TOTAL FAT	4 G	IRON	1 MG
SATURATED FAT	0.6 G	POTASSIUM	485 MG
CHOLESTEROL	19 MG	BETA CAROTENE	0.7 MG
SODIUM	105 MG	VITAMIN C	106 MG
DIETARY FIBER	2 G	VITAMIN E	TRACE

TOMATO-SHRIMP SAUTE

Although shrimp are higher in cholesterol than other shellfish, they can still have a place (if eaten occasionally and in moderate amounts) in a healthful diet. Shrimp are low in saturated fat, the dominant dietary factor in elevating blood cholesterol.

2 tablespoons olive oil
1½ cups diced green bell peppers
2 cloves garlic, minced
½ cup drained, sliced roasted red pepper
⅛ teaspoon red pepper flakes
1 pound medium shrimp, shelled and deveined
1½ teaspoons dried thyme
½ teaspoon freshly ground black pepper
¼ teaspoon salt
4 small plum tomatoes, sliced
¼ cup pitted black olives, sliced

1. Heat 1 tablespoon of the oil in a large nonstick skillet over medium-high heat until hot but not smoking. Add the green bell peppers and the garlic, and sauté until the garlic is golden, about 4 minutes. Add the roasted red pepper and the red pepper flakes, and cook 1 minute.

2. Add the remaining tablespoon of oil, the shrimp, thyme, pepper and salt. Cook the shrimp mixture, stirring occasionally, until the shrimp turn pink and are barely cooked, 3 to 6 minutes.

3. Gently stir in the tomatoes and olives, and cook until the shrimp are opaque throughout and the tomatoes are heated through, about 2 minutes.

Makes 4 servings

NUTRITION INFORMATION
values are per serving

• • •

CALORIES	229	CALCIUM	93 MG
TOTAL FAT	11 G	IRON	4 MG
SATURATED FAT	2 G	POTASSIUM	483 MG
CHOLESTEROL	175 MG	BETA CAROTENE	0.8 MG
SODIUM	366 MG	VITAMIN C	72 MG
DIETARY FIBER	2 G	VITAMIN E	TRACE

HOLIDAY SCAMPI

The name *scampi*—actually the Italian word for prawns, or large shrimp—has been given to a favorite Italian-American restaurant dish in which shrimp are cooked with butter, white wine and garlic. Here, cholesterol-free olive oil replaces the butter and, for a novel flavor twist, a mixture of lemon juice and mellow balsamic vinegar stands in for the wine.

1 pound medium shrimp
1 tablespoon olive oil
3 medium carrots, julienned
1 cup diced celery
¼ cup chopped parsley
1 tablespoon chopped chives
2 garlic cloves, minced
2 tablespoons fresh lemon juice
2 tablespoons balsamic vinegar
¼ cup fresh basil leaves, finely chopped, or 2 teaspoons dried basil
Lemon slices and parsley sprigs, for garnish (optional)

1. Shell and devein the shrimp, leaving the tails attached.

2. Heat the olive oil in a large nonstick skillet over medium-high heat. Add the carrots and celery, 2 tablespoons of the parsley, the chives and garlic, and sauté until the vegetables are tender, 4 to 5 minutes.

3. Add the shrimp, lemon juice, vinegar and basil, and stir-fry until the shrimp turn pink and opaque, 5 to 6 minutes. Sprinkle with the remaining 2 tablespoons parsley.

4. Divide the shrimp and vegetables evenly among six dinner plates. Garnish with lemon slices and parsley sprigs, if desired. *Makes 4 servings*

NUTRITION INFORMATION
values are per serving

• • •

CALORIES	154	CALCIUM	91 MG
TOTAL FAT	5 G	IRON	3 MG
SATURATED FAT	0.7 G	POTASSIUM	465 MG
CHOLESTEROL	117 MG	BETA CAROTENE	9 MG
SODIUM	162 MG	VITAMIN C	17 MG
DIETARY FIBER	2 G	VITAMIN E	1 MG

FISH STEW WITH PEPPERS

Since fish cooks so quickly, it is added just minutes before the stew is done. Because you don't need to start by browning the fish in fat (as you would when stewing beef), the total fat content of this dish remains extremely low.

> 1/4 pound whitefish fillet, cut into 1-inch pieces
> 1 1/2 pounds boiling potatoes
> 1 medium-size green bell pepper
> 1 medium-size red onion
> 1 garlic clove
> One 14-ounce can plum tomatoes, with their liquid
> 1 bay leaf
> 1 teaspoon dried dill
> 3/4 teaspoon sugar
> 1/4 teaspoon ground black pepper
> Pinch of salt

1. Check the fish for any visible bones and remove.

2. Wash the potatoes and bell pepper; peel the onion and garlic. Slice the potatoes, pepper and onion 1/4 inch thick, and mince the garlic; set aside.

3. Combine the tomatoes and their liquid, the onions, garlic and bay leaf in a large nonstick skillet, and bring to a boil over medium-high heat, stirring to break up the tomatoes. Add the potatoes, dill and sugar, and stir to combine. Cover the pan, reduce the heat to medium and simmer, turning the potatoes occasionally, 15 minutes, or until the potatoes are just tender. Add the bell pepper, cover and cook 5 minutes more. Add the fish, black pepper and salt, cover and cook 2 to 3 minutes, or until the fish is opaque.

4. Remove the bay leaf, divide the stew among 4 bowls and serve.   *Makes 4 servings*

NUTRITION INFORMATION
values are per serving

• • •

CALORIES	213	CALCIUM	55 MG
TOTAL FAT	2 G	IRON	3 MG
SATURATED FAT	0.3 G	POTASSIUM	998 MG
CHOLESTEROL	17 MG	BETA CAROTENE	TRACE
SODIUM	218 MG	VITAMIN C	53 MG
DIETARY FIBER	4 G	VITAMIN E	TRACE

SEAFOOD STEW

Many people mistakenly believe that lobster is loaded with cholesterol: The half-pound of lobster meat in this stew has less cholesterol than one egg.

> 1 pound cod, cut into 1 1/2-inch chunks
> 12 cherrystone clams
> 1 tablespoon olive oil
> 1 cup chopped onions
> 2 garlic cloves, minced
> 1 1/4 pounds potatoes, cut into 1/4-inch-thick slices
> 1 cup chopped celery
> 1 teaspoon saffron threads, or less to taste
> 2 tablespoons chopped fresh basil, or 2 teaspoons dried basil
> 1 teaspoon dried thyme
> 1/2 teaspoon red pepper flakes
> 1 cup dry vermouth
> One 35-ounce can Italian plum tomatoes, with their liquid
> 1/2 pound shelled lobster tail, cut into 1 1/2-inch chunks

1. Check the cod for any visible bones and remove. Discard any opened clams and wash the remaining clams in several changes of cold water; refrigerate until needed.

2. Heat the oil in a large pot over medium heat until hot but not smoking. Add the onions and garlic, and cook about 5 minutes, or until the onion is soft. Add the potatoes, celery, saffron, basil, thyme, red pepper flakes, vermouth and tomatoes with their liquid, breaking up the tomatoes with the back of a spoon; stir well. Bring the stew to a boil, then reduce the heat and simmer, covered, 15 minutes. Add the lobster, cod and clams and cook another 10 minutes, or until the seafood is just cooked through. Discard any clams that have not opened. Ladle the stew into bowls and serve.   *Makes 6 servings*

NUTRITION INFORMATION
values are per serving

• • •

CALORIES	285	CALCIUM	138 MG
TOTAL FAT	4 G	IRON	10 MG
SATURATED FAT	0.6 G	POTASSIUM	1357 MG
CHOLESTEROL	87 MG	BETA CAROTENE	0.7 MG
SODIUM	477 MG	VITAMIN C	43 MG
DIETARY FIBER	3 G	VITAMIN E	TRACE

Seafood Stew

OYSTER STEW

A change from the traditional oyster stew—a rich blend of oysters, butter and cream—this warming chowder is filled with a colorful variety of vegetables and lightened with skim milk instead of cream.

1 tablespoon vegetable oil
3 tablespoons unbleached all-purpose flour
2 cups skim milk
¾ pound all-purpose potatoes, diced (2 cups)
1 cup low-sodium chicken stock
1½ cups grated carrots
¾ cup each coarsely diced red and yellow bell pepper
¾ cup sliced mushroom caps
¼ cup thinly sliced scallions
¼ cup minced shallots
12 small fresh oysters, shelled, with their liquor reserved
2 tablespoons chopped fresh parsley
1 teaspoon Worcestershire sauce
1 teaspoon grated lemon zest
½ teaspoon salt
Dash of hot pepper sauce
1½ cups coarsely chopped spinach leaves

1. Heat the oil in a medium-size heavy-gauge saucepan over medium heat until hot but not smoking. Add the flour and cook, stirring, 3 minutes (the mixture should be dry but not browned). Slowly add the milk one-third at a time, whisking constantly until smooth. Add the potatoes and ½ cup of the stock, reduce the heat to low and cook about 20 minutes, or until the potatoes are tender.

2. Meanwhile, in a medium-size nonstick skillet over medium heat, cook the carrots, bell peppers, mushrooms, scallions and shallots in the remaining stock about 5 minutes, or until the vegetables are slightly wilted. Add the oysters and their liquor and cook until the oysters' edges are ruffled and the oysters are firm.

3. Add the contents of the skillet to the saucepan, then add the parsley, Worcestershire sauce, lemon zest, salt and hot pepper sauce, and stir to combine. Stir in the spinach and cook until just wilted; serve immediately.   *Makes 4 servings*

NUTRITION INFORMATION
values are per serving

• • •

CALORIES	241	CALCIUM	210 MG
TOTAL FAT	5 G	IRON	4 MG
SATURATED FAT	0.8 G	POTASSIUM	1040 MG
CHOLESTEROL	16 MG	BETA CAROTENE	9 MG
SODIUM	451 MG	VITAMIN C	80 MG
DIETARY FIBER	4 G	VITAMIN E	4 MG

SHEPHERD'S PIE

Black beans replace lamb in this updated classic. Even with cheese in the topping, it's still a lowfat meal.

1½ cups cooked black beans (¾ cup dried)
1 cup tomato sauce
2 tablespoons tomato paste
1 cup chopped onion
¼ teaspoon dried oregano, crumbled
¾ teaspoon salt
Black pepper
1 pound all-purpose potatoes, peeled, boiled and mashed
½ cup shredded part-skim mozzarella
2 tablespoons nonfat sour cream
1 tablespoon butter, softened

1. In a medium-size saucepan stir together the beans, tomato sauce and paste, onion, oregano, ¼ cup of water, ¼ teaspoon of salt, and pepper to taste, and bring to a boil over medium heat. Reduce the heat, cover and simmer 20 minutes, or until the liquid is thickened and the onions are translucent. Spread the mixture in a shallow 1½-quart casserole and set aside to cool.

2. Preheat the oven to 350°.

3. Place the mashed potatoes in a large bowl. Add the mozzarella, sour cream, butter, the remaining ½ teaspoon of salt and pepper to taste, and beat until well blended. Spread the potato mixture evenly over the beans. Score the potato topping with a fork and bake the pie 45 minutes, or until the topping is bubbly and golden. *Makes 4 servings*

NUTRITION INFORMATION
values are per serving

• • •

CALORIES	311	CALCIUM	145 MG
TOTAL FAT	6 G	IRON	3 MG
SATURATED FAT	3 G	POTASSIUM	1091 MG
CHOLESTEROL	16 MG	BETA CAROTENE	0.5 MG
SODIUM	945 MG	VITAMIN C	30 MG
DIETARY FIBER	6 G	VITAMIN E	TRACE

SPANAKOPITA

Paper-thin phyllo, a Greek pastry dough, contains no fat. However, in this and many other recipes the dough must be brushed with margarine to keep it supple enough to be folded over the filling.

2 cups plain lowfat yogurt
1 pound spinach
¾ cup lowfat cottage cheese (1%)
3 tablespoons unbleached all-purpose flour
1 cup chopped scallions
¼ cup chopped fresh parsley
1 tablespoon chopped fresh dill, or 1 teaspoon dried dill
2 teaspoons grated lemon zest
½ teaspoon white pepper
¼ teaspoon salt
3 tablespoons margarine
8 sheets phyllo dough

1. To make the yogurt cheese, place a cheesecloth-lined strainer over a bowl. Spoon the yogurt into the strainer, cover it with plastic wrap and refrigerate 24 hours, or until the yogurt is the consistency of thick sour cream. You should have about 1 cup of yogurt cheese. (Discard the whey, or reserve it to use in soups or in baking recipes requiring buttermilk or sour milk.)

2. Trim and thoroughly wash but do not dry the spinach. Place it in a large saucepan over medium-high heat, cover and cook, stirring occasionally, 1 to 2 minutes, or until the spinach is wilted. Drain it in a colander, pressing out as much of the water as possible, then set the spinach aside to drain and cool completely.

3. Preheat the oven to 375°.

4. In a large bowl stir together the yogurt cheese, cottage cheese, flour, scallions, parsley, dill, lemon zest, pepper and salt. Squeeze any excess moisture from the spinach. Coarsely chop the spinach and add it to the cheese mixture; set aside.

5. Melt the margarine in a small saucepan over medium-low heat; set aside.

6. Unfold the phyllo and cover it with a damp kitchen towel (keep the phyllo covered while you work to keep it from drying out). Place 1 sheet of phyllo in a 9-inch tart pan (preferably with a removable bottom), and brush it lightly with margarine. Place another sheet of phyllo in the pan at right angles to the first to form a cross, and brush it with margarine. Layer in the remaining phyllo sheets in crisscross fashion to form an even overhang of pastry around the pan, brushing each sheet with margarine.

7. Spoon the cheese mixture into the pan and bring the overhanging edges of the phyllo over it to cover it completely. Brush the top with the remaining margarine and bake the spanakopita 15 to 20 minutes, or until golden brown.

8. Remove the sides of the pan, leaving the spanakopita on the pan bottom, and transfer it to a platter. (If using a regular tart pan, serve directly from the pan.) Cut the spanakopita into quarters and serve.

Makes 4 servings

NUTRITION INFORMATION
values are per serving

• • •

CALORIES	378	CALCIUM	376 MG
TOTAL FAT	11 G	IRON	6 MG
SATURATED FAT	3 G	POTASSIUM	1037 MG
CHOLESTEROL	9 MG	BETA CAROTENE	5 MG
SODIUM	478 MG	VITAMIN C	49 MG
DIETARY FIBER	4 G	VITAMIN E	10 MG

VEGETABLE QUESADILLAS

This Tex-Mex take on the grilled cheese sandwich makes a fine light lunch or breakfast. Grating the cheese "stretches" it so you can use less than usual.

2 flour tortillas
2 fresh plum tomatoes, sliced
½ red bell pepper, finely chopped
½ yellow bell pepper, finely chopped
2 scallions, finely chopped
1 large carrot, grated
½ cup grated Monterey Jack cheese
½ cup plain lowfat yogurt
2 tablespoons Spicy Salsa (page 54) or bottled salsa
10 watercress sprigs, trimmed

1. Heat a medium-size nonstick skillet over medium heat. Place a tortilla in the skillet and warm it 2 to 3 minutes. Turn the tortilla in the skillet and place half of the tomatoes, bell peppers, scallions and carrot on one half of the tortilla. Top the vegetables with half of the cheese, yogurt, salsa and watercress. Fold the tortilla over the filling and cook another 3 minutes, or until the cheese melts.

2. Transfer the quesadilla to a plate, cover it with foil to keep it warm and make another quesadilla in the same fashion.

Makes 2 servings

NUTRITION INFORMATION
values are per serving

• • •

CALORIES	221	CALCIUM	288 MG
TOTAL FAT	7 G	IRON	2 MG
SATURATED FAT	3 G	POTASSIUM	477 MG
CHOLESTEROL	16 MG	BETA CAROTENE	6 MG
SODIUM	138 MG	VITAMIN C	75 MG
DIETARY FIBER	3 G	VITAMIN E	TRACE

BLACK BEAN AND CORN CHILI

Even though this chili is meatless, the combination of beans and corn provides high-quality protein. You can double or triple the recipe for a crowd.

½ cup coarsely chopped onion
2 garlic cloves, chopped
1 tablespoon safflower oil
1½ cups cooked black beans
1 cup canned tomatoes, with their liquid
1 tablespoon tomato paste
1 cup frozen corn kernels
1 tablespoon chili powder
1 teaspoon ground cumin
1 teaspoon sugar
½ cup diced green bell pepper

1. Sauté the onion and garlic in the oil in a medium-size saucepan over medium heat 1 to 2 minutes, or until the onion is translucent. Add the beans, tomatoes and their liquid, tomato paste, corn, chili

Vegetable Quesadillas

powder, cumin and sugar, and stir to combine. Reduce the heat, cover the pan and simmer the mixture 15 to 20 minutes.

2. Add the bell pepper and cook the chili another 5 minutes. Ladle the chili into 4 bowls and serve.

Makes 4 servings

NUTRITION INFORMATION
values are per serving

• • •

CALORIES	191	CALCIUM	54 MG
TOTAL FAT	4 G	IRON	3 MG
SATURATED FAT	0.4 G	POTASSIUM	565 MG
CHOLESTEROL	0 MG	BETA CAROTENE	0.8 MG
SODIUM	154 MG	VITAMIN C	26 MG
DIETARY FIBER	5 G	VITAMIN E	2 MG

BAKED MACARONI AND CHEESE

Mustard and Worcestershire sauce complement the Cheddar flavor; skim milk makes a lowfat sauce.

¼ cup margarine
1 cup coarsely chopped onion
⅓ cup unbleached all-purpose flour
1 cup skim milk
1 cup chopped fresh tomatoes
¼ cup chopped fresh parsley
1 tablespoon coarse-grain Dijon mustard
1 tablespoon Worcestershire sauce
¼ teaspoon black pepper
10 ounces (2½ cups) elbow macaroni
¼ cup grated Cheddar cheese

1. For the sauce, melt the margarine in a medium-size saucepan over medium heat. Add the onion, and cook, stirring, 5 minutes, or until the onion is translucent. Add the flour and stir until well blended. Slowly add the milk, stirring constantly to prevent lumps from forming. Cook the sauce, stirring frequently, another 3 to 5 minutes, or until thickened. Stir in the tomatoes, parsley, mustard, Worcestershire sauce and pepper, then remove the pan from the heat, cover and set aside.

2. Preheat the oven to 350°.

3. Meanwhile, bring a large pot of water to a boil. Cook the macaroni 8 minutes, or according to the package directions, until al dente. Drain the macaroni and transfer it to a 1½-quart baking dish. Add the sauce and stir well. Spread the cheese over the macaroni and bake 10 to 15 minutes, or until the macaroni is heated through and the cheese is melted. Divide the macaroni among 6 plates and serve.

Makes 6 servings

NUTRITION INFORMATION
values are per serving

• • •

CALORIES	322	CALCIUM	110 MG
TOTAL FAT	10 G	IRON	3 MG
SATURATED FAT	3 G	POTASSIUM	301 MG
CHOLESTEROL	6 MG	BETA CAROTENE	TRACE
SODIUM	143 MG	VITAMIN C	15 MG
DIETARY FIBER	TRACE	VITAMIN E	6 MG

STUFFED PARATHAS

Indian breads are practically a whole cuisine in themselves, from brittle, peppery *papadums* to puffy deep-fried *pooris* to substantial griddle-baked *parathas*. These *parathas* have a spicy legume filling that makes them a complete, protein-rich meal. You can make the stuffed breads ahead of time and reheat them, covered with foil on a baking sheet, in a 350° oven for 10 minutes.

¼ cup dried chickpeas
½ cup yellow lentils
½ cup chopped onion
1 low-sodium vegetable bouillon cube
2 tablespoons minced fresh ginger
1½ tablespoons no-salt-added tomato paste
1 tablespoon vinegar
2 teaspoons honey
1 teaspoon ground cumin
⅓ teaspoon red pepper flakes
½ teaspoon salt
1 cup whole-wheat flour
1 cup bread flour, approximately
1½ tablespoons olive oil

1. Bring the chickpeas and 2 cups of water to a simmer in a medium-size saucepan, and cook 2 minutes. Cover the pan and refrigerate overnight.

2. Bring the chickpeas to a boil over medium heat, cover and cook 15 minutes. Add the lentils, onion and bouillon cube, and simmer 45 minutes. Reduce the heat to low, add the ginger, tomato paste, vinegar, honey, cumin, pepper and ¼ teaspoon of the salt, and cook, uncovered, stirring occasionally, 10 minutes. Remove the pan from the heat and set aside to cool.

3. For the dough, place the whole-wheat flour, 1 cup of the bread flour, 1 tablespoon of the oil and the remaining salt in a food processor. With the machine running, add ½ cup plus 2 tablespoons of water and process 45 seconds, or until a smooth, elastic dough is formed. Place the dough in a plastic bag, close the bag and set the dough aside to rest in a warm place about 30 minutes.

4. Lightly flour a work surface and roll out the dough into a 15-inch disk. Brush the dough with the remaining oil, then roll it into a log. With a rolling pin, flatten the log slightly, sealing the ends. Cut the log crosswise into 12 equal pieces. Place one piece of dough on the work surface and roll it out to a 5-inch disk. Place a scant 2 tablespoons of the chickpea mixture on the circle of dough, bring the edges together in the center and pinch them to seal the paratha. Turn the paratha over and flatten it to a 4-inch disk. Repeat with the remaining dough, placing the parathas on a sheet of waxed paper.

5. Heat a medium-size nonstick skillet over medium heat. Place 3 parathas at a time, seam side down, in the skillet and cook 5 minutes, then turn them and cook 3 minutes more. Turn them again and cook for another minute. Cook the remaining parathas in the same fashion. Divide the parathas among 4 plates and serve.

Makes 4 servings

NUTRITION INFORMATION
values are per serving

• • •

CALORIES   426   CALCIUM   62 MG
TOTAL FAT   7 G   IRON   6 MG
SATURATED FAT   0.9 G   POTASSIUM   636 MG
CHOLESTEROL   0 MG   BETA CAROTENE   TRACE
SODIUM   280 MG   VITAMIN C   6 MG
DIETARY FIBER   9 G   VITAMIN E   3 MG

LENTIL CROQUETTES WITH SPICY RAITA

Lentils (and other legumes) in a rainbow of colors, cooked into saucelike *dals*, are a staple of Indian menus. Here, lentils are formed into highly seasoned patties and served with a yogurt sauce.

2¼ cups cooked lentils, cooked very soft (1 cup dried)
1 cup minced onion
1 teaspoon minced garlic
½ teaspoon salt
¼ teaspoon ground cumin
¼ teaspoon curry powder
⅛ teaspoon celery salt
¾ cup dry bread crumbs
2 tablespoons vegetable oil
Spicy Raita (recipe follows)

1. Preheat the oven to 350°.

2. In a medium-size bowl, stir together the lentils, onion, garlic, salt and spices. Stir in half of the bread crumbs. With wet hands, shape the lentil mixture into 8 patties.

3. Spread the remaining bread crumbs on a plate. One at a time, dredge the patties in the crumbs, turning to coat them evenly.

4. Heat the oil in a large ovenproof skillet over medium-low heat until hot but not smoking. Fry the croquettes 2 minutes on each side, or until crisp and browned, then place the skillet in the oven and bake 20 minutes. Serve the croquettes with Spicy Raita.

Makes 4 servings

NUTRITION INFORMATION
values are per serving

• • •

CALORIES   322   CALCIUM   66 MG
TOTAL FAT   8 G   IRON   6 MG
SATURATED FAT   1 G   POTASSIUM   646 MG
CHOLESTEROL   0 MG   BETA CAROTENE   0 MG
SODIUM   476 MG   VITAMIN C   6 MG
DIETARY FIBER   8 G   VITAMIN E   8 MG

SPICY RAITA

Refreshing, yogurt-based *raita* is just one of the array of chutneys and relishes that accompany Indian meals. Perhaps the most familiar *raita* is made with grated cucumbers and mint and seasoned with cumin—just the thing to cool the palate after a bite of pungently spiced food. This carrot-and-scallion *raita* could be used as a salad dressing or dip as well as a condiment.

> 1 cup grated carrots
> ½ cup plain lowfat yogurt
> ½ cup thinly sliced scallions
> 1 tablespoon honey
> 1½ teaspoons olive oil
> ½ teaspoon minced garlic
> ½ teaspoon red pepper flakes
> Black pepper to taste

Combine all the ingredients in a small bowl and stir together until smooth. Refrigerate the raita until ready to serve.   *Makes 4 servings*

NUTRITION INFORMATION
values are per serving

• • •

CALORIES	65	CALCIUM	68 MG
TOTAL FAT	2 G	IRON	TRACE
SATURATED FAT	0.5 G	POTASSIUM	196 MG
CHOLESTEROL	2 MG	BETA CAROTENE	5 MG
SODIUM	30 MG	VITAMIN C	9 MG
DIETARY FIBER	1 G	VITAMIN E	TRACE

SPICED LENTILS AND PEAS WITH BROWN RICE

This lowfat, high-protein dish is solidly satisfying, thanks to brown rice and a trio of legumes: lentils, yellow split peas and sweet green peas.

> ¾ cup brown rice
> 2 tablespoons low-sodium chicken stock
> 1 cup chopped onion
> 2 garlic cloves, minced
> 1¼ cups cooked yellow split peas (½ cup dried)
> 1¼ cups cooked lentils (½ cup dried)
> 2 teaspoons ground cumin
> 1 teaspoon ground coriander
> 1 teaspoon turmeric
> ¾ teaspoon salt
> ¼ teaspoon black pepper
> One 10-ounce package frozen green peas, thawed
> ½ cup plain lowfat yogurt

1. Bring 1½ cups of water to a boil in a medium-size saucepan. Stir in the rice, reduce the heat to low, cover and cook 40 minutes, or until the water is completely absorbed. Remove the pan from the heat and set aside.

2. Combine the stock, onion and garlic in a large saucepan and cook over medium heat 3 minutes. Add the split peas, lentils, cumin, coriander, turmeric, salt, pepper and ⅔ cup of water; reduce the heat to low, cover and cook, stirring occasionally, 10 minutes. Add the green peas and cook another 5 minutes, or until the peas are hot.

3. Divide the rice among 4 plates and spoon the lentil mixture on top. Top each serving with 2 tablespoons of yogurt.   *Makes 4 servings*

NUTRITION INFORMATION
values are per serving

• • •

CALORIES	393	CALCIUM	128 MG
TOTAL FAT	2 G	IRON	7 MG
SATURATED FAT	0.4 G	POTASSIUM	886 MG
CHOLESTEROL	2 MG	BETA CAROTENE	TRACE
SODIUM	494 MG	VITAMIN C	11 MG
DIETARY FIBER	12 G	VITAMIN E	3 MG

Lentil Pilaf

LENTIL PILAF

Lentils cook in much less time than beans and they require no presoaking. If you chop and begin to sauté the vegetables just before the lentils are done, you can have this satisfying main dish on the table in about 45 minutes.

1 cup yellow lentils
2 teaspoons turmeric
2 tablespoons safflower oil
2 garlic cloves, finely chopped
½ pound fresh tomatoes, coarsely chopped
1 cup coarsely chopped carrots
1 cup coarsely chopped green beans
1 cup coarsely chopped scallions
2 tablespoons chopped fresh parsley
¾ teaspoon ground cumin
¼ teaspoon salt

1. Place the lentils and 1 teaspoon of the turmeric in a medium-size saucepan with 2 cups of water and bring to a boil over medium-high heat. Cover the pan, reduce the heat to low and simmer 30 minutes, or until the lentils are just tender; set aside to keep warm.

2. Heat 1 tablespoon of the oil in a medium-size nonstick skillet over medium-high heat. Add the garlic and sauté 30 seconds, or just until fragrant. Add the tomatoes, carrots, green beans, scallions, parsley, cumin and salt, and cook, stirring frequently, 5 minutes, or until the vegetables just begin to color. Add the lentils and any liquid in the saucepan, the remaining oil and turmeric, and cook, stirring, another 5 minutes, or until the lentils are heated through and the vegetables are crisp-tender.

Makes 4 servings

NUTRITION INFORMATION
values are per serving

• • •

CALORIES 273	CALCIUM 75 MG
TOTAL FAT 8 G	IRON 7 MG
SATURATED FAT 0.8 G	POTASSIUM 927 MG
CHOLESTEROL 0 MG	BETA CAROTENE 7 MG
SODIUM 158 MG	VITAMIN C 34 MG
DIETARY FIBER 9 G	VITAMIN E 5 MG

VEGETABLE GUMBO

Tomatoes, okra and bell peppers, traditional ingredients in the Creole stew called gumbo, provide most of the fiber here. For a heartier meal, ladle this stew over brown rice, which will add even more fiber.

2 tablespoons unbleached all-purpose flour
1 tablespoon vegetable oil
3 cups canned plum tomatoes, with their liquid
1 cup coarsely chopped onion
1 cup coarsely chopped green bell pepper
1 cup chopped celery
½ teaspoon dried thyme
1 bay leaf
2 tablespoons chopped fresh parsley
¼ teaspoon hot pepper sauce, or to taste
¼ teaspoon salt
¼ teaspoon black pepper
10 ounces whole okra, trimmed

1. Stir the flour and oil together in a medium-size saucepan over medium heat for about 2 minutes, or until the flour is browned.

2. Add the tomatoes and their liquid, the onion, bell pepper, celery, thyme, bay leaf, parsley, hot pepper sauce, salt and black pepper. Reduce the heat to low and simmer, uncovered, 20 minutes.

3. Add the okra and cook another 10 minutes.

4. Remove and discard the bay leaf, then ladle the gumbo into 4 bowls and serve.   *Makes 4 servings*

NUTRITION INFORMATION
values are per serving

• • •

CALORIES	132	CALCIUM	130 MG
TOTAL FAT	4 G	IRON	2 MG
SATURATED FAT	0.6 G	POTASSIUM	857 MG
CHOLESTEROL	0 MG	BETA CAROTENE	1 MG
SODIUM	460 MG	VITAMIN C	68 MG
DIETARY FIBER	4 G	VITAMIN E	3 MG

TOMATO AND BASIL TART WITH CHEVRE

For this quiche-like tart, fat-free phyllo pastry (sold at gourmet shops and many supermarkets) takes the place of a heavy pie crust. Uncharacteristically, the phyllo is not brushed with butter or margarine.

1½ pounds fresh plum tomatoes
2 tablespoons low-sodium chicken stock
1 cup chopped onion
3 cups chopped fresh spinach
2 cups diced summer squash
2 cups chopped fresh mushrooms
¼ cup chopped fresh basil
1 garlic clove, minced
¼ teaspoon salt
¼ teaspoon black pepper
4 sheets phyllo dough
3 large eggs
¼ cup plain lowfat yogurt
Pinch of grated nutmeg
2 ounces chèvre (mild goat cheese), cut into small pieces.

1. Preheat the oven to 350°.

2. Peel, seed and chop the tomatoes and set aside in a colander to drain.

3. Heat the stock in a large nonstick skillet over high heat. Add the onion, reduce the heat to medium and cook, stirring occasionally, 5 minutes. Add the tomatoes, spinach, squash, mushrooms, basil, garlic, salt and pepper, and cover the skillet. Cook, stirring occasionally, another 5 minutes. Uncover the skillet and cook, stirring, 2 minutes more, or until the spinach is wilted. Set aside to cool.

4. Separate the sheets of phyllo. Fit one sheet into an 8½-inch tart pan, folding in the edges to leave a 2-inch overhang. Repeat with the remaining phyllo.

5. In a small bowl whisk together the eggs, yogurt and nutmeg.

6. Using a slotted spoon to drain the vegetables well, spoon them into the tart pan. Pour the egg mixture over the vegetables and dot with chèvre. Roll and crimp the edges of the phyllo to form a rim and spray it with nonstick cooking spray.

7. Bake the tart 40 minutes, or until the filling is set and the pastry is light golden. Let the tart stand 5 minutes, then cut it into quarters and serve.

Makes 4 servings

NUTRITION INFORMATION
values are per serving

• • •

CALORIES	259	CALCIUM	167 MG
TOTAL FAT	8 G	IRON	5 MG
SATURATED FAT	3 G	POTASSIUM	1018 MG
CHOLESTEROL	167 MG	BETA CAROTENE	3 MG
SODIUM	313 MG	VITAMIN C	57 MG
DIETARY FIBER	4 G	VITAMIN E	2 MG

EGGPLANT-TOFU CASSEROLE

Pillow-like blocks of firm tofu, drained in a strainer and squeezed dry in paper towels, lend a solid, meaty quality—as well as protein and B vitamins—to vegetarian casseroles. Tofu can also be blended with ricotta cheese as a lower-fat filling for pasta shells.

1½ pounds eggplant
½ teaspoon Oriental sesame oil
1 cup finely chopped onion
¾ cup chopped red bell pepper
2 garlic cloves, minced

bs

pray a baking sheet

vise, place them cut
40 minutes, or until

medium-size non-
dd the onion, bell
ut 15 minutes, or

scoop the cooked
nd mash it with a

fork. Add the sautéed vegetables, tofu, Swiss cheese, 2 tablespoons of Parmesan, all but 2 tablespoons of the bread crumbs, the parsley, salt and spices, and stir well.

5. Transfer the mixture to a 1-quart baking dish, sprinkle with the remaining bread crumbs and Parmesan and bake 30 minutes. *Makes 4 servings*

NUTRITION INFORMATION
values are per serving

• • •

CALORIES	225	CALCIUM	203 MG
TOTAL FAT	10 G	IRON	6 MG
SATURATED FAT	1 G	POTASSIUM	529 MG
CHOLESTEROL	13 MG	BETA CAROTENE	TRACE
SODIUM	336 MG	VITAMIN C	43 MG
DIETARY FIBER	5 G	VITAMIN E	TRACE

BROWN RICE AND VEGETABLE RISOTTO

For a traditional Italian *risotto*, short-grain arborio rice is first sautéed, then stirred constantly as stock is gradually added over a period of about 20 minutes. Here, brown rice is used, and the stirring time cut, but the rice is still deliciously creamy.

2 tablespoons plus 1 teaspoon margarine
2 cups broccoli florets
1 cup julienned carrots
1 cup parsnips, sliced ⅛ inch thick
1½ cups low-sodium chicken stock
½ teaspoon dried oregano
½ teaspoon black pepper
1½ cups chopped scallions
1 cup brown rice
¼ cup grated Parmesan cheese
¼ cup chopped fresh parsley

1. Melt 1 tablespoon of the margarine in a large nonstick skillet over medium-high heat. Add the broccoli, carrots and parsnips, and cook, stirring, 2 minutes, or until the vegetables are well coated with margarine. Add ¼ cup of the stock, ¼ teaspoon of the oregano and ¼ teaspoon of the pepper, cover and cook 2 minutes more. Stir in the scallions.

p. 119

#2

Remove the pan from the heat, transfer the vegetables to a bowl and cover it loosely to keep warm.

2. Melt the remaining margarine in the skillet over medium-high heat. Add the rice, and sauté 2 minutes. Add ¾ cup of water, the remaining stock, oregano and pepper. Cover the pan, reduce the heat to medium-low and simmer 45 minutes, or until the rice is tender and the liquid is almost completely absorbed. Stir in the vegetables, Parmesan and parsley, and cook, stirring, over medium-high heat 1 minute, or until heated through. Divide the risotto among 4 plates and serve.

Makes 4 servings

NUTRITION INFORMATION
values are per serving

• • •

CALORIES	326	CALCIUM	155 MG
TOTAL FAT	11 G	IRON	3 MG
SATURATED FAT	3 G	POTASSIUM	606 MG
CHOLESTEROL	6 MG	BETA CAROTENE	8 MG
SODIUM	367 MG	VITAMIN C	69 MG
DIETARY FIBER	8 G	VITAMIN E	5 MG

AFRICAN CURRY WITH BROWN RICE

This filling entrée, adapted from West African cooking, is a nutritional standout. One serving supplies about the half the recommended daily fiber intake, twice the recommended amount of beta carotene, nearly half the potassium you need each day and more than your daily requirement of vitamin C.

    1 cup brown rice
    One 35-ounce can plum tomatoes, with their liquid
    14 ounces unpeeled sweet potatoes, cut into
        ½-inch-thick slices
    ½ cup sliced onion
    4 garlic cloves, crushed and peeled
    2 tablespoons curry powder
    20 pitted prunes
    1 cup coarsely chopped scallions
    ½ cup chopped fresh coriander
    2 tablespoons peanut butter
    ¼ teaspoon salt

African Curry with Brown Rice

1. Bring 2½ cups of water to a boil in a medium-size saucepan. Stir in the rice, cover, reduce the heat to low and cook 45 minutes, or until the rice is tender and the water is completely absorbed.

2. Meanwhile, place the tomatoes and their liquid, the potatoes, onion, garlic and curry powder in a large saucepan. Bring to a boil over medium-high heat, reduce the heat to medium-low and simmer 20 minutes, or until the potatoes are tender. Stir in the remaining ingredients, and cook, stirring occasionally, 10 minutes. Divide the rice among 4 plates and top with the curry. *Makes 4 servings*

NUTRITION INFORMATION
values are per serving

• • •

CALORIES	404	CALCIUM	162 MG
TOTAL FAT	6 G	IRON	5 MG
SATURATED FAT	0.9 G	POTASSIUM	1356 MG
CHOLESTEROL	0 MG	BETA CAROTENE	12 MG
SODIUM	594 MG	VITAMIN C	71 MG
DIETARY FIBER	11 G	VITAMIN E	6 MG

VEGETABLE SUSHI ROLLS

An Asian market will supply you with everything you need to prepare this Japanese specialty. Stock up on unseasoned rice vinegar (milder than most Western vinegars), short-grain brown rice, fragrant dark sesame oil, reduced-sodium soy sauce, firm tofu and delicate sheets of mineral-rich *nori* (dried seaweed). For successful sushi-making, you need slightly sticky rice. If the rice has been cooked in advance and refrigerated (which will dry it out slightly), warm the rice for 5 minutes in a tightly covered pot with a half-cup of water.

1 tablespoon plus 2 teaspoons Japanese rice vinegar
1 tablespoon sugar
¼ teaspoon salt
2 cups cooked short-grain brown rice (¾ cup raw),
*   at room temperature (see headnote)*
1¼ teaspoons Oriental sesame oil
1 tablespoon plus 1 teaspoon reduced-sodium soy sauce
½ teaspoon sherry

¼ teaspoon grated fresh ginger
3½ ounces firm tofu, cut into ½ x 3½-inch strips
¼ teaspoon grated orange zest
Two 7 x 8-inch sheets nori (Japanese dried seaweed), or
*   2 large cabbage leaves*
10 fresh basil leaves
¼ red bell pepper, cut into ¼-inch-wide strips
1 scallion, julienned
¼ avocado, peeled and cut into ½-inch-thick slices
1 carrot, finely julienned

1. In a small saucepan, heat the vinegar, sugar and salt until the sugar dissolves.

2. Place the rice in a medium-size bowl and toss it lightly with the vinegar mixture and 1 teaspoon of the oil.

3. In a small bowl, combine the remaining oil, 1 teaspoon of soy sauce, the sherry and ginger. Add the tofu and toss to combine; set aside.

4. Combine the orange zest and remaining soy sauce in a small bowl; set aside.

5. If using cabbage leaves, bring a large pot of water to a boil. Blanch the leaves 15 seconds, or just until wilted. Cool the leaves under cold water, pat dry with paper towels and cut out the center ribs.

6. Place a sheet of nori, shiny side down, or a cabbage leaf, on a clean dishcloth so that a short side of the nori or leaf is toward you. Spread 1 cup of rice evenly over the nori or leaf, leaving ½-inch borders at the top and bottom.

7. Using half of the ingredients, arrange the filling on the rice in the following manner: About one-third of the way from the top, lay the basil leaves in a row. Place the tofu strips horizontally on top of the basil. Arrange the bell pepper strips horizontally below the tofu, then add rows of scallion strips, avocado slices and carrot strips below the peppers.

8. Pick up the near edge of the dishcloth and the nori (or cabbage leaf) and begin rolling it tightly away from you, holding the filling in place with your fingers. When the edges of the nori or leaf meet, peel back the dishcloth so it does not catch in the roll. When the roll is completely formed, squeeze it gently; the nori or leaf should stick to itself: Moisten it slightly with water if it does not stick.

9. Set the roll aside for a few minutes, then carefully remove the dishcloth and transfer the roll to a cutting board. Using a sharp serrated knife, cut the roll crosswise into 8 slices. Make a second sushi roll in the same fashion, then arrange 8 slices on each of 2 plates. *Makes 2 servings*

STUFFED SQUASH WITH CHEESE

Acorn squash is an excellent source of potassium. Rice and vegetables are the major components of the stuffing, and the topping is part-skim mozzarella.

2 medium-size acorn squash (about 3 pounds total weight)
3 tablespoons butter or margarine
1 tablespoon minced garlic
1 cup peeled, diced eggplant
1 cup diced red bell pepper
2 cups cooked brown rice (⅔ cup raw)
¼ cup chopped fresh parsley
1 tablespoon balsamic vinegar
¾ teaspoon dried oregano, crumbled
¼ teaspoon black pepper
Pinch of salt
¾ cup grated part-skim mozzarella

1. Preheat the oven to 375°.

2. Using a large, heavy knife, carefully halve the squash lengthwise. Place the halves cut side down on a foil-lined baking sheet and bake 20 minutes, or until the flesh is barely tender. (The squash will be cooked further after it is stuffed.) Leave the oven set at 375°.

3. Let the squash cool slightly, then remove and discard the seeds and stringy membranes. Using a teaspoon, scoop out and reserve the flesh, leaving a ¼-inch-thick shell and being careful not to pierce the skin; set aside the flesh and hollowed-out squash.

4. For the stuffing, melt 2 tablespoons of the butter in a medium-size skillet over medium heat. Add the garlic and sauté 15 seconds, then add the egg-plant and sauté 2 to 3 minutes, or until the eggplant begins to soften. Add the bell pepper and continue cooking, stirring occasionally, 2 minutes. Add the remaining butter, the reserved squash flesh, the rice, parsley, vinegar, oregano, pepper and salt, and stir to combine thoroughly.

5. Divide the mixture among the squash shells, top with the mozzarella and bake 10 to 15 minutes, or until the filling is heated through.

Makes 4 servings

BAKED POTATOES WITH RATATOUILLE

Forget about butter and sour cream: Fat-free *ratatouille*, a Provençal vegetable stew, is a much more satisfying topping for baked potatoes.

4 baking potatoes
1 medium onion, sliced
1 medium eggplant, diced
1 medium zucchini, diced
1 medium yellow squash, diced
1 small green bell pepper, diced
1 small red bell pepper, diced
One 15-ounce can whole peeled tomatoes, with their liquid
1 garlic clove, crushed
½ teaspoon dried oregano, crumbled
¼ teaspoon red pepper flakes
2 tablespoons chopped fresh parsley

1. Preheat the oven to 350°.

2. Scrub and dry the potatoes and prick the skins a few times with a fork. Bake the potatoes about 1 hour, or until easily pierced with a fork.

3. Meanwhile, combine all the remaining ingredients except the parsley in a large nonstick skillet. Sauté over medium-high heat, breaking up the tomatoes with a spoon, for about 8 minutes, or until the vegetables begin to soften. Cover the skillet, reduce the heat to low and simmer 20 minutes.

4. Halve the baked potatoes lengthwise without cutting through the bottom skin. Separate the halves and top each potato with ratatouille. Sprinkle with chopped parsley. *Makes 4 servings*

NUTRITION INFORMATION
values are per serving

• • •

CALORIES	284	CALCIUM	98 MG
TOTAL FAT	0.7 G	IRON	4 MG
SATURATED FAT	0.1 G	POTASSIUM	1421 MG
CHOLESTEROL	0 MG	BETA CAROTENE	0.6 MG
SODIUM	194 MG	VITAMIN C	78 MG
DIETARY FIBER	8 G	VITAMIN E	TRACE

POTATO AND SPINACH CASSEROLE

Whenever possible, cook potatoes without peeling them. Many of this vegetable's nutrients, including potassium, B vitamins, iron and fiber, are concentrated in or just beneath the skin.

4 baking potatoes (about 2 pounds)
½ teaspoon minced fresh rosemary, or 1½ teaspoons dried rosemary, crumbled
½ cup sliced onions
2 cups fresh spinach leaves, chopped
1½ cups skim milk
1 egg
¼ cup grated Parmesan cheese
1 tablespoon dry bread crumbs

1. Preheat the oven to 350°.

2. Scrub and dry the potatoes and slice them ¼ inch thick. Place half of the slices in a 1½-quart baking dish and sprinkle with half of the rosemary. Top the potatoes with half of the onions and spinach. Repeat the layers.

3. Beat together the milk, egg and 3 tablespoons of the Parmesan; pour the mixture over the vegetables. Cover the dish with foil and bake 50 minutes.

4. Meanwhile, combine the bread crumbs with the remaining Parmesan; set aside.

5. Remove the casserole from the oven and top it with the Parmesan mixture. Return the casserole to the oven and bake, uncovered, another 10 minutes. *Makes 4 servings*

NUTRITION INFORMATION
values are per serving

• • •

CALORIES	295	CALCIUM	247 MG
TOTAL FAT	3 G	IRON	4 MG
SATURATED FAT	2 G	POTASSIUM	1133 MG
CHOLESTEROL	59 MG	BETA CAROTENE	1 MG
SODIUM	205 MG	VITAMIN C	35 MG
DIETARY FIBER	5 G	VITAMIN E	1 MG

HERBED POTATOES AU GRATIN

Potato casseroles can be loaded with fat, but this dish, which gets its flavor from herbs and onions, is topped with just 2 tablespoons of cheese.

1½ pounds new potatoes
1 tablespoon butter, melted
1 tablespoon unbleached all-purpose flour
¼ cup chopped fresh parsley
1½ teaspoons fresh rosemary
1 teaspoon minced garlic
¼ teaspoon black pepper
1½ cups skim milk
¾ cup sliced onions
2 tablespoons grated Swiss cheese

1. Preheat the oven to 375°.

2. Slice the unpeeled potatoes ¼ inch thick and place them in a bowl of cold water.

3. Melt the butter in a small saucepan over medium-low heat. Stir in the flour, half the parsley, the rosemary, garlic and pepper. Gradually add the milk, stirring until thick and smooth; set aside.

4. Drain and dry the potatoes; place half in a 9-inch round baking dish. Top with half the onions, then layer in the remaining potatoes and onions. Pour on the sauce, cover the dish with foil and bake 30 minutes. Stir the potatoes gently and bake for another 30 minutes. Stir again, sprinkle the cheese on top and bake, uncovered, 10 to 15 minutes more, or until the cheese is golden brown. Sprinkle with the remaining parsley and serve. *Makes 4 servings*

NUTRITION INFORMATION
values are per serving

• • •

CALORIES 241 CALCIUM 178 MG
TOTAL FAT 4 G IRON 2 MG
SATURATED FAT 3 G POTASSIUM 809 MG
CHOLESTEROL 12 MG BETA CAROTENE TRACE
SODIUM 99 MG VITAMIN C 25 MG
DIETARY FIBER 4 G VITAMIN E TRACE

ROASTED VEGETABLES WITH GARLIC SAUCE

Don't hesitate to use the full two *heads* (not cloves) of garlic called for here. Slow roasting will mellow the garlic's pungency to a mild sweetness.

2 small new potatoes, or 1 medium-size baking potato
1 medium-size sweet potato
1 small acorn squash
1 medium-size pear
½ teaspoon olive oil
2 medium-size turnips, trimmed
2 medium-size beets, stems trimmed to 1 inch
2 medium-size parsnips, trimmed
2 medium-size red onions
2 heads of garlic
½ teaspoon salt
¾ cup nonfat sour cream
Black pepper

1. Preheat the oven to 500°.
2. Halve the potatoes lengthwise, quarter the squash and halve the pear; brush the cut sides lightly with oil. Leave the turnips, beets, parsnips and

onions whole. Peel the outer skin from the garlic heads but do not peel or separate the cloves. Arrange the vegetables and pear in a roasting pan, placing the cut vegetables and pear halves cut side up, and sprinkle with salt. Roast about 30 minutes, or until the vegetables are tender when pierced with a fork. Remove the garlic; cover the pan with foil to keep warm.

3. For the sauce, separate the garlic cloves and squeeze the cloves out of their skins into a bowl; discard the skins. Using a fork, mash the garlic and mix in the sour cream and pepper to taste. Arrange the vegetables and pear on a platter and serve the garlic sauce on the side. *Makes 2 servings*

NUTRITION INFORMATION
values are per serving

• • •

CALORIES 513 CALCIUM 226 MG
TOTAL FAT 2 G IRON 5 MG
SATURATED FAT 0.3 G POTASSIUM 2032 MG
CHOLESTEROL 0 MG BETA CAROTENE 8 MG
SODIUM 776 MG VITAMIN C 88 MG
DIETARY FIBER 17 G VITAMIN E 3 MG

FRITTATA WITH GREENS AND TOFU

A *frittata*, or Italian open-face omelet, is often made with an assortment of vegetables. This one features nutrient-packed dark leafy greens.

1 pound trimmed mustard, turnip or collard greens, coarsely chopped, or 10-ounce package frozen greens, thawed
1½ teaspoons olive oil
½ cup coarsely chopped shallots
6 garlic cloves, minced
2 whole anchovies, bone in, rinsed, dried and finely chopped
¼ teaspoon red pepper flakes
1 teaspoon dried thyme
6 ounces firm tofu, cut into ¼-inch cubes
3 large eggs
3 tablespoons skim milk
¼ teaspoon salt
1½ ounces part-skim mozzarella, cut into thin strips

Roasted Vegetables with Garlic Sauce

1. If using fresh greens, place them in a large non-stick skillet with ½ cup water; cover and cook over medium-low heat about 20 minutes, or until tender. Uncover the skillet and cook until the moisture evaporates. Transfer the greens to a large bowl; you should have about 2 cups. If using frozen greens, drain and squeeze dry enough greens to measure 2 cups; set aside.

2. Heat the oil in a large nonstick skillet over medium heat. Add the shallots, garlic, anchovies, red pepper flakes and thyme, and cook about 10 minutes, or until the shallots and garlic are softened. Add the greens and tofu to the skillet, toss to coat well and distribute the mixture evenly in the skillet.

3. In a medium-size bowl beat together the eggs, milk and salt, and pour the mixture into the skillet, pressing the egg mixture evenly into the greens and tofu with a wooden spoon. Cook, covered, over medium heat 3 to 4 minutes, or until the eggs are set. Lay the mozzarella strips on top of the frittata, reduce the heat to low, cover and cook about 1 minute, or just until the cheese melts. Serve hot or warm.

Makes 4 servings

NUTRITION INFORMATION
values are per serving

• • •

CALORIES	231	CALCIUM	380 MG
TOTAL FAT	12 G	IRON	8 MG
SATURATED FAT	3 G	POTASSIUM	545 MG
CHOLESTEROL	168 MG	BETA CAROTENE	7 MG
SODIUM	361 MG	VITAMIN C	26 MG
DIETARY FIBER	2 GM	VITAMIN E	TRACE

GREEN TAMALE PIE

The original (ground beef) version of this American family favorite weighs in with some 20 grams of fat. Filling the pie with beans and vegetables instead of meat eliminates most of the fat while adding potassium, vitamin C and fiber. Though crowned with grated Cheddar, this savory pie has only 3 grams of fat.

2 cups frozen lima beans, thawed
1 cup washed, trimmed spinach leaves
2 scallions, trimmed and coarsely chopped
2 tablespoons tomato paste

1 garlic clove
4 teaspoons chili powder
1 cup coarsely chopped green bell pepper
½ cup corn kernels
1½ cups yellow cornmeal
Pinch of salt
¼ cup grated Cheddar cheese

1. Place the beans, spinach, scallions, tomato paste, garlic and 2 teaspoons of the chili powder in a food processor or blender and process 1 to 2 minutes, or until puréed, scraping down the sides of the container with a rubber spatula as necessary. Stir in the bell pepper and corn, and set aside.

2. Preheat the oven to 350°.

3. Spray a heavy-gauge ovenproof skillet (preferably cast iron) with nonstick cooking spray; set aside. (If you do not have an ovenproof skillet, wrap the handle of the skillet in a double thickness of foil.)

4. In a medium-size saucepan over medium heat, combine the cornmeal, salt, remaining chili powder and 2½ cups of cold water, and cook, stirring constantly, 2 to 3 minutes, or until the mixture thickens and comes to a boil. Remove the pan from the heat and spread two-thirds of the cornmeal mixture in the prepared skillet. Spoon the lima bean purée over it, top with the remaining cornmeal mixture and sprinkle the pie with cheese.

5. Bake the tamale pie 30 minutes, or until the cheese is melted and the top is lightly browned. To serve, cut the pie into 6 wedges. *Makes 6 servings*

NUTRITION INFORMATION
values are per serving

• • •

CALORIES	248	CALCIUM	71 MG
TOTAL FAT	3 G	IRON	3 MG
SATURATED FAT	1 G	POTASSIUM	572 MG
CHOLESTEROL	5 MG	BETA CAROTENE	1 MG
SODIUM	170 MG	VITAMIN C	29 MG
DIETARY FIBER	8 G	VITAMIN E	5 MG

TORTILLAS RANCHERAS

Beans—*frijoles*—are a staple in Mexican kitchens and are gaining popularity north of the border as the basis for substantial, delicious and nutritious soups, casseroles and salads. Mixed with vegetables and served atop tortillas, black beans make a brunch dish that will satisfy even the heartiest of appetites.

1½ cups diced plum tomatoes
1 cup diced yellow bell pepper
1 cup diced red bell pepper
½ cup finely chopped scallions
¼ cup chopped fresh coriander
¼ cup freshly squeezed lime juice
Pinch of grated lime zest
½ teaspoon chili powder
½ teaspoon ground cumin
Pinch of red pepper flakes, or to taste
1½ cups cooked black beans (¾ cup dried)
2 teaspoons vegetable oil
Four 7-inch flour tortillas
3 cups shredded Romaine lettuce
⅓ cup unsalted roasted peanuts

1. In a medium-size bowl stir together the tomatoes, bell peppers, scallions. coriander, lime juice, lime zest, chili powder, cumin and pepper flakes. Add the black beans and stir to combine; set aside.

2. Heat ½ teaspoon of the oil in a medium-size nonstick skillet over medium-high heat. Place a tortilla in the skillet and cook about 1 minute on each side, or until it is warmed and softened. Repeat with the remaining tortillas and place them on 4 plates. Top each tortilla with shredded Romaine, spoon the tomato-bean mixture on top and sprinkle with peanuts.   *Makes 4 servings*

NUTRITION INFORMATION
values are per serving

• • •

CALORIES	303	CALCIUM	100 MG
TOTAL FAT	11 G	IRON	4 MG
SATURATED FAT	1 G	POTASSIUM	632 MG
CHOLESTEROL	0 MG	BETA CAROTENE	1 MG
SODIUM	13 MG	VITAMIN C	77 MG
DIETARY FIBER	5 G	VITAMIN E	2 MG

VEGETABLE-CHEESE BURRITOS

These burritos boast a flavor you won't find in the burritos you get at your local Mexican restaurant. The tortillas are filled with arugula (a tart salad green), Greek feta cheese and roasted bell peppers. (See page 157 for information on roasting peppers.)

2 packed cups arugula, watercress or spinach leaves,
* coarsely chopped*
1 large tomato, cored and cut into 1-inch pieces
¾ cup crumbled feta cheese
1 tablespoon minced red onion
1 red bell pepper, roasted, peeled and finely diced
1 garlic clove, minced
1 tablespoon red wine vinegar, preferably balsamic
1½ teaspoons dried oregano
Six 8-inch flour tortillas

1. Combine the chopped greens, tomato, feta, onion, bell pepper, garlic and vinegar in a large bowl.

2. Heat a large skillet over high heat. Sprinkle ¼ teaspoon of the oregano over the surface of the skillet. When the oregano is fragrant and just beginning to smoke, place one tortilla on top of it and heat about 30 seconds. Remove the tortilla from the skillet and place one-sixth of the vegetable mixture in the center of the tortilla. Fold the bottom third of the tortilla over the filling, then roll the sides together loosely. Repeat with the remaining oregano, tortillas and filling, then divide the filled burritos among 3 plates and serve.   *Makes 3 servings*

NUTRITION INFORMATION
values are per serving

• • •

CALORIES	297	CALCIUM	282 MG
TOTAL FAT	10 G	IRON	4 MG
SATURATED FAT	4 G	POTASSIUM	362 MG
CHOLESTEROL	25 MG	BETA CAROTENE	1 MG
SODIUM	334 MG	VITAMIN C	73 MG
DIETARY FIBER	3 G	VITAMIN E	N/A

PESTO PIZZA

Homemade pizza is fresh and hot every time, and you can customize it to your own tastes. For variety, top this basil-scented pie with peppers and mushrooms instead of the eggplant and tomatoes called for here, or replace the Parmesan with a goat cheese such as Bucheron or Montrachet.

1¼ teaspoons dry yeast
Pinch of sugar
¾ cup unbleached all-purpose flour
¼ cup whole-wheat flour
1 tablespoon olive oil
¼ teaspoon plus a pinch of salt
5 large garlic cloves
⅓ cup chopped fresh basil
2 tablespoons grated Parmesan cheese
1 tablespoon chopped walnuts
½ pound red onions
½ pound eggplant
¾ pound fresh plum tomatoes
½ cup shredded part-skim mozzarella

1. In a medium-size bowl stir together the yeast, sugar and 6 tablespoons of warm water (105-115°); set aside 5 minutes. Add the all-purpose flour, 3 tablespoons of the whole-wheat flour, the oil and ¼ teaspoon of the salt, and mix well to form a dough.

2. Flour a work surface with 1½ teaspoons of the whole-wheat flour and knead the dough 5 minutes. Rinse and dry the bowl. Place the dough in the bowl, cover with a damp kitchen towel and set aside to rise in a draft-free place 40 minutes, or until doubled in bulk.

3. Meanwhile, for the pesto, bring a small saucepan of water to a boil. Add the garlic cloves, and cook 5 minutes. Peel the garlic cloves and place them in a food processor or blender. Add the basil, Parmesan, walnuts, the remaining salt and ¼ cup of water. Process the mixture 1 minute, or until thick and smooth; set aside.

4. Peel and trim the onions. Trim the eggplant and tomatoes. Cut the onions, eggplant and tomatoes into thin slices; set aside.

5. Preheat the oven to 500°.

6. Punch down the dough. Flour the work surface and a rolling pin with the remaining whole-wheat flour and roll out the dough to a 12-inch round. Transfer it to a pizza pan or baking sheet and

crimp the edges of the dough to form a rim. Spread the pesto evenly over the crust and top it with onions, eggplant and tomatoes. Sprinkle the pizza with mozzarella and bake 15 minutes, or until the cheese is bubbly.   *Makes 4 servings*

NUTRITION INFORMATION
values are per serving
• • •

CALORIES	263	CALCIUM	196 MG
TOTAL FAT	8 G	IRON	3 MG
SATURATED FAT	3 G	POTASSIUM	519 MG
CHOLESTEROL	10 MG	BETA CAROTENE	0.6 MG
SODIUM	290 MG	VITAMIN C	23 MG
DIETARY FIBER	4 G	VITAMIN E	1 MG

POTATO PIZZAS

When not laden with fatty sausage, a heavy layer of high-fat cheese and lots of oil, pizza makes an ideal dinner. This vegetable-topped, cheese-dusted pie is a good source of niacin and potassium, and it also supplies more than 5 grams of dietary fiber—about one-fourth of the recommended daily amount.

1 package dry yeast
2⅓ cups unbleached all-purpose flour, approximately
1 tablespoon margarine, melted
½ teaspoon salt, approximately
½ pound small red potatoes
1 medium-size red onion
4 firm-ripe plum tomatoes
1 tablespoon cornmeal
1 tablespoon olive oil
1 tablespoon grated Parmesan cheese
1 teaspoon dried oregano, crumbled
¼ teaspoon ground black pepper
¼ cup chopped fresh parsley

1. Place the yeast in a large bowl and add ⅔ cup of warm water (105-115°) and stir to combine; set aside 3 to 5 minutes. Add ⅓ cup of the flour and stir until smooth, then add the margarine, ½ teaspoon of salt and the remaining flour, and stir until the mixture forms a cohesive dough. Transfer the dough to a lightly floured board and knead 5 to 10 minutes, or

Potato Pizzas

until the dough is smooth and elastic. Place the dough in a medium-size bowl, cover it with a damp kitchen towel and set it aside in a warm place to rise 1 hour, or until the dough is doubled in bulk.

2. Meanwhile, wash the potatoes, place them in a small saucepan with cold water to cover and bring to a boil over medium-high heat. Reduce the heat to medium and simmer, uncovered, 10 to 15 minutes, or until the potatoes are just tender when pierced with a sharp knife. Drain the potatoes and set them aside to cool.

3. When the dough has risen, punch it down and divide it into 4 equal pieces. Wrap each piece in plastic wrap and refrigerate until needed. Peel the onion, then cut the tomatoes, onion and potatoes into ¼-inch-thick slices; cover them loosely with plastic wrap and set aside.

4. Preheat the oven to 500°.

5. Dust a work surface and a rolling pin with cornmeal. Roll each portion of dough into a ball, flatten it into a disk, then roll it out to a 7-inch circle

about ⅛ inch thick. Place the circles of dough on a nonstick baking sheet. Top each pizza crust with onions, then with potato and tomato slices. Drizzle the oil over the pizzas, then sprinkle each one with Parmesan, oregano, pepper and a pinch of salt.

6. Bake the pizzas 10 minutes, then reduce the oven temperature to 400° and bake 5 to 7 minutes more, or until the crusts are golden. Sprinkle the pizzas with parsley and serve. *Makes 4 servings*

NUTRITION INFORMATION
values are per serving

• • •

CALORIES	407	CALCIUM	54 MG
TOTAL FAT	8 G	IRON	5 MG
SATURATED FAT	1 G	POTASSIUM	460 MG
CHOLESTEROL	1 MG	BETA CAROTENE	TRACE
SODIUM	301 MG	VITAMIN C	19 MG
DIETARY FIBER	5 G	VITAMIN E	3 MG

CORNMEAL-CRUST PIZZA WITH MUSHROOM SAUCE

Italians cook cornmeal into a thick porridge called *polenta*, which, when cooled, can be cut with a knife. The crust for this pizza is made from a *polenta*-like mixture that is formed into a round and baked.

1½ cups stoneground cornmeal
¼ cup grated Parmesan cheese
2 teaspoons olive oil
¾ pound fresh mushrooms, trimmed and thinly sliced
1 medium-size onion, peeled and finely chopped
1 garlic clove, crushed
1 cup canned crushed tomatoes
¼ teaspoon dried oregano, crumbled
¼ teaspoon dried basil, crumbled
⅛ teaspoon red pepper flakes
1 cup shredded Swiss cheese

1. For the crust, bring 3½ cups of water to a boil in a large saucepan.

2. Meanwhile, mix 1 cup of cold water with the cornmeal to make a thick paste. Stir the cornmeal mixture into the boiling water and cook, stirring constantly, 10 to 12 minutes, or until thick and smooth. Remove the pan from the heat, stir in the Parmesan, and mix well.

3. Spread the mixture evenly in a nonstick 12-inch pizza pan or spread it in a 12-inch round on a large baking sheet, smoothing it with a spatula. Let the crust stand at room temperature at least 1 hour, or until thoroughly cool and dry on the surface.

4. Preheat the oven to 350°.

5. Bake the crust 45 minutes.

6. Meanwhile, for the sauce, heat the oil in a large nonstick skillet and add the mushrooms, onion and garlic. Cook, stirring, until any liquid evaporates and the mushrooms are lightly browned. Add the tomatoes, herbs and pepper flakes, and cook over low heat, stirring occasionally, another 5 minutes.

7. Spread the sauce over the crust, top with the Swiss cheese and bake about 5 minutes, or until bubbly and hot.   *Makes 4 servings*

NUTRITION INFORMATION
values are per serving

• • •

CALORIES	358	CALCIUM	373 MG
TOTAL FAT	14 G	IRON	3 MG
SATURATED FAT	7 G	POTASSIUM	654 MG
CHOLESTEROL	30 MG	BETA CAROTENE	TRACE
SODIUM	285 MG	VITAMIN C	14 MG
DIETARY FIBER	9 G	VITAMIN E	2 MG

SPAGHETTI WITH TURKEY-TOMATO SAUCE

Turkey breast has the lowest fat content of any meat or poultry, so substituting turkey for ground beef, pork or lamb is one of the simplest ways to reduce your consumption of fat. Although ground turkey breast is not as juicy as ground beef, the difference is not detectable in this flavorful sauce.

6 garlic cloves
1 medium onion
½ pound ground skinless turkey breast
1½ teaspoons dried oregano, crumbled
¾ teaspoon salt
½ teaspoon black pepper
1 tablespoon olive oil
One 35-ounce can no-salt-added whole tomatoes,
* with their liquid*
2 tablespoons tomato paste
1 bay leaf
½ pound whole-wheat or regular spaghetti

1. Lightly bruise 3 of the garlic cloves; set aside. Mince the remaining 3 garlic cloves. Coarsely chop the onion.

2. In a small bowl stir together the turkey, minced garlic, ½ teaspoon of the oregano, ½ teaspoon of the salt and ¼ teaspoon of the pepper.

3. Heat the oil in a medium-size saucepan over medium heat. Add the turkey mixture, the onion and the bruised garlic cloves, and cook, stirring frequently to break up the turkey, 3 to 5 minutes, or until the turkey turns white and begins to brown.

4. Add the tomatoes with their liquid, the tomato paste, bay leaf and remaining oregano, salt and pepper. Bring the mixture to a boil, breaking up the tomatoes with a spoon. Reduce the heat to medium-low and simmer 20 minutes, stirring occasionally.

5. Remove and discard the garlic and the bay leaf.

6. About 15 minutes before the sauce is done, bring a large pot of water to a boil. Cook the spaghetti 10 to 12 minutes, or according to the package directions until al dente.

7. Drain the spaghetti and divide it among 4 plates. Spoon some sauce over each serving.

Makes 4 servings

NUTRITION INFORMATION
values are per serving
• • •

CALORIES	383	CALCIUM	114 MG
TOTAL FAT	7 G	IRON	5 MG
SATURATED FAT	1 G	POTASSIUM	915 MG
CHOLESTEROL	31 MG	BETA CAROTENE	1 MG
SODIUM	531 MG	VITAMIN C	44 MG
DIETARY FIBER	2 G	VITAMIN E	TRACE

TURKEY TETRAZZINI

Here is an example of how you can eliminate the salt from recipes by flavoring foods with onions, herbs and small amounts of sharp-flavored cheese.

1 cup low-sodium chicken stock
1½ cups sliced fresh mushrooms
1 cup chopped red onion
1 cup frozen corn kernels
⅓ cup skim milk
1 tablespoon sherry
1 tablespoon plus 2 teaspoons cornstarch
½ pound skinless cooked turkey breast, cut into cubes
1 cup frozen peas
¼ cup chopped fresh parsley
½ pound fettuccine
2 tablespoons grated Parmesan cheese

1. Bring the stock to a boil in a medium-size saucepan over medium-high heat. Add the mushrooms, onion and corn, reduce the heat to medium and simmer the mixture 8 to 10 minutes, or until the mushrooms are tender.

2. Meanwhile, in a small bowl stir together the milk, sherry and cornstarch until well blended.

3. Return the stock to a boil, stir in the cornstarch

Linguine with Tuna Sauce

mixture and boil 2 minutes, or until the sauce thickens. Add the turkey, peas and parsley, remove the pan from the heat, cover and set aside to keep warm.

4. Bring a large pot of water to a boil, add the fettuccine and cook 10 minutes, or according to the package directions until al dente; drain and transfer to a serving bowl.

5. Stir in the turkey mixture and toss until combined, then sprinkle the pasta with Parmesan.

Makes 6 servings

NUTRITION INFORMATION
values are per serving

• • •

CALORIES 285	CALCIUM 74 MG
TOTAL FAT 3 G	IRON 3 MG
SATURATED FAT 1 G	POTASSIUM 443 MG
CHOLESTEROL 31 MG	BETA CAROTENE TRACE
SODIUM 120 MG	VITAMIN C 9 MG
DIETARY FIBER 2 G	VITAMIN E TRACE

LINGUINE WITH TUNA SAUCE

Three ounces of drained oil-packed white tuna contains about 7 grams of fat. But the same amount of water-packed tuna contains only 2 grams of fat.

1 tablespoon olive oil
¼ cup chopped onion
1 garlic clove, crushed
One 12-ounce can crushed tomatoes
One 12½-ounce can water-packed tuna, drained
¼ cup black olives, slivered
2 tablespoons red wine
1 small bay leaf
¾ teaspoon chopped fresh oregano, or ¼ teaspoon dried oregano, crumbled
¼ teaspoon red pepper flakes
1 pound linguine or fettuccine
2 tablespoons chopped fresh parsley

1. Heat the oil in a large saucepan. Add the onion and cook until translucent. Add the garlic and brown slightly. Add all the remaining ingredients except the linguine and parsley and bring to a boil. Reduce the heat and simmer 20 minutes.

2. Bring a large saucepan of water to a boil. Ten minutes before the sauce is done, cook the linguine until al dente.

3. Drain the linguine in a colander, then transfer to 4 plates. Top with the sauce and sprinkle with chopped parsley. *Makes 4 servings*

NUTRITION INFORMATION
values are per serving

• • •

CALORIES	580	CALCIUM	90 MG
TOTAL FAT	8 G	IRON	6 MG
SATURATED FAT	1 G	POTASSIUM	724 MG
CHOLESTEROL	37 MG	BETA CAROTENE	TRACE
SODIUM	569 MG	VITAMIN C	16 MG
DIETARY FIBER	TRACE	VITAMIN E	TRACE

SHRIMP AND PENNE WITH TOMATO SAUCE AND MINT

Penne is a quill-shaped pasta; if desired, use another medium-size pasta, such as ziti, in this dish.

¼ cup low-sodium chicken stock
2 cups julienned fennel
1 cup finely chopped onion
1 garlic clove, minced
One 28-ounce can plum tomatoes, with their liquid
¼ pound small shelled, deveined shrimp
½ pound penne, cooked and drained
1 cup finely chopped fresh mint
⅛ teaspoon each salt and black pepper

1. For the tomato sauce, combine the stock, fennel, onion and garlic in a large nonstick skillet, and cook over medium heat, stirring occasionally, about 5 minutes, or until the vegetables are soft.

2. Purée the tomatoes with their liquid in a food processor or blender, then add the purée to the skil-

let. Increase the heat to medium-high and cook 15 minutes, or until the sauce is slightly thickened.

3. Meanwhile, bring a medium-size saucepan of water to a boil. Cook the shrimp 4 minutes, then drain, cool under cold water and drain again. Reserving 4 cooked shrimp for garnish, coarsely chop the remaining shrimp.

4. Place the penne in a large bowl, add the chopped shrimp and the tomato sauce and toss to combine. Add the mint, salt and pepper and toss again. Divide the penne among 4 bowls, garnish each serving with a whole shrimp and serve immediately. *Makes 4 servings*

NUTRITION INFORMATION
values are per serving

• • •

CALORIES	308	CALCIUM	128 MG
TOTAL FAT	2 G	IRON	6 MG
SATURATED FAT	0.3 G	POTASSIUM	727 MG
CHOLESTEROL	44 MG	BETA CAROTENE	2 MG
SODIUM	480 MG	VITAMIN C	49 MG
DIETARY FIBER	2 G	VITAMIN E	0 MG

SOPA SECA

Although it may sound like a contradiction in terms, the literal translation of the name of this Mexican dish is "dry soup." The pasta, vegetables and shrimp are cooked in broth until most of the liquid is absorbed.

1 cup low-sodium chicken stock
2 garlic cloves, chopped
½ teaspoon dried oregano, crumbled
¼ teaspoon red pepper flakes
⅛ teaspoon black pepper
7 ounces medium-size unshelled shrimp
2 cups diced green bell peppers
2 cups chopped onions
One 14-ounce can plum tomatoes, with their liquid
½ pound vermicelli, broken into 2-inch pieces (2 cups)
3 tablespoons chopped fresh coriander

1. In a large skillet bring 2 cups of water, the stock, garlic, oregano, red pepper flakes and black pepper to a boil over medium heat. Add the shrimp and bell peppers, and cook 3 minutes, or until the shrimp turn bright pink. Using a slotted spoon, remove the shrimp and bell peppers; set aside.

2. Add the onions and the tomatoes with their liquid to the soup and return to a boil over medium-high heat. Add the vermicelli, and cook, stirring frequently, 8 to 10 minutes, or until the pasta is tender and most of the liquid has been absorbed.

3. Return the shrimp and bell peppers to the pan, then stir in the coriander and serve.

Makes 4 servings

NUTRITION INFORMATION
values are per serving

• • •

CALORIES	333	CALCIUM	98 MG
TOTAL FAT	3 G	IRON	5 MG
SATURATED FAT	0.4 G	POTASSIUM	641 MG
CHOLESTEROL	78 MG	BETA CAROTENE	0.6 MG
SODIUM	405 MG	VITAMIN C	66 MG
DIETARY FIBER	2 G	VITAMIN E	N/A

STIR-FRIED VEGETABLES AND SHRIMP ON FETTUCCINE

This filling one-dish meal supplies about half of your daily protein requirement and also provides plenty of beta carotene and good amounts of potassium, iron and vitamin C. The recipe calls for tamari, a mellow, unrefined soy sauce sold in health-food stores and some Asian grocery stores. If tamari is not available, substitute reduced-sodium soy sauce.

½ pound green beans
½ pound yellow squash
¼ pound carrots
6 ounces shelled, deveined shrimp
2 tablespoons vegetable oil
2 teaspoons minced garlic
4 thin slices fresh ginger
½ pound fettuccine
¼ pound bean sprouts
½ cup low-sodium chicken stock
2 teaspoons tamari

2 teaspoons cornstarch
⅔ cup chopped scallions

1. Wash and trim the beans, squash and carrots. Cut the beans into 2-inch lengths, the squash into 2 x ¼-inch sticks and the carrots into ¼-inch-thick diagonal slices. Slice the shrimp in half lengthwise; set aside.

2. Heat 1 tablespoon of the oil in a medium-size skillet over medium heat until hot but not smoking. Add the shrimp, 1 teaspoon of the garlic and 2 slices of the ginger, and stir-fry about 2 minutes, or until the shrimp turn pink. Transfer the shrimp, garlic and ginger to a bowl; cover loosely and set aside. Wipe out the skillet with paper towels.

3. Bring 3 quarts of water to a boil in a large pot over medium-high heat. Cook the fettuccine 10 to 12 minutes, or according to the package directions until al dente.

4. Meanwhile, heat the remaining oil in the skillet over medium-high heat. Add the remaining garlic and ginger, the beans, squash, carrots and bean sprouts, and cook, stirring, 2 minutes, or until the vegetables are crisp-tender.

5. Mix the stock, tamari and cornstarch in a cup, add the mixture to the vegetables and bring to a boil, stirring constantly. Add the shrimp and scallions, and stir to combine. Remove the pan from the heat and set aside.

6. Drain the fettuccine thoroughly and divide it among 4 plates. Top the fettuccine with the shrimp and vegetables.

Makes 4 servings

NUTRITION INFORMATION
values are per serving

• • •

CALORIES	382	CALCIUM	91 MG
TOTAL FAT	9 G	IRON	5 MG
SATURATED FAT	1 G	POTASSIUM	629 MG
CHOLESTEROL	66 MG	BETA CAROTENE	6 MG
SODIUM	272 MG	VITAMIN C	33 MG
DIETARY FIBER	2 G	VITAMIN E	7 MG

SPINACH LASAGNA

This meatless but filling lasagna is low in total fat and saturated fat because it is made with part–skim mozzarella and lowfat cottage cheese.

½ pound fresh mushrooms, sliced
2 garlic cloves, crushed
1 cup chopped onion
Two 16-ounce cans tomato purée
1 tablespoon dried basil
2 teaspoons dried oregano
2 tablespoons chopped fresh parsley
¼ teaspoon salt
¼ teaspoon freshly ground black pepper
¼ teaspoon red pepper flakes
One 10-ounce package of whole-wheat or spinach
    lasagna noodles
Two 10-ounce packages frozen chopped spinach, thawed
1 tablespoon olive oil
Pinch of freshly grated nutmeg
2 cups lowfat cottage cheese (1%)
2 tablespoons lowfat milk (1%)
2 ounces part-skim mozzarella, shredded
2 tablespoons grated Parmesan cheese

1. Bring a large saucepan of water to a boil.

2. Meanwhile, combine the mushrooms, garlic and all but 2 tablespoons of the onion in a large nonstick skillet; cover and cook over medium heat, stirring often, about 5 minutes, or until the vegetables soften.

3. Add the tomato purée to the skillet. Stir in the basil, oregano, parsley, a pinch of salt and pepper and the red pepper flakes; partially cover and simmer for 30 minutes, stirring occasionally.

4. Cook the lasagna noodles according to the package directions; drain and set aside.

5. Preheat the oven to 350°.

6. Squeeze the excess water from the spinach. Cook the reserved onion in the oil in a nonstick skillet until softened. Add the spinach and cook, stirring, until the liquid evaporates. Add the remaining salt and pepper and the nutmeg, and remove the skillet from the heat.

7. Place the cottage cheese and milk in a blender and blend until smooth; set aside.

8. Spread a little tomato sauce on the bottom of a 9 x 13-inch baking dish. Form a layer using one third of the noodles, one third of the tomato sauce, half of the cottage cheese, half of the spinach and half of the shredded mozzarella. Repeat with one third of the noodles and the remaining cottage cheese, mozzarella and spinach. Top with the remaining noodles, tomato sauce and the grated Parmesan. Cover loosely with foil and bake 50 to 60 minutes, or until bubbly; remove the foil during the last 10 minutes. Let the lasagna stand 10 minutes before serving.

Makes 6 servings

NUTRITION INFORMATION
values are per serving
• • •

CALORIES	377	CALCIUM	305 MG
TOTAL FAT	6 G	IRON	5 MG
SATURATED FAT	2 G	POTASSIUM	1231 MG
CHOLESTEROL	10 MG	BETA CAROTENE	4 MG
SODIUM	563 MG	VITAMIN C	67 MG
DIETARY FIBER	6 G	VITAMIN E	3 MG

PASTA WITH CREAMY CORIANDER PESTO

Fresh basil is the main ingredient in traditional Genovese pesto; fresh coriander (also called cilantro or Chinese parsley) makes a fragrant and appealing pesto as well. Serve this pasta side dish with simple broiled or baked chicken or fish.

2 ounces linguine
½ cup lowfat cottage cheese (1%)
¼ cup fresh coriander leaves
½ teaspoon salt
2½ teaspoons olive oil
3 garlic cloves, peeled and thinly sliced
¼ teaspoon red pepper flakes, or to taste

1. Bring a large pot of water to a boil. Cook the linguine according to the package directions until al dente; drain and set aside.

2. While the pasta is cooking, place the cottage cheese, coriander leaves and salt in a food processor or blender and process until smooth; set aside.

3. In a small skillet, heat the oil, garlic and red pepper flakes over very low heat about 5 minutes, or until the garlic is golden. Remove the skillet from the heat, add the drained linguine and the sauce, and toss until well combined.   *Makes 2 servings*

CALORIES	207	CALCIUM	66 MG
TOTAL FAT	7 G	IRON	2 MG
SATURATED FAT	1 G	POTASSIUM	170 MG
CHOLESTEROL	3 MG	BETA CAROTENE	0 MG
SODIUM	768 MG	VITAMIN C	8 MG
DIETARY FIBER	0 G	VITAMIN E	TRACE

FETTUCCINE WITH VEGETABLES

Any dish made with dairy products and a variety of vegetables is sure to supply substantial amounts of potassium. The milk and cheese—as well as enriched pasta—are also among the best sources of B vitamins.

½ pound green beans
½ pound yellow squash
1 cup lowfat cottage cheese (1%)
⅓ cup skim milk
2 tablespoons chopped fresh parsley
1 tablespoon margarine
½ pound red onions, sliced
2 garlic cloves, chopped
¾ pound fettuccine
1½ cups frozen corn kernels
½ teaspoon dried summer savory or basil
¼ teaspoon white pepper
Pinch of salt
1 tablespoon grated Parmesan cheese

1. Cut the beans into 2-inch lengths. Halve the squash lengthwise and slice it ¼ inch thick; set aside.
2. For the sauce, process the cottage cheese in a blender until smooth. With the machine running, add the milk, and process 5 seconds. Stir in the parsley; set aside.
3. Bring a large pot of water to a boil.
4. Meanwhile, melt the margarine in a medium-size skillet over medium heat. Add the onions and garlic, and cook, stirring, 5 minutes.

5. Cook the fettuccine 8 to 10 minutes, or according to the package directions until al dente.
6. Meanwhile, add the beans, squash, corn, savory, pepper and salt to the skillet, and cook, stirring frequently, 10 minutes, or until the vegetables are crisp-tender.
7. Drain the fettuccine and transfer it to a large serving bowl. Add the cheese sauce and vegetables, and toss to combine. Sprinkle the pasta and vegetables with Parmesan and serve.

Makes 4 servings

CALORIES	494	CALCIUM	150 MG
TOTAL FAT	6 G	IRON	5 MG
SATURATED FAT	1 G	POTASSIUM	639 MG
CHOLESTEROL	4 MG	BETA CAROTENE	0.5 MG
SODIUM	311 MG	VITAMIN C	27 MG
DIETARY FIBER	2 G	VITAMIN E	2 MG

PENNE WITH RED PEPPER SAUCE

You don't have to drink orange juice every day to get your vitamin C: Red bell peppers are among the top vegetable sources of this vitamin. Some of the others are broccoli, Brussels sprouts, cauliflower, kale, cabbage and chili peppers.

2 large red bell peppers, halved and cored
¼ pound green beans
6 ounces penne or other pasta
1 tablespoon olive oil
2 medium shallots, finely chopped
2 garlic cloves, minced
½ cup white wine
½ cup low-sodium chicken stock
1 medium-size tomato, chopped
2 small leeks, washed and cut crosswise into ¼-inch pieces
1 large yellow bell pepper, cut into ¼-inch-wide strips
1 teaspoon chopped fresh rosemary
½ teaspoon salt
¼ teaspoon black pepper
2 tablespoons goat cheese, crumbled (1 ounce)

1. Preheat the broiler.

2. Broil the red bell peppers about 5 inches from the heat, turning frequently, until they are charred all over. Place the peppers in a paper bag and let them steam 15 minutes.

3. Meanwhile, bring a medium-size saucepan and a large pot of water to a boil. Blanch the green beans in the saucepan about 5 minutes, or until just tender; drain and cool under cold water. Cook the pasta in the large pot of boiling water according to the package directions until al dente; set aside to drain.

4. Chop the red bell peppers, place them in a blender and purée; set aside.

5. Heat the oil in a large nonstick skillet over medium heat. Add the shallots and garlic, and sauté 1 minute. Cover and cook 4 minutes, or until the shallots are soft. Add the wine and stock, bring to a gentle boil and cook about 3 minutes, or until the liquid is reduced to about ¾ cup. Add the tomato, leeks and yellow pepper, and simmer about 3 minutes, or until the liquid is reduced to about ½ cup. Add the green beans, red pepper purée, rosemary, salt, black pepper and half of the goat cheese, and simmer 1 minute.

6. Toss the sauce with the pasta, then add the remaining cheese and toss again. *Makes 2 servings*

NUTRITION INFORMATION
values are per serving

• • •

CALORIES	567	CALCIUM	152 MG
TOTAL FAT	13 G	IRON	9 MG
SATURATED FAT	3 G	POTASSIUM	945 MG
CHOLESTEROL	8 MG	BETA CAROTENE	2 MG
SODIUM	787 MG	VITAMIN C	267 MG
DIETARY FIBER	4 G	VITAMIN E	TRACE

Penne with Red Pepper Sauce

PASTA AND CAULIFLOWER WITH SESAME SAUCE

The vegetables that are tossed with the pasta make for generous portions while adding only about 30 calories per serving. For convenience, the cauliflower and pasta are cooked in the same pot of water.

4 cups cauliflower florets
½ cup plain lowfat yogurt
1 tablespoon plus 1 teaspoon Oriental sesame oil
1 tablespoon toasted sesame seeds
1 teaspoon lemon juice
1 large red bell pepper, cut into ¼-inch-wide strips
½ pound spinach rotelle (spiral pasta)
½ teaspoon salt
¼ teaspoon red pepper flakes
Black pepper

1. Bring a large sauce pan of water to a boil. Add the cauliflower and cook it 10 minutes, or until fork-tender. (If you prefer crisp-tender cauliflower, cook it 8 minutes.)

2. Meanwhile, for the sauce, in a large bowl whisk together the yogurt, oil, sesame seeds and lemon juice. Add the bell pepper strips and toss to coat; set aside.

3. Reserving the boiling water, use a slotted spoon to transfer the cauliflower to a colander; cool under cold running water and drain.

4. Cook the pasta in the boiling water 8 minutes, or according to package directions until al dente; cool under cold water and drain thoroughly.

5. Add the pasta and cauliflower to the sauce and toss until well combined. Add the salt and red pepper flakes and black pepper to taste, and toss again.

Makes 4 servings

NUTRITION INFORMATION
values are per serving

• • •

CALORIES	321	CALCIUM	154 MG
TOTAL FAT	7 G	IRON	3 MG
SATURATED FAT	1 G	POTASSIUM	581 MG
CHOLESTEROL	2 MG	BETA CAROTENE	TRACE
SODIUM	193 MG	VITAMIN C	120 MG
DIETARY FIBER	3 G	VITAMIN E	2 MG

PASTA WITH GOAT CHEESE AND ONIONS

Goat cheese is still something of a novelty to many Americans, but its unique flavor merits attention. Young goat cheeses, such as Bucheron, are soft, spreadable and only mildly tart; well-aged cheeses range from tangy to pungent and from firm to rock-hard. Although French goat cheese—*chèvre*—is the world standard, American cheesemakers have begun to produce cheeses that rival those from France.

6 ounces mild French goat cheese, such as Bucheron
½ cup skim milk
1 medium-size red onion
½ teaspoon olive oil
½ pound capelletti or small shell pasta
Black pepper
*¼ cup minced fresh herbs in any combination, such as
    basil, chives, Italian parsley, coriander, thyme
    or rosemary*
1½ teaspoons shaved or grated Parmesan cheese

1. Bring enough water to a boil in the bottom of a double boiler so that the boiling water will just touch the top pan. When the water boils, place the cheese in the top pan and heat, stirring with a whisk, until the cheese is completely melted. Whisk in the skim milk, cover the pan and set aside.

2. Bring a large pot of water to a boil.

3. Preheat the broiler and position the rack 2 inches from the heat.

4. Slice the onion into ⅛-inch-thick wedges; do not separate the layers.

5. Place a nonstick or foil-lined baking sheet under the broiler 1 minute, or until hot. Arrange the onion wedges in a single layer on the sheet and brush the tops and sides of the slices lightly with oil. Broil the onions about 5 minutes, or until they are soft and slightly charred.

6. Cook the pasta in the boiling water according to the package directions until al dente; drain well and return it to the pot.

7. Add the cheese sauce, black pepper to taste and half the fresh herbs to the pasta, and toss until the pasta is well coated with the sauce and herbs.

8. Divide the pasta among 3 dinner plates and top with equal amounts of onions and Parmesan. Sprinkle with the remaining herbs and serve.

Makes 3 servings

NUTRITION INFORMATION
values are per serving
• • •

CALORIES 468 CALCIUM 169 MG
TOTAL FAT 14 G IRON 4 MG
SATURATED FAT 9 G POTASSIUM 275 MG
CHOLESTEROL 27 MG BETA CAROTENE TRACE
SODIUM 253 MG VITAMIN C 8 MG
DIETARY FIBER TRACE VITAMIN E TRACE

CAPELLINI WITH ARTICHOKES

Don't hesitate to use frozen vegetables. Frozen immediately after picking, they are in some cases nutritionally superior to fresh.

½ pound mushrooms
1 red onion, peeled
2 garlic cloves, peeled
1 cup low-sodium chicken stock
½ cup canned chickpeas, rinsed and drained
3 tablespoons olive oil
½ pound capellini or spaghettini
1½ cups frozen artichoke hearts, thawed and drained
1 teaspoon dried oregano, crumbled
Pinch of salt
¼ cup chopped fresh parsley
¼ teaspoon ground black pepper

1. Wash, trim and coarsely chop the mushrooms; coarsely chop the onion and garlic; set aside.
2. Place the stock and chickpeas in a medium-size saucepan and bring to a boil over medium-high heat. Cover the pan, reduce the heat to medium-low and simmer 15 minutes.
3. Meanwhile, heat 2 tablespoons of oil in a large skillet over medium-high heat. Add the onion and garlic, and cook, stirring occasionally, 10 minutes, or until softened; set aside.
4. Reserving the stock, transfer the chickpeas to a food processor or blender and process until puréed; set aside.
5. Bring a large pot of water to a boil. Cook the capellini 8 minutes, or according to the package directions until al dente.

6. Meanwhile, return the stock to a boil. Add the mushrooms, artichokes, oregano and salt, and simmer, stirring occasionally, 5 minutes. Drain the pasta, place it in a serving bowl and toss it with the remaining oil. Add the chickpea purée, the stock, vegetables, parsley and pepper, toss again and serve.
Makes 4 servings

NUTRITION INFORMATION
values are per serving
• • •

CALORIES 394 CALCIUM 70 MG
TOTAL FAT 13 G IRON 5 MG
SATURATED FAT 2 G POTASSIUM 637 MG
CHOLESTEROL 1 MG BETA CAROTENE TRACE
SODIUM 259 MG VITAMIN C 14 MG
DIETARY FIBER 2 G VITAMIN E 2 MG

PASTA-STUFFED PEPPERS

Yes, there's bacon in this recipe, but after the bacon is cooked, nearly all the fat is discarded. As a result, one of these stuffed peppers contains less fat than a half-cup serving of some bottled pasta sauces.

¼ pound fettuccine
2 strips bacon
½ cup finely chopped onion
2 red bell peppers
5 dried figs, diced
1 tablespoon grated Parmesan cheese
2 tablespoons (1 ounce) goat cheese, preferably Montrachet
¼ cup low-sodium chicken stock
¼ teaspoon salt
Black pepper

1. Bring a large pot of water to a boil. Cook the fettuccine according to the package directions until al dente; drain and set aside.
2. Cook the bacon in a small skillet over medium heat about 7 minutes, or until crisp. Drain the bacon on paper towels, crumble it and set aside.
3. Drain all but ½ teaspoon of the bacon fat from the skillet. Add the onion and 2 teaspoons of water and cook, covered, over low heat about 8 minutes, or until softened; remove the skillet from the heat and set aside.

4. Bring another large pot of water to a boil.

5. Meanwhile, cut off and reserve the tops from the bell peppers. Seed the peppers. Blanch the peppers and the tops in the boiling water about 10 minutes, or until softened but still firm enough to hold their shape. Drain the peppers and tops and set aside to cool.

6. Preheat the oven to 400°.

7. In a large bowl combine the fettuccine, bacon, onions, figs, Parmesan, goat cheese, stock, salt, and black pepper to taste, and mix well. Fill each bell pepper with half of the mixture and cover with the tops. Place the peppers in a baking dish and bake about 12 minutes, or until heated through.   *Makes 2 servings*

NUTRITION INFORMATION
values are per serving

• • •

CALORIES	451	CALCIUM	150 MG
TOTAL FAT	9 G	IRON	5 MG
SATURATED FAT	4 G	POTASSIUM	670 MG
CHOLESTEROL	15 MG	BETA CAROTENE	TRACE
SODIUM	559 MG	VITAMIN C	146 MG
DIETARY FIBER	5 G	VITAMIN E	TRACE

COLD PEANUT PASTA

Cold noodles with spicy peanut sauce is a Szechuan restaurant dish you probably have not considered making at home. By doing so, however, you can keep the fat content down and add fresh vegetables for a more healthful dish. Also, you can adjust the amount of hot pepper sauce to suit your taste for fiery foods. If you're being extra careful about sodium, substitute reduced-sodium soy sauce.

½ pound capellini or spaghettini

3 tablespoons smooth peanut butter

1 tablespoon plus 2 teaspoons Oriental sesame oil

2 tablespoons soy sauce

1 tablespoon Japanese rice vinegar

2 teaspoons brown sugar

¼ teaspoon hot pepper sauce

1 cup shredded carrots

1 cup diced green bell pepper

½ cup chopped scallions

2 tablespoons chopped fresh coriander or parsley

Cold Peanut Pasta

1. Bring a large pot of water to a boil. Cook the pasta 8 minutes, or according to the package directions until al dente.

2. Drain the pasta in a colander, rinse it under cold running water and set aside in the colander to drain again.

3. Meanwhile, for the sauce, in a small bowl stir together the peanut butter and oil until blended. Gradually add the soy sauce, vinegar, sugar, hot pepper sauce and 2 tablespoons of water, and stir until smooth.

4. Transfer the pasta to a serving bowl, add the carrots, bell pepper and scallions, and toss well. Pour on the sauce, sprinkle on the coriander and toss until the pasta and vegetables are well coated with sauce.

Makes 4 servings

NUTRITION INFORMATION
values are per serving

• • •

CALORIES	366	CALCIUM	37 MG
TOTAL FAT	13 G	IRON	3 MG
SATURATED FAT	2 G	POTASSIUM	375 MG
CHOLESTEROL	0 MG	BETA CAROTENE	5 MG
SODIUM	590 MG	VITAMIN C	31 MG
DIETARY FIBER	2 G	VITAMIN E	4 MG

ORIENTAL PASTA WITH SNOW PEAS AND PEPPERS

Generally speaking, vegetables provide the maximum amount of vitamins and minerals when they are eaten raw, but quick-cooking methods such as stir-frying or microwaving preserve most of their nutrients. The broccoli and snow peas in this Asian-inspired pasta dinner provide calcium. The bell peppers are an excellent source of vitamin C. In fact, a serving of this dish supplies more than twice the recommended daily requirement of this heart-friendly vitamin.

½ pound snow peas
1 red bell pepper
1 yellow bell pepper
2 cups broccoli florets
¾ pound linguine
¼ cup low-sodium chicken stock
2 tablespoons reduced-sodium soy sauce
2 tablespoons lemon juice
1 tablespoon vegetable oil
2 teaspoons minced fresh ginger
1 garlic clove, minced

1. Bring a large pot of water to a boil.

2. Meanwhile, string and trim the snow peas. Core and coarsely dice the bell peppers; set aside.

3. Blanch the snow peas in the boiling water 30 seconds, or until they turn bright green. Using a slotted spoon and reserving the boiling water, transfer the snow peas to a colander; cool them under cold running water and set them aside to drain. Blanch the broccoli florets 3 minutes, or until crisp-tender; using a slotted spoon, transfer them to a colander, cool and drain them.

4. Return the pot of water to a boil. Cook the linguine in the boiling water 10 minutes, or according to the package directions until al dente.

5. Meanwhile, cut the blanched snow peas in half diagonally.

6. For the dressing, combine the stock, soy sauce, lemon juice, oil, ginger and garlic in a small bowl and stir until blended; set aside.

7. Drain the linguine and transfer it to a large serving bowl. Add the snow peas, bell peppers, broccoli and dressing, and toss to combine.

Makes 4 servings

NUTRITION INFORMATION
values are per serving

• • •

CALORIES	400	CALCIUM	68 MG
TOTAL FAT	5 G	IRON	5 MG
SATURATED FAT	0.7 G	POTASSIUM	494 MG
CHOLESTEROL	TRACE	BETA CAROTENE	0.6 MG
SODIUM	363 MG	VITAMIN C	129 MG
DIETARY FIBER	3 G	VITAMIN E	5 MG

ORZO AND VEGETABLES

Pasta makes a superb endurance fuel for athletes. Although the old "carbo loading" theory has fallen from favor, sports nutritionists still recommend an everyday diet that is high in complex carbohydrates.

2 cups orzo (rice-shaped pasta)
1 tablespoon vegetable oil
⅓ cup chopped onion
2 medium zucchini, cut into 2 x ½-inch pieces
1 cup fresh or frozen corn kernels
¼ cup chopped pecans
1 tablespoon chopped fresh dill

1. Cook the orzo according to package directions until al dente. Turn the orzo into a colander and set aside to drain.

2. Heat the oil in a large skillet. Add the onion and sauté until transparent. Add the zucchini, corn and ¼ cup water to the skillet, cover and cook the vegetables over medium heat about 5 minutes, or until just tender.

3. Add the orzo, pecans and dill to the skillet, and cook, stirring, until heated through.   *Makes 4 servings*

NUTRITION INFORMATION
values are per serving

• • •

CALORIES	316	CALCIUM	30 MG
TOTAL FAT	9 G	IRON	3 MG
SATURATED FAT	1 G	POTASSIUM	356 MG
CHOLESTEROL	0 MG	BETA CAROTENE	TRACE
SODIUM	9 MG	VITAMIN C	8 MG
DIETARY FIBER	2 G	VITAMIN E	2 MG

COUSCOUS

Americans typically eat large portions of meat with small side dishes of vegetables and grains. This Moroccan-style meal, like many ethnic dishes, reverses the proportions: A generous platter of couscous is "garnished" with slivers of chicken.

2 tablespoons olive oil

½ teaspoon each ground cinnamon, cumin and paprika

2 or 3 saffron threads, crumbled

1 medium-size onion, sliced

1 cup diced parsnips

¾ cup sliced carrots

10 dried apricot halves

2 chicken thighs, skinned

1 cup canned plum tomatoes, drained and diced

1¼ cups instant couscous

½ teaspoon salt

Black pepper

2 tablespoons chopped fresh coriander

1. Heat the oil in a large heavy-gauge saucepan over medium heat. Add the cinnamon, cumin, paprika and saffron, and cook, stirring, 2 minutes, or until fragrant. Add the onion, parsnips, carrots, apricots and chicken thighs, and sauté, turning the chicken occasionally, 5 minutes.

2. Add the tomatoes and 4½ cups of water and bring to a boil over medium-high heat. Reduce the heat to low, cover the pan and simmer the mixture 30 minutes.

3. Remove the pan from the heat. Remove the chicken, bone it and cut the meat into strips; set aside.

4. Stir the couscous into the pan, cover and set aside 5 minutes. Add the salt, and pepper to taste.

5. Mound the couscous on a platter. Scatter the chicken strips over the couscous and sprinkle with coriander. *Makes 4 servings*

NUTRITION INFORMATION
values are per serving

• • •

CALORIES	417	CALCIUM	76 MG
TOTAL FAT	10 G	IRON	3 MG
SATURATED FAT	2 G	POTASSIUM	706 MG
CHOLESTEROL	25 MG	BETA CAROTENE	5 MG
SODIUM	409 MG	VITAMIN C	21 MG
DIETARY FIBER	13 G	VITAMIN E	1 MG

CAULIFLOWER–PARSLEY SALAD WITH CHICKEN

Crisp green parsley is more than just a garnish—it is an excellent source of potassium, beta carotene and vitamin C. Cauliflower belongs to the family of cruciferous plants, which also includes broccoli, cabbage and kale; vegetables in this group are rich in fiber and vitamin C.

> 1 pound skinless, boneless chicken breast
> 2¼ cups cauliflower florets
> ½ cup Japanese rice vinegar
> 3 tablespoons walnut oil
> 2 teaspoons Worcestershire sauce
> 1 teaspoon sugar
> 1 tablespoon chopped fresh tarragon, or 1 teaspoon dried tarragon
> ¼ teaspoon black pepper
> 1 papaya (about ¾ pound)
> ½ pound tomatoes
> 2 cups packed parsley
> 6 ounces breadsticks

1. Bring 2 cups of water to a boil in a small skillet over medium-high heat. Add the chicken, reduce the heat to low, partially cover the pan and simmer 10 minutes, or until the chicken is cooked through. Transfer the chicken to a plate, cover loosely with plastic wrap and set aside to cool.

2. Bring a medium-size saucepan of water to a boil. Blanch the cauliflower in the boiling water 2 to 4 minutes, or until it is tender when pierced with a knife. Drain the cauliflower, cool under cold running water and set aside to drain again.

3. For the dressing, in a small bowl stir together the vinegar, oil, Worcestershire sauce, sugar, tarragon and pepper; set aside.

4. Peel and seed the papaya and cut it into 1-inch cubes. Halve and core the tomatoes, then cut them into ½-inch-thick wedges. When the chicken is cool, cut it on the diagonal into ¼-inch-thick slices.

5. Place the cauliflower, papaya, tomatoes, chicken and parsley in a large bowl.

6. Stir the dressing to recombine it. Pour the dressing over the salad, toss it gently and serve it with the breadsticks.   *Makes 4 servings*

NUTRITION INFORMATION
values are per serving
• • •

CALORIES	423	CALCIUM	121 MG
TOTAL FAT	15 G	IRON	4 MG
SATURATED FAT	2 G	POTASSIUM	942 MG
CHOLESTEROL	69 MG	BETA CAROTENE	2 MG
SODIUM	769 MG	VITAMIN C	122 MG
DIETARY FIBER	5 G	VITAMIN E	5 MG

CHINESE CHICKEN SALAD

Nappa is one of several greens that may be called "Chinese cabbage." A tightly furled, rather oblong head of crinkled pale green leaves, nappa is an excellent choice for salads because the leaves are thinner and more delicate than those of regular cabbage.

> 1 pound skinless, boneless chicken breast
> 2 cups shredded nappa cabbage or green cabbage
> 1½ cups each julienned red, yellow and green bell pepper
> ¼ pound asparagus, blanched and cut into 1-inch pieces
> 1 cup bean sprouts
> ⅓ cup lemon juice
> 1 garlic clove, minced
> 1 tablespoon finely shredded fresh ginger
> ½ teaspoon red pepper flakes
> 3 tablespoons reduced-sodium soy sauce
> 2 tablespoons Oriental sesame oil
> 1 pound linguine, cooked, drained and cooled
> 1 small honeydew melon with rind removed, cut into thin wedges

1. Bring 2 cups of water to a boil in a small skillet over medium-high heat. Add the chicken, reduce the heat to low, partially cover the pan and simmer 10 minutes, or until the chicken is cooked through. Drain the chicken and set aside to cool.

2. Cut the cooled chicken into thin strips and transfer to a medium-size bowl. Add the cabbage, peppers, asparagus and bean sprouts.

3. For the dressing, in a small bowl stir together the lemon juice, garlic, ginger, red pepper flakes, soy sauce and sesame oil. Pour the dressing over the chicken mixture and toss to combine. Mound the linguine on a platter and top with the chicken mixture. Surround the salad with honeydew wedges.

Makes 6 servings

NUTRITION INFORMATION
values are per serving

• • •

CALORIES 504	CALCIUM 66 MG
TOTAL FAT 8 G	IRON 5 MG
SATURATED FAT 1 G	POTASSIUM 985 MG
CHOLESTEROL 46 MG	BETA CAROTENE 0.6 MG
SODIUM 367 MG	VITAMIN C 130 MG
DIETARY FIBER 3 G	VITAMIN E 3 MG

GREEN SALAD WITH CHICKEN AND MANGOES

This colorful salad is an outstanding source of potassium, beta carotene and vitamin C .

1 pound boneless, skinless chicken breast
½ cup low-sodium chicken stock
¼ cup lemon juice
2 tablespoons olive oil
1 teaspoon finely chopped fresh tarragon, or ¼ teaspoon dried tarragon, crumbled
¼ teaspoon salt
¼ teaspoon black pepper
2 heads Romaine lettuce
2 bunches watercress
2 cups diced red bell peppers
1 cup shredded red cabbage
1 cup finely chopped scallions
4 small mangoes, peeled and diced

Green Salad with Chicken and Mangoes

1. Bring 2 cups of water to a boil in a small skillet over medium-high heat. Add the chicken, reduce the heat to low, partially cover the pan and simmer 10 minutes, or until the chicken is cooked through. Drain the chicken and set it aside to cool to room temperature.

2. For the dressing, in a small bowl whisk together the stock, lemon juice, oil, tarragon, salt and black pepper; set aside.

3. Wash the Romaine and watercress. Tear the Romaine into bite-size pieces, trim the watercress and combine the greens in a large bowl. Add the bell peppers, cabbage and scallions, and toss well.

4. Cut the chicken diagonally into thin slices. Whisk the dressing briefly to reblend it. Add the chicken, mangoes and dressing to the salad and toss gently. Divide the salad among 4 plates and serve.

Makes 4 servings

NUTRITION INFORMATION
values are per serving

• • •

CALORIES	403	CALCIUM	247 MG
TOTAL FAT	11 G	IRON	5 MG
SATURATED FAT	2 G	POTASSIUM	1696 MG
CHOLESTEROL	69 MG	BETA CAROTENE	12 MG
SODIUM	274 MG	VITAMIN C	246 MG
DIETARY FIBER	12 G	VITAMIN E	3 MG

CURRIED TURKEY SALAD

The chicken or turkey salad you find at the salad bar may contain more mayonnaise than anything else. Here, sliced vegetables and chunks of fruit join good-sized turkey cubes in a lowfat dressing.

½ cup fat-free mayonnaise
½ cup plain lowfat yogurt
¼ cup buttermilk
¼ cup chopped chutney
1½ teaspoons curry powder
⅛ teaspoon ground ginger
3 cups skinless cooked turkey breast, cut into 1-inch cubes
One 13¼-ounce can juice-packed pineapple chunks, drained
1 cup thinly sliced celery
¼ cup thinly sliced scallions
½ cup frozen green peas, thawed

1 Granny Smith or other tart green apple, peeled, cored and diced
Small head leaf lettuce
2 ounces snow peas, blanched

1. Combine the mayonnaise, yogurt, buttermilk, chutney, curry powder and ginger in a small bowl; set aside.

2. In a large bowl combine the turkey, pineapple, celery, scallions, peas and apple. Add the dressing and toss to combine. Refrigerate the salad at least 2 hours, or until well chilled.

3. To serve, line a platter with lettuce and spoon the turkey salad on top. Garnish with snow peas.

Makes 4 servings

NUTRITION INFORMATION
values are per serving

• • •

CALORIES	363	CALCIUM	169 MG
TOTAL FAT	2 G	IRON	4 MG
SATURATED FAT	0.7 G	POTASSIUM	929 MG
CHOLESTEROL	102 MG	BETA CAROTENE	1 MG
SODIUM	452 MG	VITAMIN C	37 MG
DIETARY FIBER	4 G	VITAMIN E	2 MG

TURKEY–CHESTNUT SALAD

If you plan to stuff your holiday bird with chestnut dressing, buy some extra chestnuts and make this "best of the leftovers" salad the next day. Chestnuts are the only nuts that are low in fat.

10 ounces fresh chestnuts in shell (about 36 chestnuts)
4 slices whole-wheat bread
2 tablespoons plus 2 teaspoons margarine
¼ cup unbleached all-purpose flour
2 cups low-sodium chicken stock
2 cups diced yellow bell peppers
1⅓ cups diced celery
¾ teaspoon dried thyme
¼ teaspoon ground black pepper
8 cups Romaine, loosely packed, torn into bite-size pieces
2 cups sliced, cooked beets
1 pound skinless cooked turkey breast, thinly sliced

1. Using a sharp paring knife, cut an X on one flat side of each chestnut.

2. Bring 3 cups of water to a boil in a medium-size saucepan over medium-high heat and add the chestnuts. When the water returns to a boil, reduce the heat to medium-low, partially cover the pan and cook 20 minutes, or until the chestnuts are tender when pierced with a knife.

3. Meanwhile, preheat the oven to 375°.

4. Cut the bread into ¼-inch cubes, spread the cubes on a baking sheet and bake 5 minutes, or until crisp and golden; set aside to cool.

5. When the chestnuts are cooked, transfer them to a colander and cool under cold running water. Remove and discard the outer shell and inner skin. Break the chestnuts in half if they do not break into pieces as they are peeled; cover the chestnuts loosely with foil and set aside.

6. For the dressing, melt the margarine in a medium-size saucepan over medium heat. Add the flour, and cook, stirring, until the mixture forms a smooth paste. Gradually stir in the stock, bring to a boil and cook, stirring constantly, for 1 minute, or until the mixture is thickened. Stir in the bell peppers, celery, thyme and black pepper, and reduce the heat to medium-low. Partially cover the pan and simmer the mixture 1 to 2 minutes, or until the vegetables are just crisp-tender; set aside.

7. To serve, divide the Romaine among 4 plates. Arrange the beets and turkey on the Romaine, scatter the chestnuts and croutons on top and spoon the dressing over the salads. *Makes 4 servings*

NUTRITION INFORMATION
values are per serving

• • •

CALORIES	511	CALCIUM	120 MG
TOTAL FAT	11 G	IRON	6 MG
SATURATED FAT	2 G	POTASSIUM	1565 MG
CHOLESTEROL	94 MG	BETA CAROTENE	2 MG
SODIUM	386 MG	VITAMIN C	99 MG
DIETARY FIBER	13 G	VITAMIN E	7 MG

BEAN AND TUNA SALAD

The addition of sturdy white beans, carrots, celery, scallions and a robust rosemary dressing transforms everday canned tuna into a filling lunch that is low in fat and high in fiber. Slices of French bread round out the meal nicely.

6 tablespoons lemon juice
2 tablespoons olive oil
2 tablespoons chopped fresh parsley
1 teaspoon chopped fresh rosemary, or ¼ teaspoon
    dried rosemary, crushed
¼ teaspoon black pepper
Pinch of salt
2 cups diced carrots
1½ cups coarsely chopped scallions
1 cup diced celery
1 cup cooked or canned white beans
One 7-ounce can water-packed white tuna
12 large Boston lettuce leaves
6 ounces French bread

1. For the dressing, in a small bowl combine the lemon juice, oil, parsley, rosemary, pepper and salt, and whisk until blended.

2. In a large bowl toss together the carrots, scallions and celery.

3. If using canned beans, rinse them under cold running water and drain them. Drain the tuna. Add the beans and tuna to the salad, pour the dressing over it and toss it gently. Let the salad stand at room temperature at least 30 minutes, or refrigerate it at least 2 hours.

4. Meanwhile, wash and dry the lettuce. To serve, line 4 plates with lettuce leaves and spoon the tuna salad on top; serve the bread alongside.

Makes 4 servings

NUTRITION INFORMATION
values are per serving

• • •

CALORIES	368	CALCIUM	168 MG
TOTAL FAT	10 G	IRON	5 MG
SATURATED FAT	2 G	POTASSIUM	1035 MG
CHOLESTEROL	21 MG	BETA CAROTENE	14 MG
SODIUM	520 MG	VITAMIN C	43 MG
DIETARY FIBER	5 G	VITAMIN E	3 MG

FRESH TUNA NIÇOISE

If you're still making tuna salad the way your mother did, consider as an alternative this sophisticated "composed salad" from the South of France. Baked fresh tuna is arranged on individual salad plates with boiled red potatoes (tiny new potatoes are best), crisp-tender green beans and juicy tomatoes in a mustard-chive vinaigrette. Save the sliced white bread for another day and enjoy the salad with a crusty French *baguette* or *boule*.

¾ pound small red potatoes, preferably new potatoes
5 ounces green beans, cut into 1½-inch pieces (1 cup)
¾ pound fresh yellowfin tuna, ¾ inch thick
¼ cup red wine vinegar, preferably balsamic
1 tablespoon olive oil
1 tablespoon Dijon mustard
1 tablespoon chopped fresh chives
Pinch of salt
Pinch of black pepper
2 medium-size tomatoes
8 ounces Romaine lettuce, torn into bite-size pieces
6 ounces French bread, sliced

1. Bring a medium-size saucepan of water to a boil. Scrub the potatoes, place them in the boiling water, cover, reduce the heat to low and simmer 15 to 20 minutes, or until the potatoes are tender when pierced with a knife.

2. Meanwhile, bring a small saucepan of water to a boil. Blanch the green beans 2 to 3 minutes, cool under cold water and set aside in a colander to drain.

3. Preheat the oven to 375°.

4. Place the tuna in a small baking dish, add 2 tablespoons of water, cover with foil and bake 10 minutes, or until the fish flakes when tested with a knife. Transfer the tuna to a bowl and use a fork to break it into large flakes; cover loosely and set aside.

5. In a small bowl, whisk together the vinegar, oil, mustard, chives, salt and pepper; transfer half of the dressing to a medium-size bowl. When the potatoes are done, drain, cool them slightly and cut into 1-inch cubes. Add the potatoes to the larger bowl of dressing and toss to coat. Cut the tomatoes into wedges.

6. Divide the Romaine among 6 salad plates and arrange the potatoes, tomatoes, green beans and tuna on top. Pour the remaining dressing over the salads and serve with the bread.   *Makes 4 servings*

NUTRITION INFORMATION
values are per serving
• • •

CALORIES	361	CALCIUM	107 MG
TOTAL FAT	6 G	IRON	5 MG
SATURATED FAT	1 G	POTASSIUM	1111 MG
CHOLESTEROL	38 MG	BETA CAROTENE	2 MG
SODIUM	405 MG	VITAMIN C	41 MG
DIETARY FIBER	4 G	VITAMIN E	1 MG

SPICY SHRIMP SALAD WITH CONFETTI RICE

Cooking shrimp in their shells intensifies their flavor. Here, the shells, along with garlic and herbs, are also used to flavor olive oil for the dressing. Olive oil is rich in monounsaturated fats.

1 tablespoon pickling spice
1¼ pounds medium-size shrimp, in their shells
3 tablespoons olive oil
2 garlic cloves, minced
1 teaspoon each dried basil, oregano and tarragon, crushed
¼ teaspoon red pepper flakes
¼ cup buttermilk
¼ cup fresh lemon juice
1 tablespoon Dijon mustard
2 cups cooked brown rice, cooled
½ cup finely chopped red bell pepper
½ cup finely chopped green bell pepper
1 head Boston lettuce
2 tablespoons finely chopped parsley

1. Stir the pickling spice into 1 quart of water in a medium-size saucepan and bring to a boil. Add the shrimp, cover, remove the pan from the heat and let stand 6 to 8 minutes. Cool the shrimp in a colander under cold running water. Shell and devein the shrimp, reserving the shells. Transfer the shrimp to a medium-size bowl and set aside.

2. Heat the oil in a medium-size skillet and add the shrimp shells, garlic, herbs and red pepper flakes. Cover and cook the mixture 10 minutes, then strain it and add it to the shrimp.

3. Combine the buttermilk, lemon juice and mustard in a small bowl, add the mixture to the shrimp

Scallop and Orange Salad

and toss gently. Refrigerate the shrimp at least 2 hours, or overnight.

4. Combine the rice and bell peppers in a large bowl. Pour half of the dressing from the shrimp into the rice mixture; toss to combine.

5. Line a platter with lettuce and mound the rice on top. Arrange the shrimp on the rice and top with the remaining dressing. Sprinkle the shrimp with chopped parsley. *Makes 4 servings*

NUTRITION INFORMATION
values are per serving
• • •

CALORIES	366	CALCIUM	139 MG
TOTAL FAT	13 G	IRON	4 MG
SATURATED FAT	2 G	POTASSIUM	546 MG
CHOLESTEROL	177 MG	BETA CAROTENE	0.5 MG
SODIUM	283 MG	VITAMIN C	48 MG
DIETARY FIBER	2 G	VITAMIN E	2 MG

SCALLOP AND ORANGE SALAD

While pleasing luncheon guests with this attractive salad, you can also boast about its rich supply of potassium, calcium, vitamin C and fiber.

2 navel oranges
1⅓ cups orange juice
1 pound bay scallops
2 tablespoons minced fresh ginger
1 tablespoon honey
1 garlic clove, minced
¼ cup white wine vinegar
2 tablespoons olive oil
¼ teaspoon each salt and black pepper
2 cups diced red bell pepper
⅔ cup thinly sliced scallions
1 cup raw bulgur
3 cups leaf lettuce
2 cups broccoli florets, blanched

1. Grate 2 teaspoons of orange zest; set aside. Peel and section the oranges and set aside in a bowl.

2. Heat the orange juice in a large skillet over medium-high heat. Add the scallops and cook 1 to 2 minutes, or just until cooked through; drain in a strainer set over a bowl.

3. Return the orange juice to the skillet, add the ginger, honey and garlic, and bring to a boil. Reduce the heat to low and cook, stirring occasionally, 20 minutes, or until the liquid is reduced to ½ cup. Strain the liquid and set aside to cool.

4. In a large bowl whisk together the vinegar, oil, salt and black pepper. Stir in the scallops, the orange liquid, orange sections, half the orange zest, the bell pepper and half the scallions; cover and refrigerate 1 hour, or until the flavors are blended.

5. Meanwhile, place the bulgur in a medium-size bowl and add 2 cups of cold water; set aside 30 minutes. Thoroughly drain the bulgur and squeeze it as dry as possible.

6. Line 4 diner plates with lettuce and divide the bulgur among them. Arrange the scallops, broccoli and oranges on top. Drizzle some dressing over each salad and sprinkle with the remaining scallions and orange zest. *Makes 4 servings*

NUTRITION INFORMATION
values are per serving
• • •

CALORIES	410	CALCIUM	154 MG
TOTAL FAT	9 G	IRON	4 MG
SATURATED FAT	1 G	POTASSIUM	1262 MG
CHOLESTEROL	37 MG	BETA CAROTENE	2 MG
SODIUM	350 MG	VITAMIN C	225 MG
DIETARY FIBER	12 G	VITAMIN E	2 MG

TAMPA BAY HALIBUT SALAD

Make-ahead meals can be a real convenience. Chilling this salad for three to four hours actually improves it, by giving the potatoes and fish time to absorb the well-seasoned, lowfat dressing. The same holds true for most any pasta, potato or grain salad.

1 large sweet potato (about 10 ounces)
1½ pounds asparagus
1 pound boneless halibut steak, 1 inch thick
2 navel oranges
½ cup freshly squeezed orange juice

¼ cup chopped shallots
4 teaspoons olive oil
1 tablespoon Japanese rice vinegar
1 teaspoon Dijon mustard
¼ teaspoon salt
8 large Romaine lettuce leaves, washed and trimmed

1. Bring a small saucepan of water to a boil. Wash and trim the sweet potato; do not peel it. Cut the potato into 1-inch chunks and cook 20 minutes, or until tender.

2. Meanwhile, bring a large pot of water to a boil. Trim the asparagus, cut into 1-inch pieces and cook 5 to 7 minutes, or until crisp-tender. Drain, cool under cold water and set aside to drain again. When the potato is done, drain and set aside to cool.

3. Preheat the oven to 350°. Rinse and pat dry the halibut, place in a small baking pan and bake 10 minutes, or until the fish flakes when tested with a fork; set aside to cool.

4. Meanwhile, peel and section the oranges and remove the membranes; set aside.

5. For the dressing, in a small bowl combine the orange juice, shallots, oil, vinegar, mustard and salt, and whisk until blended.

6. In a large bowl combine the potato, asparagus, halibut and oranges. Add the dressing and toss gently (the fish should remain in large chunks). Cover the bowl and refrigerate the salad 3 to 4 hours, tossing twice while it is chilling.

7. To serve, line 4 plates with the Romaine and mound the halibut salad on top. *Makes 4 servings*

NUTRITION INFORMATION
values are per serving

• • •

CALORIES	324	CALCIUM	147 MG
TOTAL FAT	8 G	IRON	3 MG
SATURATED FAT	1 G	POTASSIUM	1330 MG
CHOLESTEROL	36 MG	BETA CAROTENE	9 MG
SODIUM	243 MG	VITAMIN C	111 MG
DIETARY FIBER	4 G	VITAMIN E	6 MG

POTATO-VEGETABLE SALAD WITH SALMON

All too often, storebought potato salad sacrifices the potato—a true powerhouse of nutrition—to a morass of mayo. Here's a potato salad worth the small effort of making it at home: To the potatoes (in a yogurt-based dressing) are added limas and green beans, zucchini, carrots, cabbage and radishes. The addition of salmon turns it into a lowfat main dish.

½ cup plain lowfat yogurt
2 tablespoons plus 1 teaspoon olive oil
2 tablespoons finely chopped fresh dill
1 tablespoon Dijon mustard
¼ teaspoon black pepper
1½ pounds small red potatoes, boiled, peeled and quartered
½ pound green beans, cut into 1-inch lengths and blanched
1⅓ cups grated zucchini
1 cup grated carrots
1 cup finely shredded red cabbage
¾ cup thinly sliced radishes
½ cup frozen lima beans, blanched
Two 7-ounce cans water-packed salmon
2 shallots, finely chopped
1 tablespoon chopped fresh parsley
¼ teaspoon salt

1. For the dressing, in a small bowl stir together the yogurt, oil, dill, mustard and pepper until well blended; set aside.

2. Place the potatoes, green beans, zucchini, carrots, cabbage, radishes and lima beans in a large bowl and stir to combine.

3. Drain the salmon and add it to the salad. Add the shallots, parsley and dressing and stir gently (the salmon should remain in fairly large chunks). Add the salt, stir again and serve. *Makes 6 servings*

NUTRITION INFORMATION
values are per serving

• • •

CALORIES	285	CALCIUM	229 MG
TOTAL FAT	10 G	IRON	2 MG
SATURATED FAT	2 G	POTASSIUM	1041 MG
CHOLESTEROL	38 MG	BETA CAROTENE	4 MG
SODIUM	555 MG	VITAMIN C	34 MG
DIETARY FIBER	5 G	VITAMIN E	3 MG

SALMON SALAD WITH LENTILS AND RICE

Salmon is one of the best sources of omega-3 fatty acids, the cardio-protective substances in fish oil.

1½ cups cooked lentils (½ cup dried)
1½ cups cooked brown rice (½ cup raw)
½ cup finely chopped scallions
¼ cup chopped fresh parsley
2 tablespoons red wine vinegar, preferably balsamic
1 tablespoon capers, rinsed and drained
2 teaspoons olive oil, preferably extra-virgin
¼ teaspoon salt
¼ teaspoon black pepper
⅛ teaspoon dried thyme
3 cups arugula or watercress leaves
One 7-ounce can water-packed salmon, drained
¼ cup thinly sliced radishes

1. Place the lentils and rice in a medium-size bowl. Add the scallions, parsley, vinegar, capers, oil, salt, pepper and thyme, and stir to mix well.

2. Place the greens on a platter and top with the lentil-rice mixture.

3. In a small bowl combine the salmon and radishes, breaking up the salmon with a fork. Scatter the salmon and radishes over the lentils and rice.

Makes 2 servings

NUTRITION INFORMATION
values are per serving

• • •

CALORIES	558	CALCIUM	350 MG
TOTAL FAT	12 G	IRON	8 MG
SATURATED FAT	2 G	POTASSIUM	1286 MG
CHOLESTEROL	55 MG	BETA CAROTENE	2 MG
SODIUM	850 MG	VITAMIN C	48 MG
DIETARY FIBER	12 G	VITAMIN E	5 MG

APPLE, FENNEL AND PASTA SALAD

The pasta, vegetables and diced apples are tossed with a balsamic vinegar dressing in this contemporary pasta salad. Balsamic vinegar, a unique Italian product, is aged for years in a series of vats made of different kinds of wood. Dark, syrupy and mildly sweet, it needs little or no oil to turn it into a delicious salad dressing. Serious salad makers delight in a "wardrobe" of vinegars that might also include rice vinegar and herbed, spiced or fruited vinegars.

5 ounces elbow macaroni
1½ cups frozen lima beans
¼ cup balsamic vinegar
1½ tablespoons olive oil
1 tablespoon frozen apple juice concentrate, thawed
2 teaspoons chopped fresh oregano, or ¾ teaspoon dried oregano, crumbled
½ teaspoon salt
¼ teaspoon black pepper
3 McIntosh apples (about 1 pound total weight)
2 tablespoons lemon juice
One ½-pound fennel bulb
⅔ cup thinly sliced radishes
1½ ounces Parmesan cheese
½ small head escarole

1. Bring a large saucepan of water to a boil. Add the macaroni and cook 8 minutes, or according to the package directions until al dente; drain, rinse under cold water and set aside to drain thoroughly.

2. Cook the lima beans according to the package directions; drain and set aside.

3. For the dressing, whisk together the vinegar, oil, apple juice concentrate, oregano, salt and pepper; set aside.

4. Core but do not peel the apples, then dice them and toss them with the lemon juice in a large bowl. Trim and thinly slice the fennel and add it to the apples. Add the macaroni, lima beans, radishes and dressing, and toss well.

5. Using a vegetable peeler or a sharp knife, cut the Parmesan into thin shavings; set aside.

6. To serve, wash and trim the escarole. Line a platter with escarole leaves and mound the apple mixture on top. Scatter the Parmesan shavings over the salad and serve. *Makes 4 servings*

NUTRITION INFORMATION
values are per serving
• • •

CALORIES 403   CALCIUM 254 MG
TOTAL FAT 10 G   IRON 5 MG
SATURATED FAT 3 G   POTASSIUM 860 MG
CHOLESTEROL 9 MG   BETA CAROTENE 2 MG
SODIUM 526 MG   VITAMIN C 41 MG
DIETARY FIBER 7 G   VITAMIN E 6 MG

5. Meanwhile, for the dressing, stir together the miso, ginger and pepper in a small bowl. Gradually stir in the yogurt, then add ¼ cup of cold water and stir until smoothly blended; set aside.

6. Cut the snow peas into slivers. When the pasta is done, drain, rinse under cold water and set aside to drain thoroughly.

7. To serve, place the pasta, tomatoes, carrots, snow peas and soybeans in a large bowl. Pour on the dressing, sprinkle the salad with parsley and sesame seeds, and toss gently to combine.

Makes 4 servings

PASTA–SOYBEAN SALAD WITH MISO DRESSING

Soybeans supply twice as much protein as most other legumes—and also about nine times as much fat. However, most of the fat is unsaturated, and soy beans, like all other plant-derived foods, contain no cholesterol.

¼ cup dried soybeans, soaked overnight in cold water
1 pound tomatoes
¼ pound carrots
¼ pound snow peas
½ pound radiatore (pasta ruffles) or fusilli (spiral)
1 tablespoon plus 1 teaspoon light miso
¼ teaspoon ground ginger
¼ teaspoon black pepper
¼ cup plain lowfat yogurt
1 tablespoon chopped parsley
1 teaspoon toasted sesame seeds

1. Drain the soybeans, add fresh cold water to cover and bring to a boil over medium heat. Cover the pan, reduce the heat to low and simmer 1 hour, or until the soybeans are just tender. Skim off and discard the skins, which will float to the surface.

2. While the soybeans are cooking, core the tomatoes and cut into chunks. Trim, peel and grate the carrots. Trim the snow peas. Bring a medium-size saucepan of water to a boil and blanch the snow peas 30 seconds, or until they turn bright green; rinse under cold running water and set aside to drain.

3. Drain the soybeans and set aside to cool.

4. Bring a large pot of water to a boil. Cook the pasta 10 minutes, or according to the package directions, until al dente.

NUTRITION INFORMATION
values are per serving
• • •

CALORIES 329   CALCIUM 102 MG
TOTAL FAT 4 G   IRON 5 MG
SATURATED FAT 0.4 G   POTASSIUM 719 MG
CHOLESTEROL TRACE   BETA CAROTENE 5 MG
SODIUM 244 MG   VITAMIN C 41 MG
DIETARY FIBER 3 G   VITAMIN E 1 MG

TROPICAL BEAN SALAD

Slivers of smoked turkey add a savory tang to this colorful salad. Because of their high sodium content, smoked meats and seafood are best used as flavor accents rather than as the main ingredient of a meal. You may wish to eliminate any salt in a recipe when such foods are included.

¼ cup low-sodium chicken stock
2 tablespoons Dijon mustard
2 tablespoons lemon juice
4 teaspoons olive oil
1 garlic clove, minced
Black pepper
3 tablespoons finely chopped fresh basil
1 large head Romaine lettuce
3½ cups cooked baby lima beans (2 cups dried)
3 cups fresh pineapple chunks
1 medium-size red onion, thinly sliced
6 plum tomatoes, cut into wedges
2 cups seedless grapes
2 ounces smoked turkey, cut into thin strips
12 whole toasted almonds

1. For the dressing, in a small bowl combine the stock, mustard, lemon juice, oil and garlic. Add pepper to taste and whisk until smooth. Stir in the basil; set aside.

2. Wash and trim the Romaine and cut the leaves in half crosswise; wrap the top halves in plastic wrap and refrigerate them. Cut the bottom halves of the leaves into very thin strips and place them in a large serving bowl. Add the beans, pineapple, onion, tomatoes, grapes and turkey, and toss gently to combine. Add the dressing and toss again. Cover the bowl and refrigerate 3 hours, or until the salad is well chilled and the flavors are blended.

3. To serve, arrange the reserved Romaine leaves around the edges of the salad. Scatter the almonds over the salad and serve.   *Makes 6 servings*

NUTRITION INFORMATION
values are per serving

• • •

CALORIES	298	CALCIUM	114 MG
TOTAL FAT	8 G	IRON	5 MG
SATURATED FAT	0.9 G	POTASSIUM	959 MG
CHOLESTEROL	8 MG	BETA CAROTENE	1 MG
SODIUM	141 MG	VITAMIN C	40 MG
DIETARY FIBER	3 G	VITAMIN E	1 MG

Black Bean Salad

BLACK BEAN SALAD

Legumes—dried beans and peas—are excellent sources of guar gum and pectin, two types of soluble fiber that can lower blood cholesterol levels.

⅓ cup white wine vinegar
2 tablespoons corn oil
1 tablespoon Dijon mustard
1 teaspoon Oriental sesame oil
1 garlic clove, peeled and minced
1 teaspoon dried tarragon
¼ teaspoon salt
¼ teaspoon black pepper
2 cups canned black beans, rinsed and drained
1 cup diced celery
1 red bell pepper, thinly sliced
6 ounces small fresh beets, trimmed
2 cups sliced carrots
2 cups shredded Romaine lettuce

1. In a large bowl whisk together the vinegar, corn oil, mustard, sesame oil, garlic, tarragon, salt and black pepper. Add the beans, celery and bell pepper, and toss well; set aside at room temperature.

2. Bring 2 cups of water to a boil in a medium-size saucepan over medium-high heat. Add the beets, cover the pan, reduce the heat to medium-low and simmer 15 minutes, or until the beets are tender when pierced with a sharp knife. Add the carrots and cook 5 minutes, or until crisp-tender. Drain the beets and carrots, cool under cold running water and set aside to drain.

3. Halve the beets and cut them into ¼-inch-thick slices. Add the beets, carrots and Romaine to the salad, and toss to combine. Let the salad stand at room temperature at least 1 hour before serving.

Makes 6 servings

NUTRITION INFORMATION
values are per serving

• • •

CALORIES	247	CALCIUM	76 MG
TOTAL FAT	9 G	IRON	3 MG
SATURATED FAT	1 G	POTASSIUM	853 MG
CHOLESTEROL	0 MG	BETA CAROTENE	12 MG
SODIUM	292 MG	VITAMIN C	52 MG
DIETARY FIBER	8 G	VITAMIN E	7 MG

WHITE BEANS IN PARMESAN VINAIGRETTE

Beans have twice as much protein as grains and are good sources of B vitamins and iron. This salad provides more than your daily requirement of thiamin, a B vitamin essential for turning carbohydrates into energy.

1 cup dried Great Northern beans
1 bay leaf
½ teaspoon salt
3 large plum tomatoes, peeled, seeded and coarsely chopped
2 tablespoons slivered black olives
2 tablespoons chopped scallion
3 tablespoons low-sodium chicken stock
3 tablespoons grated Parmesan cheese
2 tablespoons red wine vinegar
1 teaspoon olive oil
2 garlic cloves, minced
¼ teaspoon black pepper

1. Place the beans in a medium-size saucepan, add enough water to cover by 2 inches and bring to a boil over medium heat. Reduce the heat, add the bay leaf and salt, cover and simmer 1½ hours, or until the beans are tender, adding water if necessary to prevent the beans from drying out.

2. Drain the cooked beans. Remove and discard the bay leaf and transfer the beans to a medium-size bowl. Stir in the tomatoes, olives and scallions, and set aside.

3. For the dressing, whisk together the stock, Parmesan, vinegar, oil, garlic and pepper in a small bowl. Pour the dressing over the warm beans and toss well. Serve at room temperature.

Makes 6 servings

NUTRITION INFORMATION
values are per serving

• • •

CALORIES	238	CALCIUM	139 MG
TOTAL FAT	5 G	IRON	4 MG
SATURATED FAT	2 G	POTASSIUM	786 MG
CHOLESTEROL	4 MG	BETA CAROTENE	0.7 MG
SODIUM	518 MG	VITAMIN C	19 MG
DIETARY FIBER	4 G	VITAMIN E	TRACE

BLACK-EYED PEA AND LENTIL SALAD

Legumes such as black-eyed peas and lentils contain all of the B vitamins except B_{12}, which is not found in any foods from plant sources.

½ cup dried black-eyed peas
½ cup dried lentils
½ teaspoon plus ⅛ teaspoon salt
½ cup finely chopped onion
¼ cup chopped fresh parsley
1½ teaspoons lemon juice
1 teaspoon Dijon mustard
1 garlic clove, minced
½ teaspoon dried thyme
⅛ teaspoon black pepper
1 teaspoon olive oil
2 tablespoons low-sodium chicken stock

1. Place the peas and lentils in a medium-size saucepan with cold water to cover by 2 inches. Bring to a boil over medium heat and stir in ½ teaspoon of the salt; cover, reduce the heat to low and simmer 20 minutes, or until the peas and lentils are tender, adding more water if necessary.

2. Drain the peas and lentils and transfer them to a medium-size bowl. Stir in the onion and parsley.

3. For the dressing, in a small bowl whisk together the lemon juice, mustard, garlic, thyme, pepper and the remaining salt. Slowly whisk in the oil, then add the stock, whisking constantly. Pour the dressing over the peas and lentils and toss well.

Makes 6 servings

NUTRITION INFORMATION
values are per serving

• • •

CALORIES	215	CALCIUM	139 MG
TOTAL FAT	2 G	IRON	5 MG
SATURATED FAT	0.3 G	POTASSIUM	766 MG
CHOLESTEROL	0 MG	BETA CAROTENE	0.5 MG
SODIUM	499 MG	VITAMIN C	12 MG
DIETARY FIBER	10 G	VITAMIN E	4 MG

RED BEAN AND RICE SALAD

On Mondays, you'll find a steaming pot of red beans and rice on many a Louisiana dinner table, as the dish is usually cooked with the savory remains of the traditional Sunday ham. This nutritious legume and grain combination, however, is equally good as a salad, flavored with herbs and hot sauce instead of the ham.

2 tablespoons vegetable oil
1 cup brown rice
2½ cups low-sodium chicken stock
1 cup canned red kidney beans, rinsed and drained
¼ cup sliced celery
¼ cup chopped onion
¼ cup chopped green bell pepper
¼ cup chopped red bell pepper
1 tablespoon chopped fresh parsley
1 tablespoon red wine vinegar
½ teaspoon hot pepper sauce
2 cups shredded lettuce

1. Heat 1 tablespoon of the oil in a medium-size saucepan over medium-high heat. Add the rice and sauté until lightly browned. Add the stock and bring to a boil. Reduce the heat and simmer the rice, covered, 50 minutes, or until the rice is tender and the broth is completely absorbed. Drain the rice in a colander and set aside to cool at least 30 minutes.
2. When cool, transfer the rice to a bowl. Add the remaining oil and the other remaining ingredients except the lettuce, and toss until well combined. Cover and refrigerate 2 hours.
3. To serve, line a platter with shredded lettuce and mound the salad on top. *Makes 4 servings*

NUTRITION INFORMATION
values are per serving

• • •

CALORIES	316	CALCIUM	42 MG
TOTAL FAT	9 G	IRON	3 MG
SATURATED FAT	1 G	POTASSIUM	543 MG
CHOLESTEROL	0 MG	BETA CAROTENE	TRACE
SODIUM	324 MG	VITAMIN C	23 MG
DIETARY FIBER	7 G	VITAMIN E	6 MG

GREEK SALAD

Eliminating the oil and olives from a Greek salad cuts fat and calories considerably. A yogurt dressing and fiber-rich black-eyed peas take the place of these traditional high-fat ingredients.

1 large cucumber
½ cup plain lowfat yogurt
¼ cup chopped fresh mint
3 tablespoons lemon juice
1 teaspoon sugar
4 plum tomatoes
4 ounces Romaine lettuce, torn into bite-size pieces
2 cups cooked black-eyed peas (1 cup dried)
¼ cup chopped scallions
1 ounce feta cheese, crumbled

1. For the dressing, scrub the cucumber and halve lengthwise. Peel and seed one half, cut into large chunks and process in a food processor or blender 15 to 20 seconds, or until puréed. Add the yogurt, mint, lemon juice and sugar and process another 5 to 10 seconds, scraping down the sides of the container with a rubber spatula; set aside.
2. Cut the remaining cucumber half lengthwise into quarters, then cut crosswise into ¼-inch-thick slices. Cut the tomatoes into large dice. Place the Romaine, cucumber, tomatoes, peas and scallions in a large bowl and toss to combine. Sprinkle the feta over the salad and, just before serving, add the dressing and toss to combine. *Makes 2 servings*

NUTRITION INFORMATION
values are per serving

• • •

CALORIES	302	CALCIUM	438 MG
TOTAL FAT	5 G	IRON	4 MG
SATURATED FAT	3 G	POTASSIUM	1502 MG
CHOLESTEROL	16 MG	BETA CAROTENE	3 MG
SODIUM	225 MG	VITAMIN C	69 MG
DIETARY FIBER	14 G	VITAMIN E	5 MG

Lentils with Oranges and Arugula

LENTILS WITH ORANGES AND ARUGULA

The bright-hot flavor of fresh ginger—in the form of ginger juice—enlivens this salad. The unusual seasoning is made by squeezing freshly grated ginger root in a square of cheesecloth. A thumb-sized piece of the root will yield about two teaspoons of juice. To keep ginger root fresh, seal it in plastic wrap and then in foil, and store it in the freezer for up to a year.

½ cup dried red lentils
1 garlic clove, peeled
½ small onion
½ teaspoon turmeric
2 oranges, peeled and sectioned
½ cup sliced red onion
2 tablespoons chopped fresh mint
1 teaspoon red wine vinegar, preferably balsamic
2 teaspoons olive oil
1 teaspoon walnut oil
⅓ cup orange juice
2 teaspoons ginger juice
3 cups arugula or watercress leaves

1. Place the lentils, garlic clove, onion half and turmeric in a large saucepan. Add enough cold water to cover and bring to a boil over high heat. Reduce the heat and simmer 7 to 10 minutes, or until the lentils are tender.

2. Drain the lentils; remove and discard the garlic and onion. Transfer the lentils to a large bowl, add the oranges, red onion and mint, and toss to combine.

3. For the dressing, combine the vinegar, oils, orange juice and ginger juice in a small bowl, and whisk until blended. Pour the dressing over the lentil mixture and toss again.

4. Arrange the arugula on 2 plates and spoon the lentil mixture on top. *Makes 2 servings*

NUTRITION INFORMATION
values are per serving

• • •

CALORIES 341	CALCIUM 166 MG
TOTAL FAT 8 G	IRON 6 MG
SATURATED FAT 0.9 G	POTASSIUM 1128 MG
CHOLESTEROL 0 MG	BETA CAROTENE 2 MG
SODIUM 27 MG	VITAMIN C 122 MG
DIETARY FIBER 12 G	VITAMIN E 4 MG

SPICY POTATO AND CHICKPEA SALAD

Roasted bell peppers have an inimitable smoky flavor, and roasting peppers at home is easy: Halve, stem and seed the peppers, then cut each half in half again. Lay the pepper pieces on a foil-lined baking sheet and broil them four inches from the heat, turning them occasionally, about ten minutes, or until charred. Place the peppers in a paper bag to steam for ten minutes, then scrape off the charred skin and rinse the pepper pieces under cold running water.

1 anchovy fillet, drained
1 tablespoon olive oil
½ cup chopped onion
2 garlic cloves, chopped
2 tablespoons white wine
3 tablespoons low-sodium chicken stock
2 tablespoons sherry vinegar or red wine vinegar
¼ teaspoon salt
1 teaspoon ground cumin
¼ teaspoon paprika
⅛ teaspoon ground cloves
Pinch of ground red pepper
⅔ cup canned chickpeas, rinsed and drained
4 medium-size potatoes, boiled and cut into 1-inch pieces
1 large red bell pepper, roasted (see above), peeled and cut into ¼-inch-wide strips
4 pitted black olives, halved
¼ cup chopped scallions
1½ tablespoons chopped fresh parsley
1½ tablespoons chopped fresh coriander

1. In a medium-size skillet, heat the anchovy in the oil over medium heat, stirring with a wooden spoon, until the anchovy disintegrates and the oil is hot. Add the onion and garlic and cook 1 minute, tossing to coat with oil, then cover and cook 4 to 5 minutes, or until the onion is soft.

2. Add the wine and boil gently until almost all of the liquid has evaporated. Add the stock, vinegar, salt, cumin, paprika, cloves and ground red pepper, and simmer another 2 minutes.

3. Remove the skillet from the heat, add the chickpeas and potatoes, and toss gently. Add the pepper strips, olives, scallions, parsley and coriander and toss again. Serve the salad at room temperature.

Makes 2 servings

NUTRITION INFORMATION
values are per serving

• • •

CALORIES	483	CALCIUM	97 MG
TOTAL FAT	11 G	IRON	6 MG
SATURATED FAT	1 G	POTASSIUM	1854 MG
CHOLESTEROL	2 MG	BETA CAROTENE	0.8 MG
SODIUM	674 MG	VITAMIN C	146 MG
DIETARY FIBER	7 G	VITAMIN E	1 MG

TABBOULEH

This light, refreshing grain salad sparkles with the flavors of mint, parsley and lemon juice. It makes a fine addition to a picnic lunch.

1 cup bulgur
2 medium tomatoes, chopped
1 cup fresh parsley, chopped
1 cup fresh mint, chopped
½ cup finely chopped scallions, green and white parts
2 tablespoons lemon juice
2 tablespoons olive oil
½ teaspoon salt
Small head Romaine lettuce

1. Bring 2 cups of water to a boil in a small saucepan.

2. Place the bulgur in a large bowl and pour the boiling water over it; let stand at least 2 hours.

3. Drain the bulgur well in a strainer, pressing out the excess water. Return the bulgur to the bowl, add the tomatoes, herbs, scallions, lemon juice, oil and salt, and mix well. Line a platter with Romaine leaves and mound the tabbouleh on top. *Makes 4 servings*

NUTRITION INFORMATION
values are per serving

• • •

CALORIES	212	CALCIUM	73 MG
TOTAL FAT	8 G	IRON	3 MG
SATURATED FAT	1 G	POTASSIUM	542 MG
CHOLESTEROL	0 MG	BETA CAROTENE	2 MG
SODIUM	288 MG	VITAMIN C	50 MG
DIETARY FIBER	10 G	VITAMIN E	2 MG

WILD RICE SALAD WITH WALNUT-ORANGE DRESSING

This colorful salad, best made ahead of time for flavor as well as convenience, is an excellent source of the antioxidant vitamins C and E. Vitamin E is found in the walnut oil, wild rice and Brussels sprouts; both the Brussels sprouts and the red bell pepper are rich in vitamin C.

1 cup wild rice
One 10-ounce package frozen Brussels sprouts, thawed
⅓ cup freshly squeezed orange juice
2 tablespoons walnut oil
½ teaspoon orange extract
¼ teaspoon black pepper
Pinch of salt
1 cup slivered red bell pepper
2 tablespoons chopped fresh mint
4 large Romaine lettuce leaves

1. Bring 3½ cups of water to a boil in a medium-size saucepan over medium-high heat. Add the rice, reduce the heat to low and simmer, partially covered, 45 minutes.

2. Cut the sprouts in half and set aside to drain on paper towels.

3. Remove the pan of rice from the heat and stir in the orange juice, oil, orange extract, black pepper and salt. Stir in the Brussels sprouts, bell pepper and mint. Let the mixture cool slightly, then transfer to a large bowl, cover with plastic wrap and refrigerate overnight, stirring occasionally.

4. To serve, line a platter with the Romaine and mound the salad on top.   *Makes 4 servings*

NUTRITION INFORMATION
values are per serving

• • •

CALORIES	253	CALCIUM	36 MG
TOTAL FAT	8 G	IRON	2 MG
SATURATED FAT	0.8 G	POTASSIUM	525 MG
CHOLESTEROL	0 MG	BETA CAROTENE	0.6 MG
SODIUM	53 MG	VITAMIN C	93 MG
DIETARY FIBER	3 G	VITAMIN E	3 MG

TWO-RICE AND PASTA SALAD

Not so long ago, the weight-conscious shied away from "starches." Today we recognize complex carbohydrates—a more flattering name for starches—as the building blocks of a healthy eating plan. A lowfat dish like this one would fit perfectly into almost any weight-loss or weight-maintenance diet.

2 tablespoons dried currants
¾ teaspoon salt
½ cup wild rice
½ cup brown rice
1¾ ounces small bow-tie pasta (about ½ cup)
¾ pound Bosc pears
2 tablespoons lemon juice
¼ cup nonfat sour cream
¼ cup lowfat milk (2%)
2 tablespoons chutney
2 teaspoons curry powder
1 cup diced red bell peppers
1 cup diced carrots
½ cup chopped scallions
8 large lettuce leaves
¾ ounce shelled, toasted pistachios (about ¼ cup)

1. Place the currants in a small bowl with hot water to cover; set aside.

2. Bring 2 quarts of water to a boil in a large saucepan over medium-high heat. Add ¼ teaspoon of the salt, the wild rice and brown rice, and cook, stirring occasionally, 40 minutes. Add the pasta and cook 8 minutes. Drain the rice and pasta in a large strainer, cool under cold water and set aside to drain.

3. Core the pears, cut them into ¾-inch cubes and place them in a bowl. Add the lemon juice and toss well.

4. For the dressing, in a small bowl combine the sour cream, milk, chutney, curry powder, the remaining salt and 1 tablespoon of the lemon juice from the bowl of pears.

5. In a large bowl combine the rice and pasta with the bell peppers, carrots, scallions, pears and currants. Add the dressing and toss well, then cover the bowl and refrigerate until well chilled.

6. To serve, line 4 plates with lettuce leaves and mound the salad on top. Sprinkle the salad with pistachios and serve.   *Makes 4 servings*

NUTRITION INFORMATION
values are per serving
• • •

CALORIES 384 CALCIUM 75 MG
TOTAL FAT 8 G IRON 3 MG
SATURATED FAT 2 G POTASSIUM 596 MG
CHOLESTEROL 6 MG BETA CAROTENE 4 MG
SODIUM 536 MG VITAMIN C 64 MG
DIETARY FIBER 6 G VITAMIN E TRACE

ITALIAN BREAD SALAD

The Italians call this salad *panzanella* and make it with slightly stale, crusty Italian bread. But you can use just about any kind of reasonably firm bread. Make the salad a few hours ahead of time to give the bread and vegetables time to absorb the vinaigrette.

1 small ripe tomato
¼ cup tomato juice
3 tablespoons balsamic vinegar
2 teaspoons walnut oil
¼ teaspoon thyme
Pinch each of salt and black pepper
1 red and 1 yellow bell pepper, sliced and blanched
5 ounces green beans, trimmed and blanched
2 cups cubed whole-wheat bread (2½ slices)

1. For the dressing, core and quarter the tomato, place it in a blender and process until puréed. Add the tomato juice, vinegar, walnut oil, thyme, salt and black pepper, and process until blended.
2. Place the blanched vegetables in a large bowl, add the bread cubes and the dressing and toss to combine. Cover the bowl and refrigerate for at least 2 hours. *Makes 2 servings*

NUTRITION INFORMATION
values are per serving
• • •

CALORIES 195 CALCIUM 66 MG
TOTAL FAT 6 G IRON 4 MG
SATURATED FAT 0.6 G POTASSIUM 541 MG
CHOLESTEROL 0 MG BETA CAROTENE 1 MG
SODIUM 384 MG VITAMIN C 127 MG
DIETARY FIBER 6 G VITAMIN E 2 MG

ORZO VEGETABLE SALAD

The small pasta called *orzo* is shaped like rice (although the word *orzo* is actually Italian for "barley"). You can use *orzo* in many recipes that call for cooked rice or other grains. Conversely, you can substitute four to five cups of cooked brown or white rice—or a combination of the two—for the pasta in this salad.

1½ cups orzo
¼ cup apple juice
3 tablespoons white wine vinegar
2 tablespoons plus 2 teaspoons vegetable oil
2 teaspoons Dijon mustard
½ teaspoon ground ginger
½ teaspoon black pepper
Pinch of salt
½ pound cherry tomatoes, halved
1 cup cooked black beans (½ cup dried)
1 cup cooked green peas
1 large yellow bell pepper, diced

1. Bring a medium-size saucepan of water to a boil. Add the orzo and cook 8 to 10 minutes, or according to the package directions until al dente. Transfer the orzo to a colander, cool under cold running water and set aside to drain.
2. In a medium-size bowl combine the apple juice, vinegar, oil, mustard, ginger, pepper and salt, and stir to combine. Add the tomatoes, beans, peas, bell pepper and orzo, and stir to combine. Serve the salad at room temperature or chilled.
Makes 6 servings

NUTRITION INFORMATION
values are per serving
• • •

CALORIES 327 CALCIUM 30 MG
TOTAL FAT 7 G IRON 3 MG
SATURATED FAT 0.9 G POTASSIUM 387 MG
CHOLESTEROL 0 MG BETA CAROTENE TRACE
SODIUM 70 MG VITAMIN C 26 MG
DIETARY FIBER 2 G VITAMIN E 5 MG

THREE-MELON SALAD WITH RASPBERRY VINAIGRETTE

The choice of dressing can make or break a healthful salad: The vinaigrette used here has less than 4 grams of fat per serving—about half the fat in a tablespoon of bottled Italian dressing.

3 tablespoons raspberry vinegar, or to taste
1 tablespoon safflower oil
1 tablespoon lemon juice
½ teaspoon salt
4 cups 1-inch cantaloupe chunks
3 cups 1-inch honeydew chunks
4 cups watermelon balls or chunks
3 ounces farmer cheese or pot cheese
½ cup chopped fresh mint leaves
4 large Romaine lettuce leaves, washed and trimmed
2 tablespoons coarsely chopped pecans

1. For the dressing, in a small bowl whisk together the vinegar, oil, lemon juice and salt; set aside.

2. Combine the cantaloupe, honeydew and watermelon in a large bowl, add the dressing and toss gently. Cover the bowl and refrigerate at least 1 hour.

3. Just before serving, crumble the cheese into a small bowl, add the mint and mash with a fork to combine.

4. Line a serving platter with the Romaine leaves and mound the melon on it. Sprinkle the cheese over the melon and scatter the pecans on top.

Makes 4 servings

NUTRITION INFORMATION
values are per serving
• • •

CALORIES	239	CALCIUM	51 MG
TOTAL FAT	9 G	IRON	1 MG
SATURATED FAT	0.4 G	POTASSIUM	1089 MG
CHOLESTEROL	0 MG	BETA CAROTENE	4 MG
SODIUM	349 MG	VITAMIN C	121 MG
DIETARY FIBER	4 G	VITAMIN E	2 MG

INDONESIAN-STYLE FRUIT SALAD

Even with coconut and peanuts (traditional Indonesian ingredients), this salad is still low in total fat and saturated fat. It is also an exceptional source of potassium, beta carotene and vitamin C.

1 small jalapeño chili, finely chopped
¼ cup freshly squeezed lime juice
3 tablespoons honey
2 medium-size Delicious apples (¾ pound total weight)
1 small honeydew melon
2 pints fresh strawberries
4 kiwi fruits
2 medium-size mangoes
4 cups fresh pineapple chunks, or juice-packed pineapple chunks, drained
½ cup fresh or packaged shredded unsweetened coconut
¼ cup chopped roasted peanuts

1. For the dressing, in a small bowl combine the jalapeño with 3 tablespoons of the lime juice and the honey; set aside.

2. Core but do not peel the apples and cut them into ½-inch cubes. Place them in a small bowl and toss with the remaining lime juice.

3. Cut the honeydew melon into balls or 1-inch cubes; you should have about 4 cups. Place the melon in a large bowl.

4. Wash, hull and quarter the strawberries and add them to the bowl. Peel the kiwi fruits and mangoes, cut them into bite-size pieces and add them to the bowl. Add the apples, pineapple chunks and dressing, and toss well. Divide the salad among 6 plates, sprinkle with coconut and peanuts and serve.

Makes 6 servings

NUTRITION INFORMATION
values are per serving
• • •

CALORIES	354	CALCIUM	62 MG
TOTAL FAT	7 G	IRON	2 MG
SATURATED FAT	3 G	POTASSIUM	1141 MG
CHOLESTEROL	0 MG	BETA CAROTENE	2 MG
SODIUM	126 MG	VITAMIN C	188 MG
DIETARY FIBER	10 G	VITAMIN E	1 MG

Indonesian-Style Fruit Salad

PEAR AND ENDIVE SALAD

In this salad, which makes a luxurious luncheon or dinner dish, an inventive lowfat dressing and a small amount of pungent Gorgonzola cheese take the place of bottled blue-cheese dressing, which has about 9 grams of fat per tablespoon. Nonfat sour cream is blended with mashed pear and fruit juices to make the rich, smooth, slightly sweet dressing. Choose perfectly ripe, sweet pears for this salad: Bartlett, Anjou or Comice pears would be good choices.

1 very ripe small pear (about 3 ounces), plus 4 large pears
  (about 6 ounces each)
3 tablespoons lemon juice
3 tablespoons apple juice
1 tablespoon chopped fresh parsley
1 teaspoon sugar
1 tablespoon nonfat sour cream
6 ounces Belgian endive, separated into leaves
1 ounce Gorgonzola cheese (¼ cup)

1. For the dressing, peel and core the small pear. Cut it into large chunks, place in a small bowl and mash with a fork until smooth. Stir in 2 tablespoons of the lemon juice, the apple juice, parsley, sugar and sour cream; set aside.

2. Halve, stem and core but do not peel the remaining pears. Cut them lengthwise into ¼-inch-thick slices, place them in a medium-size bowl and toss with the remaining lemon juice.

3. Line a serving platter with the endive leaves and arrange the pear slices on top. Crumble the Gorgonzola over the pears and drizzle the dressing over the salad.

Makes 4 servings

NUTRITION INFORMATION
values are per serving

• • •

CALORIES 151	CALCIUM 82 MG
TOTAL FAT 3 G	IRON TRACE
SATURATED FAT 1 G	POTASSIUM 406 MG
CHOLESTEROL 5 MG	BETA CAROTENE 0.6 MG
SODIUM 113 MG	VITAMIN C 16 MG
DIETARY FIBER 5 G	VITAMIN E TRACE

⏶ *Sandwiches* ⏶

CHICKEN CLUB SANDWICH WITH CARROT SALAD

If sodium is a problem for you, "hold" the bacon and have an all-chicken club instead.

1½ tablespoons lowfat mayonnaise
1½ tablespoons plain lowfat yogurt
1½ cups shredded carrots
⅓ cup golden raisins
1 teaspoon lemon juice
½ teaspoon grated lemon zest
1 tablespoon spicy brown mustard
2 thin slices Canadian bacon
4 leaves Romaine lettuce
1 medium-size tomato, sliced
½ medium-size onion, sliced
2 ounces skinless cooked chicken breast, thinly sliced
6 slices whole-wheat bread

1. Mix the mayonnaise and yogurt in a cup.
2. For the carrot salad, in a small bowl stir together the carrots, raisins, lemon juice, lemon zest and half the mayonnaise mixture. Cover the bowl and refrigerate until ready to serve.
3. Stir the mustard into the remaining mayonnaise mixture, cover and refrigerate.
4. Cook the bacon in a small nonstick skillet over medium heat 1 minute on each side, or until heated through; set aside.
5. Divide the Romaine, tomato and onion into 4 portions and the chicken and bacon into 2 portions.
6. Toast the bread and spread one side of each slice with the mayonnaise mixture.
7. To assemble each sandwich, top a slice of toast with a portion of Romaine, tomato, onion and chicken; place another slice of toast on top. Add another portion of Romaine, tomato and onion, and top with bacon and the last slice of toast. Insert 2 long toothpicks or small skewers into each sandwich. Using a serrated knife, cut the sandwiches diagonally in half. Serve with the salad. *Makes 2 servings*

NUTRITION INFORMATION
values are per serving
• • •

CALORIES	442	CALCIUM	150 MG
TOTAL FAT	10 G	IRON	5 MG
SATURATED FAT	1 G	POTASSIUM	878 MG
CHOLESTEROL	37 MG	BETA CAROTENE	15 MG
SODIUM	868 MG	VITAMIN C	37 MG
DIETARY FIBER	13 G	VITAMIN E	8 MG

TURKEY SANDWICH WITH CRANBERRY CHUTNEY

Skinless turkey breast is one of the healthiest options for a meat sandwich, but turkey cold cuts may not be as wise a choice. Often, turkey roll, turkey ham and turkey salami or pastrami are made with both dark and light meat as well as high-cholesterol organ meats. Seasoned and preserved with sodium compounds such as monosodium glutamate and sodium nitrate, these cold cuts are almost always excessively high in sodium.

1 small apple, washed and cored
1 small seedless orange, washed
½ cup cranberries
2 teaspoons sugar
1 cup sliced mushrooms
8 slices whole-wheat bread
1 tablespoon whipped margarine
¼ pound thinly sliced cooked turkey breast
1 cup grated carrots
2 tomatoes, sliced
2 cups Romaine lettuce, torn into bite-size pieces

1. For the chutney, cut the apple and orange into large chunks and place them in a food processor or blender. Add the cranberries and sugar, and process, pulsing the machine on and off, about 20 seconds, or until the fruit is coarsely chopped and well mixed; set aside.

Vegetable, Chicken and Cheese Melt

2. In a small nonstick skillet cook the mushrooms with 1 tablespoon of water over medium heat, stirring often, 3 to 5 minutes, or until softened.

3. Spread one side of each slice of bread with margarine. Divide the turkey among 4 slices of bread and top it with mushrooms, carrots, tomatoes and Romaine. Spread the remaining slices of bread with chutney and place them on top of the sandwiches. (If making the sandwiches ahead of time, do not add the chutney until just before serving, or it will soak through the bread.) Cut the sandwiches in half and serve immediately.   *Makes 4 servings*

NUTRITION INFORMATION
values are per serving

• • •

CALORIES	248	CALCIUM	75 MG
TOTAL FAT	5 G	IRON	3 MG
SATURATED FAT	0.7 G	POTASSIUM	609 MG
CHOLESTEROL	24 MG	BETA CAROTENE	6 MG
SODIUM	375 MG	VITAMIN C	37 MG
DIETARY FIBER	9 G	VITAMIN E	2 MG

VEGETABLE, CHICKEN AND CHEESE MELT

If you replace a thick slice of cheese on a toasted sandwich with shredded cheese, you can use much less. The shredded cheese will melt faster, too.

1 tablespoon olive oil
1 cup chopped onion
2 garlic cloves, minced
3 red bell peppers, seeded and coarsely diced
2 medium-size zucchini, sliced ¼ inch thick
Black pepper
¼ pound skinless, boneless chicken breast,
*   cut into ½-inch chunks*
Four 2-ounce whole-wheat pita breads
½ cup shredded part-skim mozzarella (2 ounces)
3 cups washed, stemmed watercress

1. Heat 2½ teaspoons of the oil in a medium-size nonstick skillet over medium heat. Add the onion and garlic, and cook, stirring, 4 minutes. Increase the heat to medium-high, add the bell peppers and zucchini, and cook, stirring, 5 minutes. Add ½ cup of water and cook 3 minutes more. Add black pepper to taste. Using a slotted spoon, transfer the vegetables to a bowl to cool. Add the chicken to the skillet and cook, stirring, over medium heat 5 minutes, or until cooked through. Transfer the chicken to a small bowl. Wipe the skillet with paper towels; set aside.

2. Split the pita breads and sprinkle the bottom halves with mozzarella. Divide the vegetable mixture, chicken and watercress among the sandwiches and cover with the top halves of the pita breads.

3. Brush the skillet with the remaining oil and heat over medium-high heat. Place one sandwich at a time in the skillet and heat it 3 minutes, or until the cheese melts, then carefully turn and heat it 2 minutes longer.
Makes 4 servings

NUTRITION INFORMATION
values are per serving

• • •

CALORIES	309	CALCIUM	167 MG
TOTAL FAT	8 G	IRON	3 MG
SATURATED FAT	2 G	POTASSIUM	484 MG
CHOLESTEROL	25 MG	BETA CAROTENE	1 MG
SODIUM	459 MG	VITAMIN C	126 MG
DIETARY FIBER	2 G	VITAMIN E	TRACE

SMOKED SALMON SALAD SANDWICH

Flavorful smoked salmon is expensive (and high in sodium), but a little goes a long way. Ask which of the types offered in your market is the least salty.

1 cup grated carrots
1 cup grated zucchini
½ cup finely chopped celery
⅓ cup julienned radishes
¼ cup finely chopped scallions
2 tablespoons finely chopped fresh dill
2 teaspoons Dijon mustard
2 teaspoons capers, rinsed and drained
½ teaspoon grated lemon zest
2 ounces thinly sliced smoked salmon, julienned
½ cup plain lowfat yogurt
2 tablespoons nonfat sour cream
8 sprigs watercress, trimmed of coarse stems
4 slices dark pumpernickel bread

1. In a medium-size bowl toss together the carrots, zucchini, celery, radishes, scallions and dill. Stir in the mustard, capers and lemon zest, then add the salmon, yogurt and sour cream, and stir gently to combine.

2. Divide the watercress among the 4 slices of bread and spoon the salmon mixture on top to make open-faced sandwiches.
Makes 2 servings

NUTRITION INFORMATION
values are per serving

• • •

CALORIES	295	CALCIUM	218 MG
TOTAL FAT	5 G	IRON	3 MG
SATURATED FAT	0.9 G	POTASSIUM	1012 MG
CHOLESTEROL	10 MG	BETA CAROTENE	10 MG
SODIUM	803 MG	VITAMIN C	28 MG
DIETARY FIBER	8 G	VITAMIN E	1 MG

VEGETABLE-BRIE MELT

The luxurious taste and texture of Brie give this sandwich a high-fat flavor, though the topping consists mainly of vegetables. Rich-tasting Brie, incidentally, is actually lower in fat than Cheddar, muenster or Monterey Jack cheese.

1½ cups shredded spinach
1 cup shredded carrots
⅔ cup coarsely chopped mushrooms
⅓ cup coarsely chopped shallots
1½ ounces Brie, chilled and finely diced (¼ cup)
¼ cup plain lowfat yogurt
1 tablespoon Dijon mustard
¼ teaspoon black pepper
4 English muffins

1. Preheat the oven to 375°.

2. In a medium-size bowl combine the spinach, carrots, mushrooms, shallots, Brie, yogurt, mustard and pepper, and stir with a wooden spoon until well blended; set aside.

3. Split and toast the muffins, then place them cut side up on a baking sheet. Divide the vegetable mixture evenly among the muffin halves and bake 10 minutes, or until heated through. Divide the muffins among 4 plates and serve.
Makes 4 servings

CALORIES	232	CALCIUM	185 MG
TOTAL FAT	5 G	IRON	3 MG
SATURATED FAT	2 G	POTASSIUM	716 MG
CHOLESTEROL	12 MG	BETA CAROTENE	6 MG
SODIUM	609 MG	VITAMIN C	10 MG
DIETARY FIBER	3 G	VITAMIN E	TRACE

sandwich and cook another 3 to 4 minutes, or until the bread is lightly browned.   *Makes 4 servings*

CALORIES	295	CALCIUM	287 MG
TOTAL FAT	12 G	IRON	4 MG
SATURATED FAT	6 G	POTASSIUM	558 MG
CHOLESTEROL	30 MG	BETA CAROTENE	0.9 MG
SODIUM	684 MG	VITAMIN C	22 MG
DIETARY FIBER	9 G	VITAMIN E	2 MG

GRILLED VEGETABLE-CHEDDAR SANDWICH

Though reminiscent of a cheeseburger, this meatless sandwich contains just one ounce of cheese per serving—and less than half the fat of a cheeseburger.

One 6-ounce eggplant
2 cups sliced mushrooms
¼ pound Cheddar cheese, grated
1 cup thinly sliced scallions
2 cups bean sprouts
3 cups leaf lettuce, torn into bite-size pieces
8 slices whole-grain bread
2 tablespoons Dijon mustard

1. Preheat the oven to 350°.
2. Lightly spray a baking sheet with nonstick cooking spray.
3. Cut the eggplant into ¼-inch-thick slices, lay them on the baking sheet and bake 10 minutes, or until tender; set aside to cool.
4. Meanwhile, place the mushrooms in a medium-size skillet with 2 tablespoons of water and sauté over medium heat 3 to 5 minutes, or until softened.
5. Divide the cheese, mushrooms, scallions, sprouts and lettuce among 4 slices of bread and top with the eggplant slices. Spread the 4 remaining slices of bread with mustard, place them on the sandwiches and press them firmly with your hand to help hold them together during cooking.
6. Spray a large nonstick skillet with nonstick cooking spray and heat it over medium-high heat. Place a sandwich cheese side down in the skillet and heat it, pressing it with a metal spatula, 3 to 4 minutes, or until the cheese is melted, then turn the

OPEN-FACED CARROT SALAD SANDWICH

Vegetable salad sandwiches for lunch make a refreshing change from tuna or chicken salad. Here, carrot salad is bound with mashed banana rather than mayonnaise for a lower fat content and an appealing natural sweetness.

½ small banana, peeled
1 cup shredded carrots
2 teaspoons lemon juice
¼ teaspoon grated lemon zest
2 Bibb or butter lettuce leaves
1 slice whole-grain pumpernickel bread
2 thin unpeeled apple slices

1. Mash the banana in a small bowl. Add the carrots, lemon juice and lemon zest, and stir to combine.
2. Place the lettuce on the bread, top with the carrot salad and apple slices.   *Makes 1 serving*

CALORIES	175	CALCIUM	61 MG
TOTAL FAT	1 G	IRON	2 MG
SATURATED FAT	0.1 G	POTASSIUM	737 MG
CHOLESTEROL	0 MG	BETA CAROTENE	19 MG
SODIUM	193 MG	VITAMIN C	22 MG
DIETARY FIBER	6 G	VITAMIN E	1 MG

BEAN, CABBAGE AND APPLE SANDWICH

This overstuffed vegetable sandwich is packed with dietary fiber, potassium and iron.

½ cup thinly sliced red cabbage
2 strips bacon, diced
½ cup diced onion
2 garlic cloves, crushed
1½ teaspoons grated fresh ginger
1 cup chopped canned tomatoes, with their liquid
2 tablespoons molasses
1 teaspoon red wine vinegar
1 cup cooked pinto beans (½ cup dried)
1 tablespoon Dijon mustard
¾ teaspoon ginger juice (see page 156)
1 small apple, cored and thinly sliced
2 whole-wheat rolls, split

1. Blanch the cabbage in a small saucepan of boiling water 2 minutes; drain, cool under cold water and transfer to a medium-size bowl.

2. In a medium-size skillet, cook the bacon over medium-low heat about 6 minutes, or until crisp. Pour off all but 2 teaspoons of fat. Add the onion, garlic and ginger to the skillet and cook 6 to 7 minutes, or until the onion is softened. Add the tomatoes and their liquid, the molasses and vinegar, and cook about 15 minutes, or until slightly thickened. Add the beans and cook another 5 minutes, adding a few tablespoons of water if the mixture becomes too dry.

3. Meanwhile, stir together the mustard and ginger juice. Add the apple to the cabbage and toss.

4. Spread the ginger-mustard on the bottom half of each roll, top with a layer of the cabbage mixture and then with the beans. Place the tops on the sandwiches and serve. *Makes 2 servings*

NUTRITION INFORMATION
values are per serving

• • •

CALORIES	440	CALCIUM	177 MG
TOTAL FAT	7 G	IRON	6 MG
SATURATED FAT	2 G	POTASSIUM	1191 MG
CHOLESTEROL	5 MG	BETA CAROTENE	0.5 MG
SODIUM	845 MG	VITAMIN C	40 MG
DIETARY FIBER	10 G	VITAMIN E	1 MG

VEGETABLE PUREE SANDWICH

Plan ahead by cooking the carrots, turnips and sweet potatoes the night before you'll be serving these sandwiches. You can even mash the vegetables and stir in the mustard and dill in advance, but don't assemble the sandwiches ahead of time or the toast will lose its appealing crunch.

½ pound carrots
½ pound turnips
½ pound sweet potatoes
1 tablespoon Dijon mustard
2 tablespoons chopped fresh dill
1 medium-size cucumber
Eight ½-inch-thick slices Vegetable Bread (page 203)

1. Trim the carrots, peel the turnips and potatoes, and cut the vegetables into large chunks.

2. Bring 1 inch of water to a boil in a pan that will accommodate a large vegetable steamer. Place the vegetables in the steamer and cook, covered, 10 minutes, or until tender when pierced with a sharp knife; set aside to cool.

3. Place the vegetables in a medium-size bowl and mash them until smooth. Add the mustard and dill, and stir until blended; set aside.

4. Peel and slice the cucumber. Toast the bread and spread about ⅔ cup of the vegetable purée on each of 4 slices. Top the purée with cucumber slices and place a second slice of toast on each sandwich. Serve immediately. *Makes 4 servings*

NUTRITION INFORMATION
values are per serving

• • •

CALORIES	393	CALCIUM	90 MG
TOTAL FAT	4 G	IRON	5 MG
SATURATED FAT	0.7 G	POTASSIUM	768 MG
CHOLESTEROL	0 MG	BETA CAROTENE	13 MG
SODIUM	519 MG	VITAMIN C	32 MG
DIETARY FIBER	11 G	VITAMIN E	5 MG

BUTTERNUT SQUASH SANDWICH

Thick slices of butternut squash, bathed in a peanut-almond dressing, are served on whole-wheat bread for a lunch that provides plenty of energy. Save any leftover squash to serve mashed and seasoned with pumpkin pie spice and a pinch of brown sugar. Or, use it in a quick bread or cookie recipe that calls for pumpkin.

1 small butternut squash
4 whole blanched almonds
¼ cup plain lowfat yogurt
2 teaspoons peanut butter
1 scallion, trimmed and chopped
Pinch of salt
Four ½-inch-thick slices dense whole-wheat bread
2 large Romaine lettuce leaves, torn into bite-size pieces
1 small tomato, sliced
1 ounce alfalfa sprouts

1. Preheat the oven to 375°.
2. Line a baking sheet with aluminum foil.
3. Using a large, heavy knife, carefully halve the squash. Place the squash halves cut side down on the baking sheet and bake 25 minutes, or until the flesh is tender when pierced with a knife. Remove the squash from the oven and set aside to cool.
4. Meanwhile, place the almonds in a small skillet and toast them over medium-high heat 2 to 3 minutes, or until golden, tossing them frequently to prevent scorching.
5. For the dressing, place the almonds in a food processor or blender (if using a blender, coarsely chop the almonds first) and process until puréed. Add the yogurt, peanut butter, scallion and salt, and process until blended; set aside.
6. When the squash is cool enough to handle, remove and discard the seeds and stringy membranes. Peel one squash half and cut it lengthwise into four ¼-inch-thick slices. (The remaining squash can be used in Winter Squash Bread, page 208.) Dip the squash slices in the dressing and set aside.
7. Toast the bread and spread each piece with 1 tablespoon of dressing. Layer the Romaine, tomato, squash and sprouts on 2 pieces of toast and top with the remaining dressing. Place a second slice of toast on each sandwich, cut the sandwiches in half and serve immediately. *Makes 2 servings*

NUTRITION INFORMATION
values are per serving
• • •

CALORIES	274	CALCIUM	153 MG
TOTAL FAT	9 G	IRON	3 MG
SATURATED FAT	1 G	POTASSIUM	581 MG
CHOLESTEROL	2 MG	BETA CAROTENE	3 MG
SODIUM	516 MG	VITAMIN C	26 MG
DIETARY FIBER	10 G	VITAMIN E	2 MG

CHICKPEA POCKETS

A rich-tasting chickpea purée in a pita pouch captures the flavor of *felafel* (Middle Eastern deep-fried chickpea balls) without the fat.

2 garlic cloves
¾ cup cooked chickpeas
1 teaspoon lemon juice
1 teaspoon corn oil
½ teaspoon Oriental sesame oil
One 6-inch pita bread
½ cup shredded lettuce
1 small tomato, diced
3 small pitted black olives, halved

1. Blanch the garlic in boiling water 4 minutes. Drain the garlic, cool under cold water and discard the peels.
2. Combine the garlic, chickpeas, lemon juice, oils and ½ teaspoon of water in a food processor or blender, and process until puréed.
3. Halve the pita and fill the halves with the chickpea purée, lettuce, tomato and olives.
Makes 1 serving

NUTRITION INFORMATION
values are per serving
• • •

CALORIES	409	CALCIUM	122 MG
TOTAL FAT	12 G	IRON	6 MG
SATURATED FAT	1 G	POTASSIUM	667 MG
CHOLESTEROL	0 MG	BETA CAROTENE	0.7 MG
SODIUM	315 MG	VITAMIN C	23 MG
DIETARY FIBER	6 G	VITAMIN E	5 MG

Caponata Club Sandwich

CAPONATA CLUB SANDWICH

The Italian vegetable stew called *caponata* contains eggplant, zucchini and peppers. Here, the vegetables are sandwiched with prosciutto, a dry-cured ham. Use a reduced-sodium ham, if you prefer.

½ small eggplant
1 medium-size zucchini
3 large green bell peppers
1 medium-size yellow onion
2 teaspoons olive oil
2 garlic cloves, minced
2 cups salt-free canned tomatoes, with their liquid
1 tablespoon red wine vinegar, preferably balsamic
*2 tablespoons chopped fresh basil, or 2 teaspoons
    dried basil*
½ teaspoon dried oregano, crumbled
2 medium-size fresh tomatoes
1 small red onion
12 slices whole-wheat bread
6 ounces (12 slices) prosciutto or other lean cured ham
8 lettuce leaves

1. Preheat the broiler.

2. Cut the eggplant, zucchini, peppers and yellow onion into ¾-inch pieces and spread them on a large baking sheet. Broil 5 inches from the heat, stirring occasionally, 10 to 12 minutes, or until soft.

3. Heat the olive oil in a medium-size saucepan over medium-low heat. Add the garlic and broiled vegetables and sauté 2 minutes. Add the canned tomatoes and their liquid, the vinegar, basil and oregano, bring to a boil and reduce the heat to low. Simmer the mixture, uncovered, 20 minutes, or until the vegetables are tender and the liquid has evaporated; set aside to cool.

4. Slice the fresh tomatoes and red onion. Toast the bread. Spread 4 slices of toast with ¼ cup each of the vegetable mixture and top with another slice of toast. Top equally with the prosciutto, tomato, onion and lettuce, then top each with another slice of toast. Insert long picks to hold the sandwiches together and cut the sandwiches into quarters.

Makes 4 servings

NUTRITION INFORMATION
values are per serving

• • •

CALORIES	352	CALCIUM	157 MG
TOTAL FAT	8 G	IRON	5 MG
SATURATED FAT	1 G	POTASSIUM	1162 MG
CHOLESTEROL	13 MG	BETA CAROTENE	1 MG
SODIUM	972 MG	VITAMIN C	103 MG
DIETARY FIBER	12 G	VITAMIN E	1 MG

GRILLED EGGPLANT SANDWICH

These lavish mini-pizzas are stacked with eggplant and mushrooms as well as tomato sauce and cheese.

3 large plum tomatoes, peeled, seeded and chopped (2 cups)
1 cup thinly sliced mushrooms
1 tablespoon balsamic or other red wine vinegar
¼ teaspoon fennel seeds
Eight ¼-inch-thick eggplant slices (about ½ pound)
½ medium-size red onion, thinly sliced
2 teaspoons olive oil
Black pepper
1 English muffin
2 tablespoons grated fontina cheese

1. For the sauce, combine the tomatoes, mushrooms, vinegar and fennel seeds in a small nonreactive saucepan. Cook, covered, over medium heat 10 minutes, or until the juices are rendered. Uncover the pan and cook another 15 minutes, or until the sauce is thickened and reduced to about 1 cup.

2. Meanwhile, preheat the oven to 500°.

3. Place the eggplant slices on a baking sheet, top with onion slices and brush with 1 teaspoon of the oil. Sprinkle with pepper to taste, and bake 4 minutes. Brush the onions and eggplant with the remaining oil and bake another 3 to 4 minutes, or until the vegetables are soft.

4. Preheat the broiler.

5. Split and toast the English muffin. Spread the muffin halves with half of the tomato sauce and place 4 onion-topped eggplant slices on each half. Top with the remaining sauce and sprinkle with cheese. Broil the sandwiches about 1 minute, or until the cheese melts. *Makes 2 servings*

NUTRITION INFORMATION
values are per serving

• • •

CALORIES	273	CALCIUM	198 MG
TOTAL FAT	10 G	IRON	4 MG
SATURATED FAT	3 G	POTASSIUM	1101 MG
CHOLESTEROL	17 MG	BETA CAROTENE	2 MG
SODIUM	346 MG	VITAMIN C	50 MG
DIETARY FIBER	5 G	VITAMIN E	TRACE

TOFU-CARROT SANDWICHES

Make up a batch of this velvety sandwich spread on the weekend and you'll have most of your workday lunches covered. Since the tofu-carrot mixture is quite moist, carry it in a small leakproof container (such as an empty yogurt cup) and wrap the bread, Romaine and sprouts separately. Although the recipe calls for toast, you may not have access to a toaster at work: For textural contrast, use untoasted slices of a firm multi-grain bread instead.

3 cups sliced carrots
6 ounces firm tofu, well drained
1 tablespoon olive oil
2 teaspoons Dijon mustard
1 garlic clove, peeled
¼ teaspoon salt
¼ teaspoon black pepper
8 slices whole-wheat bread
8 large Romaine lettuce leaves
2 cups alfalfa sprouts

1. Bring a medium-size saucepan of water to a boil. Add the carrots and cook about 15 minutes, or until tender; drain and set aside to cool.

2. Combine the carrots, tofu, oil, mustard, garlic, salt and pepper in a food processor or blender, and process until smooth; set aside.

3. Toast the bread. Place a folded Romaine leaf on each slice of toast and top it with the carrot spread and sprouts. Cut the open-face sandwiches in half and divide among 4 plates.

Makes 4 servings

NUTRITION INFORMATION
values are per serving

• • •

CALORIES	273	CALCIUM	169 MG
TOTAL FAT	10 G	IRON	7 MG
SATURATED FAT	1 G	POTASSIUM	627 MG
CHOLESTEROL	0 MG	BETA CAROTENE	18 MG
SODIUM	558 MG	VITAMIN C	18 MG
DIETARY FIBER	10 G	VITAMIN E	2 MG

LENTIL TABBOULEH IN PITA POCKETS

Bulgur is usually the predominant ingredient in *tabbouleh*, but the nutritional value of this Middle-Eastern salad is considerably enhanced by the addition of lentils: The amino acids in legumes complement those in grains, creating complete protein.

1 cup lentils
1 cup diced onion
2 garlic cloves, minced
¾ cup bulgur
1 cup finely chopped fresh parsley
1 cup finely chopped fresh mint
1½ teaspoons dried thyme
1½ teaspoons dried oregano
Hot pepper sauce
1 tablespoon vegetable oil
1 teaspoon grated lemon zest
Eight 1-ounce pita breads
1 small cucumber
2 ounces feta cheese, rinsed and drained
8 large Romaine lettuce leaves, torn into bite-size pieces

1. Place the lentils, onion, garlic and 3 cups of water in a medium-size saucepan and cook over medium heat for 30 minutes, or until the lentils are tender. Stir in the bulgur, add half of the parsley and half of the mint, and cook over low heat 2 minutes. Add the thyme, oregano, and pepper sauce to taste, then cover the pan, remove it from the heat and set it aside to cool to room temperature. (Keep the pan covered so the bulgur will steep properly.)

2. When the lentil mixture is cool, pour off any excess liquid, pressing the mixture gently with a slotted spoon. (It should be firm enough to retain the impression of the spoon.) Transfer the mixture to a bowl and stir in the remaining mint and parsley, the oil and lemon zest. Cover the bowl and refrigerate the mixture at least 2 hours, or until well chilled.

3. Just before serving, wrap the pita breads in foil and warm them in a 200° oven.

4. Meanwhile, peel, seed and thinly slice the cucumber and finely dice the feta. Cut open one end of each pita bread. Place some Romaine in each pita. Divide the lentil mixture among the sandwiches and top with some of the feta and cucumber.

Makes 8 servings

NUTRITION INFORMATION
values are per serving
• • •

CALORIES	258	CALCIUM	113 MG
TOTAL FAT	4 G	IRON	5 MG
SATURATED FAT	1 G	POTASSIUM	498 MG
CHOLESTEROL	6 MG	BETA CAROTENE	0.6 MG
SODIUM	249 MG	VITAMIN C	16 MG
DIETARY FIBER	8 G	VITAMIN E	3 MG

SOUTH OF THE BORDER SANDWICHES

The tortillas are spread with a lowfat version of refried beans, which are traditionally made with lard.

½ cup dried black beans
1 large tomato, coarsely chopped
¼ cup chopped onion
1 tablespoon chopped fresh coriander
2 teaspoons balsamic vinegar, or to taste
4 medium-size flour tortillas
½ medium-size avocado
⅛ teaspoon salt
Black pepper
¾ cup watercress, washed and trimmed
¼ cup plain lowfat yogurt

1. Place the beans in a medium-size saucepan with cold water to cover. Cover the pan and refrigerate the beans overnight.

2. Drain the beans, add 5 cups of fresh water and bring to a boil over medium-high heat. Reduce the heat to medium-low and simmer 1 hour, or until the beans are soft. Drain, reserving 1 tablespoon of liquid; set aside to cool.

3. Preheat the oven to 350°.

4. For the salsa, in a small bowl stir together the tomato, onion, coriander and vinegar; set aside.

5. Wrap the tortillas in foil and heat them in the oven 5 minutes.

6. Meanwhile, peel the avocado half and cut it into thin slices. Using a fork or potato masher, coarsely mash the beans, adding some of the reserved cooking liquid if they are very dry. Stir in the salt and add pepper to taste.

7. Place each tortilla on a plate. Spread one half of each tortilla with one-fourth of the beans, then divide the salsa, avocado slices, watercress and yogurt among them. Fold the tortillas over the filling and serve. *Makes 4 servings*

NUTRITION INFORMATION
values are per serving

• • •

CALORIES	229	CALCIUM	105 MG
TOTAL FAT	6 G	IRON	3 MG
SATURATED FAT	0.9 G	POTASSIUM	522 MG
CHOLESTEROL	TRACE	BETA CAROTENE	0.6 MG
SODIUM	85 MG	VITAMIN C	15 MG
DIETARY FIBER	4 G	VITAMIN E	0 MG

CHILI-BEAN SLOPPY JOES

These meatless sandwiches—low in saturated fat and free of cholesterol—are as deliciously spicy and satisfying as Sloppy Joes made with ground beef.

½ pound red onions
3 tablespoons margarine
1 garlic clove, chopped
One 14-ounce can plum tomatoes, with their liquid
2 cups cooked kidney beans, or canned kidney beans, rinsed and drained
2 tablespoons tomato paste
1½ teaspoons chili powder

½ teaspoon brown sugar
Pinch of salt
Four 2-ounce whole-wheat rolls
⅔ cup shredded Romaine lettuce

1. Peel and trim the onions. Cut a 1-inch-thick slice from the center of one onion; wrap and set it aside. Coarsely chop the remaining onions.

2. Heat the margarine in a medium-size saucepan over medium heat. Add the chopped onions and garlic, and sauté 5 minutes, or until the onions are translucent. Add the tomatoes with their liquid, the beans, tomato paste, chili powder, sugar and salt, and bring the mixture to a boil. Cover the pan, reduce the heat to low and simmer the chili 20 minutes, stirring occasionally.

3. Ten minutes before serving, preheat the oven to 375°. Split the rolls, wrap them in foil and heat 10 minutes.

4. Meanwhile, cut the reserved onion into 4 slices. Place the rolls on 4 plates and top them with the bean mixture. Garnish each sandwich with Romaine and an onion slice, and serve. *Makes 4 servings*

NUTRITION INFORMATION
values are per serving

• • •

CALORIES	379	CALCIUM	117 MG
TOTAL FAT	12 G	IRON	6 MG
SATURATED FAT	2 G	POTASSIUM	884 MG
CHOLESTEROL	0 MG	BETA CAROTENE	0.8 MG
SODIUM	574 MG	VITAMIN C	27 MG
DIETARY FIBER	8 G	VITAMIN E	7 MG

HAZELNUT CHEESECAKE

Most cheesecakes are loaded with fat (16 grams per serving is not unusual) and cholesterol. This recipe cuts back on both by using part-skim ricotta cheese and lowfat yogurt—and just one egg yolk.

3 ounces roasted, hulled hazelnuts, finely ground
1 pound part-skim ricotta cheese
2 cups lowfat lemon yogurt
1 egg
1 egg white
¼ cup arrowroot
⅔ cup sugar
½ teaspoon vanilla extract
¼ teaspoon almond extract
¼ teaspoon salt
¼ teaspoon grated lemon zest

1. Preheat the oven to 300°.

2. Lightly coat a 7-inch springform pan with nonstick cooking spray.

3. Reserving 1 tablespoon of the ground hazelnuts, combine all of the remaining ingredients in a medium-size bowl and mix well. Pour the mixture into the pan and bake 1 hour. Turn off the oven and let the cake cool in the unopened oven 1½ to 2 hours, then cool the cake on a rack at room temperature another 1½ hours.

4. Remove the cake from the pan and sprinkle the top with the reserved ground hazelnuts. Refrigerate the cake 3 to 4 hours, or overnight, before serving.

Makes 10 servings

NUTRITION INFORMATION
values are per serving

• • •

CALORIES	233	CALCIUM	212 MG
TOTAL FAT	10 G	IRON	TRACE
SATURATED FAT	3 G	POTASSIUM	194 MG
CHOLESTEROL	37 MG	BETA CAROTENE	0 MG
SODIUM	149 MG	VITAMIN C	TRACE
DIETARY FIBER	TRACE	VITAMIN E	TRACE

COCOA FUDGE CAKE

Cocoa powder can stand in for baking chocolate in many recipes, saving some 10 grams of fat per ounce.

1½ cups unbleached all-purpose flour, approximately
½ cup unsweetened cocoa powder
1 teaspoon baking powder
1 teaspoon baking soda
2 tablespoons margarine
⅔ cup sugar
2 eggs
1 teaspoon vanilla extract
1½ cups buttermilk
½ cup nonfat sour cream

1. Preheat the oven to 350°. Spray an 8-inch round baking pan with nonstick cooking spray and dust it lightly with flour; set aside.

2. In a small bowl stir together 1½ cups of flour, the cocoa powder, baking powder and baking soda,

3. In a medium-size bowl cream together the margarine and sugar. Beat in the eggs one at a time. Add the vanilla and half the buttermilk, then stir in half the dry ingredients. Add the remaining buttermilk and beat until blended, then beat in the remaining dry ingredients.

4. Pour the batter into the pan and gently tap it to level the batter. Bake 35 to 40 minutes, or until a toothpick inserted into the center comes out clean and dry. Let the cake cool 5 minutes, then run a knife around the edge to loosen it and turn it out. Top each portion with some sour cream. *Makes 10 servings*

NUTRITION INFORMATION
values are per serving

• • •

CALORIES	180	CALCIUM	69 MG
TOTAL FAT	4 G	IRON	1 MG
SATURATED FAT	1 G	POTASSIUM	107 MG
CHOLESTEROL	44 MG	BETA CAROTENE	0 MG
SODIUM	177 MG	VITAMIN C	TRACE
DIETARY FIBER	TRACE	VITAMIN E	2 MG

PINEAPPLE UPSIDE-DOWN CAKE

This lightened American classic has all the old-fashioned flavor of the original—but much less fat.

¼ cup plus 2 teaspoons margarine
10 tablespoons brown sugar
One 20-ounce can juice-packed pineapple slices,
*   drained, 1 cup of juice reserved*
⅓ cup coarsely chopped dried apricots
1½ cups unbleached all-purpose flour
1¼ teaspoons baking powder
½ teaspoon baking soda
Pinch of salt
1 egg
1 cup dark raisins

1. Grease an 8-inch cake pan with 2 teaspoons of the margarine and sprinkle 2 tablespoons of sugar in the bottom. Arrange the pineapple slices in the pan, overlapping them slightly, and fill the hole in each slice with apricots. Preheat the oven to 350°.

2. In a small bowl stir together the flour, baking powder, baking soda and salt; set aside.

3. In a medium-size bowl, using an electric mixer, cream the remaining margarine and sugar. Beat in the egg, then beat in the dry ingredients and pineapple juice alternately, in 3 parts each. Stir in the raisins. Pour the batter into the pan and tap it on the countertop to settle the batter. Bake 1 hour, or until the cake is golden and pulls away from the sides of the pan.

4. Let the cake cool on a rack 5 minutes. Run a knife around the edge of the pan to loosen the cake, then place a platter over the pan and invert it. Tap it gently, then carefully lift the pan to turn out the cake.

Makes 10 servings

NUTRITION INFORMATION
values are per serving

• • •

CALORIES	260	CALCIUM	60 MG
TOTAL FAT	6 G	IRON	2 MG
SATURATED FAT	1 G	POTASSIUM	320 MG
CHOLESTEROL	21 MG	BETA CAROTENE	TRACE
SODIUM	104 MG	VITAMIN C	7 MG
DIETARY FIBER	2 G	VITAMIN E	4 MG

Fig-Berry Shortcakes

FIG-BERRY SHORTCAKES

This special-occasion dessert looks and tastes rich, and it is, indeed, a bit of an indulgence. But these fruit-and-cream-filled biscuits are also rich in calcium, fiber, and vitamin C.

5 dried figs
½ vanilla bean, split, seeds scraped out and reserved
2 cups fresh strawberries
2 cups fresh raspberries
2 tablespoons honey
8 Rich Biscuits (see headnote in Coriander and Currant
*   Scones recipe, page 214)*
½ cup Honey Cream (see page 175)

1. For the fig-berry sauce, in a 1-quart saucepan combine the figs and the vanilla bean halves and seeds, add water to cover and bring to a boil. Reduce the heat and simmer about 10 minutes, or until the figs are tender.

2. Meanwhile, wash the berries and hull and slice the strawberries. Combine 1 cup each of the raspberries and strawberries with the honey in a food processor, and purée. Strain the purée into a medium-size bowl and set aside.

3. When the figs are cooked, drain them and, when cool enough to handle, quarter them and cut into thin slices. Reserving a few berries for garnish, stir the remaining berries and the figs into the purée. Chill the mixture until ready to serve.

4. To serve, split the biscuits in half horizontally and place 2 halves on each of 4 dessert plates. Spoon one-fourth of the fig-berry sauce onto each pair of biscuit bottoms, then top with 2 tablespoons of Honey Cream. Cover with the biscuit tops and garnish with the reserved whole berries.

Makes 4 servings

HONEY CREAM

Spoon this delicious alternative to whipped cream over fresh berries, sliced peaches or warm fruit compote. Honey Cream can be made in advance, as it will keep for a week if refrigerated in a tightly covered container.

1 cup lowfat cottage cheese (1%)
2 teaspoons honey
5 tablespoons nonfat sour cream

Place the cottage cheese in a food processor or blender and purée until smooth. Transfer the cheese to a small bowl and fold in the honey and sour cream. Cover the bowl and refrigerate the mixture until ready to use.

Makes 1 cup

STRAWBERRY SHORTCAKE WITH YOGURT BISCUITS

Perfectly ripe strawberries are not only sweeter, but also contain more vitamin C than unripe berries.

1 pint fresh strawberries, hulled and sliced
4 teaspoons brown sugar
¼ cup lowfat sour cream
1½ teaspoons grated lemon zest
1¼ cups unbleached all-purpose flour, approximately
1 teaspoon baking powder
¼ teaspoon baking soda
¼ teaspoon salt
¼ teaspoon cinnamon
2½ tablespoons whipped margarine, well chilled
¼ cup plain lowfat yogurt
1 tablespoon confectioners' sugar

1. Toss the berries with 2 teaspoons of brown sugar.
2. In a small bowl mix together the sour cream, lemon zest and remaining brown sugar.
3. Preheat the oven to 450°.
4. In a large bowl stir together 1¼ cups of the flour, the baking powder, baking soda, salt and cinnamon. Cut in the margarine until the mixture resembles coarse crumbs. Add the yogurt and ¼ cup of cold water and stir briefly, then form the dough into a ball. On a lightly floured surface, knead the dough a few times, then roll it out to a ½-inch thickness.
5. Using a 3½-inch scalloped cutter, cut out 4 biscuits. Place on a baking sheet and bake 12 to 14 minutes, or until golden. Split the biscuits and place the bottom halves on 4 dessert plates. Top each with one-fourth of the strawberries and 1 tablespoon of cream; cover with the biscuit tops. Dust the shortcakes with confectioners' sugar.

Makes 4 servings

ALMOST-CHOCOLATE CUPCAKES

Made with dark, rich-tasting pumpernickel bread and sweet vanilla extract, these muffins have a mild chocolate-like flavor. They freeze well and are good to have on hand for a quick pre- or post-exercise snack or a light dessert.

3 cups fresh pumpernickel bread crumbs
  (about 6 slices of bread)
1 cup unbleached all-purpose flour
2 teaspoons baking powder
¼ teaspoon salt
2 eggs
½ cup brown sugar
1 tablespoon margarine, melted
1 teaspoon vanilla extract
1 cup skim milk

1. Preheat the oven to 375°.
2. Line 12 muffin tin cups with paper liners; set aside.
3. In a medium-size bowl combine the bread crumbs, flour, baking powder and salt; set aside.
4. In another medium-size bowl beat the eggs, then beat in the sugar, margarine and vanilla. Add half of the milk, then half of the dry ingredients, and stir until combined. Add the remaining milk and dry ingredients, and stir just until combined; do not overmix.
5. Divide the batter among the muffin cups (they will be about ¾ full) and bake 25 minutes, or until the cupcakes are browned and a toothpick inserted in a cupcake comes out clean and dry. Transfer the cupcakes to a rack to cool before serving.

Makes 12 cupcakes

NUTRITION INFORMATION
values are per cupcake

• • •

CALORIES	143	CALCIUM	81 MG
TOTAL FAT	2 G	IRON	1 MG
SATURATED FAT	0.5 G	POTASSIUM	157 MG
CHOLESTEROL	36 MG	BETA CAROTENE	0 MG
SODIUM	203 MG	VITAMIN C	TRACE
DIETARY FIBER	1 G	VITAMIN E	1 MG

PEAR CUPCAKES

These lowfat cupcakes are a healthy dessert alternative to a slice of frosted cake. To "gild the lily," brush the tops with warmed apricot jam.

1 firm-ripe Comice or Anjou pear
2 cups unbleached all-purpose flour
½ cup yellow cornmeal
2 teaspoons baking powder
2 tablespoons plus 1 teaspoon margarine
⅓ cup packed brown sugar
1 egg, lightly beaten
½ teaspoon orange extract
½ teaspoon grated orange zest
1 cup skim milk

1. Preheat the oven to 375°.
2. Line 12 muffin tin cups with paper liners; set aside.
3. Wash and core but do not peel the pear. Grate the pear into a small bowl; you should have about 1 cup.
4. In another small bowl combine the flour, cornmeal and baking powder; set aside.
5. In a medium-size bowl cream together the margarine and sugar, then gradually beat in the egg, orange extract and orange zest. Stir in the grated pear, then add half of the milk and half of the dry ingredients, and stir to combine. Add the remaining milk and dry ingredients, and stir just until combined; do not overmix.
6. Divide the batter among the muffin tin cups (they will be about ¾ full) and bake 30 to 35 minutes, or until the cupcakes are golden and a toothpick inserted in a cupcake comes out clean and dry. Transfer the cupcakes to a rack to cool before serving.-

Makes 12 cupcakes

NUTRITION INFORMATION
values are per cupcake

• • •

CALORIES	162	CALCIUM	68 MG
TOTAL FAT	3 G	IRON	2 MG
SATURATED FAT	0.6 G	POTASSIUM	110 MG
CHOLESTEROL	18 MG	BETA CAROTENE	TRACE
SODIUM	67 MG	VITAMIN C	TRACE
DIETARY FIBER	1 G	VITAMIN E	2 MG

Apple-Cinnamon Cupcakes

Cupcakes can be more than empty calories when made with nutritious ingredients like oats, dried apples, buttermilk and yogurt. For a slightly different taste, use dried pears or mixed dried fruit.

1 cup unbleached all-purpose flour
1 teaspoon baking powder
¾ teaspoon ground cinnamon
½ teaspoon baking soda
Pinch of salt
1 cup rolled oats
½ cup buttermilk
½ cup plain lowfat yogurt
2 eggs, beaten
1 cup chopped dried apples (2 ounces)
⅔ cup packed brown sugar
5 tablespoons butter, melted and cooled

1. Preheat the oven to 375°.
2. Line 12 muffin tin cups with paper liners; set aside.
3. In a small bowl combine the flour, baking powder, cinnamon, baking soda and salt.
4. In a medium-size bowl stir together the oats, buttermilk and yogurt.
5. In a large bowl stir together the eggs, apples, sugar and butter, then add the buttermilk mixture and stir to combine. Fold in the dry ingredients just until incorporated and divide the batter among the muffin tin cups.
6. Bake 20 minutes, or until a toothpick inserted in the center of a cupcake comes out clean and the tops are golden brown. Transfer the cupcakes to a rack to cool before serving.   *Makes 12 cupcakes*

NUTRITION INFORMATION
values are per cupcake
• • •

CALORIES	195	CALCIUM	68 MG
TOTAL FAT	7 G	IRON	1 MG
SATURATED FAT	4 G	POTASSIUM	159 MG
CHOLESTEROL	50 MG	BETA CAROTENE	0 MG
SODIUM	108 MG	VITAMIN C	TRACE
DIETARY FIBER	1 G	VITAMIN E	TRACE

Pumpkin Pie

Thanksgiving and Christmas dinner—two of the heaviest meals on the calendar—traditionally close with pie. The combination of a short (meaning rich in shortening) crust and cream-and-egg filling makes standard pumpkin pie a weighty finale to an already fat-laden meal. Do everyone a favor and lighten up the dessert course with this pie: Its flaky crust is made with margarine (instead of butter, lard or hydrogenated shortening), and the filling's rich texture comes from skim milk, egg whites and oat bran. If you feel the need for a creamy topping, try a dollop of sweetened yogurt cheese (see pages 188-189).

1 cup unbleached all-purpose flour, approximately
2 tablespoons granulated sugar
Pinch of salt
¼ cup margarine, well chilled
One 16-ounce can pumpkin purée
¼ cup oat bran
¼ cup packed brown sugar
¼ cup honey
¼ cup skim milk
2 egg whites, lightly beaten
2 teaspoons cornstarch
1 teaspoon ground allspice

1. In a medium-size bowl stir together 1 cup of flour, the granulated sugar and salt. Using a pastry blender or 2 knives, cut in the margarine until the mixture resembles cornmeal. Add 2 to 3 tablespoons of cold water and stir until the dough forms a mass. Knead the dough 1 minute, then form it into a ball, flatten it into a disk and wrap in plastic wrap. Refrigerate 20 minutes.
2. Preheat the oven to 425°.
3. Lightly flour a work surface and rolling pin. Roll out the dough to a 12-inch disk and carefully transfer it to a 9-inch pie pan. Press the dough into the pan, then trim and flute the edges; set aside.
4. For the filling, in a medium-size bowl combine the pumpkin purée, oat bran, brown sugar, honey, milk, egg whites, cornstarch and allspice, and stir until well blended. Pour the filling into the crust and bake the pie 15 minutes. Reduce the heat to 350° and bake 30 minutes more, or until the crust is golden and the filling is set. Let the pie cool on a rack 10 minutes and serve it warm or at room temperature.

Makes 10 servings

NUTRITION INFORMATION
values are per serving

• • •

CALORIES	167	CALCIUM	26 MG
TOTAL FAT	5 G	IRON	1 MG
SATURATED FAT	0.9 G	POTASSIUM	177 MG
CHOLESTEROL	TRACE	BETA CAROTENE	TRACE
SODIUM	30 MG	VITAMIN C	2 MG
DIETARY FIBER	0 G	VITAMIN E	3 MG

PEAR TART

A tasty dessert after dinner can help you resist late-night snacks. This fruit-and-custard pastry resembles a classic French fruit tart, but a traditional crust recipe would call for twice as much fat, and the custard might be made with as many as five egg yolks. If you enjoy this dessert, try a simple variation, sub-substituting sweet, firm apples, such as Empires or Winesaps, for the pears.

1¼ cups unbleached all-purpose flour
7 tablespoons sugar
Pinch of salt
¼ cup margarine, well chilled
2 ripe Comice or Anjou pears
1 egg plus 1 egg white
1 teaspoon almond extract

1. In a medium-size bowl stir together 1 cup of flour, 2 tablespoons of the sugar and the salt. Cut in the margarine until the mixture resembles cornmeal. Add 2 to 3 tablespoons of cold water and stir until the mixture forms a dough. Knead the dough 1 minute, then form it into a ball. Flatten it into a disk, wrap and refrigerate 20 minutes.

2. Dust a work surface and a rolling pin with 1 tablespoon of the flour. Roll out the dough to a 12-inch disk and transfer it to a 9-inch tart pan with a removable bottom. Gently press the dough into the pan, then trim the edges; set aside.

3. Preheat the oven to 425°.

4. Peel, core and quarter the pears and slice them ¼ inch thick; set aside.

5. In a small bowl beat together the whole egg, egg white, almond extract, 2 tablespoons of the sugar and the remaining flour.

6. Arrange the pears on the crust, then pour the egg mixture over them. Bake the tart 10 minutes.

7. Reduce the oven temperature to 350° and turn the pan if the crust is not browning evenly. Sprinkle the tart with the remaining sugar and bake 25 minutes more, or until the custard is set and the crust is golden brown. (Any liquid remaining on top of the custard will be absorbed as the tart cools.)

8. Let the tart cool on a rack 5 minutes, then remove the sides of the pan. Serve warm.

Makes 8 servings

NUTRITION INFORMATION
values are per serving

• • •

CALORIES	199	CALCIUM	12 MG
TOTAL FAT	7 G	IRON	1 MG
SATURATED FAT	1 G	POTASSIUM	88 MG
CHOLESTEROL	27 MG	BETA CAROTENE	0 MG
SODIUM	31 MG	VITAMIN C	2 MG
DIETARY FIBER	2 G	VITAMIN E	4 MG

APPLE-CARROT PIE

Apple pie has a wholesome image, but a nice wedge of this all-American dessert can carry a hefty load of saturated fat and calories. This overdue update has a cholesterol-free crust that's low in saturated fat and a nutrient-packed (and delicious) filling that combines apples, carrots, orange zest, cinnamon and ginger.

1½ cups plus 2 tablespoons unbleached all-purpose flour
2 tablespoons granulated sugar
Pinch of salt
7 tablespoons margarine
3 Granny Smith apples (about 1½ pounds total weight)
2 cups grated carrots
½ cup fresh bread crumbs, preferably pumpernickel
½ cup packed brown sugar
2 tablespoons orange juice
1 tablespoon grated orange zest
1 tablespoon grated fresh ginger
½ teaspoon ground cinnamon

1. In a medium-size bowl stir together 1½ cups of the flour, the granulated sugar and salt. Using a pastry blender or 2 knives, cut the margarine into the dry ingredients until the mixture resembles coarse cornmeal. Add 3 to 4 tablespoons of cold water and stir until the dough forms a cohesive mass. Knead the dough 1 minute, then form it into a ball, flatten it into a disk and wrap it in plastic wrap. Refrigerate the dough 20 minutes.

2. Meanwhile, wash and core but do not peel the apples, and cut them into ¼-inch-thick wedges.

3. In a large bowl toss together the apples, carrots, bread crumbs, brown sugar, orange juice and zest, ginger and cinnamon, making sure to coat the apples and carrots with orange juice; set aside.

4. Preheat the oven to 425°.

5. Lightly flour a work surface and rolling pin. Set aside one-third of the dough. Roll out the remaining dough to a 12-inch disk and carefully transfer it to a 9-inch pie pan. Press the dough into the pan, then fill it with the apple mixture, packing the filling down lightly. Dust the work surface and rolling pin with flour again. Roll out the remaining dough to a 9-inch

disk, place it on the filling and crimp together the edges of the bottom and top crusts. Make two or three ½-inch slashes in the top crust with a sharp knife.

6. Bake the pie 15 minutes, then reduce the oven temperature to 350° and bake 15 to 20 minutes more, or until the crust is golden brown. Let the pie cool on a rack 10 minutes and serve it warm, or cool it to room temperature. *Makes 10 servings*

NUTRITION INFORMATION
values are per serving

• • •

CALORIES	250	CALCIUM	27 MG
TOTAL FAT	9 G	IRON	2 MG
SATURATED FAT	2 G	POTASSIUM	227 MG
CHOLESTEROL	0 MG	BETA CAROTENE	4 MG
SODIUM	41 MG	VITAMIN C	7 MG
DIETARY FIBER	3 G	VITAMIN E	6 MG

Apple-Carrot Pie

NECTARINE TART

Processing rolled oats in the blender yields oat flour, which is combined with whole-wheat flour in the lemony crust for this fruit tart.

½ cup rolled oats
1 cup sifted whole-wheat flour
1 teaspoon grated lemon zest
¼ cup chilled margarine
3 to 4 tablespoons ice water
⅓ cup apricot jam
1 tablespoon lemon juice
4 ripe nectarines (about 1½ pounds), cut into ½-inch slices
2 tablespoons toasted sliced almonds

1. Place the oats in a blender and process to the consistency of coarse flour.
2. In a large bowl, combine the oats, flour and lemon zest. Cut in the margarine until the mixture resembles coarse meal. Sprinkle in the ice water 1 tablespoon at a time until the dough just holds together. Form the dough into a ball, flatten slightly, and wrap in wax paper. Allow the dough to rest 10 to 15 minutes.
3. Meanwhile, preheat the oven to 425°.
4. On a lightly floured board, roll the dough into an 11-inch disk about ⅛ inch thick. Transfer the dough to a 9-inch pie plate and flute the edge. Bake the pastry shell 12 to 15 minutes, or until lightly browned. Cool completely.
5. Meanwhile, strain the apricot jam into a small saucepan. Add the lemon juice and cook, stirring, over low heat until the jam is thinned and warmed. Brush the inside of the pastry shell lightly with the jam, arrange the nectarine slices in an attractive pattern on top and brush with the remaining jam. Sprinkle with almonds.   *Makes 6 servings*

NUTRITION INFORMATION
values are per serving

• • •

CALORIES	277	CALCIUM	29 MG
TOTAL FAT	10 G	IRON	2 MG
SATURATED FAT	2 G	POTASSIUM	363 MG
CHOLESTEROL	0 MG	BETA CAROTENE	0.5 MG
SODIUM	4 MG	VITAMIN C	6 MG
DIETARY FIBER	5 G	VITAMIN E	6 MG

MOLASSES COOKIES

One way to find the most healthful cookies is to read package labels very closely. Another way is to make these slice-and-bake molasses icebox cookies, a light but sweet lunch or snacktime treat.

½ cup light molasses
⅓ cup margarine, cut into 1-tablespoon pieces
2 cups unbleached all-purpose flour
¼ cup packed brown sugar
1 tablespoon skim milk
1 teaspoon ground ginger
½ teaspoon baking powder

1. In a medium-size saucepan heat the molasses over medium-low heat. When the molasses reaches the boiling point, stir in the margarine. When the margarine has melted, remove the pan from the heat and stir in the flour, sugar, milk, ginger and baking powder. Stir until the mixture forms a thick dough that pulls away from the sides of the pan.
2. Place the dough on a 12 x 12-inch sheet of foil and let it cool for a few minutes, then form it into a 1½-inch-thick log about 10 inches long. Wrap the dough in the foil and refrigerate it at least 3 hours, or until firm.
3. Preheat the oven to 325°.
4. Unwrap the dough and, with a sharp knife, cut it into ¼-inch-thick slices. (Dip the knife briefly into warm water between cuts if the dough sticks to it.)
5. Place the cookies ¾ inch apart on a nonstick baking sheet and bake 10 to 15 minutes, or until just firm to the touch. Transfer the cookies to a rack to cool; if not serving immediately, store them in an airtight container.   *Makes 40 cookies*

NUTRITION INFORMATION
values are per cookie

• • •

CALORIES	52	CALCIUM	12 MG
TOTAL FAT	2 G	IRON	TRACE
SATURATED FAT	0.3 G	POTASSIUM	50 MG
CHOLESTEROL	TRACE	BETA CAROTENE	0 MG
SODIUM	5 MG	VITAMIN C	TRACE
DIETARY FIBER	TRACE	VITAMIN E	1 MG

BUTTERNUT SQUASH HERMITS

Hermits, which originated in New England, are old-fashioned soft, spicy cookies filled with nuggets of dried fruit. These hermits are made with little shortening, but the squash that goes into them makes for moist cookies that are good "keepers"—a good choice for stocking the cookie jar.

1 cup cooked butternut squash, or ¾ pound uncooked
 butternut squash
1 cup unbleached all-purpose flour
1 cup rolled oats
1 teaspoon baking soda
¾ teaspoon ground ginger
¼ teaspoon ground allspice
Pinch of salt
¼ cup margarine, softened
⅓ cup packed brown sugar
1 egg
½ teaspoon vanilla extract
½ cup each diced dried apricots, dried currants and prunes

1. If using uncooked squash, preheat the oven to 375°.
2. Using a large, heavy knife, carefully halve the squash lengthwise. Place the halves cut side down on a foil-lined baking sheet and bake 25 minutes, or until tender. Let the squash cool, then remove and discard the seeds and stringy membranes. Scoop out enough squash flesh to measure 1 cup; reserve any remaining squash for another use. Leave the oven at 375°.
3. Lightly spray 2 baking sheets with nonstick cooking spray.
4. In a medium-size bowl stir together the flour, oats, baking soda, ginger, allspice and salt; set aside.
5. In a large bowl, using an electric mixer, cream the margarine and sugar until thoroughly blended. Beat in the egg, then gradually beat in the squash and vanilla. Add the dry ingredients and beat 5 to 10 seconds, or just until mixed, then stir in the apricots, currants and prunes.
6. Drop the dough by rounded teaspoons onto the baking sheets and bake 12 minutes, or until the cookies are golden at the edges. Transfer the cookies to racks to cool and repeat with the remaining dough. *Makes 96 cookies*

NUTRITION INFORMATION
values are per cookie
• • •
CALORIES 23 CALCIUM 4 MG
TOTAL FAT 0.6 G IRON TRACE
SATURATED FAT 0.1 G POTASSIUM 36 MG
CHOLESTEROL 2 MG BETA CAROTENE TRACE
SODIUM 11 MG VITAMIN C TRACE
DIETARY FIBER TRACE VITAMIN E TRACE

APPLE-PUMPKIN CHEWIES

These soft cookies pack well, making them ideal for lunchboxes, brown bags or knapsacks. Canned pumpkin, the surprising substitute for shortening here, keeps the fat content down to the absolute minimum. Thick applesauce or prune butter (puréed prunes) can also replace the shortening in this and other simple cookie recipes.

2 large Granny Smith apples
1 cup canned pumpkin
¼ cup molasses
¼ cup packed brown sugar
1 teaspoon grated lemon zest
½ teaspoon vanilla extract
1 cup unbleached all-purpose flour
¼ cup rolled oats
1½ teaspoons baking powder
½ teaspoon ground ginger
Pinch of salt
1 egg, lightly beaten

1. Preheat the oven to 350°.
2. Spray a nonstick baking sheet with nonstick cooking spray; set aside.
3. Wash and core but do not peel the apples. Grate the apples into a medium-size bowl; you should have about 2 cups. Add the pumpkin, molasses, sugar, lemon zest and vanilla, and stir to combine; set aside.
4. In a large bowl stir together the flour, oats, baking powder, ginger and salt, and make a well in the center. Add the pumpkin mixture and the egg, and stir just until combined.

5. Drop the batter by tablespoons onto the baking sheet and bake 35 minutes, or until the cookies are golden. Transfer the cookies to a rack to cool. Repeat with the remaining batter. If not serving the cookies immediately, store them in an airtight container. When fresh, they have a moist center; after a few days they will be firmer and chewier.

Makes 48 cookies

NUTRITION INFORMATION
values are per cookie

• • •

CALORIES	27	CALCIUM	12 MG
TOTAL FAT	0.2 G	IRON	TRACE
SATURATED FAT	0 G	POTASSIUM	45 MG
CHOLESTEROL	4 MG	BETA CAROTENE	0 MG
SODIUM	14 MG	VITAMIN C	TRACE
DIETARY FIBER	TRACE	VITAMIN E	TRACE

FRUIT FOLD-UPS

Pass up the sugary Danish on the office snack cart and treat yourself instead to one of these rich-tasting fruit- and nut-filled mini-pastries. The dough for this type of cookie is usually made with cream cheese—which has 10 grams of fat per ounce. Here, however, lowfat cottage cheese (plus a small amount of margarine) make a rich, easy to handle dough that envelops a filling of jam, nuts and raisins.

1 cup unbleached all-purpose flour, approximately
2 tablespoons sugar
2 tablespoons margarine, well chilled
½ cup lowfat cottage cheese (1%)
½ cup dark raisins
3 tablespoons coarsely chopped walnuts
¼ teaspoon ground cinnamon
¼ teaspoon vanilla extract
3 tablespoons strawberry jam

1. In a medium-size bowl stir together 1 cup of the flour and the sugar. Using a pastry blender or 2 knives, cut in the margarine until the mixture resembles coarse crumbs. Stir in the cottage cheese, then gather the dough into a ball and knead it a few times in the bowl. Loosely cover the bowl of dough and refrigerate 1 hour.

2. Combine the raisins and walnuts on a cutting board and chop them finely; transfer to a small bowl and stir in the cinnamon and vanilla extract.

3. Preheat the oven to 325°.

4. Line a large baking sheet with foil; set aside.

5. Lightly flour a work surface and rolling pin. Divide the dough into 2 equal pieces, roll out each piece into a 5 x 12-inch rectangle and place one rectangle with a long side toward you. Brush the bottom half with half of the jam, sprinkle it with half of the raisin mixture and fold the top half of the dough over to cover the filling. Cut the folded strip crosswise into eight 1½-inch-wide cookies.

6. Place the cookies 2 inches apart on the baking sheet and make 8 more cookies in the same fashion. Bake 30 minutes, or until the cookies are golden brown, then transfer them to racks to cool.

Makes 16 cookies

NUTRITION INFORMATION
values are per cookie

• • •

CALORIES	87	CALCIUM	11 MG
TOTAL FAT	2 G	IRON	TRACE
SATURATED FAT	0.4 G	POTASSIUM	60 MG
CHOLESTEROL	TRACE	BETA CAROTENE	0 MG
SODIUM	30 MG	VITAMIN C	TRACE
DIETARY FIBER	TRACE	VITAMIN E	1 MG

BISCOTTI

The Italian word *biscotti* means "cooked twice," referring to the fact that after an initial baking, these cookies are returned to the oven to dry and crisp. These crunchy anise-scented biscuits are not overly sweet: Serve them with hot or cold drinks, and adopt the Italian custom of dipping them into your beverage between bites.

3 cups unbleached all-purpose flour
1 teaspoon baking powder
Pinch of salt
5 tablespoons margarine
⅔ cup sugar
3 eggs
1 tablespoon grated lemon zest
1 tablespoon lemon juice

¾ teaspoon anise extract

1 cup currants

¾ cup chopped dried apricots

1. Preheat the oven to 350°.

2. In a medium-size bowl combine the flour, baking powder and salt; set aside.

3. In another medium-size bowl, using an electric mixer, cream together the margarine and sugar. Beat in the eggs, one at a time, then beat in the lemon zest and juice and the anise extract. Gradually add the dry ingredients, beating constantly 1 to 2 minutes, or until almost incorporated. Add the currants and apricots, and beat 1 minute more, or just until combined.

4. Divide and shape the dough into two 2½-inch-thick loaves. Place them on a nonstick baking sheet and bake 30 minutes, or until just beginning to brown. Transfer the loaves to a rack and let them cool 45 minutes.

5. Preheat the broiler.

6. Place the loaves on a cutting board and, with a serrated knife, cut them diagonally into ⅜-inch-thick slices. Lay the slices on a baking sheet and broil 5 inches from the heat 1 minute, or until lightly browned. Carefully turn the biscotti and brown another minute. Transfer them to a rack to cool, then store in an airtight container. *Makes 48 biscotti*

NUTRITION INFORMATION
values are per cookie

• • •

CALORIES	67	CALCIUM	10 MG
TOTAL FAT	2 G	IRON	TRACE
SATURATED FAT	0.3 G	POTASSIUM	68 MG
CHOLESTEROL	13 MG	BETA CAROTENE	0 MG
SODIUM	13 MG	VITAMIN C	TRACE
DIETARY FIBER	TRACE	VITAMIN E	TRACE

Biscotti

OATMEAL–BANANA BARS

Bar cookies are easy to make; these are especially quick because the wet ingredients are mixed in a blender, then simply stirred into the dry ingredients.

1 teaspoon margarine, softened
2 cups rolled oats
¾ cup whole-wheat flour
½ cup packed light brown sugar
½ cup chopped walnuts or pecans
½ cup raisins
2½ teaspoons baking powder
½ teaspoon cinnamon
¼ teaspoon nutmeg
½ teaspoon grated orange zest
1 cup lowfat milk (1%)
2 eggs plus 1 egg white
6 tablespoons margarine, melted
3 medium-size bananas, puréed (1¼ cups)

1. Preheat the oven to 350°.
2. Using the softened margarine, lightly grease a 9 x 13-inch baking pan. Line the pan with wax paper and very lightly grease the paper.
3. Combine the oats, flour, sugar, nuts, raisins, baking powder, spices and orange zest in a large bowl; set aside.
4. Combine the milk, eggs and egg white, margarine and bananas in a blender, and process until smooth. Add the contents of the blender to the dry ingredients and stir to mix well.
5. Spread the batter in the prepared pan, smoothing the top with a spatula. Bake 25 to 30 minutes, or until the edges pull away slightly from the sides of the pan and the top is lightly browned. Place the pan on a rack to cool and then cut into bars.

Makes 24 bars

NUTRITION INFORMATION
values are per bar

• • •

CALORIES	132	CALCIUM	48 MG
TOTAL FAT	6 G	IRON	TRACE
SATURATED FAT	1 G	POTASSIUM	171 MG
CHOLESTEROL	18 MG	BETA CAROTENE	0 MG
SODIUM	46 MG	VITAMIN C	2 MG
DIETARY FIBER	1 G	VITAMIN E	3 MG

PEACH AND OATMEAL CRISP

If you find plain fruit boring for dessert, but know you're better off without heavy pastry and whipped cream, try this light and luscious treat instead: a fruit crisp with a crunchy oatmeal crust and an orange-flavored yogurt topping.

2 cups fresh or frozen unsweetened peach slices
¼ cup dried currants
1 tablespoon honey
¼ teaspoon ground cinnamon
¼ teaspoon vanilla extract
1 cup rolled oats
3 tablespoons unbleached all-purpose flour
1½ teaspoons light brown sugar
4 teaspoons butter or margarine
1 cup plain lowfat yogurt
1 teaspoon orange juice

1. Preheat the oven to 325°.
2. Reserving 8 thin peach slices for the garnish, in a medium-size bowl combine the remaining peaches, the currants, honey, cinnamon and vanilla. Spread the mixture evenly in an 8-inch square pan.
3. For the topping, in a small bowl stir together the oats, flour and sugar, then work in the butter with your fingers until the mixture is crumbly. Sprinkle the topping over the peaches and bake 45 minutes, or until the topping is browned. Let the crisp cool 5 minutes.
4. Meanwhile, stir together the yogurt and orange juice in a small bowl. Divide the peach crisp among 4 plates and top each serving with ¼ cup of the yogurt mixture and 2 of the reserved peach slices.

Makes 4 servings

NUTRITION INFORMATION
values are per serving

• • •

CALORIES	273	CALCIUM	135 MG
TOTAL FAT	6 G	IRON	2 MG
SATURATED FAT	3 G	POTASSIUM	462 MG
CHOLESTEROL	14 MG	BETA CAROTENE	TRACE
SODIUM	86 MG	VITAMIN C	6 MG
DIETARY FIBER	1 G	VITAMIN E	TRACE

APPLE CRISP

The usual proportion of ingredients in a fruit crisp topping are one part butter to two parts flour and two parts sugar. Here, the proportions are altered so that healthy helpings of rolled oats and whole-wheat flour are blended with much smaller quantities of butter and sugar. The cholesterol content of this dessert is already modest, but you can substitute an equal amount of vegetable-oil margarine for the butter if you desire a cholesterol-free dessert.

8 medium-size apples, peeled, cored and cut into wedges
¼ cup granulated sugar
1 tablespoon lemon juice
1 teaspoon ground cinnamon
1 cup rolled oats
½ cup whole-wheat flour
⅓ cup packed brown sugar
¼ teaspoon salt
¼ cup unsalted butter, softened

1. Preheat the oven to 350°.

2. In a 2-quart baking dish, toss together the apples, granulated sugar, lemon juice and cinnamon.

3. In a large bowl combine the oats, flour, brown sugar and salt. Cut in the butter to make a crumbly mixture. Spread the topping over the apples, cover the dish loosely with foil and bake 30 minutes, then remove the foil and bake another 10 minutes, or until the topping is brown and the apples are soft.

Makes 8 servings

NUTRITION INFORMATION
values are per serving

• • •

CALORIES	255	CALCIUM	27 MG
TOTAL FAT	7 G	IRON	1 MG
SATURATED FAT	4 G	POTASSIUM	265 MG
CHOLESTEROL	15 MG	BETA CAROTENE	0 MG
SODIUM	20 MG	VITAMIN C	7 MG
DIETARY FIBER	4 G	VITAMIN E	1 MG

BLUEBERRY COBBLER

Cobbler is a warm fruit dessert that is topped with a rich, sweet biscuit dough and is often served with cream. If you like, garnish each serving of this berry cobbler with a spoonful of lowfat vanillla yogurt.

2 cups fresh or frozen unsweetened blueberries, thawed
3 tablespoons maple syrup
½ cup unbleached all-purpose flour, approximately
¾ teaspoon baking powder
½ teaspoon ground cinnamon
⅛ teaspoon salt
1 tablespoon plus 1½ teaspoons margarine, melted
1 tablespoon skim milk
1 teaspoon grated lemon zest

1. Preheat the oven to 400°.

2. Lightly spray a 9-inch pie plate with nonstick cooking spray; set aside.

3. If using fresh berries, wash, dry, stem and pick them over. In a small saucepan, combine the blueberries and maple syrup and cook over medium heat, stirring occasionally, 5 minutes, or until the berries are very soft; remove the pan from the heat and set aside.

4. In a medium-size bowl combine ½ cup of flour, the baking powder, cinnamon and salt, and stir to combine. Stir in the margarine, milk and lemon zest, and mix until a soft dough forms. Turn the dough onto a lightly floured surface and roll it out with a floured rolling pin to a 9-inch disk about ⅛ inch thick.

5. Stir the berry mixture, pour it into the pie plate and lay the crust on top. Bake the cobbler 25 minutes. Let it cool 5 minutes before serving, then cut it into quarters and serve warm.

Makes 4 servings

NUTRITION INFORMATION
values are per serving

• • •

CALORIES	177	CALCIUM	66 MG
TOTAL FAT	5 G	IRON	1 MG
SATURATED FAT	0.9 G	POTASSIUM	118 MG
CHOLESTEROL	TRACE	BETA CAROTENE	0 MG
SODIUM	129 MG	VITAMIN C	10 MG
DIETARY FIBER	2 G	VITAMIN E	3 MG

RICOTTA MOUSSE WITH CHUNKY PINEAPPLE SAUCE

Heavy cream and raw eggs are standard ingredients in mousse recipes. Cooks concerned with heart health and food safety, however, will appreciate this delicate mousse in which lowfat dairy products stand in for the cream and the egg is thoroughly cooked. Add a colorful fruit sauce and the result is a luxurious dessert that is low in fat while supplying substantial amounts of beta carotene and potassium.

1 large egg yolk
½ cup lowfat milk (2%)
¼ cup sugar
1 envelope unflavored gelatin
1 teaspoon grated orange zest
1 cup part-skim ricotta cheese
½ cup orange juice
¼ teaspoon vanilla extract
½ cup chopped fresh mint leaves, plus 4 mint sprigs for garnish
¼ cup chopped dried apricots
1½ cups drained juice-packed pineapple chunks
6 tablespoons lemon juice
1 teaspoon grated lemon zest
4 cups diced cantaloupe

1. In the bottom pan of a double boiler bring enough water to a simmer so that the simmering water will not touch the top pan.

2. For the mousse, place the egg yolk and milk in the top pan and cook, whisking constantly, over the simmering water 10 minutes, or until the mixture begins to thicken slightly. Add the sugar, gelatin and orange zest, and cook, stirring constantly, 8 minutes, or until the mixture is quite thick. Transfer to a medium-size bowl and set aside to cool about 15 minutes.

3. Meanwhile, in a food processor or blender, combine the ricotta, orange juice and vanilla, and process 1 minute. Add the chopped mint and process another 20 seconds. Fold the ricotta mixture into the gelatin mixture, then fold in the apricots until well blended. Spoon the mousse into four 4-ounce custard cups, cover and refrigerate at least 1 hour, or overnight.

4. For the sauce, in a small saucepan combine the pineapple, lemon juice and lemon zest, and cook over medium heat 5 minutes. Transfer the mixture to a food processor or blender and process 10 seconds, or just until roughly chopped. Cover and refrigerate the sauce until ready to serve.

5. To unmold the mousses, dip each custard cup in a bowl of hot water 10 to 15 seconds, then invert it on a plate. Surround each mousse with 1 cup of cantaloupe and spoon some of the pineapple sauce over the cantaloupe.   *Makes 4 servings*

NUTRITION INFORMATION
values are per serving

• • •

CALORIES	320	CALCIUM	255 MG
TOTAL FAT	7 G	IRON	2 MG
SATURATED FAT	4 G	POTASSIUM	986 MG
CHOLESTEROL	75 MG	BETA CAROTENE	4 MG
SODIUM	113 MG	VITAMIN C	107 MG
DIETARY FIBER	3 G	VITAMIN E	TRACE

CHOCOLATE BANANA CREAM

Chocolate is a concentrated source of fat; the darker and less sweet the chocolate is, the more fat it contains. So perhaps the best advice for committed chocolate lovers is this: Enjoy your favorite flavor in small quantities in desserts like this velvety pudding, which blends just a half-ounce of semisweet chocolate with fruit and lowfat yogurt.

2 tablespoons sugar
½ ounce semisweet chocolate
2 bananas, peeled
1½ cups plain lowfat yogurt

1. In a small saucepan heat the sugar, chocolate and 1 tablespoon of water over very low heat, stirring constantly, until the chocolate is melted; remove the pan from the heat and set aside.

2. Purée the bananas in a food processor or blender. Add the yogurt and the chocolate mixture, and process 5 to 10 seconds, scraping down the sides of the container with a rubber spatula. Divide the mixture among 4 dessert dishes and refrigerate 2 to 3 hours, or until well chilled.   *Makes 4 servings*

Ricotta Mousse with Chunky Pineapp'

NUTRITION INFORMATION
values are per serving

• • •

CALORIES 146   CALCIUM 160 MG

TOTAL FAT 3 G   IRON TRACE

SATURATED FAT 1 G   POTASSIUM 439 MG

CHOLESTEROL 5 MG   BETA CAROTENE 0 MG

SODIUM 60 MG   VITAMIN C 6 MG

DIETARY FIBER TRACE   VITAMIN E TRACE

INDIVIDUAL RICOTTA CHEESECAKES WITH PEACH PUREE

Cheesecake, that ever-popular dessert, need not include cream cheese, sour cream, butter or a large quantity of eggs: In these crustless single-serving cheesecakes, part-skim ricotta cheese is the main ingredient. Although many cheesecakes are baked for about an hour, these are not baked at all. A one-yolk stovetop custard is combined with the ricotta, then the mixture is spooned into molds and chilled until set. A lemony peach purée, made from dried fruit, adds interest to this simple dessert.

1 cup dried peaches
½ cup plus 1 tablespoon sugar
5 tablespoons plus 1 teaspoon lemon juice
1 large egg yolk
½ cup skim milk
1 envelope unflavored gelatin
1 teaspoon grated lemon zest
Pinch of salt
1¼ cups part-skim ricotta cheese
½ teaspoon vanilla extract

1. For the peach purée, in a medium-size bowl combine the peaches and ¾ cup of warm water and set aside to soak 30 minutes.

2. Transfer the peaches and the soaking liquid to a food processor or blender, add 4 tablespoons of the sugar and 4 teaspoons of the lemon juice, and process until puréed. Return the purée to the bowl, cover with plastic wrap and refrigerate at least 1 hour, or until well chilled.

3. In the bottom of a double boiler bring enough water to a simmer so that the simmering water will not touch the top pan.

4. Combine the egg yolk and milk in the top pan and cook, whisking constantly, about 5 minutes, or until the mixture is light-colored and thick. Stir in the gelatin, lemon zest, salt and remaining sugar, and continue to cook, whisking, about 4 minutes, or until the gelatin dissolves and the custard thickens. Transfer the custard to a large bowl and set aside to cool, stirring occasionally to speed the cooling.

5. Place the ricotta in a food processor or blender and process until smooth. Add the vanilla and the remaining lemon juice, and process until blended

6. Using a rubber spatula, gently fold the ricotta mixture into the custard.

7. Spoon the mixture into four shallow 4-ounce molds or custard cups. Cover the molds with plastic wrap and refrigerate at least 1 hour.

8. To serve, turn the individual cheesecakes out onto dessert plates and spoon equal amounts of the peach purée over them.   *Makes 4 servings*

NUTRITION INFORMATION
values are per serving

• • •

CALORIES 342   CALCIUM 266 MG

TOTAL FAT 8 G   IRON 2 MG

SATURATED FAT 4 G   POTASSIUM 621 MG

CHOLESTEROL 78 MG   BETA CAROTENE 0.5 MG

SODIUM 151 MG   VITAMIN C 13 MG

DIETARY FIBER 4 G   VITAMIN E TRACE

CHEESECAKE CUPS

Instead of the usual combination of graham-cracker crumbs and butter, the crust for these mini-cheesecakes is made from toasted pumpernickel bread crumbs and honey.

1 quart plain lowfat yogurt
3 tablespoons sugar
1 teaspoon grated lemon zest
1 teaspoon vanilla extract
2 slices pumpernickel bread
2 tablespoons honey
1 cup drained juice-packed mandarin orange sections

1. Place a cheesecloth-lined strainer over a medium-size bowl. Spoon the yogurt into the strainer, cover it with plastic wrap and refrigerate 4 to 6 hours.

2. Leaving the yogurt in the strainer, stir in the sugar, lemon zest and vanilla. Cover the strainer with plastic wrap and refrigerate another 4 to 6 hours, or overnight. You should have 1¾ to 2 cups of yogurt cheese, depending on the type of yogurt used and the length of time it is drained. (Discard the whey, or reserve it to use in recipes for baked goods requiring buttermilk or sour milk. Remember, however, that the whey is slightly sweetened and flavored with lemon and vanilla.)

3. Preheat the oven to 375°.

4. For the crust, place the bread in the oven and toast it 10 to 15 minutes, or until it is dry.

5. Place the bread in a food processor or blender and process until it is reduced to crumbs. Add the honey and process another 5 seconds, or until blended.

6. Divide the crumb mixture among 8 dessert dishes or custard cups and press it into the bottom of each dish to form a crust.

7. Divide the yogurt cheese mixture among the dishes. Arrange some orange sections on top of each portion and serve.   *Makes 8 servings*

NUTRITION INFORMATION
values are per serving

• • •

CALORIES	139	CALCIUM	217 MG
TOTAL FAT	2 G	IRON	9 MG
SATURATED FAT	1 G	POTASSIUM	345 MG
CHOLESTEROL	7 MG	BETA CAROTENE	TRACE
SODIUM	125 MG	VITAMIN C	12 MG
DIETARY FIBER	TRACE	VITAMIN E	TRACE

QUINOA PUDDING

Quinoa, a South American grain that resembles millet, has been described by the National Academy of Sciences as "one of the best sources of protein in the vegetable kingdom." Like all grains, it is also an abundant source of complex carbohydrates.

½ cup quinoa
2 eggs
1 cup skim milk
3 tablespoons brown sugar
1 teaspoon almond extract
1 cup cooked brown rice
½ cup chopped dried figs
¼ cup rolled oats

1. Place the quinoa in a large bowl and rinse it thoroughly in several changes of cold water. (The grain may have a residue of its natural bitter-tasting coating; rinsing will remove it.) Skim and discard any grains or fragments that float to the surface.

2. Place the quinoa in a medium-size saucepan with 1 cup of water and bring to a boil over medium-high heat. Cover the pan, reduce the heat to low and simmer 10 to 15 minutes, or until the quinoa is transparent and all the water is absorbed. Remove the pan from the heat and set aside.

3. Preheat the oven to 375°.

4. Beat the eggs in a medium-size bowl. Stir in the milk, sugar and almond extract, then add the quinoa, rice, figs and oats, and stir well. Pour the mixture into a deep 1½-quart baking dish and place it in a larger pan. Add enough boiling water to the pan to reach halfway up the side of the dish. Bake the pudding 45 minutes, or until set and golden on top. Let the pudding cool 10 minutes and serve.   *Makes 6 servings*

NUTRITION INFORMATION
values are per serving

• • •

CALORIES	214	CALCIUM	103 MG
TOTAL FAT	3 G	IRON	2 MG
SATURATED FAT	0.7 G	POTASSIUM	369 MG
CHOLESTEROL	72 MG	BETA CAROTENE	0 MG
SODIUM	49 MG	VITAMIN C	TRACE
DIETARY FIBER	3 G	VITAMIN E	TRACE

APRICOT AND PRUNE FLANS

A Spanish dish akin to the French *crème caramel*, a dessert *flan* is a molded custard baked in a shallow pan, like a tart. It is usually made with whole milk or cream, but skim milk works perfectly well here because the custard is thickened with flour. The apricots and prunes create an appetizing interplay of textures and also supply good amounts of both potassium and beta carotene.

¾ cup dried apricot halves
¾ cup pitted prunes
2 eggs
⅓ cup honey
⅔ cup unbleached all-purpose flour
1¾ cups skim milk

1. Place the apricots and prunes in a medium-size bowl, add boiling water to cover and set aside to soak 1 hour.
2. Preheat the oven to 350°.
3. For the custard, in a small bowl beat together the eggs and honey until smooth. Gradually whisk in the flour, then stir in the milk.
4. Drain the fruit and divide it among six 8-ounce custard cups or ramekins. Divide the custard among the cups and bake 1 hour, or until the custard is set and golden brown around the edges. Serve the flans warm, or cover them, refrigerate until well chilled and serve cold. *Makes 6 servings*

NUTRITION INFORMATION
values are per serving

• • •

CALORIES	245	CALCIUM	117 MG
TOTAL FAT	2 G	IRON	2 MG
SATURATED FAT	0.6 G	POTASSIUM	537 MG
CHOLESTEROL	72 MG	BETA CAROTENE	0.9 MG
SODIUM	61 MG	VITAMIN C	2 MG
DIETARY FIBER	3 G	VITAMIN E	TRACE

RAISIN-WALNUT BAKED APPLES

A classic "comfort food," baked apples are a welcome treat on a chilly evening. You might want to bake a few extra apples, then wrap and refrigerate them to pack as portable breakfasts for the family.

4 large baking apples, such as Rome (about 2¼ pounds
*   total weight)*
⅔ cup dark raisins
¼ cup coarsely chopped walnuts
¼ cup packed brown sugar
2 tablespoons freshly squeezed lemon juice
1 teaspoon ground cinnamon
½ cup plain lowfat yogurt

1. Preheat the oven to 350°.
2. Core each apple from the stem end without cutting through the bottom and hollow out a good-size cavity for the filling. Pare a 1-inch strip of peel from the circumference of each apple to prevent splitting during baking; set aside.
3. In a small bowl stir together the raisins, walnuts, sugar, 1 tablespoon of the lemon juice and the cinnamon. Divide the filling among the apples, then place them in an 8-inch square baking pan. Pour 3 cups of hot tap water into the pan and bake the apples 1 hour, or until they are very tender; remove them from the oven and set aside to cool slightly.
4. Meanwhile, in another small bowl stir together the yogurt and remaining lemon juice. Top each apple with a dollop of the yogurt mixture and serve. *Makes 4 servings*

NUTRITION INFORMATION
values are per serving

• • •

CALORIES	331	CALCIUM	107 MG
TOTAL FAT	6 G	IRON	2 MG
SATURATED FAT	0.9 G	POTASSIUM	616 MG
CHOLESTEROL	2 MG	BETA CAROTENE	0 MG
SODIUM	30 MG	VITAMIN C	18 MG
DIETARY FIBER	7 G	VITAMIN E	3 MG

Papaya and Apples with Berry Sauce

PAPAYA AND APPLES WITH BERRY SAUCE

Raspberries and papaya contribute most of the fiber in this refreshing fruit dessert, but the apple peel supplies some fiber as well. To get the most from apples, make it a habit to use them unpeeled. If you prefer not to use the liqueur in this sauce, substitute 2 teaspoons of orange juice.

1 Granny Smith apple
1 papaya
2 teaspoons lemon juice
1 cup fresh or unsweetened frozen blackberries or raspberries
2 teaspoons Cointreau or other orange liqueur (optional)
1 teaspoon honey
2 tablespoons nonfat sour cream

1. Core but do not peel the apple; peel and seed the papaya. Cut both fruits into ½-inch cubes.

2. In a large bowl toss the apple cubes with the lemon juice; set aside.

3. In a blender combine the berries, liqueur, if using, and honey, and process until just combined.

4. Add the papaya cubes to the apple cubes and toss gently. Divide the mixture among 4 plates and spoon the berry sauce over the fruit. Top each serving with 1½ teaspoons of sour cream.

Makes 4 servings

NUTRITION INFORMATION
values are per serving

• • •

CALORIES	83	CALCIUM	35 MG
TOTAL FAT	0.4 G	IRON	TRACE
SATURATED FAT	0 G	POTASSIUM	332 MG
CHOLESTEROL	0 MG	BETA CAROTENE	1 MG
SODIUM	12 MG	VITAMIN C	63 MG
DIETARY FIBER	4 G	VITAMIN E	TRACE

FLAMBEED BANANAS AND APPLES

Bananas and pistachio nuts are excellent sources of potassium and magnesium; the pistachios are used only as a garnish because they are high in fat.

> 2 tablespoons unsweetened frozen apple juice concentrate
> Pinch of ground nutmeg
> 1 banana
> 1 apple
> 1½ teaspoons margarine
> 1 tablespoon rum
> 2 teaspoons chopped pistachios

1. In a cup stir together the apple juice concentrate and nutmeg; set aside.
2. Peel the banana and cut it into ½-inch diagonal slices.
3. Core but do not peel the apple and slice it into ¼-inch-thick wedges.
4. In a medium-size nonstick skillet melt the margarine over medium-high heat. Add the apples, and cook, turning the slices to cook them evenly, 1 minute, or until they just begin to brown. Add the banana slices, and cook, turning them to coat them with margarine, 30 to 60 seconds, or until they just begin to soften. Add the apple juice mixture, bring to a boil and cook 1 minute; set aside.
5. In a small skillet heat the rum over low heat 10 to 15 seconds. Carefully ignite the rum with a match and pour the burning rum over the fruit. When the flame goes out, divide the fruit and sauce between 2 plates and top with pistachios.   *Makes 2 servings*

NUTRITION INFORMATION
values are per serving

• • •

CALORIES	179	CALCIUM	12MG
TOTAL FAT	5 G	IRON	TRACE
SATURATED FAT	0.9 G	POTASSIUM	409 MG
CHOLESTEROL	0 MG	BETA CAROTENE	0 MG
SODIUM	5 MG	VITAMIN C	9 MG
DIETARY FIBER	3 G	VITAMIN E	3 MG

POACHED PEARS WITH BLUE-CHEESE FILLING

Many of the vitamins in fruit are protected by the skin, so it's best not to peel the pears until just before you cook them. Use a sharp knife or a swivel-bladed parer to remove the thinnest possible layer of peel.

> 3 firm, ripe Bosc pears
> 1½ cups dry white wine
> ⅓ cup sugar
> 2 tablespoons golden raisins
> 3 ounces Roquefort or other blue cheese
> 4 fresh mint leaves for garnish

1. Peel the pears and, using an apple corer, core them through the stem end to form a hollow for the filling.
2. Place the pears, wine and sugar in a medium-size nonreactive saucepan, cover and poach over medium-low heat, turning the pears occasionally, 25 minutes. Add the raisins and continue cooking another 20 minutes, or until the pears are just tender. (The cooking time will vary with the ripeness of the pears.) Reserving the poaching liquid, remove the pears from the pan and set them aside to cool.
3. Place the cheese in a small bowl and, using a wooden spoon, cream it until soft and fluffy. Transfer the cheese to a pastry bag fitted with a large plain tip and pipe it into the hollows in the pears. Stand the pears on a platter.
4. Return the poaching liquid to medium-high heat and cook, uncovered, about 10 minutes, or until it becomes syrupy. Brush the pears with the syrup, garnish each pear with a mint leaf and spoon the raisins around the platter. Serve some syrup and raisins with each pear.   *Makes 3 servings*

NUTRITION INFORMATION
values are per serving

• • •

CALORIES	319	CALCIUM	183 MG
TOTAL FAT	9 G	IRON	1 MG
SATURATED FAT	5 G	POTASSIUM	441 MG
CHOLESTEROL	21 MG	BETA CAROTENE	0 MG
SODIUM	403 MG	VITAMIN C	7 MG
DIETARY FIBER	4 G	VITAMIN E	N/A

CRANBERRY POACHED PEARS WITH YOGURT

Cranberry juice is an excellent source of vitamin C. You'll find unsweetened cranberry juice at health-food stores; if it is not available, use regular or low-calorie cranberry juice.

2 cups unsweetened cranberry juice
2 teaspoons sugar
2 teaspoons grated lemon zest
1 teaspoon grated orange zest
1 teaspoon vanilla extract
1 cinnamon stick
4 whole cloves
2 large pears, peeled, halved and cored
1 cup plain lowfat yogurt
2 tablespoons toasted sesame seeds

1. In a medium-size nonreactive saucepan combine the cranberry juice, sugar, lemon zest, orange zest, vanilla, cinnamon stick and cloves, and bring to a boil over medium-high heat. Reduce the heat to low and simmer the mixture 5 minutes.

2. Add the pear halves and simmer another 15 minutes, turning occasionally. Remove the pan from the heat; remove and discard the cinnamon stick and the cloves.

3. Transfer the pear halves and poaching liquid to a bowl and set aside to cool to room temperature, basting the pears often with the liquid if they are not completely immersed.

4. Refrigerate the pears at least 30 minutes, or until well chilled. To serve, divide the pear halves between 2 dessert plates, spoon ½ cup of yogurt over each serving and sprinkle with sesame seeds.

Makes 2 servings

NUTRITION INFORMATION
values are per serving

• • •

CALORIES	192	CALCIUM	181 MG
TOTAL FAT	4 G	IRON	2 MG
SATURATED FAT	0.9 G	POTASSIUM	390 MG
CHOLESTEROL	4 MG	BETA CAROTENE	0 MG
SODIUM	46 MG	VITAMIN C	63 MG
DIETARY FIBER	5 G	VITAMIN E	1 MG

FRUIT WITH LEMON YOGURT SAUCE

A variety of fresh fruit can help to keep low-calorie meals interesting while providing important nutrients. Thanks to rapid shipping of fresh produce, you can enjoy nutritious fruits such as Hawaiian pineapples and papayas throughout the year.

1 cup plain lowfat yogurt
1 tablespoon granulated sugar
2 teaspoons lemon juice
1½ teaspoons grated lemon zest
1 cup diced cantaloupe
1 cup diced honeydew
1 cup diced fresh pineapple
1 cup sliced fresh strawberries
½ cup fresh raspberries
½ cup seedless red grapes
½ cup diced papaya
2 tablespoons chopped walnuts

1. For the sauce, in a small bowl stir together the yogurt, sugar, lemon juice and lemon zest; set aside.

2. Place all the fruit in a large bowl and toss gently to coat the fruit with the sauce.

3. Divide the fruit mixture between 4 bowls, top each serving with half the sauce and sprinkle with walnuts.

Makes 4 servings

NUTRITION INFORMATION
values are per serving

• • •

CALORIES	318	CALCIUM	268 MG
TOTAL FAT	8 G	IRON	1 MG
SATURATED FAT	2 G	POTASSIUM	1217 MG
CHOLESTEROL	7 MG	BETA CAROTENE	2 MG
SODIUM	100 MG	VITAMIN C	146 MG
DIETARY FIBER	6 G	VITAMIN E	2 MG

FRUIT KEBABS WITH COCONUT SAUCE

These three-fruit kebabs served with a creamy low-fat dipping sauce are the perfect dessert for a picnic or cookout. If you're eating outdoors on a hot day, place the bowl of dip in a larger bowl of ice to keep it chilled. Feel free to substitute or add other fruits according to what looks good at the market: Try melon balls or peach or nectarine cubes.

½ cup lowfat cottage cheese (1%)
2 tablespoons lowfat vanilla yogurt
2 tablespoons sweetened flaked coconut
1 tablespoon sugar
2 cups fresh strawberries
6 ounces black grapes, stemmed (1 cup)
½ large pineapple, halved lengthwise and cut into
    ½-inch-thick triangles

1. For the sauce, combine the cottage cheese, yogurt, coconut and sugar in a food processor or blender, and process until smooth, scraping down the sides of the container with a rubber spatula. Transfer the sauce to a small bowl.

2. Thread the berries, grapes and pineapple pieces alternately on each of 8 bamboo skewers and serve with the coconut sauce.   *Makes 4 servings*

NUTRITION INFORMATION
values are per serving

• • •

CALORIES	136	CALCIUM	52 MG
TOTAL FAT	2 G	IRON	TRACE
SATURATED FAT	0.3 G	POTASSIUM	322 MG
CHOLESTEROL	2 MG	BETA CAROTENE	TRACE
SODIUM	129 MG	VITAMIN C	56 MG
DIETARY FIBER	3 G	VITAMIN E	TRACE

Fruit Kebabs with Coconut Sauce

LEMON–LIME SHERBET

Skim milk forms the base of this dessert, which contains less than half a gram of fat and just 2 milligrams of cholesterol per serving. A half-cup of premium ice cream, by contrast, can pack in as much as 24 grams of fat and 30 milligrams of cholesterol.

2 large lemons
1 lime
⅓ cup nonfat dry milk
1 cup skim milk
¼ cup sugar

1. Grate enough lemon and lime zest to measure 1 teaspoon each. Halve and squeeze the fruit. You should have about ⅔ cup lemon juice and 3 tablespoons lime juice; set aside.

2. In a medium-size bowl combine the nonfat dry milk and the lemon and lime juices and zest. Whisk in the skim milk and sugar, and continue whisking until smooth.

3. Pour the mixture into an ice-cube tray (leave in the dividers to help the mixture freeze more quickly). Freeze the sorbet 3 hours, or until firm.

4. Transfer the sherbet to a food processor and process it, pulsing the machine on and off, about 15 seconds, or just until spoonable. Divide the sherbet among 4 dessert dishes and serve. *Makes 4 servings*

NUTRITION INFORMATION
values are per serving

• • •

CALORIES	101	CALCIUM	151 MG
TOTAL FAT	0.2 G	IRON	TRACE
SATURATED FAT	0.1 G	POTASSIUM	263 MG
CHOLESTEROL	2 MG	BETA CAROTENE	0 MG
SODIUM	63 MG	VITAMIN C	24 MG
DIETARY FIBER	TRACE	VITAMIN E	TRACE

RUBY SORBET

The secret ingredient in this jewel-toned sorbet is beet juice, which contributes a gentle sweetness in addition to lending the dessert a vibrant ruby hue. After draining the juice, set aside the cooked beets to use in a salad or side dish.

3 pounds fresh beets
4½ cups pear or apple juice
3 medium-size Bosc pears
1 tablespoon grated lemon zest

1. Wash, trim, peel and quarter the beets. Place the beets and the pear juice in a large nonreactive saucepan. Bring to a boil over medium heat, reduce the heat to low and simmer about 15 minutes, or until the beets are tender. Meanwhile, peel, core and halve the pears.

2. Turn the beets and the cooking liquid into a strainer set over a large bowl; do not press the beets. Set aside the bowl of liquid and reserve the beets for another use.

3. Return the liquid to the pan, add the pears and lemon zest, and simmer over medium heat 5 minutes. Remove the pan from the heat and let the pears cool 20 minutes.

4. Purée the pears and liquid in a food processor or blender. Pour the purée into a shallow pan and freeze 3 hours, or until firm.

5. Let the sorbet thaw at room temperature 5 minutes, then scoop it into the food processor or blender and process it about 45 seconds, or just until spoonable, pulsing the machine on and off once or twice. Scoop the sorbet into 4 dessert dishes and serve. *Makes 4 servings*

NUTRITION INFORMATION
values are per serving

• • •

CALORIES	207	CALCIUM	36 MG
TOTAL FAT	0.8 G	IRON	1 MG
SATURATED FAT	0 G	POTASSIUM	503 MG
CHOLESTEROL	0 MG	BETA CAROTENE	0 MG
SODIUM	25 MG	VITAMIN C	10 MG
DIETARY FIBER	4 G	VITAMIN E	N/A

RASPBERRY FREEZE WITH LEMON SAUCE

Frozen fruits, such as the raspberries used in this dessert, are fine substitutes for fresh. The fruit is picked at its peak ripeness and is flash-frozen, which preserves most of its nutrients. Just be sure the fruit you buy is unsweetened—not packed in sugar or syrup. Frozen cherries, peaches and blueberries are sold in most supermarkets.

Two 12-ounce packages frozen unsweetened raspberries
  (3 cups), partially thawed
½ cup frozen apple juice concentrate, thawed
½ cup lowfat milk (2%)
¼ cup evaporated skimmed milk
1½ teaspoons cornstarch
2 teaspoons grated lemon zest
2 large egg whites
2 tablespoons sugar
1 tablespoon lemon juice
2 tablespoons chopped fresh mint, plus mint springs for
  garnish

1. For the raspberry freeze, in a food processor or blender combine the raspberries and apple juice concentrate and process until puréed. Put the purée through a food mill or force it through a sieve to remove the seeds, then transfer it to a freezer container and freeze it at least 3 hours.

2. Meanwhile, make the sauce: In a medium-size saucepan stir together the lowfat milk, evaporated milk and cornstarch until smooth. Add 1 teaspoon of the lemon zest and bring the mixture to a boil over medium heat, stirring constantly; remove the pan from the heat and set aside.

3. In a medium-size bowl whisk together the egg whites, sugar and lemon juice until frothy, then gradually whisk in the hot milk mixture. Return the mixture to the saucepan, add the mint and cook over low heat, stirring constantly, 5 minutes, or until the sauce is thickened. Transfer the sauce to a small bowl, cover and refrigerate until well chilled.

4. To serve, let the raspberry mixture thaw at room temperature 30 minutes, or until soft enough to scoop. Divide the lemon sauce among 4 dessert dishes. Scoop the raspberry freeze into the dishes and garnish with mint springs and the remaining lemon zest.   *Makes 4 servings*

NUTRITION INFORMATION
values are per serving

• • •

CALORIES	206	CALCIUM	132 MG
TOTAL FAT	2 G	IRON	1 MG
SATURATED FAT	0.4 G	POTASSIUM	547 MG
CHOLESTEROL	3 MG	BETA CAROTENE	TRACE
SODIUM	70 MG	VITAMIN C	47 MG
DIETARY FIBER	8 G	VITAMIN E	TRACE

RYE BREAD

Bread—low in fat and rich in complex carbohydrates—is often the most healthful part of a sandwich. This hearty rye, made with whole-wheat as well as rye flour, will improve any meal.

1½ cups light rye flour
1 cup whole-wheat flour
1 cup unbleached all-purpose flour, approximately
½ teaspoon salt
1 package dry yeast
2 tablespoons molasses
1 tablespoon cider vinegar
2 tablespoons malted grain beverage mix,
*   such as Postum*
3 tablespoons margarine, melted
2 teaspoons caraway seeds

1. In a medium-size bowl stir together the rye flour, whole-wheat flour, 1 cup of all-purpose flour and the salt, and make a well in the center; set aside.

2. Place the yeast in a small bowl, add ¼ cup of warm water (105-115°) and set aside 2 to 3 minutes.

3. Meanwhile, in a small bowl stir together the molasses, vinegar, grain beverage and ¾ cup of warm water. Pour the yeast mixture, the molasses mixture, the margarine and caraway seeds into the dry ingredients, and stir to form a dough.

4. Turn the dough onto a lightly floured board and knead it 5 to 7 minutes, or until smooth and elastic. Transfer the dough to a medium-size bowl, cover it with a damp kitchen towel and set aside in a warm place to rise 1 hour, or until doubled in bulk.

5. Punch down the dough and knead it 2 minutes on a lightly floured surface. Return the dough to the bowl, cover and let it rise about 30 minutes, or until almost doubled in bulk.

6. Spray a 9 x 5-inch loaf pan with nonstick cooking spray and dust it lightly with flour.

7. Punch down the dough again and roll it into a ball with your hands, then flatten it into an 8-inch disk. Roll up the dough to form a log. Place the dough in the prepared pan and set it aside to rise, uncovered, 30 minutes.

8. Preheat the oven to 450°.

9. Bake the bread 10 minutes, then reduce the oven temperature to 325° and bake 35 minutes more, or until the loaf is golden brown and sounds hollow when tapped. Turn the bread out on a rack to cool at least 10 minutes before cutting it.

Makes 16 slices

NUTRITION INFORMATION
values are per slice
• • •

CALORIES	120	CALCIUM	17 MG
TOTAL FAT	3 G	IRON	1 MG
SATURATED FAT	0.4 G	POTASSIUM	133 MG
CHOLESTEROL	0 MG	BETA CAROTENE	0 MG
SODIUM	69 MG	VITAMIN C	TRACE
DIETARY FIBER	2 G	VITAMIN E	2 MG

HEARTY WHOLE-WHEAT LOAF

Many supermarket breads labeled "wheat" are made with refined white flour, not whole-wheat flour. This fiber-packed loaf is the real thing.

5½ cups whole-wheat flour
2 cups rye flour
1 cup wheat bran
½ cup wheat germ
2 packages dry yeast
2 teaspoons salt
¾ cup skim milk
½ cup corn oil
½ cup dark molasses
2 eggs
1 tablespoon cornmeal

1. Combine 3 cups of the whole-wheat flour, the rye flour, bran and wheat germ in a large bowl.

2. Transfer 3 cups of this mixture to a second large bowl and stir in the yeast and salt.

3. In a small saucepan combine the milk, oil, molasses and 1 cup of water. Heat over low heat until the mixture registers 120° on a kitchen thermometer.

4. Gradually add the liquid mixture to the flour-yeast mixture, beating constantly with an electric mixer on low speed just until blended. Increase the speed to medium and beat another 2 minutes. Reserving 1 egg white, beat in the remaining yolk and whole egg and an additional 2 cups of the flour mixture, and beat for another 2 minutes. Stir in the remaining flour mixture and enough of the remaining whole-wheat flour to make a soft dough.

5. Turn the dough onto a lightly floured work surface and knead about 10 minutes, or until smooth and elastic. Add more whole-wheat flour if the dough is too sticky.

6. Spray a bowl with nonstick cooking spray. Shape the dough into a ball and place it in the bowl, turning the dough to coat it lightly with the spray. Cover the bowl and let the dough rise in a warm place about 1 hour, or until doubled in size.

7. Punch down the dough and turn onto a lightly floured surface. Invert the bowl over the dough and let the dough rest another 15 minutes.

8. Sprinkle a baking sheet with cornmeal. Shape the dough into an oval and transfer to the baking sheet. Cover with a kitchen towel and let rise in a warm place until doubled in size.

9. Preheat the oven to 350°.

10. Cut three ⅛-inch-deep slits across the top of the loaf. Mix the reserved egg white with 1 tablespoon of water and brush the bread with the mixture. Bake the bread on the baking sheet 50 to 60 minutes, or until the loaf sounds hollow when tapped.

11. Remove the bread from the oven and transfer to a rack to cool. Serve the bread slightly warm.

Makes 20 slices

NUTRITION INFORMATION
values are per slice

• • •

CALORIES	247	CALCIUM	87 MG
TOTAL FAT	7 G	IRON	3 MG
SATURATED FAT	1 G	POTASSIUM	489 MG
CHOLESTEROL	21 MG	BETA CAROTENE	0 MG
SODIUM	234 MG	VITAMIN C	TRACE
DIETARY FIBER	5 G	VITAMIN E	6 MG

WHOLE-WHEAT QUICK BREAD

A thick slice of this easy-to-bake bread is a good foundation for breakfast. Top it with a fruit spread or part-skim ricotta or mozzarella cheese.

½ cup unbleached all-purpose flour, approximately
1½ cups whole-wheat flour
1 teaspoon baking powder
¾ teaspoon baking soda
Pinch of salt
1 cup buttermilk
⅓ cup honey
1 tablespoon margarine, melted and cooled
1 egg, lightly beaten

1. Preheat the oven to 350°.

2. Spray an 8-inch round baking pan with nonstick cooking spray and dust it with all-purpose flour.

3. In a medium-size bowl stir together the whole-wheat flour, ½ cup of the all-purpose flour, the baking powder, baking soda and salt, and make a well in the center.

4. In a small bowl stir together the buttermilk, honey, margarine and egg, then add this mixture to the dry ingredients and stir just until combined.

5. Turn the batter into the pan and bake 35 minutes, or until a toothpick inserted in the center of the bread comes out clean and dry. Turn the bread out onto a rack to cool, then cut it into 8 wedges.

Makes 8 servings

NUTRITION INFORMATION
values are per wedge

• • •

CALORIES	184	CALCIUM	71 MG
TOTAL FAT	3 G	IRON	1 MG
SATURATED FAT	0.7 G	POTASSIUM	162 MG
CHOLESTEROL	28 MG	BETA CAROTENE	0 MG
SODIUM	171 MG	VITAMIN C	TRACE
DIETARY FIBER	3 G	VITAMIN E	2 MG

Oatmeal Bread

OATMEAL BREAD

Oatmeal (in any form) is a whole-grain product and, therefore, retains its healthful bran layer. Oat bran is rich in soluble fiber, which has been shown to reduce blood cholesterol. Although the initial excitement about oat bran as a cholesterol "cure-all" has died down, oatmeal remains a nutritious, lowfat choice as a breakfast cereal or baking ingredient. Either old-fashioned or quick-cooking rolled oats may be used to make this fiber-rich bread.

2 cups whole-wheat flour
2½ cups unbleached all-purpose flour, approximately
1¼ cups rolled oats
1 package quick-acting dry yeast
Pinch of salt
1 cup skim milk
2 tablespoons brown sugar
1 egg

1. In a medium-size bowl stir together the whole-wheat flour, 1½ cups of the all-purpose flour, 1 cup of the oats, the yeast and salt, and make a well in the center; set aside.

2. Combine the milk, sugar and 1 cup of water in a small saucepan over low heat and bring it to 110° (just warm to the touch). Meanwhile, separate the egg; place the white in a small bowl, cover with plastic wrap and refrigerate. Beat the yolk in a small bowl, then beat in ¼ cup of the milk mixture. Add both milk mixtures to the dry ingredients, and stir until a dough forms.

3. Turn the dough onto a lightly floured board and knead it 5 to 7 minutes, kneading in the remaining all-purpose flour as needed. Place the dough in a medium-size bowl, cover it with a damp kitchen towel and set aside in a warm place to rise 45 minutes, or until doubled in bulk.

4. Preheat the oven to 400°.

5. Spray a baking sheet with nonstick cooking spray. Punch the dough down and knead it on a lightly floured board 1 to 2 minutes. Form the dough into an 8-inch round and place it on the baking sheet; set aside, uncovered, 15 minutes.

6. Beat the egg white and spread it generously over the top of the loaf with a pastry brush, then sprinkle the loaf with the remaining oats. Bake 25 minutes, or until the bread is golden brown and sounds hollow when tapped on the bottom. Cool the bread on a rack before slicing. *Makes 16 slices*

NUTRITION INFORMATION
values are per slice

• • •

CALORIES	166	CALCIUM	34 MG
TOTAL FAT	1 G	IRON	2 MG
SATURATED FAT	0.3 G	POTASSIUM	156 MG
CHOLESTEROL	14 MG	BETA CAROTENE	0 MG
SODIUM	22 MG	VITAMIN C	TRACE
DIETARY FIBER	3 G	VITAMIN E	TRACE

WHOLE-GRAIN SODA BREAD

Irish soda bread is traditionally made with white flour. Here, however, whole-wheat flour, wheat berries (whole, unmilled kernels of wheat) and oatmeal make for a more nutritious loaf.

¼ cup wheat berries
¾ cup dark raisins
1 cup whole-wheat flour
½ cup unbleached all-purpose flour
½ cup rolled oats
¼ cup chopped walnuts
¼ cup dark brown sugar
2 teaspoons caraway seeds
2 teaspoons baking powder
1 teaspoon baking soda
¼ teaspoon salt
1 cup plus 2 teaspoons buttermilk
1 large egg
1 tablespoon oil

1. Place the wheat berries in a small bowl, add ½ cup of boiling water and set aside to soak 1 hour, or until soft.

2. Place the raisins in another small bowl, add hot water to cover and set aside to soak.

3. Preheat the oven to 375°.

4. Lightly spray a 9-inch round baking pan with nonstick cooking spray; set aside.

5. Drain the wheat berries and raisins.

6. In a large bowl stir together the whole-wheat flour, all-purpose flour, oats, walnuts, sugar, caraway seeds, baking powder, baking soda and salt, and make a well in the center. Pour in 1 cup of the buttermilk, the egg and oil, and stir to blend. Add the drained wheat berries and raisins, and stir just until the mixture holds together as a soft dough; do not overmix.

7. Spoon the dough into the prepared pan, mounding it slightly in the center, and brush it with the remaining 2 teaspoons of buttermilk.

8. Bake the bread in the center of the oven 35 to 40 minutes, or until the loaf is golden brown and sounds hollow when tapped on the bottom. Transfer the loaf to a wire rack to cool 10 minutes, then cut it into 12 wedges. *Makes 12 servings*

NUTRITION INFORMATION
values are per wedge

• • •

CALORIES	376	CALCIUM	156 MG
TOTAL FAT	8 G	IRON	3 MG
SATURATED FAT	1 G	POTASSIUM	430 MG
CHOLESTEROL	37 MG	BETA CAROTENE	0 MG
SODIUM	385 MG	VITAMIN C	1 MG
DIETARY FIBER	5 G	VITAMIN E	4 MG

DOSAS

In India, the griddle-baked breads called *dosas* are served plain or stuffed with a filling. This unfilled version makes a tasty breakfast bread, and a nice change from toast or English muffins. Top the *dosas* with chunky fruit butter or lowfat cottage cheese.

1⅓ cups yellow cornmeal
⅓ cup whole-wheat flour
⅓ cup unbleached all-purpose flour
½ teaspoon salt
⅔ cup cooked brown rice
1 cup skim milk

1. In a medium-size bowl combine the cornmeal, whole-wheat flour, all-purpose flour and salt. Add the rice, milk and ¾ cup of water, and stir until the mixture forms a batter. Cover the bowl with plastic wrap and set aside at room temperature 1 hour.

2. Spray a large nonstick skillet with nonstick cooking spray and heat it over medium-high heat. Pour in 4 scant ¼-cup portions of batter and cook them about 2½ minutes, or until tiny holes form in the surface and the batter appears slightly dry. Turn the dosas and cook for another 2 minutes, or until the second side is dry. Serve the dosas hot or warm; they may also be eaten cold but they will not be as tender. *Makes 12 dosas*

NUTRITION INFORMATION
values are per dosa

• • •

CALORIES	100	CALCIUM	29 MG
TOTAL FAT	0.5 G	IRON	1 MG
SATURATED FAT	0.1 G	POTASSIUM	84 MG
CHOLESTEROL	TRACE	BETA CAROTENE	0 MG
SODIUM	100 MG	VITAMIN C	TRACE
DIETARY FIBER	1 G	VITAMIN E	TRACE

FOCACCIA

An Italian flatbread that resembles a pizza crust, *focaccia* is sometimes topped with herbs or with vegetables. Here, fresh and dried herbs, colorful bell peppers and ground turkey (seasoned to taste like Italian sausage) turn the *focaccia* into a light meal.

 1 package dry yeast
 3 cups unbleached all-purpose flour, approximately
 3 tablespoons margarine, melted and cooled
 Pinch of salt
 ¼ pound ground skinless turkey breast
 2 garlic cloves, minced
 ¼ teaspoon black pepper
 ¼ teaspoon dried oregano, crumbled
 1 medium-size onion
 1 red and 1 yellow bell pepper
 2 tablespoons chopped fresh basil or marjoram, plus additional herb leaves for garnish (optional)
 1 tablespoon olive oil
 ¼ cup grated Parmesan cheese

1. Place the yeast in a small bowl and add ⅓ cup of warm water (105-115°); set aside 5 minutes.

2. Combine the yeast mixture and 1½ cups of flour in a food processor and process 5 to 10 seconds, or until a ball of dough forms. If the dough does not form a ball, with the machine running add 1 to 2 tablespoons of water and pulse the processor on and off 2 or 3 times. The dough will be tight and dry, not smooth and elastic like bread dough. Place the dough in a lightly floured bowl, cover with a damp kitchen towel and set aside in a warm place to rise 2 hours, or until the dough is doubled in bulk.

3. Punch down the dough and divide it into 4 pieces. Place the dough in the food processor, add 1½ cups of the flour, the margarine, salt, and ¼ cup of warm water, and process 10 to 15 seconds, or until the dough again forms a ball. If necessary, add 1 to 2 tablespoons of water as before. Return the dough to the bowl, cover and let it rise 2½ hours, or until doubled in bulk.

4. Meanwhile, in a small bowl stir together the turkey, garlic, black pepper and oregano until well combined; cover and refrigerate. Peel, trim and thinly slice the onion. Stem and seed the bell peppers and cut them into slivers.

5. Preheat the oven to 400°.

6. Punch down the dough, form it into a ball and then flatten it into a disk. Roll it out on a lightly floured board to a 10 x 14-inch oval about ¼ inch thick and transfer it to a baking sheet. With your fingertips make shallow indentations on the surface of the dough. Scatter the onions, bell peppers and chopped basil over the dough.

7. Using a teaspoon, form small balls of the turkey mixture and place them on the focaccia, then sprinkle with oil and Parmesan and bake the focaccia 15 to 20 minutes, or until the peppers begin to brown and the Parmesan is golden. Garnish with additional basil, if desired, then cut the focaccia into 6 wedges and serve. *Makes 6 servings*

NUTRITION INFORMATION
values are per wedge

• • •

CALORIES	394	CALCIUM	86 MG
TOTAL FAT	13 G	IRON	4 MG
SATURATED FAT	2 G	POTASSIUM	186 MG
CHOLESTEROL	16 MG	BETA CAROTENE	TRACE
SODIUM	126 MG	VITAMIN C	36 MG
DIETARY FIBER	2 G	VITAMIN E	5 MG

WINTER SQUASH BREAD

For a light tender texture when making quick breads (those leavened with baking powder or soda rather than yeast), mix the batter just until blended after adding the flour—don't beat it vigorously. This bread's appealing golden color signals the presence of beta carotene. This nutrient is found in most orange-yellow fruits and vegetables, and also in dark green vegetables such as broccoli and spinach.

    1 cup cooked Hubbard or other winter squash,
        or 1 small uncooked squash
    6 ounces dried peaches
    ½ cup apple juice
    2 cups unbleached all-purpose flour, approximately
    ½ cup sugar
    2 teaspoons baking powder
    1 teaspoon ground allspice
    ½ teaspoon salt
    ¼ teaspoon baking soda
    2 eggs, beaten
    1 tablespoon corn oil

1. If using uncooked squash, preheat the oven to 375°.

2. Using a large, heavy knife, carefully halve the squash. Place the halves cut side down on a foil-lined baking sheet and bake 25 to 35 minutes, or until the flesh is tender when pierced with a knife. Reduce the oven temperature to 350°, remove the squash from the oven and set aside to cool. Meanwhile, coarsely chop the peaches.

3. Bring the apple juice to a boil in a small saucepan over medium heat. Remove the pan from the heat and stir in the peaches; set aside. When the squash is cool enough to handle, remove and discard the seeds and stringy membranes. Measure 1 cup of the cooked flesh into a small bowl and mash it with a fork; set aside. Reserve any remaining squash for another use.

Winter Squash Bread

4. Spray a 9 x 5-inch loaf pan with nonstick cooking spray and dust it lightly with flour.

5. In a large bowl stir together 2 cups of flour, the sugar, baking powder, allspice, salt and baking soda, and make a well in the center. Add the peaches and apple juice, the eggs, oil and mashed squash, and mix just until blended.

6. Turn the batter into the prepared pan and bake 1 hour and 15 minutes, or until the loaf pulls away from the sides of the pan. Let the bread cool in the pan 15 minutes, then turn it out onto a rack to cool completely before slicing it.   *Makes 16 slices*

NUTRITION INFORMATION
values are per slice

• • •

CALORIES	131	CALCIUM	35 MG
TOTAL FAT	2 G	IRON	1 MG
SATURATED FAT	0.4 G	POTASSIUM	173 MG
CHOLESTEROL	27 MG	BETA CAROTENE	0.5 MG
SODIUM	126 MG	VITAMIN C	2 MG
DIETARY FIBER	2 G	VITAMIN E	TRACE

VEGETABLE BREAD

Top a slice of this savory bread, delicately redolent of scallions and garlic, with sliced turkey breast and a little sharp mustard. The addition of mashed kidney beans and grated carrots to the bread gives you a sandwich and a salad all in one. Although draining and rinsing the canned beans removes a substantial percentage of their sodium, you are better off using freshly cooked dried beans, which are virtually sodium-free. Cook a big batch so you can make a bean-based meal the same day without extra effort.

1 cup cooked kidney beans, or canned kidney beans, rinsed and drained
2 cups grated carrots
1½ cups finely chopped scallions
2 garlic cloves, minced
1 package dry yeast
3 cups unbleached all-purpose flour
1¼ cups whole-wheat flour, approximately
1 teaspoon salt
½ teaspoon black pepper
2 tablespoons margarine

1. Mash the beans in a medium-size bowl, then add the carrots, scallions and garlic, and stir until combined; set aside.

2. Place the yeast in a small bowl, add ¾ cup of warm water (105-115°) and set aside 2 to 3 minutes. Meanwhile, in a large bowl stir together the all-purpose flour, 1 cup of the whole-wheat flour, the salt and pepper, and make a well in the center. Pour in the yeast mixture, the vegetables and the margarine, and stir until well combined; the mixture will form a fairly sticky dough.

3. Flour a work surface with 2 tablespoons of the whole-wheat flour. Knead the dough 5 to 7 minutes, or until smooth and elastic, kneading in more flour if necessary. Transfer the dough to a medium-size bowl, cover it with a damp kitchen towel and set aside in a warm place to rise 1 to 1½ hours, or until doubled in bulk.

4. Punch down the dough. Sprinkle another 2 tablespoons of the whole-wheat flour on the work surface and knead the dough 2 minutes. Return the dough to the bowl, cover and let it rise about 1 hour, or until almost doubled in bulk.

5. Spray a baking sheet with nonstick cooking spray.

6. Punch down the dough again and knead it briefly on a lightly floured surface. Form the dough into a 7-inch round and place it on the baking sheet to rise, uncovered, 30 minutes.

7. Preheat the oven to 425°.

8. Bake the bread 10 minutes, then reduce the oven temperature to 325° and bake 45 to 50 minutes more, or until the loaf is golden brown and sounds hollow when tapped. Turn the bread out on a rack to cool at least 10 minutes before slicing it.

Makes 16 slices

NUTRITION INFORMATION
values are per slice

• • •

CALORIES	155	CALCIUM	24 MG
TOTAL FAT	2 G	IRON	2 MG
SATURATED FAT	0.3 G	POTASSIUM	185 MG
CHOLESTEROL	0 MG	BETA CAROTENE	3 MG
SODIUM	192 MG	VITAMIN C	6 MG
DIETARY FIBER	3 G	VITAMIN E	2 MG

PUMPKIN-SPICE BREAD

Moist vegetable-based quick breads freeze particularly well. For convenience, freeze individually wrapped portions of this slightly sweet bread. Take one with you to work—it will thaw by mid-morning so you can enjoy it as a healthful alternative to a Danish or doughnut. Briefly warming the bread in a microwave or toaster oven will enhance its spicy flavor and fragrance.

½ cup buttermilk
1 tablespoon butter or margarine
2 tablespoons honey
2 teaspoons dry yeast
½ cup cooked or canned pumpkin
½ teaspoon ground allspice
Pinch of salt
½ cup raisins
2½ cups unbleached all-purpose flour, approximately

1. Warm the buttermilk and butter in a small saucepan over low heat until the butter melts and the mixture is just tepid. Meanwhile, in a small bowl stir together the honey, yeast and 2 tablespoons of warm water (105-115°); set aside 10 minutes.

2. In a large bowl stir together the pumpkin, allspice and salt. Stir in the buttermilk and yeast mixtures and the raisins, then gradually add enough flour to form a dough that pulls away from the sides of the bowl.

3. Turn the dough out onto a lightly floured board and knead it with floured hands 5 to 10 minutes, or until the dough is smooth and elastic, kneading in more flour if necessary.

4. Spray a large bowl with nonstick cooking spray. Place the dough in the bowl, cover it with a kitchen towel and let rise in a draft-free place 30 to 45 minutes, or until doubled in bulk.

5. Spray a baking sheet with nonstick cooking spray. Punch the dough down and shape it into a round loaf. Place the loaf on the baking sheet and let it rise again 20 to 30 minutes, or until doubled in bulk. Meanwhile, preheat the oven to 375°.

6. With a single-edge razor blade or sharp scissors, cut a cross in the top of the loaf. Bake the bread about 35 minutes, or until the loaf sounds hollow when tapped. Transfer the loaf to a rack to cool before cutting it into 8 thick slices.

Makes 8 slices

NUTRITION INFORMATION
values are per slice

CALORIES	211	CALCIUM	33 MG
TOTAL FAT	2 G	IRON	2 MG
SATURATED FAT	1 G	POTASSIUM	186 MG
CHOLESTEROL	4 MG	BETA CAROTENE	0 MG
SODIUM	50 MG	VITAMIN C	1 MG
DIETARY FIBER	2 G	VITAMIN E	TRACE

BUTTERMILK BANANA BREAD

This currant-studded quick bread contains less fat than most banana breads. The recipe offers a good use for overripe bananas (which are at their sweetest and best for baking). If you can't bake right away, peel the bananas, wrap them in foil or plastic wrap and freeze them to use another day. Thaw the frozen bananas in the refrigerator before mashing them.

1¼ cups unbleached all-purpose flour
½ teaspoon baking soda
¼ teaspoon salt
1 large egg
⅓ cup honey
2 tablespoons vegetable oil
¼ cup buttermilk
1 cup mashed ripe banana
¼ cup currants
¼ cup chopped walnuts

1. Preheat the oven to 350°.

2. Spray a 9 x 5-inch loaf pan with nonstick cooking spray; set aside.

3. In a small bowl combine the flour, baking soda and salt; set aside.

4. In a large bowl, using an electric mixer, beat together the egg, honey and oil until smooth. Add half of the flour mixture and beat until smooth. Beat in the buttermilk, then add the remaining flour mixture, blending well after each addition. Add the mashed banana and blend well. Add the currants and walnuts, and stir until combined.

5. Pour the batter into the pan and bake 50 minutes, or until the bread is firm and brown. A toothpick inserted into the loaf should come out almost dry. Turn the bread out onto a rack to cool completely before slicing it. *Makes 16 slices*

NUTRITION INFORMATION
values are per slice

• • •

CALORIES 110 CALCIUM 13 MG
TOTAL FAT 3 G IRON 1 MG
SATURATED FAT 0.5 G POTASSIUM 109 MG
CHOLESTEROL 13 MG BETA CAROTENE 0 MG
SODIUM 68 MG VITAMIN C 2 MG
DIETARY FIBER TRACE VITAMIN E 2 MG

SCALLION-CHEESE BREAD

With a good sharp cheese, a little goes a long way. Look for a well-aged Cheddar; some of the best come from England, Vermont, New York and Canada.

½ cup buttermilk
2 tablespoons lemon juice
1 tablespoon margarine
1 package dry yeast (2 teaspoons)
1½ cups whole-wheat flour, approximately
1½ cups unbleached all-purpose flour
1 tablespoon sugar
½ teaspoon salt
1 cup chopped scallions
1½ ounces sharp Cheddar cheese, grated (scant ½ cup)

1. Combine the buttermilk, lemon juice and margarine in a small skillet over medium heat, and warm the mixture just until tepid; remove from the heat and set aside.

2. Place the yeast in a small bowl and add ⅓ cup of warm water (105-115°); set aside 5 minutes. Meanwhile, in a large bowl combine 1½ cups of the whole-wheat flour, the all-purpose flour, sugar and salt, and make a well in the center.

3. Pour the buttermilk and yeast mixtures into the dry ingredients and stir to form a dough. Turn the dough out on a lightly floured surface and knead it 8 to 10 minutes, or until smooth and elastic. Return the dough to the bowl, cover with a damp kitchen towel and set aside in a draft-free place to rise 1 hour, or until doubled in bulk.

4. Punch down the dough and knead it 2 minutes. Return the dough to the bowl, cover and let it rise 45 minutes, or until almost doubled in bulk.

5. Punch down the dough again and roll it out on a lightly floured surface to a 10 x 15-inch rectangle. Sprinkle the scallions and cheese evenly over the dough. Starting with a long edge, roll up the dough and filling, jelly-roll fashion, as tightly as possible. Tuck in the ends to seal them and place the bread seam-side down on a baking sheet to rise, uncovered, 30 minutes.

6. Preheat the oven to 350°.

7. Bake the bread 30 to 40 minutes, or until it is golden brown and sounds hollow when tapped. Cool the bread on a rack at least 10 minutes before slicing it. *Makes 16 slices*

NUTRITION INFORMATION
values are per slice

• • •

CALORIES 107 CALCIUM 39 MG
TOTAL FAT 2 G IRON 1 MG
SATURATED FAT 0.8 G POTASSIUM 99 MG
CHOLESTEROL 3 MG BETA CAROTENE TRACE
SODIUM 93 MG VITAMIN C 4 MG
DIETARY FIBER 2 G VITAMIN E 1 MG

CORNMEAL MUFFINS

These lowfat, slightly sweet muffins are a far cry from oversized bakery muffins (really cupcakes) that can be packed with 20 or more grams of fat.

½ cup buttermilk
1 tablespoon plus 1 teaspoon unsalted butter or margarine, melted and cooled
1 egg, beaten
½ cup yellow cornmeal
⅓ cup unbleached all-purpose flour
¼ cup packed brown sugar
2 teaspoons baking powder
Pinch of salt

1. Preheat the oven to 375°.

2. Line 12 muffin tin cups with paper liners.

3. In a medium-size bowl stir together the buttermilk, butter and egg until blended.

4. In another medium-size bowl combine the cornmeal, flour, sugar, baking powder and salt. Add the dry ingredients to the buttermilk mixture and stir just to combine; do not overmix.

5. Divide the batter among the muffin tin cups and bake 20 minutes, or until the muffins are golden brown and a toothpick inserted into the center of a muffin comes out clean.   *Makes 12 muffins*

NUTRITION INFORMATION
values are per muffin

• • •

CALORIES	73	CALCIUM	50 MG
TOTAL FAT	2 G	IRON	TRACE
SATURATED FAT	1 G	POTASSIUM	50 MG
CHOLESTEROL	22 MG	BETA CAROTENE	0 MG
SODIUM	77 MG	VITAMIN C	TRACE
DIETARY FIBER	TRACE	VITAMIN E	TRACE

CORNMEAL-CHEESE ENGLISH MUFFINS

The ricotta topping served with these muffins is a good lowfat source of calcium. Add a glass of juice or a piece of fruit and you have a complete breakfast.

1 package dry yeast
1½ tablespoons honey
1 cup frozen corn kernels
1¼ cups unbleached all-purpose flour, approximately
1 cup plus 2 teaspoons cornmeal
1 cup whole-wheat flour
¼ cup blue cheese, crumbled
1 large egg white
2 teaspoons vegetable oil
¾ teaspoon salt
¾ teaspoon black pepper
½ cup part-skim ricotta cheese
2 tablespoons finely chopped scallions

1. Place the yeast in a small cup, add ¼ cup warm water (105-115°) and ½ tablespoon of the honey and set aside for about 5 minutes, or until foamy.

2. Meanwhile, place the corn in a food processor and process for about 10 seconds, or until chopped. Remove about half of the corn and set aside. Add 1¼

cups of the all-purpose flour, 1 cup of the cornmeal, the whole-wheat flour, blue cheese, egg white, oil, salt and pepper to the food processor and cover it.

3. After 5 minutes, stir the yeast mixture. Start the food processor, pour in the yeast mixture through the feed tube and process about 40 seconds. Add the reserved chopped corn kernels and process another 5 seconds; the dough should form a ball.

4. Place the dough in a medium-size bowl, cover it with a kitchen towel and set aside in a warm place to rise 1 hour, or until the dough is doubled in bulk.

5. Sprinkle a baking sheet with the remaining 2 teaspoons of cornmeal.

6. Punch down the dough and on a lightly floured board roll it out to a ⅜-inch thickness. Using a 3½-inch biscuit cutter, cut out 6 rounds of dough. Transfer the muffins to the baking sheet, cover with a towel and set aside in a warm place to rise 25 minutes. or until the muffins are about 1½ times their original size.

7. Heat a medium-size nonstick skillet over medium heat. Using a metal spatula place 3 muffins in the skillet and cook about 6 minutes, or until the bottoms of the muffins are golden brown. Turn the muffins and cook another 6 minutes. Transfer the cooked muffins to a wire rack to cool and cook the remaining muffins in the same fashion.

8. Just before serving, stir together the ricotta and scallions in a small bowl. Split and toast the muffins, then spread each half with 2 teaspoons of the ricotta spread and serve.   *Makes 6 muffins*

NUTRITION INFORMATION
values are per muffin

• • •

CALORIES	367	CALCIUM	126 MG
TOTAL FAT	7 G	IRON	3 MG
SATURATED FAT	3 G	POTASSIUM	276 MG
CHOLESTEROL	13 MG	BETA CAROTENE	TRACE
SODIUM	438 MG	VITAMIN C	2 MG
DIETARY FIBER	5 G	VITAMIN E	3 MG

Cornmeal-Cheese English Muffins

RYE APPLESAUCE MUFFINS

When buying rye flour, choose medium or dark flour over light: As with wheat flour, the darker flour contains more fiber than the light. Dark rye flour also has a more assertive rye flavor. Choose unsweetened applesauce at the supermarket—or use homemade.

    ⅔ cup rye flour
    ½ cup unbleached all-purpose flour
    ½ cup whole-wheat flour
    ⅓ cup rye flakes
    ½ teaspoon salt
    1 tablespoon baking powder
    1 teaspoon ground ginger
    ½ teaspoon ground cardamom
    1 cup chunky applesauce
    ¾ cup plus 2 tablespoons skim milk
    ¼ cup honey
    3 tablespoons vegetable oil
    1 large egg, lightly beaten
    1 teaspoon grated lemon zest

1. Preheat the oven to 400°.

2. Spray 12 muffin tin cups with nonstick cooking spray or line them with paper liners.

3. Sift together the dry ingredients onto a sheet of waxed paper, then resift into a large bowl.

4. In a medium-size bowl combine the applesauce, milk, honey, oil, egg and lemon zest. Pour the applesauce mixture over the dry ingredients and stir just until combined. Do not overmix.

5. Divide the batter equally among the muffin cups and bake about 20 minutes, or until a toothpick inserted in the center of a muffin comes out clean.

Makes 12 muffins

NUTRITION INFORMATION
values are per muffin

• • •

CALORIES	135	CALCIUM	79 MG
TOTAL FAT	4 G	IRON	1 MG
SATURATED FAT	0.6 G	POTASSIUM	137 MG
CHOLESTEROL	18 MG	BETA CAROTENE	0 MG
SODIUM	177 MG	VITAMIN C	TRACE
DIETARY FIBER	1 G	VITAMIN E	3 MG

ZUCCHINI-RAISIN MUFFINS

Whole-grain muffins make excellent snacks. These contain whole grains in three forms—rolled oats, whole-bran cereal and whole-wheat flour.

    1½ cups buttermilk
    1 cup rolled oats
    ½ cup ready-to-eat whole-bran cereal
    2 tablespoons margarine
    2 tablespoons light brown sugar
    1 large egg, lightly beaten
    1 cup whole-wheat flour
    1 teaspoon baking powder
    1 teaspoon baking soda
    ¼ teaspoon salt
    ¼ teaspoon ground cinnamon
    1 cup grated zucchini, squeezed dry
    ½ cup dark raisins
    ¼ cup dry-roasted cashews, coarsely chopped

1. Preheat the oven to 400°.

2. Spray 12 muffin tin cups with nonstick cooking spray or line them with paper liners.

3. In a medium-size bowl stir together the buttermilk, oats and cereal; set aside 30 minutes.

4. In another medium-size bowl, using an electric mixer, cream together the margarine and brown sugar. Beat in the egg, then stir in the flour, baking powder, baking soda, salt and cinnamon.

5. Add the flour mixture to the oats mixture and stir to combine. Stir in the zucchini, raisins and cashews, divide the batter among the muffin cups and bake 35 minutes, or until a toothpick inserted in the center of a muffin comes out clean.

Makes 12 muffins

NUTRITION INFORMATION
values are per muffin

• • •

CALORIES	150	CALCIUM	72 MG
TOTAL FAT	5 G	IRON	2 MG
SATURATED FAT	1 G	POTASSIUM	257 MG
CHOLESTEROL	19 MG	BETA CAROTENE	TRACE
SODIUM	217 MG	VITAMIN C	3 MG
DIETARY FIBER	3 G	VITAMIN E	3 MG

PEACH MUFFINS

Although made with little fat, these honey-sweetened muffins are so moist they can be eaten without butter or jam. The bran cereal adds fiber.

1¼ cups unbleached all-purpose flour
1 cup ready-to-eat whole-bran cereal
½ cup whole-wheat flour
1 teaspoon baking powder
1 teaspoon baking soda
¼ teaspoon ground cinnamon
1½ cups buttermilk
¼ cup honey
3 tablespoons vegetable oil
2 large eggs, lightly beaten
1½ cups dried peaches, coarsely diced

1. Preheat the oven to 375°.
2. Spray 18 muffin tin cups with nonstick cooking spray or line them with paper liners.
3. In a large bowl stir together the all-purpose flour, cereal, whole-wheat flour, baking powder, baking soda and cinnamon, and make a well in the center.
4. In a medium-size bowl beat together the buttermilk, honey, oil and eggs. Pour the buttermilk mixture into the dry ingredients, add the peaches and stir just until combined.
5. Divide the batter among the muffin cups and bake 20 to 25 minutes, or until the muffins are lightly browned. *Makes 18 muffins*

NUTRITION INFORMATION
values are per muffin
• • •

CALORIES	140	CALCIUM	48 MG
TOTAL FAT	3 G	IRON	2 MG
SATURATED FAT	0.6 G	POTASSIUM	263 MG
CHOLESTEROL	24 MG	BETA CAROTENE	0.6 MG
SODIUM	145 MG	VITAMIN C	3 MG
DIETARY FIBER	3 G	VITAMIN E	3 MG

ORANGE-PRUNE MUFFINS

Prunes are an exceptional source of soluble fiber, which helps lower blood cholesterol.

12 pitted prunes, cut into eighths
¼ cup orange juice
¾ cup buttermilk
1 tablespoon grated orange zest
1¾ cups unbleached all-purpose flour
1 teaspoon baking powder
½ teaspoon baking soda
½ teaspoon salt
¼ cup vegetable oil
2 tablespoons molasses
2 tablespoons dark brown sugar
1 egg
1 cup cooked cracked wheat (⅓ cup raw)

1. Preheat the oven to 400°.
2. Spray 12 muffin tin cups with nonstick cooking spray or line them with paper liners.
3. Cook the prunes and orange juice in a small saucepan over medium-low heat 4 minutes, or until the liquid has nearly evaporated. Remove from the heat and stir in the buttermilk and orange zest.
4. In a large bowl combine the flour, baking powder, baking soda and salt; make a well in the center.
5. In another medium-size bowl combine the oil, molasses, sugar and egg, and mix until blended. Add the prunes and cracked wheat, and mix until blended. Pour the mixture into the well in the dry ingredients and stir just until combined.
6. Divide the batter among the muffin cups and bake 20 minutes, or until the muffins are firm and browned. *Makes 12 muffins*

NUTRITION INFORMATION
values are per muffin
• • •

CALORIES	172	CALCIUM	52 MG
TOTAL FAT	5 G	IRON	1 MG
SATURATED FAT	0.8 G	POTASSIUM	168 MG
CHOLESTEROL	18 MG	BETA CAROTENE	TRACE
SODIUM	171 MG	VITAMIN C	4 MG
DIETARY FIBER	2 G	VITAMIN E	4 MG

Blueberry-Oat Bran Muffins

BLUEBERRY-OAT BRAN MUFFINS

For a more satisfying texture and enhanced nutritional value, you can substitute oat bran or rolled oats for up to one-third of the flour in most of your favorite muffin recipes.

1½ cups fresh or unsweetened frozen blueberries, thawed
1 cup buttermilk
¼ cup honey
2 tablespoons sunflower oil
2 egg whites, lightly beaten
1 cup rolled oats
1 cup oat bran
½ cup unbleached all-purpose flour
2 teaspoons baking powder
Pinch of salt

1. Preheat the oven to 375°.

2. Spray 12 muffin tin cups with nonstick cooking spray or line them with paper liners.

3. If using fresh blueberries, wash, dry and pick them over.

4. In a small bowl stir together the buttermilk, honey, oil and egg whites.

5. In a large bowl stir together the oats, oat bran, flour, baking powder and salt, and make a well in the center. Pour in the milk mixture and the blueberries, and stir just until combined; do not overmix.

6. Divide the batter among the muffin cups and bake 25 minutes, or until a toothpick inserted into the center of a muffin comes out clean and dry.

Makes 12 muffins

NUTRITION INFORMATION
values are per muffin

• • •

CALORIES	136	CALCIUM	70 MG
TOTAL FAT	4 G	IRON	1 MG
SATURATED FAT	0.4 G	POTASSIUM	203 MG
CHOLESTEROL	TRACE	BETA CAROTENE	0 MG
SODIUM	42 MG	VITAMIN C	TRACE
DIETARY FIBER	1 G	VITAMIN E	TRACE

WHOLE-WHEAT CRANBERRY MUFFINS

Whipped margarine, used in this recipe, is lower in calories and fat than stick margarine because air is beaten into it. However, low-calorie imitation or diet margarines, in which some of the oil is replaced by water, do not work well in baking.

1 cup whole-wheat flour
½ cup unbleached all-purpose flour
2 teaspoons baking powder
½ teaspoon ground cinnamon
Pinch of salt
½ cup skim milk
¼ cup whipped margarine, melted and cooled
¼ cup honey
1 large egg, lightly beaten
1½ cups cranberries, coarsely chopped

1. Preheat the oven to 400°.
2. Lightly spray 10 muffin tin cups with nonstick cooking spray or line them with paper liners; set aside.
3. In a large bowl stir together the flours, baking powder, cinnamon and salt.
4. In a small bowl stir together the milk, margarine, honey and egg. Add the milk mixture to the dry ingredients and stir vigorously 30 seconds. Stir in the cranberries.
5. Divide the batter among the muffin cups and bake 30 minutes, or until the tops are golden and a toothpick inserted in a muffin comes out clean.

Makes 10 muffins

NUTRITION INFORMATION
values are per muffin

• • •

CALORIES	139	CALCIUM	63 MG
TOTAL FAT	4 G	IRON	1 MG
SATURATED FAT	0.8 G	POTASSIUM	100 MG
CHOLESTEROL	22 MG	BETA CAROTENE	0 MG
SODIUM	124 MG	VITAMIN C	2 MG
DIETARY FIBER	2 G	VITAMIN E	2 MG

SWEET POTATO BISCUITS

It takes just a little ingenuity to update and improve good old-fashioned recipes. Here, sweet potato adds a rich golden color and a delectable flavor—as well as beta carotene—to the biscuits.

2 tablespoons plus 2 teaspoons margarine
1 cup unbleached all-purpose flour, approximately
1 tablespoon brown sugar
2 teaspoons baking powder
Pinch of salt
1 cup mashed cooked sweet potato
1 tablespoon skim milk

1. Preheat the oven to 450°.
2. Cut the margarine into small pieces. Combine 1 cup of flour, the sugar, baking powder and salt in a food processor. Add the margarine while pulsing the machine on and off 5 to 10 seconds, or until the mixture resembles coarse cornmeal.
3. With the machine running, add the sweet potato and milk, and process for another 5 to 10 seconds, or just until combined. (To mix the dough by hand, stir together the dry ingredients in a medium-size bowl. Cut the margarine into the dry ingredients with a pastry blender or 2 knives. Add the potato and milk and stir until combined.)
4. Remove the dough from the processor or bowl, form it into a ball with your hands and then flatten the dough into a disk.
5. Lightly flour a work surface and a rolling pin, and roll the dough out to a ½-inch thickness. Using a 2-inch biscuit cutter, cut 12 biscuits and place them on a baking sheet. Bake the biscuits 10 minutes, or until they are light golden brown. Serve warm.

Makes 12 biscuits

NUTRITION INFORMATION
values are per biscuit

• • •

CALORIES	97	CALCIUM	41 MG
TOTAL FAT	3 G	IRON	TRACE
SATURATED FAT	0.5 G	POTASSIUM	70 MG
CHOLESTEROL	TRACE	BETA CAROTENE	3 MG
SODIUM	64 MG	VITAMIN C	5 MG
DIETARY FIBER	1 G	VITAMIN E	3 MG

CORNMEAL BISCUITS

Nothing could be more inviting than hot biscuits for breakfast. These cornmeal biscuits, made with about half the usual amount of fat, can be quickly mixed in the food processor; you knead the dough for only a few seconds, and the biscuits take just ten minutes to bake.

2 cups unbleached all-purpose flour, approximately
⅔ cup yellow cornmeal
1 tablespoon sugar
2 teaspoons baking powder
Pinch of salt
3 tablespoons butter or margarine, well chilled
¾ cup skim milk

1. Preheat the oven to 425°.
2. In a medium-size bowl stir together 2 cups of the flour, the cornmeal, sugar, baking powder and salt; transfer the mixture to a food processor.
3. Cut the butter into small pieces, add it to the dry ingredients and process, pulsing the processor on and off, about 10 seconds, or until the mixture resembles coarse meal. Add the milk and process another 10 seconds, or until the dough forms a cohesive mass. To mix the dough by hand, cut the butter into the dry ingredients with a pastry blender or 2 knives, then add the milk and stir until combined.
4. Turn the dough out onto a lightly floured board and knead it gently for 30 seconds, or just until smooth. Roll it out with a floured rolling pin to a ¾-inch thickness.
5. Using a floured 2-inch biscuit cutter, cut out 16 biscuits and place them on a baking sheet. Reroll and cut any scraps of dough, then bake the biscuits 10 minutes, or until golden. Serve warm.

Makes 16 biscuits

NUTRITION INFORMATION
values are per biscuit
• • •

CALORIES	104	CALCIUM	40 MG
TOTAL FAT	2 G	IRON	1 MG
SATURATED FAT	1 G	POTASSIUM	46 MG
CHOLESTEROL	6 MG	BETA CAROTENE	0 MG
SODIUM	72 MG	VITAMIN C	TRACE
DIETARY FIBER	TRACE	VITAMIN E	TRACE

BUTTERMILK-SOY BISCUITS

Instead of solid shortening such as butter or lard, these golden-topped biscuits are made with safflower oil, which is one of the oils lowest in saturated fat. Canola oil and sunflower oil are also good choices.

1½ cups unbleached flour
½ cup lowfat soy flour
2 teaspoons baking powder
1 teaspoon baking soda
¼ teaspoon salt
3 tablespoons safflower oil
¾ cup plus 1 tablespoon buttermilk
1 tablespoon sunflower seeds

1. Preheat the oven to 450°.
2. Lightly spray a large baking sheet with nonstick cooking spray.
3. In a medium-size bowl stir together the dry ingredients using a fork. Add the oil and ¾ cup of the buttermilk, and stir until a soft dough forms and leaves the sides of the bowl. Transfer the dough to a floured board and knead 8 times, then roll the dough out with a floured rolling pin to a ½-inch thickness.
4. Using a floured 2-inch biscuit cutter, cut the dough into 12 biscuits. Place the biscuits on the baking sheet, brush the tops with the remaining buttermilk and sprinkle with sunflower seeds. Bake on the middle rack of the oven 10 to 12 minutes, or until golden. Serve warm.

Makes 12 biscuits

NUTRITION INFORMATION
values are per biscuit
• • •

CALORIES	113	CALCIUM	62 MG
TOTAL FAT	4 G	IRON	1 MG
SATURATED FAT	0.5 G	POTASSIUM	144 MG
CHOLESTEROL	TRACE	BETA CAROTENE	0 MG
SODIUM	181 MG	VITAMIN C	TRACE
DIETARY FIBER	TRACE	VITAMIN E	2 MG

POTATO ROLLS

You can make these rolls with either white or sweet potatoes. Sweet potatoes are a far better source of beta carotene than white potatoes, but white potatoes have much more potassium. The raisins are also an excellent souce of potassium.

¼ pound white or sweet potato
1 cup buttermilk
1 cup dark raisins
2 tablespoons vegetable oil
2 tablespoons sugar
1 package dry yeast
3¼ cups unbleached all-purpose flour, approximately
2 tablespoons nonfat dry milk
Pinch of salt

1. Place the potato in a small saucepan with cold water to cover, and bring to a boil over medium-high heat. Cover the pan, reduce the heat to medium-low, and cook the potato 20 minutes, or until tender when pierced with a knife. When the potato is cooked, set it aside to cool slightly; reserve the cooking water.

2. Peel the potato, mash it in a small bowl, then stir in the buttermilk, raisins and oil; set aside.

3. In a small bowl combine ¼ cup of the warm cooking water and 1 tablespoon of sugar. Add the yeast and let the mixture stand 1 to 2 minutes, or until the yeast begins to foam. Meanwhile, combine 3¼ cups of the flour, the nonfat dry milk, the remaining sugar and the salt in a medium-size bowl, and make a well in the center. Pour in the potato and yeast mixtures and stir until well combined.

4. Turn the dough onto a lightly floured surface and knead it 5 to 7 minutes, or until smooth, dusting it with more flour if necessary to prevent sticking. Place the dough in a clean medium-size bowl, cover it with a kitchen towel and set aside in a warm place to rise 40 minutes, or until doubled in bulk.

5. Punch down the dough and knead it on a floured surface 1 minute. Roll it into a 20-inch-long rope about 2 inches thick, cut the rope into ten 2-inch sections and place them on a baking sheet. Set aside to rise 25 minutes.

6. Preheat the oven to 350°.

7. Bake the rolls 15 to 20 minutes, or until golden brown on top. Let cool slightly before serving.

Makes 10 rolls

NUTRITION INFORMATION
values are per roll, made with white potato
• • •

CALORIES	247	CALCIUM	48 MG
TOTAL FAT	3 G	IRON	2 MG
SATURATED FAT	0.6 G	POTASSIUM	248 MG
CHOLESTEROL	1 MG	BETA CAROTENE	0 MG
SODIUM	44 MG	VITAMIN C	2 MG
DIETARY FIBER	2 G	VITAMIN E	2 MG

GINGER SCONES

Scones, a type of rich biscuit, are popular throughout the British Isles, where oven- or griddle-baked scones are offered warm as a teatime treat. These dense yet tender quick breads are often made with cream; however, buttermilk (which despite its name is low in fat) works just fine. Instead of the traditional toppings of jam, butter or thick cream, offer these spicy scones with an all-fruit spread and a dollop of lowfat yogurt or nonfat cream cheese.

1½ cups unbleached all-purpose flour
½ cup whole-wheat flour
2 tablespoons sugar
2 teaspoons baking powder
Pinch of salt
3 tablespoons plus 1 teaspoon margarine
1 tablespoon plus 1 teaspoon crystallized ginger, finely chopped (½ ounce)
2 teaspoons grated orange zest
¼ teaspoon ground ginger
⅔ cup buttermilk

1. Preheat the oven to 425°.

2. Combine the all-purpose flour, whole-wheat flour, sugar, baking powder and salt in a food processor. Add the margarine and process, pulsing the machine on and off, 5 to 10 seconds, or until the mixture resembles coarse cornmeal. Add the crystallized ginger, orange zest and ground ginger, then, with the machine running, add the buttermilk and process until the dough begins to clump together. Knead the dough briefly by hand until it is smooth. (To mix the dough by hand, stir together the dry ingredients in a large bowl. Using a pastry blender or 2 knives, cut in the margarine until the mixture resembles coarse cornmeal. Stir in the remaining ingredients, then knead until smooth.)

3. Divide the dough into 6 equal pieces (do not roll them into smooth balls), place them on a baking sheet and lightly shape them into mounds. Bake the scones 12 to 15 minutes, or until they are golden brown on top. Serve warm.   *Makes 6 scones*

NUTRITION INFORMATION
values are per scone

• • •

CALORIES	240	CALCIUM	103 MG
TOTAL FAT	7 G	IRON	2 MG
SATURATED FAT	1 G	POTASSIUM	121 MG
CHOLESTEROL	0 MG	BETA CAROTENE	0 MG
SODIUM	148 MG	VITAMIN C	1 MG
DIETARY FIBER	2 G	VITAMIN E	5 MG

OATMEAL SCONES

These raisin-studded scones are formed in a time-honored fashion, by rolling the dough into a flat round and then cutting it into wedges. If the wedges are left unseparated before baking, they will have crusty tops but tender sides; separating them by moving them an inch apart on the baking sheet will produce an all-over golden crust. Oatmeal scones are delicious with apples and a bit of cheese.

1⅓ cups unbleached all-purpose flour, approximately
1 cup rolled oats
1 tablespoon sugar
1 teaspoon baking soda
Pinch of salt
¼ cup butter, well chilled
⅔ cup buttermilk
⅓ cup golden raisins

1. Preheat the oven to 400°.
2. In a food processor combine 1⅓ cups of the flour, the oats, sugar, baking soda and salt.
3. Cut the butter into small pieces, add it to the dry ingredients and process, pulsing the machine on and off, 10 seconds, or until the mixture resembles coarse cornmeal. Add the buttermilk and process another 10 seconds, or until the dough forms a ball. (To mix by hand, cut the butter into the dry ingredients

with a pastry blender or 2 knives, then add the buttermilk and stir until the dough forms a ball.)

4. Turn the dough out onto a lightly floured board and gently knead in the raisins 1 minute, or until the dough is smooth.

5. Using a lightly floured rolling pin, roll the dough out into an 8½-inch disk about ½ inch thick. Place it on a baking sheet and with a sharp knife lightly score it into 8 wedges. (For scones with an all-over crust, cut the wedges apart completely and place them 1 inch apart.) Bake 15 minutes, or until golden. Cool slightly, then cut the scones along the scored lines. Serve warm.   *Makes 8 scones*

NUTRITION INFORMATION
values are per scone

• • •

CALORIES	199	CALCIUM	37 MG
TOTAL FAT	7 G	IRON	2 MG
SATURATED FAT	4 G	POTASSIUM	142 MG
CHOLESTEROL	16 MG	BETA CAROTENE	0 MG
SODIUM	200 MG	VITAMIN C	TRACE
DIETARY FIBER	1 G	VITAMIN E	TRACE

CORIANDER AND CURRANT SCONES

These fragrant scones make a great breakfast or snack. By modifying the recipe slightly, you can make Rich Biscuits for the Fig-Berry Shortcakes recipe on page 174. To make the biscuits, omit the whole-wheat pastry flour and use 2 cups of unbleached flour instead. Omit the coriander, orange zest and currants. Roll out the dough ¼ inch thick and cut out eight 3½-inch rounds or hearts with a biscuit cutter, then bake as directed below.

1 cup whole-wheat pastry flour
1 cup unbleached all-purpose flour
2 teaspoons baking powder
2½ teaspoons ground coriander
½ teaspoon sugar
3 tablespoons unsalted butter, well chilled
½ cup currants or raisins
1 tablespoon grated orange zest
¾ cup buttermilk

1. Combine the dry ingredients in a medium-size bowl and stir well. With a pastry blender or 2 knives, cut in the butter until the mixture resembles coarse cornmeal. Scatter in the currants and orange zest, then, with a fork, stir in the buttermilk until just combined. Turn the dough out onto a floured board and knead it with floured hands 3 or 4 times.

2. Spray a baking sheet with nonstick cooking spray. Divide the dough into 6 equal portions and shape each into a ball. Place the balls of dough on the baking sheet. With a sharp knife cut a cross in the top of each. Refrigerate the dough 15 minutes.

3. Meanwhile, preheat the oven to 425°.

4. Bake the scones about 15 minutes, or until golden brown. Serve warm.   *Makes 6 scones*

NUTRITION INFORMATION

values are per scone

• • •

CALORIES	247	CALCIUM	117 MG
TOTAL FAT	7 G	IRON	3 MG
SATURATED FAT	4 G	POTASSIUM	202 MG
CHOLESTEROL	18 MG	BETA CAROTENE	0 MG
SODIUM	131 MG	VITAMIN C	2 MG
DIETARY FIBER	1 G	VITAMIN E	TRACE

WHOLE-WHEAT HAZELNUT POPOVERS

All of an egg's fat and cholesterol is in its yolk. Using mostly whites, as you do here, keeps the fat and cholesterol content of baked goods low. Serve the popovers with a bowl of soup, or fill their hollow centers with a light seafood or chicken salad.

1 cup lowfat milk (1%), approximately
1 egg
2 egg whites
½ cup whole-wheat flour
½ cup unbleached all-purpose flour
¼ teaspoon salt
2 tablespoons finely ground toasted hazelnuts

1. Preheat the oven to 400°.

2. Spray 10 popover pan cups or muffin tin cups with nonstick cooking spray. Place the pans in the oven to heat. Meanwhile, combine 1 cup of milk with the remaining ingredients in a blender and process just until smooth. (Or, combine the ingredients in a medium-size bowl and whisk until smooth.) Do not overblend or overbeat; the batter should be the consistency of heavy cream. Add 1 to 3 tablespoons more milk if necessary.

3. Working quickly, fill the hot popover pans about two-thirds full; if using muffin tins, fill them almost to the top. Bake the popovers 20 minutes, then, without opening the oven, reduce the temperature to 350° and bake another 20 to 25 minutes.

4. Remove the popovers from the pans and quickly prick the bottom of each one with a small sharp knife. Reduce the oven temperature to 200° and return the popovers to the oven to crisp 15 minutes. They can be held in the oven for up to 40 minutes, if necessary. Serve warm.

Makes 10 large popovers

NUTRITION INFORMATION

values are per popover

• • •

CALORIES	75	CALCIUM	39 MG
TOTAL FAT	2 G	IRON	TRACE
SATURATED FAT	0.4 G	POTASSIUM	91 MG
CHOLESTEROL	22 MG	BETA CAROTENE	0 MG
SODIUM	83 MG	VITAMIN C	TRACE
DIETARY FIBER	1 G	VITAMIN E	TRACE

Whole-Wheat Hazelnut Popovers

STEAMED BROWN BREAD

Steamed brown bread served with a fragrant pot of baked beans is a time-honored Sunday dinner in New England. The slightly sweet bread presents an appetizing counterpoint to the savory beans. Slices of this lowfat brown bread also make delicious sandwiches when spread with nonfat cream cheese.

½ cup dark raisins
½ cup whole-wheat flour
¾ cup cornmeal
½ cup rye flour
2 teaspoons baking soda
1 cup lowfat milk (2%)
½ cup molasses
¼ cup honey
1 tablespoon distilled white vinegar
1 teaspoon grated orange zest

1. Preheat the oven to 300°.

2. Lightly spray three clean 1-pound (2-cup) cans with nonstick cooking spray.

3. Place the raisins in a small bowl, add boiling water to cover and set aside to soak 15 minutes; drain and pat dry. Toss the raisins with 1 tablespoon of the whole-wheat flour; set aside.

4. In a large bowl combine the remaining whole-wheat flour, the cornmeal, rye flour and baking soda, and make a well in the center.

5. In a medium-size bowl whisk together the milk, molasses, honey, vinegar and orange zest.

6. Pour the milk mixture into the dry ingredients and stir to moisten, then mix the batter until smooth. Stir in the raisins.

7. Ladle the batter into the cans, filling them about two-thirds full. Cover each can with a double thickness of foil, pressing it around the rim to seal it, and secure it with string or tape. Place the cans in a large roasting pan, casserole or Dutch oven and add boiling water to a depth of 2 inches. Cover the pan (use foil if the pan does not have a cover) and bake the breads 3 hours.

8. Run a knife around the edges of the cans to loosen the bread, then slide the loaves out of the cans. Place the loaves on a baking sheet and bake about 10 minutes, or until the crust appears dry. Cut each loaf into eight ½-inch-thick slices.

Makes three loaves, 12 servings

NUTRITION INFORMATION
values are per serving

• • •

CALORIES	146	CALCIUM	123 MG
TOTAL FAT	0.9 G	IRON	3 MG
SATURATED FAT	0.3 G	POTASSIUM	515 MG
CHOLESTEROL	2 MG	BETA CAROTENE	0 MG
SODIUM	161 MG	VITAMIN C	TRACE
DIETARY FIBER	2 G	VITAMIN E	TRACE

☕ Breakfast ☕

BREAKFAST COBBLER

Biscuit-topped cobblers are most often served for dessert, but the ingredients in this one add up to a healthful breakfast. There are four different fruits, including fiber-rich prunes and dried apricots; rolled oats (a breakfast classic); and skim milk.

2 pears
8 dried apricot halves
6 prunes
1 cup juice-packed pineapple chunks, drained, ⅓ cup juice reserved
3 tablespoons honey
½ cup rolled oats
1½ cups sifted unbleached all-purpose flour
1½ teaspoons baking powder
½ teaspoon salt
½ teaspoon ground cinnamon
½ cup skim milk
¼ cup vegetable oil
1 tablespoon brown sugar

1. Preheat the oven to 425°.

2. Peel and core the pears and cut them into 1-inch cubes; you should have about 1½ cups. Place the pears in an ovenproof skillet. Quarter the apricot halves and prunes and add them to the skillet. Add the pineapple and juice, 1 tablespoon of the honey and ⅓ cup of water, and bring to a boil. Reduce the heat to medium-low and cook 7 minutes, or until the pears are tender and the liquid is reduced by at least half. Remove the skillet from the heat and set aside.

3. Reserving 1 tablespoon of oats, combine the remaining oats, the flour, baking powder, salt and cinnamon in a medium-size bowl and make a well in the center.

4. In a small bowl, combine the remaining honey, the milk, oil and sugar. Pour the mixture into the well in the dry ingredients and stir just until combined.

5. Drop the batter by tablespoonsful onto the fruit in the skillet and sprinkle it with the reserved oats. Bake the cobbler 12 minutes, or until the topping is firm and browned.

Makes 8 servings

NUTRITION INFORMATION
values are per serving

• • •

CALORIES	271	CALCIUM	78 MG
TOTAL FAT	8 G	IRON	2 MG
SATURATED FAT	1 G	POTASSIUM	300 MG
CHOLESTEROL	TRACE	BETA CAROTENE	TRACE
SODIUM	199 MG	VITAMIN C	5 MG
DIETARY FIBER	3 G	VITAMIN E	6 MG

FRIED OATMEAL

Sometimes sold as Scottish or Irish oats, steel-cut oats can be found in health food stores or gourmet shops. They boast a more robust flavor and texture than rolled oats, but take considerably longer to cook.

½ cup steel-cut oats
3 tablespoons dark raisins
2 teaspoons sugar
1 teaspoon corn oil
1 teaspoon unsalted butter
2 teaspoons unbleached all-purpose flour
¼ teaspoon ground cinnamon
4 teaspoons pure maple syrup

1. Combine the oats with 2 cups of water in a small saucepan and cook, uncovered, over low heat about 45 minutes, or until the oatmeal is soft and the liquid is almost totally absorbed. Add the raisins and sugar and cook 1 minute, then increase the heat to high and cook, stirring, 1 minute, or until any excess liquid evaporates.

2. Spread the oatmeal in a thin layer in a 9 x 5-inch loaf pan and smooth the top with a spatula. Lay a sheet of plastic wrap on the surface of the oatmeal and refrigerate at least 2 hours, or until firm. (The oatmeal can be prepared the night before.)

3. Using a metal spatula, loosen the edges of the oatmeal and turn it out onto a plate. Cut the sheet of oatmeal in half lengthwise, then crosswise to make 4 equal pieces.

4. Heat the oil in a nonstick skillet over medium heat. When the oil is hot, add the butter. When the butter melts, dust the oatmeal slices with flour and cook them about 2 minutes on each side, or until well browned. Divide the slices between 2 plates, sprinkle with cinnamon and drizzle each serving with 2 teaspoons of maple syrup.

Makes 2 servings

NUTRITION INFORMATION
values are per serving

• • •

CALORIES	289	CALCIUM	46 MG
TOTAL FAT	7 G	IRON	2 MG
SATURATED FAT	2 G	POTASSIUM	297 MG
CHOLESTEROL	6 MG	BETA CAROTENE	0 MG
SODIUM	4 MG	VITAMIN C	TRACE
DIETARY FIBER	6 G	VITAMIN E	2 MG

BROWN RICE CEREAL WITH FRUIT AND ALMONDS

Brown rice, apricots, apples and spices cook up into a delicious hot breakfast with none of the refined sweeteners (sugar, dextrose or corn syrup) usually added to packaged breakfast cereals.

2 cups brown rice
¼ teaspoon ground allspice
Pinch of salt
½ cup dried apricots, cut into thin strips
½ cup slivered toasted almonds
1 Delicious apple, cored and chopped
2 cups lowfat milk (2%)

1. Place the rice, allspice, salt and 1 quart of water in a medium-size saucepan and bring to a boil over medium heat. Cover the pan, reduce the heat to low and cook 40 minutes, or until the rice is tender and the water is absorbed. Add the apricots and cook another 5 minutes.

2. Divide the cereal among 4 bowls, sprinkle with almonds and chopped apple, and pour ½ cup of milk over each serving. *Makes 6 servings*

NUTRITION INFORMATION
values are per serving

• • •

CALORIES	375	CALCIUM	152 MG
TOTAL FAT	9 G	IRON	2 MG
SATURATED FAT	2 G	POTASSIUM	528 MG
CHOLESTEROL	6 MG	BETA CAROTENE	0.5 MG
SODIUM	69 MG	VITAMIN C	2 MG
DIETARY FIBER	5 G	VITAMIN E	TRACE

QUICK OATS WITH MIXED FRUIT

Apple pie would not be a heart-wise breakfast choice, but this hot cereal cooked in apple juice with dried fruit, honey and cinnamon has all the fragrance of a freshly baked pie.

¾ cup apple juice
⅔ cup quick-cooking oats
Pinch of salt
Pinch of ground cinnamon
⅓ cup mixed dried fruit, finely chopped
2 tablespoons honey
⅔ cup skim milk

Brown Rice Cereal with Fruit and Almonds

1. In a small saucepan stir together the apple juice, oats, salt, cinnamon and ¾ cup of water and bring to a boil over medium-high heat. Reduce the heat to low, cover the pan and simmer 1 minute, or until the liquid is absorbed; remove the pan from the heat.

2. Stir in the fruit and honey, cover the pan and let stand 2 minutes, or until the fruit is softened. Divide the oatmeal between 2 bowls and pour some milk over each serving. *Makes 2 servings*

NUTRITION INFORMATION
values are per serving

• • •

CALORIES	292	CALCIUM	281 MG
TOTAL FAT	2 G	IRON	7 MG
SATURATED FAT	0.4 G	POTASSIUM	546 MG
CHOLESTEROL	1 MG	BETA CAROTENE	TRACE
SODIUM	402 MG	VITAMIN C	2 MG
DIETARY FIBER	4 G	VITAMIN E	3 MG

BREAKFAST INDIAN PUDDINGS

Dark molasses, the traditional sweetener for this homey New England dish, is a good source of calcium; the combination of molasses, milk and yogurt provides nearly half the calcium you need each day.

⅔ cup yellow cornmeal
¼ cup dark molasses
2 large eggs
1½ teaspoons ground cinnamon
1 teaspoon ground ginger
½ teaspoon ground nutmeg
Pinch of salt
2 cups lowfat milk (2%)
1 cup apricot nectar
1 teaspoon vanilla extract
8 dried apricots
½ cup plain lowfat yogurt

1. Preheat the oven to 325°.

2. In a large bowl whisk together the cornmeal, molasses, eggs, 1¼ teaspoons of the cinnamon, the ginger, nutmeg and salt; set aside.

3. Heat the milk, apricot nectar and vanilla in a medium-size saucepan over medium-high heat until hot. Whisk 1 cup of the hot liquid into the cornmeal mixture, then whisk in the remaining liquid. Return the mixture to the saucepan and cook, whisking constantly, for 2 minutes, or until it thickens and starts to bubble. Divide the mixture among four 1-cup ramekins and bake for about 40 minutes, or until firm and browned on top.

4. Let the puddings cool at room temperature about 30 minutes. (If making them the night before, cover and refrigerate them when cool; reheat them in a 350° oven 20 minutes.)

5. A few minutes before serving, place the apricots in a small bowl and add boiling water to cover; let stand 1 minute. Drain the apricots and cut them into strips. Top each pudding with 2 tablespoons of yogurt and some apricot strips, and sprinkle with the remaining cinnamon. *Makes 4 servings*

NUTRITION INFORMATION
values are per serving

• • •

CALORIES	328	CALCIUM	375 MG
TOTAL FAT	6 G	IRON	6 MG
SATURATED FAT	3 G	POTASSIUM	1213 MG
CHOLESTEROL	117 MG	BETA CAROTENE	1 MG
SODIUM	167 MG	VITAMIN C	2 MG
DIETARY FIBER	3 G	VITAMIN E	TRACE

BULGUR-BANANA PORRIDGE

Bulgur, a popular main-dish grain in the Middle East, consists of kernels of whole wheat that have been steamed and then crushed. Here, bulgur is baked with bananas and maple syrup to make a hearty, high-energy breakfast.

2 bananas, peeled and mashed
1 egg, lightly beaten
1 tablespoon pure maple syrup
2 teaspoons cornstarch
½ teaspoon vanilla extract
¼ teaspoon ground nutmeg
¼ teaspoon ground cinnamon

½ cup bulgur
2 cups skim milk
½ ounce toasted almonds, slivered

1. Preheat the oven to 325°.

2. Place the bananas in a medium-size saucepan. Add the egg, maple syrup, cornstarch, vanilla, nutmeg and cinnamon, and stir well. Add the bulgur, then gradually stir in the milk. Bring to a boil over medium-high heat and cook, stirring constantly, 1 minute, or until well blended and thickened.

3. Transfer the porridge to a 1-quart baking dish and bake 25 minutes, or until set. Stir the porridge, divide it among 4 bowls and top each portion with almonds.   *Makes 4 servings*

NUTRITION INFORMATION
values are per serving

• • •

CALORIES	215	CALCIUM	184 MG
TOTAL FAT	4 G	IRON	1 MG
SATURATED FAT	0.9 G	POTASSIUM	553 MG
CHOLESTEROL	55 MG	BETA CAROTENE	0 MG
SODIUM	83 MG	VITAMIN C	6 MG
DIETARY FIBER	5 G	VITAMIN E	TRACE

MILLET PORRIDGE WITH APRICOTS

Millet, like all grains, is an excellent source of lowfat protein. A serving of this porridge, made with skim milk, provides about 5 grams of protein—more than you would get from half an ounce of cheese.

1 cup apple cider
½ cup skim milk
¾ teaspoon grated lemon zest
½ teaspoon salt
½ cup millet
½ cup coarsely chopped unsulfured dried apricots
2 tablespoons unsweetened shredded coconut
1 teaspoon butter

1. Combine the apple cider, milk and 1½ cups of water in a medium-size nonreactive saucepan and bring to a boil over medium-high heat. Add the

lemon zest and salt, then slowly stir in the millet. Cover the pan, reduce the heat to low and simmer 20 minutes.

2. Add the apricots and coconut, and cook, covered, another 20 minutes, or until the millet is creamy, adding more water if all of the water evaporates before the millet is cooked. Remove the pan from the heat and stir in the butter.   *Makes 4 servings*

NUTRITION INFORMATION
values are per serving

• • •

CALORIES	189	CALCIUM	50 MG
TOTAL FAT	3 G	IRON	2 MG
SATURATED FAT	2 G	POTASSIUM	335 MG
CHOLESTEROL	3 MG	BETA CAROTENE	0.7 MG
SODIUM	296 MG	VITAMIN C	1 MG
DIETARY FIBER	5 G	VITAMIN E	TRACE

GRAPE AND NUT CEREAL

Even hearty appetites will be sated by this generous breakfast, a crunchy combination of toast cubes, oats, fresh and dried fruit, and almond-flavored yogurt.

1 slice raisin bread
2 tablespoons rolled oats
⅓ cup plain lowfat yogurt
¼ teaspoon almond extract
Pinch of ground cinnamon
½ ounce dried pears
1 teaspoon brown sugar
¼ cup each seedless red and green grapes
2 tablespoons roasted unsalted peanuts, coarsely chopped

1. Preheat the oven to 375°.

2. Meanwhile, cut the bread into ½-inch cubes and spread them and the oats on a foil-lined baking sheet. Bake 5 to 10 minutes, or until the bread is golden brown; set aside to cool.

3. Stir together the yogurt, almond extract and cinnamon in a cup. Dice the pears; set aside.

4. To serve, place the bread cubes, oats and pears in a cereal bowl and stir to combine. Spoon the yogurt mixture on top and sprinkle it with the sugar. Add the grapes and peanuts, toss gently and serve immediately.   *Makes 1 serving*

GRANOLA

Commercial granolas, despite their "health food" image, can contain quite a lot of saturated fat from the coconut oil and coconut they're frequently made with. This toasted cereal includes the minimum amount of polyunsaturated safflower oil (some oil is needed to keep the oats from burning) and lots of dried fruit.

3 cups rolled oats
½ cup sunflower seeds
3 tablespoons sesame seeds
¼ cup wheat germ
¼ teaspoon ground cinnamon
6 tablespoons safflower oil
¼ cup honey
¾ cup chopped dried apples
¾ cup golden raisins

1. Preheat the oven to 350°.

2. Combine the oats, sunflower seeds, sesame seeds, wheat germ and cinnamon in a large bowl.

3. In a small bowl, stir together the oil and honey; pour this mixture over the oat mixture and toss to coat the dry ingredients. Spread the mixture in two shallow 9 x 13-inch baking pans and bake on the middle rack of the oven 15 minutes, stirring frequently. Allow the granola to cool.

4. When cool, stir the dried apples and raisins into the cooled granola. Store in a covered container in the refrigerator.   *Makes about 5½ cups*

NUTRITION INFORMATION
values are per ¼ cup

• • •

CALORIES	140	CALCIUM	26 MG
TOTAL FAT	7 G	IRON	1 MG
SATURATED FAT	0.6 G	POTASSIUM	98 MG
CHOLESTEROL	0 MG	BETA CAROTENE	0 MG
SODIUM	4 MG	VITAMIN C	TRACE
DIETARY FIBER	1 G	VITAMIN E	2 MG

NUTRITION INFORMATION
values are per serving

• • •

CALORIES	364	CALCIUM	197 MG
TOTAL FAT	12 G	IRON	2 MG
SATURATED FAT	2 G	POTASSIUM	603 MG
CHOLESTEROL	5 MG	BETA CAROTENE	0 MG
SODIUM	152 MG	VITAMIN C	7 MG
DIETARY FIBER	3 G	VITAMIN E	N/A

COUSCOUS-CURRANT CEREAL

For this unusual hot cereal, couscous—tiny grains of semolina-flour pasta—is cooked in apple juice. The delicate pasta cooks in just five minutes—off the heat, so you needn't watch it constantly.

2 cups apple juice
Pinch of ground cinnamon
1 cup instant couscous
½ cup dried currants
1 cup skim milk
4 strawberries, hulled

1. Place the apple juice and cinnamon in a small nonreactive saucepan and bring to a boil over high heat. Remove the pan from the heat and add the couscous and currants; cover and set aside 5 minutes.

2. Meanwhile, warm the milk in another small saucepan over medium-low heat.

3. Fluff the couscous with a fork and divide it among 4 bowls. Top each serving with a strawberry and serve with the warm milk.   *Makes 4 servings*

NUTRITION INFORMATION
values are per serving

• • •

CALORIES	305	CALCIUM	112 MG
TOTAL FAT	0.6 G	IRON	2 MG
SATURATED FAT	0.2 G	POTASSIUM	495 MG
CHOLESTEROL	1 MG	BETA CAROTENE	0 MG
SODIUM	41 MG	VITAMIN C	5 MG
DIETARY FIBER	7 G	VITAMIN E	TRACE

Bran Cereal with Date Milk

Bran cereal can be every bit as toothsome as heavily sugared breakfast foods when you pour on a fruit-sweetened lowfat milk mixture. The combination of bran cereal, dates and strawberries adds up to an outstanding 18 grams of dietary fiber—nearly a full day's requirement.

¼ cup fresh strawberries
¼ cup lowfat cottage cheese (1%)
2 ounces pitted dates (5 dates)
3 tablespoons skim milk
¼ teaspoon vanilla extract
½ cup wheat-bran morsels cereal

1. Wash, hull and halve the strawberries; set aside.

2. Combine the cottage cheese, dates, milk and vanilla in a blender, and process about 10 seconds, or until the mixture is thick and smooth, scraping down the sides of the container with a rubber spatula as necessary.

3. Place the cereal in a bowl and pour the milk mixture over it. Top the cereal with the strawberries and serve. *Makes 1 serving*

NUTRITION INFORMATION
values are per serving

• • •

CALORIES	338	CALCIUM	143 MG
TOTAL FAT	2 G	IRON	8 MG
SATURATED FAT	0.4 G	POTASSIUM	1268 MG
CHOLESTEROL	3 MG	BETA CAROTENE	0 MG
SODIUM	517 MG	VITAMIN C	44 MG
DIETARY FIBER	18 G	VITAMIN E	2 MG

Muesli

Muesli was created early in this century by a Swiss physician who was a proponent of the healing qualities of uncooked foods. The mixture of grains and fresh or dried fruits is moistened with milk or yogurt. The original recipe called for grated apple, and, indeed, the recipe is open to all sorts of tasty improvisations. You might try different kinds of dried fruit or substitute almonds for the hazelnuts.

2 cups rolled oats
1 cup skim milk
¼ cup dried currants or raisins
¼ cup apple juice
2 tablespoons honey
1 cup plain lowfat yogurt
½ cup minced dried apples
¼ cup minced dried apricots
¼ cup finely chopped hazelnuts
¼ cup brown sugar
2 tangerines, peeled, sectioned and seeded

1. Place the oats in a medium-size bowl, pour in the milk and stir well. In a small bowl, combine the currants and apple juice. Set aside both mixtures 30 minutes.

2. Stir the honey into the yogurt; set aside.

3. Add the currants and apple juice, the dried fruit, hazelnuts and sugar to the oats, and stir well.

4. Divide the muesli among 4 bowls and top each serving with ¼ cup of yogurt and some tangerine sections. *Makes 4 servings*

NUTRITION INFORMATION
values are per serving

• • •

CALORIES	423	CALCIUM	241 MG
TOTAL FAT	7 G	IRON	3 MG
SATURATED FAT	1 G	POTASSIUM	775 MG
CHOLESTEROL	5 MG	BETA CAROTENE	0.6 MG
SODIUM	89 MG	VITAMIN C	15 MG
DIETARY FIBER	5 G	VITAMIN E	TRACE

Muesli

BROWN RICE GINGERBREAD PANCAKES

When you include lowfat dairy products like buttermilk and part-skim ricotta in your breakfast, you keep your calorie, fat and cholesterol intake low and get plenty of calcium. This festive breakfast dish also supplies a good amount of potassium, which works with calcium to keep your heart and other muscles functioning properly.

½ cup brown rice
2 tablespoons lemon juice
2 tablespoons honey
2 teaspoons cornstarch
1 cup unbleached all-purpose flour
¼ cup chopped walnuts
1 teaspoon baking powder
½ teaspoon baking soda
¾ teaspoon ground cinnamon
½ teaspoon ground cloves
¾ cup buttermilk

3 tablespoons molasses
2 egg whites
1 tablespoon grated fresh ginger
¼ cup part-skim ricotta cheese

1. Bring 1¼ cups of water to a boil in a small saucepan over medium heat. Add the rice, cover the pan, reduce the heat to low and cook 30 minutes, or until the rice is just tender and the water is absorbed. Remove the pan from the heat and let cool until the rice is just warm. (You can also cook the rice in advance or use 1½ cups leftover rice.)

2. Meanwhile, for the sauce, in a small saucepan stir together the lemon juice, honey, cornstarch and 2 tablespoons of water. Bring the sauce to a boil over medium heat, stirring constantly, and boil 30 seconds, or until the sauce thickens. Remove the pan from the heat and set aside to cool.

3. Stir together the flour, walnuts, baking powder, baking soda, cinnamon and cloves in a large bowl, and make a well in the center. Pour in the buttermilk, molasses, egg whites and ginger, and stir until combined. Stir the rice to break it up, then add it to the batter and stir just until combined.

4. Preheat the oven to 200°.

5. Heat a medium-size nonstick skillet over medium-low heat. Using 2 tablespoons of batter for each, make 3 pancakes. Cook 3 minutes, or until bubbles form on the tops of the pancakes, then turn them and cook another 3 minutes, or until golden. Transfer the pancakes to a heatproof platter, cover with foil and place in the oven to keep warm. Make another 5 batches of pancakes in the same fashion.

6. To serve, fold the ricotta into the sauce. Divide the pancakes among 6 plates and top each serving with a heaping tablespoon of sauce.

Makes 6 servings

NUTRITION INFORMATION
values are per serving

• • •

CALORIES	249	CALCIUM	182 MG
TOTAL FAT	5 G	IRON	3 MG
SATURATED FAT	1 G	POTASSIUM	476 MG
CHOLESTEROL	4 MG	BETA CAROTENE	0 MG
SODIUM	192 MG	VITAMIN C	3 MG
DIETARY FIBER	2 G	VITAMIN E	1 MG

BANANA PANCAKES WITH STRAWBERRY SAUCE

Dry toast and coffee, once the recommended "diet" breakfast, has been replaced by delicious, high-fiber, nutrient-rich meals. These pancakes, for instance, are made without butter or oil, and the fresh strawberry topping is a high-fiber alternative to bottled pancake syrups, which often consist of nothing but refined sugar and have no nutritional value. When raspberries or blueberries are in season, you can use them instead of strawberries.

1 cup fresh strawberries
2 tablespoons plus 2 teaspoons sugar
½ teaspoon cornstarch
1 egg
¾ cup buttermilk
½ cup mashed banana
¼ cup skim milk
1⅓ cups unbleached all-purpose flour
1 teaspoon baking soda
½ teaspoon baking powder
½ teaspoon ground cinnamon

1. For the sauce, combine the strawberries, 2 teaspoons of the sugar and 1 teaspoon of water in a small saucepan, cover and cook over medium-low heat 10 minutes, or until the strawberries are tender. Increase the heat to medium-high and bring the mixture to a boil.

2. Meanwhile, stir together the cornstarch and 1 teaspoon of water in a cup. Add this mixture to the sauce and cook 1 minute, or until thickened. Remove the pan from the heat and mash the strawberries with a fork. Cover the pan to keep warm and set aside.

3. In a small bowl beat together the egg, buttermilk, banana and skim milk; set aside.

4. In a medium-size bowl stir together the flour, the remaining sugar, the baking soda, baking powder and cinnamon, and make a well in the center. Add the egg mixture and stir until well blended.

5. Spray a large nonstick skillet with nonstick cooking spray and heat it over medium-high heat. Pour in four ¼-cup portions of batter and spread them with a spoon to form 5-inch pancakes. Cook the pancakes 2 minutes, or until bubbles appear on the tops and the bottoms are golden. Turn the pancakes and cook another 2 minutes, or until the second side is golden. Transfer the pancakes to a plate and cover them with foil to keep warm. Make 4 more pancakes in the same fashion. Divide the pancakes among 4 plates, spoon the strawberry sauce over them and serve.

Makes 4 servings

NUTRITION INFORMATION
values are per serving

• • •

CALORIES	266	CALCIUM	118 MG
TOTAL FAT	3 G	IRON	2 MG
SATURATED FAT	0.8 G	POTASSIUM	330 MG
CHOLESTEROL	55 MG	BETA CAROTENE	0 MG
SODIUM	315 MG	VITAMIN C	24 MG
DIETARY FIBER	3 G	VITAMIN E	TRACE

BLUEBERRY CORNMEAL PANCAKES

A cup of fresh blueberries contains about one-third of your daily requirement of vitamin C. Adding the berries to these cornmeal pancakes also gives you a good deal of fiber. Other berries or chopped fresh fruits, such as ripe peaches or pears, would also work well in these pancakes.

1¼ cups unbleached all-purpose flour
1 cup yellow or white cornmeal
1½ teaspoons baking soda
1 teaspoon baking powder
Pinch of salt
2¼ cups buttermilk
2 eggs, separated, plus 1 egg white
3 tablespoons dark brown sugar
2 cups fresh or unsweetened frozen blueberries, thawed
1 tablespoon vegetable oil

1. In a small bowl, stir together the flour, cornmeal, baking soda, baking powder and salt; set aside.

2. In a large bowl, whisk together the buttermilk, egg yolks and sugar; set aside.

3. In another large bowl, using an electric mixer, beat the egg whites until stiff peaks form.

4. Add the dry ingredients to the buttermilk mixture and stir until blended, then gently fold in the egg whites. Stir in the blueberries.

5. Heat ½ teaspoon of oil in a large nonstick skillet over medium heat. Using ¼ cup of batter for each pancake, make 4 pancakes, cooking them about 4 minutes on each side or until golden brown. Make 5 more batches of pancakes in the same fashion, adding ½ teaspoon of oil to the skillet before cooking each batch.   *Makes 6 servings*

NUTRITION INFORMATION
values are per serving

• • •

CALORIES	317	CALCIUM	160 MG
TOTAL FAT	6 G	IRON	3 MG
SATURATED FAT	1 G	POTASSIUM	300 MG
CHOLESTEROL	74 MG	BETA CAROTENE	TRACE
SODIUM	408 MG	VITAMIN C	7 MG
DIETARY FIBER	3 G	VITAMIN E	3 MG

BUTTERMILK CORNMEAL PANCAKES

It's not just the ingredients you choose but also the cooking methods you use that keep a heart-healthy diet on track. A nonstick skillet lets you prepare these fluffy pancakes without greasing the pan.

1 cup stone-ground yellow cornmeal
½ cup unbleached flour
1 tablespoon baking powder
½ teaspoon baking soda
¼ teaspoon salt
1 egg
1¼ cups buttermilk, approximately
1 tablespoon safflower oil

1. Combine the dry ingredients in a large bowl. Add the egg, 1¼ cups of the buttermilk and the oil, and stir to mix thoroughly. If the batter is too thick, stir in additional buttermilk by the tablespoon.

2. Preheat a nonstick griddle or a large nonstick skillet. Using a scant ¼ cup batter for each, make 4 pancakes. Cook until bubbles just begin to form on the tops of the pancakes and the bottoms are lightly browned. Turn and cook the other side until lightly browned. Make 2 more batches of pancakes in the same fashion.   *Makes 4 servings*

NUTRITION INFORMATION
values are per serving

• • •

CALORIES	249	CALCIUM	238 MG
TOTAL FAT	7 G	IRON	2 MG
SATURATED FAT	1 G	POTASSIUM	238 MG
CHOLESTEROL	56 MG	BETA CAROTENE	TRACE
SODIUM	560 MG	VITAMIN C	TRACE
DIETARY FIBER	5 G	VITAMIN E	1 MG

Sweet Potato Pancakes

Potato pancakes are usually made from white potatoes and fried in quite a bit of fat. These crisp-crusted sweet-potato cakes supply significantly more beta carotene and are cooked in much less fat.

⅓ cup unbleached all-purpose flour
¼ cup skim milk
1 egg, beaten
2 tablespoons brown sugar
½ teaspoon ground ginger
1 pound sweet potatoes, peeled and grated (4 cups)
¼ cup chopped scallions
2 tablespoons vegetable oil

1. In a large bowl beat together the flour, milk, egg, sugar and ginger. Stir in the grated potatoes and the scallions.

2. In a large nonstick skillet, heat 1½ teaspoons of the oil over medium-high heat until it barely begins to smoke. Drop six ¼-cup portions of the potato mixture into the skillet and cook 1 minute. Using a spatula, flatten the mixture into ¼-inch-thick cakes, then reduce the heat to medium and cook 2 to 3 minutes more.

3. Turn the pancakes, add 1½ teaspoons of oil and cook another 5 minutes, shaking the pan to keep the pancakes from sticking. Turn the pancakes again and drizzle 2 to 3 tablespoons of water into the pan. Increase the heat to medium-high and cook, pressing the pancakes with the spatula to brown them evenly, 2 minutes more, or until the pancakes are golden brown all over. Transfer the pancakes to a platter and cover loosely with foil.

4. Repeat with the remaining potato mixture, divide the pancakes among 6 plates and serve.

Makes 6 servings

Nutrition Information
values are per serving

• • •

CALORIES	157	CALCIUM	36 MG
TOTAL FAT	6 G	IRON	1 MG
SATURATED FAT	0.9 G	POTASSIUM	163 MG
CHOLESTEROL	36 MG	BETA CAROTENE	6 MG
SODIUM	25 MG	VITAMIN C	11 MG
DIETARY FIBER	2 G	VITAMIN E	6 MG

Buckwheat–Wild Rice Waffles

Egg whites can be substituted for whole eggs in many waffle and pancake recipes, thereby cutting fat.

1 cup unbleached all-purpose flour
¾ cup light buckwheat flour
2 teaspoons baking powder
¼ teaspoon salt
3 tablespoons honey
2 tablespoons vegetable oil
1½ cups lowfat milk (2%)
3 large egg whites
¾ cup cold cooked wild rice (about 3 tablespoons raw)
1 cup thinly sliced cantaloupe
1 cup fresh raspberries or frozen unsweetened raspberries, thawed
3 tablespoons pure maple syrup

1. In a large bowl stir together the flours, baking powder and salt, and make a well in the center. Pour in the honey and oil and and mix until blended. Add the milk and stir until the batter is fairly smooth.

2. Preheat the oven to 200°. Spray a nonstick waffle iron with nonstick cooking spray and preheat it.

3. In a large bowl, using an electric mixer, beat the egg whites until soft peaks form. Gently fold the egg whites into the batter, then fold in the wild rice.

4. Pour 1 cup of batter into the waffle iron and cook 2 to 3 minutes, or until the waffle is golden. Transfer the waffle to an ovenproof platter and place it in the oven to keep warm. Using the remaining batter, make 5 more waffles in the same fashion.

5. Divide the waffles among 6 plates and top each waffle with cantaloupe, berries, and 1½ teaspoons of maple syrup.

Makes 6 servings

Nutrition Information
values are per serving

• • •

CALORIES	305	CALCIUM	165 MG
TOTAL FAT	7 G	IRON	2 MG
SATURATED FAT	1 G	POTASSIUM	386 MG
CHOLESTEROL	5 MG	BETA CAROTENE	0.5 MG
SODIUM	250 MG	VITAMIN C	17 MG
DIETARY FIBER	4 G	VITAMIN E	5 MG

Buckwheat-Wild Rice Waffles

RAISIN WAFFLES WITH FRUIT SAUCE

The fat in coconut is highly saturated, but as with most high-fat foods, you can use just a modest amount without incurring serious dietary damage.

½ cup diced fresh pineapple
¼ cup dried apricots, cut into ¼-inch strips
½ cup golden raisins
1 cinnamon stick
½ teaspoon grated lime zest
1 tablespoon pure maple syrup
1 cup unbleached all-purpose flour
1½ teaspoons sugar
¾ teaspoon baking powder
⅛ teaspoon baking soda
1 egg, separated
¼ cup buttermilk
1 tablespoon plus 1½ teaspoons margarine,
    melted and cooled
2 tablespoons shredded unsweetened coconut

1. For the sauce, in a small nonreactive saucepan stir together the pineapple, apricots, ¼ cup of the raisins, the cinnamon stick, lime zest and 6 table-spoons of water . Cover and bring the sauce to a boil, then reduce the heat and simmer, stirring occasion-ally, 30 minutes. Stir in the maple syrup.

2. While the sauce is cooking, in a large bowl stir together the flour, sugar, baking powder and baking soda, and set aside.

3. In a small bowl whisk together the egg yolk, buttermilk and margarine until well blended.

4. In another large bowl, using an electric mixer, beat the egg white until stiff peaks form.

5. Add the buttermilk mixture to the dry ingredi-ents and stir until blended, then stir in the remaining raisins. Using a rubber spatula, fold in the egg whites.

6. Spray a waffle iron with nonstick cooking spray and preheat it. (If your waffle iron does not have a nonstick surface, spray it with nonstick cook-ing spray before heating it. Do not respray the hot iron.) Pour in one-third of the batter, spread it even-ly with a rubber spatula, and bake 2 to 3 minutes, or until the waffle is browned and crisp. Make two more waffles in the same fashion.

7. Place each waffle on a plate, top with the fruit sauce and sprinkle with coconut. *Makes 3 servings*

NUTRITION INFORMATION
values are per serving

• • •

CALORIES	394	CALCIUM	122 MG
TOTAL FAT	10 G	IRON	4 MG
SATURATED FAT	3 G	POTASSIUM	3 MG
CHOLESTEROL	72 MG	BETA CAROTENE	0.5 MG
SODIUM	156 MG	VITAMIN C	6 MG
DIETARY FIBER	2 G	VITAMIN E	5 MG

YOGURT WAFFLES

Most people associate homemade waffles with leisurely weekend mornings, but they can also be a handy convenience food: Store them in the freezer and reheat them at breakfast time. These delicately crisp waffles actually improve with freezing. Place them in plastic sandwich bags, squeeze out as much air as possible and seal shut. To reheat the waffles, pop them in a toaster or heat them in a 375° oven or toaster-oven 10 minutes. Boost the calcium content of the waffles by spreading them with yogurt, or top them with fresh berries for added fiber.

2 cups unbleached all-purpose flour
1½ teaspoons baking powder
½ teaspoon baking soda
2 tablespoons butter or margarine
2 cups plain lowfat yogurt
2 tablespoons brown sugar
1 egg, separated, plus 1 egg yolk

1. In a large bowl stir together the flour, baking powder and baking soda.

2. Melt the butter in a small saucepan over low heat. When the butter is melted, remove the pan from the heat and stir in the yogurt and sugar; set aside.

3. In another large bowl, using an electric mixer, beat the egg white until stiff but not dry; set aside.

4. Lightly beat the egg yolks; add the yolks and the yogurt mixture to the dry ingredients and stir to combine. Stir half of the beaten egg white into the batter, then fold in the remaining egg white.

5. Spray a waffle iron with nonstick cooking spray and preheat it. (If your waffle iron does not have a nonstick surface, spray it with nonstick cooking spray before heating it. Do not respray the hot iron.) Using ¼ cup of batter for each individual waffle, pour the batter onto the waffle iron and spread it with the back of a spoon (it is thicker than the usual waffle batter). Cook the waffles about 4 minutes, or until crisp and brown. Repeat with the remaining batter. *Makes 5 servings*

NUTRITION INFORMATION
values are per serving

• • •

CALORIES	329	CALCIUM	244 MG
TOTAL FAT	9 G	IRON	3 MG
SATURATED FAT	4 G	POTASSIUM	303 MG
CHOLESTEROL	103 MG	BETA CAROTENE	0 MG
SODIUM	296 MG	VITAMIN C	TRACE
DIETARY FIBER	1 G	VITAMIN E	TRACE

FRENCH TOAST WAFFLES

If the usual breakfast choices are geting boring, here is a simple but appetizing way to perk up your morning meal: Bake French toast in a waffle iron instead of browning it in a skillet. Made with raisin bread and topped with cinnamon, the toast has a gentle sweetness although no refined sugar is added. You may be better able to resist the temptation of a mid-morning Danish or doughnut if you've had this pastry-like treat for breakfast.

1 egg, beaten
½ cup skim milk
¼ teaspoon ground cinnamon
4 slices raisin bread
2 tablespoons unsweetened apple butter

1. Preheat a nonstick waffle iron. (If your waffle iron does not have a nonstick surface, spray it with nonstick cooking spray before heating it. Do not respray the hot iron.)
2. Beat together the egg, milk and cinnamon in a shallow bowl. Dip the bread in the milk mixture, turning it to coat both sides.
3. Place the bread in the waffle iron and cook it 2 minutes, or until golden brown. Divide the toast waffles among 2 plates and top each serving with 1 tablespoon of apple butter. *Makes 2 servings*

NUTRITION INFORMATION
values are per serving

• • •

CALORIES	236	CALCIUM	146 MG
TOTAL FAT	5 G	IRON	2 MG
SATURATED FAT	1 G	POTASSIUM	303 MG
CHOLESTEROL	108 MG	BETA CAROTENE	0 MG
SODIUM	251 MG	VITAMIN C	TRACE
DIETARY FIBER	1 G	VITAMIN E	TRACE

FRENCH TOAST FINGERS WITH APPLE PUREE

A warm fruit sauce tops this whole-wheat French toast. The apple purée is so easy to make that you might want to cook up a double or triple batch for other uses: Stir the spicy purée into plain yogurt or serve it with poultry.

4 Granny Smith apples, peeled, cored and thinly sliced (about 18 ounces total weight)
1 cup apple juice
1 teaspoon lemon juice
Pinch of grated lemon zest
Pinch of pumpkin-pie spice
⅔ cup golden raisins
¼ cup chopped walnuts
3 large eggs plus 4 egg whites
3 tablespoons skim milk
1 teaspoon vanilla extract
¼ teaspoon ground cinnamon
1 tablespoon plus 2 teaspoons vegetable oil
12 slices whole-wheat bread

1. Cook the apples, apple juice, lemon juice, zest and pumpkin-pie spice in a medium-size saucepan over medium heat 10 minutes; process in a food processor or blender until puréed but still chunky. Stir in the raisins and walnuts, return the purée to the pan and cover to keep warm.
2. In a large, shallow bowl whisk together the eggs, egg whites and milk. Add the vanilla and cinnamon; set aside.
3. Heat 2 teaspoons of oil in a large nonstick skillet over medium-high heat. Dip 4 slices of bread into the egg mixture, place them in the skillet and cook 3

minutes. Turn the toast and cook another 3 minutes, or until well browned. Dip and cook the remaining bread in the same fashion, adding oil as necessary. Cut each piece of French toast into 4 strips, and top each serving with apple purée.   *Makes 6 servings*

NUTRITION INFORMATION
values are per serving

• • •

CALORIES	361	CALCIUM	80 MG
TOTAL FAT	12 G	IRON	3 MG
SATURATED FAT	2 G	POTASSIUM	348 MG
CHOLESTEROL	107 MG	BETA CAROTENE	0 MG
SODIUM	394 MG	VITAMIN C	5 MG
DIETARY FIBER	8 G	VITAMIN E	5 MG

ORANGE–NUTMEG PAN TOAST

Treat yourself to this high-carbohydrate, lowfat French toast after a morning workout.

1 egg
½ cup skim milk
1 teaspoon grated orange zest
¼ teaspoon ground nutmeg
8 slices whole-wheat French bread, ½ inch thick
¼ cup pure maple syrup
1 tablespoon confectioners' sugar

1. Place the egg, milk, 2 tablespoons of water, the orange zest and nutmeg in a large shallow pan, and whisk to combine.

Orange-Nutmeg Pan Toast

2. Place the bread slices in the egg mixture to coat one side, then immediately turn the bread. Let the bread stand at least 10 minutes.

3. Warm the syrup in a small saucepan.

4. Heat a nonstick griddle or nonstick skillet over medium heat. Brown both sides of the bread slices on the griddle or in the skillet. Sprinkle with sugar and serve with the warm syrup.   *Makes 4 servings*

NUTRITION INFORMATION
values are per serving

• • •

CALORIES	224	CALCIUM	106 MG
TOTAL FAT	4 G	IRON	2 MG
SATURATED FAT	0.5 G	POTASSIUM	201 MG
CHOLESTEROL	54 MG	BETA CAROTENE	0 MG
SODIUM	389 MG	VITAMIN C	1 MG
DIETARY FIBER	6 G	VITAMIN E	TRACE

RASPBERRY-ORANGE FRENCH TOAST

Pick up French toast "to go" at a fast-food restaurant and you'll be taking on 10 to 20 more grams of fat than are in this delicious fruit-sauced toast.

¾ *cup skim milk*
¼ *cup orange juice*
1½ *teaspoons grated orange zest*
2 *eggs*
½ *teaspoon ground cinnamon*
¼ *teaspoon ground nutmeg*
8 *slices whole-wheat bread*
3 *cups fresh or frozen unsweetened raspberries, thawed*
2 *tablespoons brown sugar*
1 *tablespoon plus 1½ teaspoons margarine*
8 *orange segments, for garnish*

1. In a medium-size bowl whisk together the milk, orange juice, orange zest, eggs, cinnamon and nutmeg.

2. Lay the bread slices in a large baking pan and pour the milk mixture over them, turning the bread once to coat it with the mixture; set aside 20 minutes. Tilt the pan occasionally to enable the bread to absorb all the liquid.

3. Meanwhile, combine the raspberries and sugar in a food processor or blender and process until puréed. Strain the purée through a sieve, then transfer it to a small pitcher and set aside.

4. Melt half the margarine in a large nonstick skillet over medium-high heat. Add 4 slices of bread and cook 4 minutes on each side, or until golden brown. Melt the remaining margarine in the skillet and cook the remaining bread in the same fashion. Divide the French toast among 4 plates, top each serving with sauce and garnish with orange segments.

Makes 4 servings

NUTRITION INFORMATION
values are per serving

• • •

CALORIES	302	CALCIUM	146 MG
TOTAL FAT	10 G	IRON	3 MG
SATURATED FAT	2 G	POTASSIUM	424 MG
CHOLESTEROL	107 MG	BETA CAROTENE	TRACE
SODIUM	376 MG	VITAMIN C	41 MG
DIETARY FIBER	10 G	VITAMIN E	4 MG

FRUIT AND RICE FRITTERS

Fritters are—by definition—fried, but these are cooked in just a fraction of the oil needed for deep-frying. The brown rice and the dried peaches, pears and apricots are excellent sources of fiber. Make the fritters the day after you've had brown rice for dinner, cooking extra with this in mind.

5 *dried pear halves*
5 *dried peach halves*
5 *dried apricots*
4 *tablespoons whole-wheat flour*
1½ *cups cooked brown rice (½ cup raw)*
1 *large egg, separated, plus 2 large egg whites*
1 *tablespoon toasted sesame seeds*
¼ *teaspoon salt*
¼ *teaspoon pumpkin-pie spice*
2 *tablespoons vegetable oil*

1. Finely chop the dried fruit, place it in a medium-size bowl with the flour and toss to coat the fruit. Add the rice, egg yolk, sesame seeds, salt and pumpkin-pie spice, and mix well; set aside.

2. In a large bowl, using an electric mixer, beat the egg whites until stiff. Gently fold them into the rice mixture.

3. Heat the oil in a large nonstick skillet over medium heat. Using ½ cup of batter for each, make 3 fritters, flattening them with a spatula to a ½-inch thickness. Cook 2 to 3 minutes, then turn and cook another 2 to 3 minutes, or until the fritters are golden on both sides. Make 3 more fritters in the same fashion and serve immediately.   *Makes 6 servings*

NUTRITION INFORMATION
values are per serving

• • •

CALORIES	221	CALCIUM	38 MG
TOTAL FAT	7 G	IRON	2 MG
SATURATED FAT	1 G	POTASSIUM	365 MG
CHOLESTEROL	36 MG	BETA CAROTENE	TRACE
SODIUM	120 MG	VITAMIN C	2 MG
DIETARY FIBER	4 G	VITAMIN E	4 MG

WHOLE-WHEAT CREPES WITH MIXED FRUIT

These fruit-filled crêpes need no heavy sauce or creamy topping. A serving gives you more than half your daily requirement of vitamin C.

1 cup whole-wheat flour
3 tablespoons sugar
3 large eggs
1 cup frozen unsweetened blueberries, thawed and drained
2 oranges, peeled, halved and cut crosswise into thin slices
2 tablespoons honey
2 tablespoons lemon juice
¼ teaspoon ground cardamom
2 kiwi fruit, peeled, halved and thinly sliced
1 tablespoon vegetable oil

1. For the crêpe batter, place the flour, sugar, eggs and 1½ cups of water in a food processor or blender and process 1 minute. Transfer the batter to a bowl, cover and refrigerate until needed. (The batter may be made up to 3 hours in advance.)

2. For the filling, combine the blueberries, orange slices, honey, lemon juice and cardamom in a medi-

um-size saucepan, and cook over medium heat 5 minutes, or until the fruit is slightly softened; transfer to a bowl.

3. Drain the kiwi slices, add them to the bowl and toss gently; set aside at room temperature.

4. Preheat the oven to 200°.

5. To make the crêpes, stir the batter well to re-blend it. Heat a medium-size nonstick skillet over medium-high heat and brush it lightly with oil. Pour in ¼ cup of batter and swirl the pan to coat the bottom evenly. Cook the crêpe 1½ minutes, then turn it and cook another 30 seconds. Transfer the cooked crêpe to a heatproof plate, cover it loosely with foil and place it in the oven to keep warm. Repeat to make a total of 8 crêpes.

6. Reserve ½ cup of filling. To assemble the crêpes, lay each browned side down on a small plate, spoon about ¼ cup of filling on top and fold the sides of the crêpe over the filling. Top each crêpe with a spoonful of the remaining filling.

Makes 8 servings

NUTRITION INFORMATION
values are per serving

• • •

CALORIES	165	CALCIUM	35 MG
TOTAL FAT	4 G	IRON	1 MG
SATURATED FAT	0.9 G	POTASSIUM	224 MG
CHOLESTEROL	80 MG	BETA CAROTENE	TRACE
SODIUM	26 MG	VITAMIN C	38 MG
DIETARY FIBER	4 G	VITAMIN E	2 MG

BUCKWHEAT CREPES WITH ORANGES

A company brunch can be a healthy feast if you replace eggs Benedict or quiche Lorraine with fruit-filled crêpes that have just 1 gram of fat. Oranges and other citrus fruits are the best year-round sources of vitamin C.

1 large egg
½ cup lowfat milk (1 %)
2 tablespoons buckwheat flour
2 tablespoons unbleached all-purpose flour
4 navel oranges

¾ cup orange juice, approximately
2 tablespoons honey
2 tablespoons Cointreau or other orange liqueur

1. In a food processor or blender process the egg, milk and flours until smooth. Transfer the batter to a bowl, cover and refrigerate 1 hour.

2. Meanwhile, using a vegetable peeler, strip the colored zest from 1 orange and cut enough into thin strips to measure 2 tablespoons; set aside.

3. Working over a bowl to catch the juice, peel and section all 4 oranges, removing the membranes; set aside.

4. Spray a nonstick crêpe pan or small nonstick skillet with nonstick cooking spray, then heat it over medium-high heat. Stir the batter, then spoon 2 tablespoons of batter into the pan and swirl to coat the bottom of the pan evenly. Cook about 1 minute, or until the bottom of the crêpe is browned, then turn and cook about 15 seconds. Transfer the crêpe to a platter. Make another 5 crêpes in the same fashion.

5. Pour the juice from the bowl of oranges into a measuring cup and add enough additional orange juice to measure 1 cup. Combine the juice, honey and Cointreau in a small nonreactive saucepan and bring to a boil over high heat. Cook, stirring occasionally, 10 minutes, or until the syrup is reduced to ¼ cup. Add the oranges and cook 2 minutes, or until heated through.

6. Lay each crêpe browned side down on a plate, spoon some oranges and syrup on top and fold the crêpe over the filling. Garnish with strips of orange zest. *Makes 6 servings*

NUTRITION INFORMATION
values are per serving

• • •

CALORIES	141	CALCIUM	86 MG
TOTAL FAT	1 G	IRON	TRACE
SATURATED FAT	0.5 G	POTASSIUM	354 MG
CHOLESTEROL	36 MG	BETA CAROTENE	TRACE
SODIUM	22 MG	VITAMIN C	89 MG
DIETARY FIBER	TRACE	VITAMIN E	TRACE

SKILLET CORNBREAD WITH PRUNES

A substantial wedge of this golden skillet-baked bread can be a wholesome breakfast all by itself. Made with grains, milk and fruit, it's a welcome change from the everyday bowl of cereal.

¼ cup margarine
1½ cups unbleached all-purpose flour
½ cup yellow cornmeal
¼ cup brown sugar
2½ teaspoons baking powder
1 egg, lightly beaten
1 cup buttermilk
1 cup coarsely chopped pitted prunes

1. Preheat the oven to 375°.

2. Melt the margarine in a 9-inch ovenproof nonstick skillet over medium-low heat. (If you do not have an ovenproof nonstick skillet, wrap the handle of the skillet in a double thickness of foil.)

3. Meanwhile, in a medium-size bowl combine the flour, cornmeal, sugar and baking powder, and make a well in the center.

4. Swirl the skillet to coat it completely with margarine, then pour the margarine into the well in the dry ingredients, leaving a coating of margarine on the skillet. Add the egg, buttermilk and prunes to the bowl, and stir just until the dry ingredients are incorporated; do not overmix.

5. Turn the batter into the skillet, spread it evenly with a rubber spatula and bake 30 minutes, or until the bread is golden on top. A toothpick inserted in the center of the bread should come out clean and dry.

6. Let the bread cool in the pan on a rack, then cut it into 8 wedges. *Makes 8 servings*

NUTRITION INFORMATION
values are per serving

• • •

CALORIES	264	CALCIUM	117 MG
TOTAL FAT	7 G	IRON	2 MG
SATURATED FAT	1 G	POTASSIUM	270 MG
CHOLESTEROL	28 MG	BETA CAROTENE	TRACE
SODIUM	134 MG	VITAMIN C	1 MG
DIETARY FIBER	3 G	VITAMIN E	5 MG

Five-Vegetable Hash Browns

FIVE-VEGETABLE HASH BROWNS

Sautéing carrots, parsnips, sweet potatoes and turnips along with white potatoes transforms this all-time favorite breakfast dish into a far more healthful meal, rich in beta carotene and vitamin C.

1 pound small red potatoes
½ pound carrots
½ pound parsnips
¼ pound sweet potatoes
¼ pound turnips
1 medium-size onion
2 ounces shallots
2 teaspoons margarine
1 tablespoon olive oil
2 teaspoons sugar
¼ teaspoon salt
Black pepper
¼ cup chopped fresh parsley

1. Wash and trim the red potatoes, carrots, parsnips, sweet potatoes and turnips, and cut them into ½-inch-thick slices.

2. Bring ¾ cup of water to a boil in a large non-stick skillet over medium-high heat. Add the vegetables, return the water to a boil and cover the skillet. Cook 5 to 7 minutes, or until the vegetables are crisp-tender, stirring the vegetables several times.

3. Meanwhile, peel and thinly slice the onion and shallots. Transfer the cooked vegetables to a bowl and cover loosely with foil.

4. Wipe the skillet with paper towels. Melt the margarine in the skillet over medium heat, then add the onion and shallots, and sauté 2 minutes, or until the onion is soft.

5. Drain and discard any liquid from the bowl and return the vegetables to the skillet, then add the oil, sugar and salt. Cook the vegetables, stirring frequently from the bottom of the pan, 10 to 15 minutes, or until tender and browned. Add pepper to taste and sprinkle the vegetables with parsley. Divide the vegetables among 4 plates and serve.

Makes 4 servings

MORNING FRUIT AND YOGURT BOWL

The combination of cottage cheese, yogurt and almonds not only provides lots of lowfat protein, it also gives you one-fourth of your daily calcium requirement. In addition, the fruit in this recipe supplies plenty of potassium.

⅓ cup plain lowfat yogurt
3 tablespoons lowfat cottage cheese (1%)
2 teaspoons brown sugar
½ teaspoon coconut extract
2 tablespoons rolled oats
6 almonds, coarsely chopped
⅓ cup strawberries
⅓ cup seedless green grapes
1 banana
1 tablespoon dark raisins
2 teaspoons chopped fresh mint

1. Process the yogurt, cottage cheese, sugar and coconut extract in a blender about 15 seconds, or until smooth. Transfer the mixture to a bowl, cover and refrigerate.
2. Preheat the oven to 375°.
3. Spread the oats and almonds in a shallow pan and toast in the oven, shaking the pan occasionally, 5 minutes, or until golden. Remove the pan from the oven and set aside to cool.
4. Meanwhile, hull and halve the strawberries. Place the grapes and berries in a medium-size bowl.
5. Just before serving, peel the banana, cut it into large chunks, and add it to the bowl with the other fruit. Spoon the yogurt mixture on top. Scatter the oats, almonds, raisins and mint over the yogurt and serve.   *Makes 1 serving*

NUTRITION INFORMATION
values are per serving
• • •

CALORIES	376	CALCIUM	219 MG
TOTAL FAT	6 G	IRON	2 MG
SATURATED FAT	2 G	POTASSIUM	1024 MG
CHOLESTEROL	7 MG	BETA CAROTENE	TRACE
SODIUM	233 MG	VITAMIN C	46 MG
DIETARY FIBER	5 G	VITAMIN E	2 MG

NUTRITION INFORMATION
values are per serving
• • •

CALORIES	242	CALCIUM	67 MG
TOTAL FAT	6 G	IRON	2 MG
SATURATED FAT	0.9 G	POTASSIUM	763 MG
CHOLESTEROL	0 MG	BETA CAROTENE	10 MG
SODIUM	189 MG	VITAMIN C	28 MG
DIETARY FIBER	7 G	VITAMIN E	3 MG

HERBED MELON WITH YOGURT SAUCE

Basil and black pepper provide a savory counterpoint to the sweetness of melon, mint and honey.

2 tablespoons honey
1½ tablespoons lemon juice
¼ cup minced fresh basil
2 tablespoons minced fresh mint
½ teaspoon coarsely ground black pepper
1 medium-size cantaloupe
1 cup plain lowfat yogurt

1. Combine 1 tablespoon of the honey, the lemon juice, 1½ tablespoons of the basil, ½ tablespoon of the mint and ¼ teaspoon of the pepper in a large bowl.
2. Cut the cantaloupe into 1½-inch cubes, add it to the bowl and toss to coat; set aside.
3. Combine the yogurt, the remaining honey, herbs and pepper in a small bowl and stir well. Let the sauce stand 15 minutes to allow the flavors to blend. To serve, divide the cantaloupe and sauce between two large shallow bowls.   *Makes 2 servings*

NUTRITION INFORMATION
values are per serving
• • •

CALORIES	241	CALCIUM	288 MG
TOTAL FAT	3 G	IRON	2 MG
SATURATED FAT	1 G	POTASSIUM	1193 MG
CHOLESTEROL	7 MG	BETA CAROTENE	5 MG
SODIUM	106 MG	VITAMIN C	121 MG
DIETARY FIBER	2 G	VITAMIN E	TRACE

ORANGES WITH THREE-FRUIT SAUCE

A serving of this luscious combination of fruits, milk and nuts supplies almost twice as much potassium as an 8-ounce glass of orange or grapefruit juice—and slightly more vitamin C. You also get the fiber that the juice lacks.

½ cup unsweetened apple juice
⅓ cup dried apricots
4 large navel oranges
1½ cups cantaloupe chunks
½ cup fresh or frozen unsweetened raspberries, thawed
½ cup evaporated skimmed milk
1 ounce toasted hazelnuts, chopped

1. Place the apple juice and apricots in a small saucepan and bring to a boil over medium-high heat. Reduce the heat to low and simmer, partially covered, 10 minutes, or until the apricots are soft.
2. Meanwhile, peel and section the oranges, removing the membranes; set aside.
3. For the sauce, transfer the apricots and their cooking liquid to a food processor or blender and process 5 to 10 seconds, or until puréed, scraping down the sides of the container with a rubber spatula. Add the cantaloupe and process until puréed, then add the raspberries and process until puréed. Add ¼ cup of milk and process 5 seconds, or until the sauce is blended and slightly thickened, then stir in the remaining milk.
4. Divide the sauce among 4 bowls and top it with the orange sections. Sprinkle each portion with hazelnuts and serve. *Makes 4 servings*

NUTRITION INFORMATION
values are per serving
• • •

CALORIES 217 · CALCIUM 191 MG
TOTAL FAT 5 G · IRON 1 MG
SATURATED FAT 0.4 G · POTASSIUM 837 MG
CHOLESTEROL 1 MG · BETA CAROTENE 2 MG
SODIUM 45 MG · VITAMIN C 128 MG
DIETARY FIBER 3 G · VITAMIN E TRACE

TOMATO-LEMON BREAKFAST SHAKE

A breakfast-in-a-glass can be a great source of dietary fiber if you start with whole fruits and vegetables rather than with juice. To save time, cook the carrots the day before (or save some leftover carrots from the previous night's dinner).

1 large carrot
1 cup plain lowfat yogurt
⅔ cup drained canned tomatoes
1 tablespoon sugar
1 teaspoon grated lemon zest
Ice cubes (optional)

1. Trim and peel the carrot and cut it into ½-inch chunks.
2. Place the carrot in a small saucepan with 1 cup of water and bring to a boil over high heat. Reduce the heat to low and simmer, partially covered, 5 minutes. Drain the cooked carrot and place it in the refrigerator to cool about 15 minutes.
3. Place the carrot in a food processor or blender and process until puréed. Add the yogurt, tomatoes, sugar and lemon zest, and process 1 minute, or until smooth, scraping down the sides of the container with a rubber spatula if necessary. Pour the shake into a tall glass, over ice if desired, and serve.
Makes 1 serving

NUTRITION INFORMATION
values are per serving
• • •

CALORIES 261 · CALCIUM 484 MG
TOTAL FAT 4 G · IRON 2 MG
SATURATED FAT 2 G · POTASSIUM 1178 MG
CHOLESTEROL 14 MG · BETA CAROTENE 16 MG
SODIUM 451 MG · VITAMIN C 37 MG
DIETARY FIBER 4 G · VITAMIN E TRACE

Appendix

The Fat and Cholesterol Content of Foods

This chart is designed to help you reduce the amount of fat and cholesterol you consume each day. Refer to it often as you begin *The Healthy Heart Solution* program, then use it as necessary to help in maintaining your "daily fat target" (see page 28). The amount of fat in a serving of each food is listed in grams; cholesterol is listed in milligrams.

DAIRY AND EGGS

	Fat (g)	Sat Fat (g)	Chol (mg)	Cal		Fat (g)	Sat Fat (g)	Chol (mg)	Cal
CHEESE					**MILK AND CREAM**				
American, 1 oz	9	6	26	105	Buttermilk, 1 cup	2	1	9	99
American spread, 1 oz	6	4	15	81	Chocolate milk, whole, 1 cup	8	5	31	208
Blue, 1 oz	8	5	21	99	Eggnog, 1 cup	19	11	149	342
Brie, 1 oz	8	5	28	93	Evaporated milk, skim, 1 cup	1	0	9	199
Camembert, 1 oz	7	4	20	84	Heavy cream, 2 tbsp	11	7	41	103
Cheddar, 1 oz	9	6	29	113	Half and half, 1 tbsp	2	1	6	20
Colby, 1 oz	9	6	27	110	Milk, 2% fat, 1 cup	5	3	18	121
Cottage, creamed, ½ cup	5	3	17	117	Milk, 1% fat, 1 cup	3	2	10	102
Cottage, lowfat, ½ cup	2	1	10	101	Milk, skim, 1 cup	0	0	4	86
Cream, 1 oz	10	6	31	98	Milk, whole, 1 cup	8	5	33	150
Feta, 1 oz	6	4	25	74	Sour cream, ¼ cup	12	8	26	124
Fontina, 1 oz	9	5	32	109					
Gouda, 1 oz	8	5	32	100	**YOGURT**				
Monterey, 1 oz	8	5	25	105	Lowfat, fruit, 1 cup	2	2	10	231
Mozzarella, part-skim, 1 oz	5	3	16	71	Lowfat, plain, 1 cup	4	2	14	144
Mozzarella, regular, 1 oz	6	4	22	79	Nonfat, plain, 1 cup	0	0	4	125
Muenster, 1 oz	8	5	27	103	Whole milk, plain, 1 cup	8	5	29	139
Parmesan, 2 tbsp	4	2	8	50					
Provolone, 1 oz	8	5	19	99	**EGGS**				
Ricotta, part-skim, ½ cup	10	6	38	171	Egg, whole	5	2	212	75
Ricotta, whole-milk, ½ cup	16	10	63	216	Egg, yolk	5	2	213	59
Swiss, 1 oz	8	5	26	105	Egg, white	0	0	0	17

FAT AND OILS

	Fat (g)	Sat Fat (g)	Chol (mg)	Cal		Fat (g)	Sat Fat (g)	Chol (mg)	Cal
Butter, 1 tbsp	11	7	31	100	Peanut oil, 1 tbsp	14	2	0	119
Canola oil, 1 tbsp	14	1	0	124	Safflower oil, 1 tbsp	14	1	0	120
Cocoa butter, 1 tbsp	14	8	0	120	Sesame oil, 1 tbsp	14	2	0	120
Coconut oil, 1 tbsp	14	12	0	120	Sunflower oil, 1 tbsp	14	1	0	120
Corn oil, 1 tbsp	14	2	0	120					
Lard, 1 tbsp	13	5	7	115	**SALAD DRESSINGS**				
Olive oil, 1 tbsp	14	2	0	119	Blue cheese, 2 tbsp	16	3	5	151
Palm oil, 1 tbsp	14	7	0	120	French, low calorie, 2 tbsp	2	0	0	40
Margarine, liquid, 1 tbsp	11	2	0	98	French, regular, 2 tbsp	12	3	0	129
Margarine, soft tub, 1 tbsp	11	2	0	97	Italian, low calorie, 2 tbsp	3	0	2	32
Margarine, stick, 1 tbsp	11	2	0	98	Italian, regular, 2 tbsp	14	2	20	140
Mayonnaise, imitation, 2 tbsp	6	1	7	69	Russian, low calorie, 2 tbsp	1	0	2	47
Mayonnaise, regular, 2 tbsp	22	3	17	201	Russian, regular, 2 tbsp	16	2	6	153

POULTRY (4 oz except where indicated)

	Fat (g)	Sat Fat (g)	Chol (mg)	Cal
CHICKEN				
Chicken frankfurter	9	2	45	116
Chicken liver, simmered	6	2	721	179
Chicken roll, light-meat, 2 slices	8	2	57	180
Chicken wings, with skin, roasted, 4 wings	26	7	114	394
Chicken wings, with skin, batter-dipped, fried, 4 wings	43	11	155	635
Chicken wings, without skin, roasted, 4 wings	7	2	71	171
Dark meat, with skin, roasted	18	5	104	289
Dark meat, without skin, roasted	11	3	106	234
Dark meat, with skin, batter-dipped, fried	21	6	101	340
Light meat, with skin, roasted	12	3	96	254
Light meat, with skin, batter-dipped, fried	18	5	96	31
Light meat, without skin, roasted	5	1	97	198
Capon, with skin, roasted	13	4	98	262
GOOSE				
With skin, roasted	25	8	104	349
Without skin, roasted	14	5	110	272
TURKEY				
Breast meat, with skin, roasted	4	1	103	174
Breast meat, without skin, roasted	1	0	95	154
Dark meat, with skin, roasted	13	4	102	253
Dark meat, without skin, roasted	8	3	97	214
Light meat, with skin, roasted	10	3	87	225
Light meat, without skin, roasted	4	1	79	179
Turkey bologna, 2 slices	9	3	56	113
Turkey frankfurter	8	3	48	102
Turkey ham, 2 slices	3	1	32	73
Turkey roll, light-meat, 2 slices	4	1	24	83
DUCK				
With skin, roasted	32	11	96	385
Without skin, roasted	13	5	102	230

BEEF (4 oz except where indicated)

	Fat (g)	Sat Fat (g)	Chol (mg)	Cal
Beef frankfurter (cured)	32	14	70	360
Bottom round, trimmed, select cut, braised	7	3	109	229
Bottom round, trimmed, prime cut, braised	10	4	109	251
Brisket, trimmed, braised	15	5	106	275
Chuck, blade roast, trimmed, select cut, braised	16	6	121	293
Chuck, blade roast, untrimmed, choice cut, braised	35	15	118	443
Corned beef, cooked	22	7	112	286
Eye of round, trimmed, select cut, roasted	4	1	79	177
Flank, trimmed, select cut	14	6	78	258
Ground beef, lean, baked	21	8	89	306
Ground beef, extra-lean, broiled	19	7	96	292
Ground beef, regular, broiled	24	9	103	329
Liver, pan fried	9	3	549	247
Pastrami	33	12	106	398
Porterhouse, trimmed, broiled	12	5	91	249
Prime rib, trimmed, broiled	38	16	97	447
Rib eye, trimmed, choice cut, broiled	13	5	91	257
Rib eye, untrimmed, choice cut, broiled	25	10	95	350
Ribs, select cut, broiled	12	5	87	235
Round, trimmed, select cut, broiled	8	3	94	210
Sirloin, trimmed, broiled	9	3	101	222
Sirloin, untrimmed, broiled	20	8	103	311
T-bone steak, trimmed, choice cut, broiled	12	5	91	244
T-bone steak, untrimmed, choice cut, broiled	28	12	96	369
Tenderloin, trimmed, prime cut, broiled	14	5	97	261
Tenderloin, untrimmed, prime cut, broiled	27	11	90	368
Top loin, trimmed, select cut, broiled	10	4	88	227
Top loin, trimmed, prime cut, broiled	27	11	90	368
Top round, trimmed, prime cut, broiled	10	4	96	245
Top round, untrimmed, prime cut, broiled	13	5	97	270

PORK (4 oz cooked except where indicated)

	Fat (g)	Sat Fat (g)	Chol (mg)	Cal		Fat (g)	Sat Fat (g)	Chol (mg)	Cal
Bacon, 3 slices	9	3	16	109	Ham, fresh, butt half	9	3	108	233
Blade loin	16	6	95	264	Ham, fresh, shank half	12	4	104	243
Boston butt, fresh	18	7	107	292	Kielbasa, 1 oz	8	2	10	80
Canadian bacon, 2 slices	8	3	58	185	Loin, roast	9	3	88	213
Center loin	9	3	93	228	Pepperoni, 1 oz	13	5	22	148
Center rib, boneless	11	4	92	244	Picnic shoulder, fresh	14	5	129	280
Country-style ribs	11	4	92	247	Sirloin	11	4	96	241
Ground pork	23	9	106	336	Spareribs	34	13	137	449
Ham, cured, extra-lean	6	2	60	164	Tenderloin	7	3	106	211
Ham, cured, lean	7	2	62	177	Top loin	9	3	90	229

FISH AND SHELLFISH (4 oz except where indicated)

	Fat (g)	Sat Fat (g)	Chol (mg)	Cal		Fat (g)	Sat Fat (g)	Chol (mg)	Cal
Anchovy, canned, 5 fillets	2	0	17	42	Oysters, cooked	6	1	123	155
Bluefish, cooked	5	1	67	178	Perch, cooked	1	0	130	133
Carp, cooked	8	2	95	184	Pike, cooked	1	0	57	128
Catfish, cooked	6	1	82	165	Salmon, pink, canned	7	2	61	135
Caviar, 2 tbsp	6	1	188	81	Salmon, sockeye, fresh, cooked	12	2	99	245
Cod, cooked	1	0	62	119	Sardines, canned in oil, with bones	13	2	161	236
Clams, breaded, fried	13	3	69	229	Scallops, breaded and fried	13	3	69	244
Clams, cooked	2	0	76	168	Scallops, cooked	1	0	60	127
Crab, Alaskan king, cooked	2	0	60	110	Shrimp, breaded and fried	14	2	201	274
Crayfish, cooked	2	0	202	129	Shrimp, cooked	1	0	221	112
Grouper, cooked	1	0	53	133	Snapper, cooked	2	0	53	145
Haddock, cooked	1	0	84	127	Squid, fried	8	2	295	198
Halibut, cooked	3	0	46	159	Swordfish, cooked	6	2	57	176
Herring, cooked	10	2	67	178	Trout, rainbow, cooked	5	1	83	171
Lobster, cooked	1	0	82	111	Tuna light, canned in oil	9	2	20	224
Mackerel, cooked	20	5	85	297	Tuna light, canned in water	1	0	20	148
Monkfish, cooked	2	0	35	107	Tuna, blue fin, fresh, cooked	7	2	56	208
Mussels, cooked	5	1	63	195					

LEGUMES

	Fat (g)	Sat Fat (g)	Chol (mg)	Cal		Fat (g)	Sat Fat (g)	Chol (mg)	Cal
Black beans, cooked, 1 cup	1	0	0	227	Navy beans, cooked, 1 cup	1	0	0	258
Blackeyed peas, cooked, 1 cup	1	0	0	198	Pink beans, cooked, 1 cup	1	0	0	252
Broad beans, cooked, 1 cup	1	0	0	187	Pinto beans, cooked, 1 cup	1	0	0	234
Chickpeas, cooked, 1 cup	4	1	0	269	Refried beans, canned, 1 cup	3	1	0	271
Cranberry beans, cooked, 1 cup	1	0	0	241	Soybeans, cooked, 1 cup	15	2	0	298
Great northern beans, cooked, 1 cup	1	0	0	209	Split peas, cooked, 1 cup	1	0	0	231
Kidney beans, canned, 1 cup	1	0	0	225	Tempeh, ½ cup	6	1	0	165
Lentils, cooked, 1 cup	1	0	0	230	Tofu, 4 oz	6	1	0	94
Lima beans, cooked, 1 cup	1	0	0	216	White beans, cooked, 1 cup	1	0	0	254
					Yellow beans, cooked, 1 cup	2	0	0	255

NUTS AND SEEDS

	FAT (g)	SAT FAT (g)	CHOL (mg)	CAL		FAT (g)	SAT FAT (g)	CHOL (mg)	CAL
Almonds, 1 oz	15	1	0	167	Macadamias, roasted in oil, 1 oz	22	3	0	204
Almond butter, 2 tbsp	19	2	0	203	Peanuts, roasted in oil, 1 oz	14	2	0	165
Beechnuts, 1 oz	14	2	0	164	Peanut butter, 2 tbsp	16	3	0	188
Brazil nuts, 1 oz	19	5	0	186	Pecans, 1 oz	19	2	0	189
Cashews, dry roasted, 1 oz	13	3	0	163	Pinenuts, 1 oz	14	2	0	146
Cashew butter, 2 tbsp	14	3	0	167	Pistachios, 1 oz	14	2	0	164
Chestnuts, roasted, 1 oz	1	0	0	70	Pumpkin seeds, roasted, 1 oz	6	1	0	127
Coconut, dried, shredded, sweetened, 1 oz	10	9	0	142	Sesame seeds, 1 tbsp	4	1	0	47
Filberts, 1 oz	19	1	0	188	Sunflower seeds, 1 oz	14	1	0	162
Hazelnuts, 1 oz	18	1	0	179	Tahini, 2 tbsp	16	2	0	179
					Walnuts, 1 oz	18	2	0	182

BREADS AND GRAINS

	FAT (g)	SAT FAT (g)	CHOL (mg)	CAL		FAT (g)	SAT FAT (g)	CHOL (mg)	CAL
BREADS					Puffed wheat, ½ cup	0	0	0	44
Bagel, plain	2	0	0	200	Raisin Bran, 1 cup	1	0	0	180
Bread, French, 1 slice	1	0	0	100	Rice Krispies, 1 cup	0	0	0	111
Bread, Italian, 1 slice	0	0	0	85	Shredded Wheat, 1 cup	1	0	0	151
Bread, (oatmeal, white, wheat, whole-wheat, rye), 1 slice	1	0	0	65	Wheaties, 1 cup	0	0	0	101
Breadcrumbs, dry, grated, 1 cup	5	2	5	390	**CRACKERS**				
Croissant	12	4	13	235	Graham crackers, plain, 2	1	0	0	60
Danish, fruit, 2½ oz	13	4	56	235	Matzoh, 1 board	1	0	0	115
Doughnut, glazed, 2½ oz	13	5	21	235	Melba toast, plain, 4	0	0	0	80
English muffin	1	0	0	140	Rice cakes, 1 piece	0	0	0	35
Pancake, from mix, 1 (4")	2	1	16	60	Rye wafers, 4	2	1	0	110
Pita bread	1	0	0	165	Saltines, 4	1	1	4	50
Tortilla, corn	1	0	0	65	Snack type, round, 4	4	1	0	60
Tortilla, flour	3	1	0	59	Wheat, thin type, 4	1	1	0	35
Waffle, from mix, 3 oz	8	3	59	205	Whole wheat, 4	4	1	0	70
CEREALS, HOT, COOKED					**GRAINS AND PASTA**				
Corn grits, 1 cup	0	0	0	145	Amaranth, uncooked, ½ cup	6	2	0	367
Cream of Rice, 1 cup	0	0	0	127	Barley, cooked, 1 cup	1	0	0	193
Cream of Wheat, 1 cup	0	0	0	133	Buckwheat, uncooked, 1 cup	6	1	0	583
Farina, 1 cup	0	0	0	117	Bulgur, uncooked, 1 cup	0	0	0	151
Oatmeal, 1 cup	2	0	0	145	Couscous, cooked, 1 cup	0	0	0	200
Oat bran, 1 cup	2	0	0	88	Egg noodles, cooked, 1 cup	2	0	52	212
Wheatena, 1 cup	1	0	0	136	Noodles, chow mein, canned, 1 cup	14	2	0	237
CEREALS, READY-TO-EAT					Pasta, cooked, 1 cup	1	0	0	197
All Bran, 1 cup	2	0	0	209	Quinoa, uncooked, ½ cup	5	1	0	318
Cheerios, 1 cup	1	0	0	88	Rice, brown, cooked, 1 cup	2	0	0	216
Corn flakes, 1 cup	0	0	0	109	Rice, white, cooked, 1 cup	0	0	0	264
Granola, ⅓ cup	5	3	0	125	Rice, wild, cooked, 1 cup	1	0	0	166
Puffed rice, ½ cup	0	0	0	56	Wheat germ, toasted, ¼ cup	3	1	0	108

FRUITS AND JUICES

	Fat (g)	Sat Fat (g)	Chol (mg)	Cal		Fat (g)	Sat Fat (g)	Chol (mg)	Cal
Apple, 1 medium	0	0	0	81	Grapes, 10	0	0	0	36
Apple juice, 1 cup	0	0	0	117	Honeydew melon, 4-oz slice	0	0	0	45
Applesauce, unsweetened, 1 cup	0	0	0	105	Kiwi, 1	0	0	0	46
Apricots, 3	0	0	0	51	Nectarine, 1 medium	1	0	0	67
Apricots, canned in juice, 1 cup	0	0	0	119	Orange, 1 medium	0	0	0	62
Apricots, dried, 5 medium halves	0	0	0	43	Orange juice, 1 cup	0	0	0	112
Avocado, 1 medium	31	5	0	324	Peach, 1 medium	0	0	0	37
Banana, 1 medium	1	0	0	105	Peaches, canned in juice, 1 cup	0	0	0	109
Blackberries, 1 cup	1	0	0	75	Pear, 1 medium	1	0	0	98
Blueberries, 1 cup	1	0	0	81	Pineapple, fresh, 1 cup	1	0	0	76
Cantaloupe, ½	1	0	0	93	Pineapple, canned in juice, 2 slices	0	0	0	70
Cherries, 10	1	0	0	49	Pineapple juice, 1 cup	0	0	0	140
Cranberry juice cocktail, 1 cup	0	0	0	144	Plum, 1 medium	0	0	0	36
Cranberry sauce, canned, 1 cup	0	0	0	418	Prunes, 5	0	0	0	100
Dates, 5	0	0	0	116	Prune juice, 1 cup	0	0	0	182
Figs, 5	1	0	0	237	Raisins, 1 oz	0	0	0	84
Grape juice, 1 cup	0	0	0	154	Raspberries, 1 cup	1	0	0	60
Grapefruit, ½ medium	0	0	0	39	Strawberries, whole, 1 cup	1	0	0	45
Grapefruit juice, unsweetened, 1 cup	0	0	0	94	Tangerine, 1 medium	0	0	0	37
					Watermelon, diced, 1 cup	1	0	0	51

VEGETABLES AND JUICES

	Fat (g)	Sat Fat (g)	Chol (mg)	Cal		Fat (g)	Sat Fat (g)	Chol (mg)	Cal
Artichoke, cooked, 1 cup	0	0	0	55	Peas, cooked, 1 cup	0	0	0	125
Asparagus, cooked, 4 spears	0	0	0	15	Peppers, sweet, raw, 1	0	0	0	20
Bamboo shoots, cooked, 1 cup	0	0	0	14	Potato, baked with skin, 1 large	0	0	0	220
Beans, snap, cooked, 1 cup	0	0	0	45	Potatoes, french fried, in vegetable oil, 2 oz	8	3	0	160
Bean sprouts, raw, 1 cup	0	0	0	30					
Beets, cooked, 1 cup	0	0	0	55	Potatoes, mashed, with milk and margarine, 1 cup	9	2	4	225
Broccoli, cooked, 1 cup	0	0	0	45					
Brussels sprouts, cooked, 1 cup	1	0	0	60	Potato salad, with mayonnaise, 1 cup	21	4	170	360
Cabbage, raw, 1 cup	0	0	0	15					
Carrot, raw, 1 medium	0	0	0	30	Pumpkin, canned, 1 cup	1	0	0	85
Cauliflower, cooked, 1 cup	0	0	0	30	Radishes, raw, 1 cup	1	0	0	20
Celery, 1 stalk	0	0	0	5	Sauerkraut, 1 cup	0	0	0	45
Corn, cooked, 1 cup	0	0	0	135	Spinach, raw, 1 cup	0	0	0	10
Cucumber, 6 large slices	0	0	0	5	Squash, summer, cooked, 1 cup	1	0	0	35
Eggplant, cooked, 1 cup	0	0	0	25	Sweet potatoes, baked, 1 medium	0	0	0	115
Jerusalem artichoke, raw, 1 cup	0	0	0	115	Tomatoes, canned, 1 cup	1	0	0	50
Kale, cooked, 1 cup	1	0	0	40	Tomatoes, raw, 1 medium	0	0	0	25
Leeks, cooked, 1 cup	0	0	0	32	Tomato juice, 1 cup	0	0	0	40
Lettuce, 1 cup	0	0	0	10	Tomato paste, ¼ cup	1	0	0	55
Mushrooms, raw, 1 cup	0	0	0	20	Tomato sauce, 1 cup	0	0	0	75
Okra, 8 pods	0	0	0	25	Turnips, cooked, 1 cup	0	0	0	30
Onions, chopped, ¼ cup	0	0	0	14	Vegetable juice cocktail, 1 cup	0	0	0	45
Parsnips, cooked, 1 cup	0	0	0	125	Water chestnuts, 1 cup	0	0	0	70

SWEETS AND SNACKS

	FAT (g)	SAT FAT (g)	CHOL (mg)	CAL		FAT (g)	SAT FAT (g)	CHOL (mg)	CAL
CAKES (2-oz slice)					**FROZEN DESSERTS**				
Angelfood	0	0	0	125	Frozen yogurt, lowfat, ½ cup	3	2	10	115
Carrot, with cream cheese					Fruit and juice bars	0	0	0	70
frosting	16	3	56	289	Ice cream, ½ cup	7	4	30	135
Cheesecake	14	8	128	210	Ice cream, premium, ½ cup	12	7	44	175
Coffee cake	5	2	35	173	Ice milk, ½ cup	3	2	9	92
Devil's food, with chocolate					Sherbet, ½ cup	2	1	7	135
frosting	6	3	28	143	Sorbet, ½ cup	0	0	0	100
Gingerbread	4	1	1	175					
					PIES (2-oz slice)				
CANDY (1 oz)					Apple	14	4	0	304
Caramels	3	2	1	115	Blueberry	13	3	0	285
Chocolate, milk, with almonds	10	5	5	150	Custard	17	11	6	341
Fudge	3	2	1	115	Lemon meringue	11	3	107	266
Jelly beans	0	0	0	105	Pecan	24	4	71	431
Marshmallows	0	0	0	90	Pumpkin	13	6	82	240
CONDIMENTS					**PUDDINGS**				
Chocolate topping, fudge type,					Chocolate, ½ cup	4	2	15	150
2 tbsp	5	3	0	125	Custard, baked, 1 cup	15	7	278	305
Honey, 1 tbsp	0	0	0	65	Rice, ½ cup	4	2	15	155
Jam or jelly, 1 tbsp	0	0	0	55	Tapioca, ½ cup	4	2	15	145
Maple syrup, 2 tbsp	0	0	0	122					
					SNACK FOODS				
COOKIES					Cheese puffs, 1 oz	8	4	0	160
Chocolate chip, 4 small	11	4	18	185	Popcorn, 1 cup, air popped	0	0	0	30
Fig bars, 4	4	1	27	210	Popcorn, popped in oil,				
Oatmeal raisin, 4	10	3	2	245	with 1 tbsp butter, 1 cup	15	8	31	155
Peanut butter, 4	14	4	22	245	Potato chips, 1 oz	10	3	0	150
Shortbread, 4	8	3	27	155	Pretzels, 1 oz	1	0	0	111
Vanilla wafers, 4	3	1	10	74	Tortilla chips, 1 oz	8	1	0	142

FAST FOOD

	FAT (g)	SAT FAT (g)	CHOL (mg)	CAL		FAT (g)	SAT FAT (g)	CHOL (mg)	CAL
Cheeseburger, single, plain,					French fries, fried in vegetable oil,				
on bun	15	6	50	319	regular order	12	4	0	235
Cheeseburger, 2 patties,					Hamburger, single, plain, on bun	12	5	35	275
with condiments,					Onion rings, 8-9 rings	16	7	14	276
on double-decker bun	35	13	93	650	Pancakes, 3 with butter and syrup	14	6	58	520
Chicken, fried, dark meat,					Pizza, cheese, one slice	3	2	9	140
2 pieces	27	7	166	431	Potato, baked, with				
Chicken breast sandwich,					cheese sauce and broccoli	21	9	20	403
grilled	29	5	43	490	Roast beef sandwich, plain	14	4	51	346
English muffin, with egg, cheese,					Salad, tossed, with chicken	2	1	72	105
Canadian bacon	20	9	234	383	Taco, beef, 1 small	21	11	56	369
Fish sandwich, with tartar sauce	23	5	55	431	Turkey sandwich, homemade	5	1	60	490

Healthy Dining Out

There is no reason not to eat in restaurants—and enjoy yourself—when you're on a lowfat diet. In fact, with a few precautions, you can eat very healthfully when dining out. While you may not be able to precisely calculate the number of grams of fat in a restaurant meal, do your best to estimate, and be sure to record those estimates in your fat diary (see pages 26–27). The following general guidelines, and suggestions for what to order and go easy on for specific cuisines, will help you keep your restaurant meals relatively low in fat.

- If bread is served, ask that the butter be removed from the table. The crusty, flavorful breads offered in quality restaurants are usually quite tasty without butter.
- Ask how foods are prepared. Requests to make slight alterations in a dish can usually be honored without any problem. For example, ask that the dish be prepared without added butter, oil or salt.
- In general, choose items that are poached, steamed, broiled or roasted. Avoid the creamed, pan–fried and sautéed as well as the "buttery," "cheesy" and "crispy." Ask that meat or seafood be broiled without fat.
- Request that all salad dressings, sauces and toppings be served on the side and use them sparingly. Hollandaise, béarnaise, rémoulade, mayonnaise, tartar sauce, sour cream and gravy are all exceedingly high in fat. Brown sauces—such as bordelaise—are wine–based and may be lower in fat if they have been skimmed and no butter has been added (ask before ordering). Tomato sauces, too, are likely to be lower in fat.
- Remove the skin from poultry and trim all visible fat from meat before eating it.
- If portion sizes are large (especially meat), consider sharing an entrée. Alternatively, you can take half of the entrée home in a "doggie bag" and save it for another meal.
- If you can't resist a rich dessert, share it. Or order sorbet or fruit.

ITALIAN

Order often	Minestrone; bean soup; seafood salad; marinated calamari; steamed mussels; steamed or boiled artichokes; any pasta with tomato sauce, marinara sauce, clam sauce, puttanesca sauce or primavera sauce (unless cream–based); any baked or broiled fish; veal or chicken marsala, cacciatore or piccata; pizza with vegetable toppings, such as broccoli, mushrooms, peppers, onions, tomatoes or eggplant.
Go easy on	Stuffed clams; stuffed mushrooms; stuffed artichokes; deep–fried mozzarella; fried calamari; cheese– or meat–filled pastas, such as ravioli, manicotti, lasagna, tortellini, baked ziti or cannelloni; any dish with Alfredo sauce or another cream– or cheese–based sauce; pesto sauce, meat sauce, carbonara sauce; dishes that include pancetta; veal, chicken or eggplant Parmesan; pizza with meat toppings or extra cheese.

FRENCH

Order often Consommé; stock–based soups; gazpacho; salad niçoise; steamed or boiled artichokes; steamed mussels; meat, fish or chicken with bordelaise sauce, or some other wine–based sauce; any dish prepared à la Provençale (with tomatoes, wine and herbs); bouillabaisse; ratatouille; steamed vegetables.

Go easy on Cream–based soups; coquilles St. Jacques; pâté de foie gras; stuffed artichokes; mussels au gratin (with cheese), or any dish prepared au gratin; any dish prepared with béarnaise, béchamel, hollandaise, velouté or Mornay sauce; soufflé; fondue; sweetbreads, kidneys or liver; duck dishes.

CHINESE

Order often Wonton soup; hot and sour soup; steamed dumplings; steamed vegetables; stir–fried or steamed sliced chicken (usually white meat), beef or seafood with vegetables; steamed rice; lo mein with vegetables, chicken or shrimp; bean curd (tofu) with vegetables; moo shu chicken or shrimp.

Go easy on Egg drop soup; spare ribs; fried dumplings; noodles with sesame sauce; lobster Cantonese–style; General Tso's chicken; egg foo yong; lobster sauce; fried rice; crispy noodles; dishes made with diced chicken (usually dark meat); any duck dish.

JAPANESE

Order often Miso soup; clear soup; braised or grilled beef, chicken or fish; chicken teriyaki; stir–fried, steamed or pickled vegetables; tofu dishes; steamed rice.

Go easy on Fried tofu; fried chicken, shrimp, fish or vegetable tempura or agemono; gyoza (fried dumplings); chicken or pork katsu (fried cutlets).

MEXICAN

Order often Gazpacho; black bean soup; salsa; enchiladas, burritos or soft tacos with chicken, seafood, or vegetables; chicken fajitas; rice.

Go easy on Nachos; chiles con queso; guacamole; chorizo; chiles rellenos; chimichangas; flautas; crispy tacos, refried beans; dishes with mole sauce; beef enchiladas, tacos, burritos or fajitas.

INDIAN

Order often	Mulligatawny soup; lentil soup; papadum (crispy lentil wafers); chapati (un-leavened whole-wheat bread); raita (chopped raw vegetables with yogurt sauce); dal (lentil sauce); tandoori chicken, shrimp, lobster or fish; chicken or vegetable curry; fish masala (fish cubes cooked in gravy); basmati rice, plain or with shrimp, chicken or vegetables; chutney.
Go easy on	Coconut soup; pakoras (fried pieces of fish, meat or vegetables) ; paratha (but-tered unleavened flat bread); poori (fried, unleavened whole-wheat bread); any dishes cooked with nuts, cream, butter or cheese.

STEAKHOUSE

Order often	French onion soup (without cheese); Manhattan clam chowder; shrimp cock-tail; London broil; filet mignon; round steak; plain baked potato; steamed vegetables; broiled or baked seafood; broiled or baked chicken breast.
Go easy on	New England clam chowder; Buffalo chicken wings; potato skins, porterhouse steak; T-bone steak; sirloin steak; prime rib; french fries; vegetables with cheese sauce; coleslaw; stuffed seafood or chicken dishes.

FAST FOOD

Order often	Tossed green salad; plain hamburger; roast beef sandwich; grilled or broiled chicken breast sandwich; plain baked potato; grilled or broiled fish sandwich; fried chicken breast with the skin removed; hotcakes without butter.
Go easy on	Large specialty burgers; bacon burgers, cheeseburgers; fried chicken or fish sandwich; chicken nuggets; french fries; crispy fried chicken with the skin; dark-meat fried chicken; egg and sausage sandwich; croissant sandwich.

SALAD BARS

Choose often	Fresh vegetables (avocados excluded); kidney beans; chickpeas; fresh fruit; tofu; white-meat chicken or turkey (remove the skin before eating).
Go easy on	Olives; avocados; marinated artichoke hearts; sunflower seeds; ham; cheese; coleslaw; potato salad; pasta salad; marinated bean salads; tuna salad; chick-en salad; salad dressings.

The New Food Labels

By May 1994, all food manufacturers will be required by the Food and Drug Administration to display a new standardized food label (though many foods may have the new label before the start date). The new label is a vast improvement over the old one. It will make sticking to your fat target simple, since all food labels will be required to carry grams of total fat and grams of saturated fat. The sample label below shows you what the new label will look like.

Serving sizes will now be standardized across product lines, making it easier to compare the nutritional content between brands.

The new labels set forth the daily value, and give the percentage of the daily value, for each nutrient. You can ignore the percentages for fat, since on The Healthy Heart Solution program you only count grams of total fat. However, you might want to use the percent of the daily value for other nutrients, such as sodium, cholesterol, dietary fiber, and so on.

Nutrition Facts

Serving Size ½ cup (114g)
Servings Per Container 4

Amount Per Serving

Calories 90   Calories from Fat 30

	% Daily Value*
Total Fat 3g	**5%**
Saturated Fat 0g	**0%**
Cholesterol 0g	**0%**
Sodium 300mg	**13%**
Total Carbohydrate 13g	**4%**
Dietary Fiber 3g	**12%**
Sugars 3g	
Protein 3g	

Vitamin A	80%	•	Vitamin C	60%
Calcium	4%	•	Iron	4%

* Percent Daily Values are based on a 2000 calorie diet. Your daily values may be higher or lower depending on your calorie needs:

	Calories	2,000	2,500
Total Fat	Less than	65g	80g
Sat Fat	Less than	20g	25g
Cholesterol	Less than	300mg	300mg
Sodium	Less than	2,400mg	2,400mg
Total Carbohydrate		300mg	375mg
Fiber		25mg	30mg

Calories per gram:
Fat 9   •   Carbohydrate 4g   •   Protein 4

Dietary fiber and sugars will now be listed under carbohydrate.

The old labels gave detailed information about the vitamins and minerals that most people easily got enough of—such as B vitamins—but ignored the nutrients that people needed to worry about getting too much of—such as fat and saturated fat. The new labels correct this imbalance by giving not only the grams of fat per serving, but also the grams of saturated fat.

The new labels use an average daily intake of 2000 calories a day and 65 grams of fat, which translates to 30 percent of calories from fat.

The new labels will now list the number of calories per gram for fat, carbohydrates and protein.

INDEX